150 Years of Lancashire Cricket

Lancashire County
Cricket Club

1864 – 2014

Max Books in association with Lancashire CCC

First published in the UK in 2014 by Max Books
in association with Lancashire County Cricket Club

A CIP catalogue record for this title is available from the British Library

ISBN: 978-0-9562224-7-3

Cover Design by Peter Devine
Typeset and Design by Andrew Searle
Photography by Simon Pendrigh, John Dawson and Lancashire CCC

Printed and bound in the UK by CPI Colour

MAX BOOKS
Epworth House
34 Wellington Road
Nantwich Cheshire CW5 7BX
Tel: 01270 625278
Email: maxcricket@btinternet.com

Introduction

THIS BOOK has very much been a team effort, with Andy Searle, Paul Edwards, Graham Hardcastle and myself aiming to compile a year by year history of this great club. We have been helped along the way by Ken Grime, Alan West, Simon Pendrigh, Chris Ostick and others.

The book is a compilation written by different authors, and as such reflects the different eras of the club. Andy Searle wrote up to the first World War, Paul Edwards from 1915-1962 and Graham Hardcastle from 1963 to 2013 (with the advent of one-day cricket). I have written the player profiles and I have also included five administrators and finished off with one of Lancashire's famous Presidents.

Many thanks to Lancashire CCC for all the help and encouragement with the project and to the players who have contributed the forewords so willingly. Quite a strong team! In helping compile this book you perchance to dream:

Of Brian Statham shirt billowing in the wind bowling from the new pavilion end and forming Lancashire's deadliest new-ball partnership with the sublime Ted McDonald. Of Hornby and Barlow once more stepping onto the pitch from different pavilions (amateur and professional), but this time the new Media Centre and The Pavilion. Of Johnny Briggs and Muttiah Muralitharan bowling in tandem. Eddie Paynter getting to grips with Twenty20 cricket. Jack Bond captaining the great side of the 1920s and Ken Cranston complete with cravat once more leading a Lancashire side out onto the pitch. Of Harry Makepeace and RG Barlow opening the innings against the old enemy Yorkshire – certainly no fours before lunch! Spectators once more revelling in the artistry of Reggie Spooner and JT Tyldesley. Of AC MacLaren amassing huge scores with Neil Fairbrother. Cyril Washbrook and Vernon Royle patrolling the covers and Warren Hegg and George Duckworth battling behind the stumps. Glen Chapple opening the bowling with Walter Brearley. Fred Reynolds walking across the practice ground, shotgun cocked ready to shoot pigeons! In the press box reporting the scene, Archie Ledbrooke, John Kay, Brian Bearshaw, Colin Evans, Chris Ostick and, of course, Sir Neville Cardus. And gazing on the scene from the committee room, sit AN Hornby, Tommy Higson, Cedric Rhoades and Michael Cairns, kept in order by Jim Cumbes.

We wanted to make this book a fitting tribute to Lancashire's 150th anniversary and part of the proceeds from the book are going towards the Lancashire Foundation and also to be used for Lancashire heritage. I hope this book will bring back many memories for people and help young cricketers dream that one day they too will step onto the hallowed turf of Old Trafford as a Lancashire player.

Rev. Malcolm G Lorimer
January 2014

Acknowledgements

WE WOULD like to thank Lancashire County Cricket Club and all who have helped and encouraged us with this book, especially Daniel Gidney, Geoff Durbin, Lee Morgan, Ken Grime and Paul Holliday. Also, Michael Cairns and David Hodgkiss in particular and members of the Lancashire Board for giving us permission for the book as part of the 150th Anniversary celebrations.

Many thanks to all the Lancashire cricketers, both former and present day, who have helped with interviews and information. Especially, we would like to thank those who contributed to the forewords.

We have had full access to the photographic archives of Lancashire CCC and used photographs from that extensive collection. We have also had photographs from the collections of Keith Hayhurst, Tony Laughton and Malcolm Lorimer. Simon Pendrigh, Lancashire's official photographer, has provided the recent colour photographs, whilst the earlier ones are from John Dawson and are copyright of Lancashire CCC. Thanks to Roger Mann for the photo of Rev. F.W. Wright and Bodyline Books for the photograph of AC MacLaren and WG Grace.

We would also like to thank Peter Devine for the cover design, Mark Taylor for the records section, Alan West for proofreading and also Keith Hayhurst, Geoff Ogden and Ken Thomas for their advice.

A big thank you to Andy Searle, who has written the first 50 years and also compiled and typeset the book, doing all the page make-ups. That he did it whilst living in Bulgaria shows the wonders of the Internet.

Paul Edwards, who has written the years 1915 to 1962, and Graham Hardcastle – 1963 to 2013 – have written to the deadlines set, and we wish another group of writers well when Lancashire celebrate 200 years!

We have drawn extensively on earlier histories, notably those by Archie Ledbrooke, John Kay, Brian Bearshaw, Eric Midwinter, Peter Wynne-Thomas and Colin Evans, and also local newspaper records. Particularly useful for the early history of the club has been the research done by the late Don Ambrose for the Lancashire Cricket Archive.

We would also like to thank Chris Ostick from the *Manchester Evening News* and Richard Hobson from *The Times* for their help.

Whilst every effort has been made to make sure that none of the material or photographs in this book breaches any copyright, if anyone has any issue with anything in this book regarding copyright, please contact Max Books (details on verso page).

Forewords

BROUGHT UP on Stockport Road a decent throw from Levenshulme Cricket Club, it was somewhat natural that I was attracted to the game from a very early age. As is so often the case I was seriously encouraged to play the game by Jack Boaz, a teacher at Alma Park School and through the teachers associated with Manchester and Lancashire Schoolboys and later the Lancashire Federation. Upon leaving school I would have dearly loved to have joined the groundstaff at Old Trafford. However, my parents (quite correctly in hindsight) insisted that I continue my education by gaining entrance to the famous Hollins College in Manchester.

At that time it seemed that I had some future potential and was invited to Old Trafford at any time that my studies permitted, which led to me playing a number of 2nd XI and numerous Club and Ground games. Unfortunately, while I was supremely confident playing league cricket, I found playing on the main square alongside many famous players intimidating. After a couple of seasons faced with serious competition, it became clear that I was not to be offered a contract. Looking back it was a wonderful experience which taught me so much about life, particularly leadership (Geoff Edrich) and operating in a team environment.

Lancashire chairman Michael Cairns presents Jimmy Anderson with a silver salver at the Ashes Test of 2013 at Emirates Old Trafford to mark his achievement of passing 300 Test match wickiss. The pair are flanked by Bob Willis and Sir Ian Botham, the only two other living England cricketers to have achieved the feat.

Tommy Burrows, the then Chairman of Lancashire CCC was immensely helpful in providing an introduction for me to obtain a dream job where I was able to work and have sufficient time to enjoy a very successful period playing cricket in the south of England. By 1965, and with two children, I had to get serious about life outside cricket, so I went back to University in the United States, which led to me joining the PanAm and Inter-Continental Hotels Corporation, which kept me out of the UK for 25 years and meant that it was unlikely that I would ever return to the North West. However, as a result of remaining in contact with my lifelong friend Jack Simmons I did return to Old Trafford in 1999 to see if I could provide some help with the club's ancillary businesses.

As they say, the rest is history, but it's much more than that for me. I have to say that when I first returned to Old Trafford the ground, to my surprise, looked so small, regrettably tatty and in need of serious investment. At the same time the memories came flooding back – walking down the steps following Geoff Edrich, Brian Booth and Ken Grieves, only for me to be confronted by a member saying, "Oh no, not you again", the Committee Room, which I had never been in as I thought being summoned there was only to receive bad news, and the many hours spent on the practice ground, which by the time of my return had been converted to a car park.

On a positive note, my circumspection and any semblance of inferiority had totally disappeared. I vividly recall my first committee meeting as a co-opted member in charge of the newly-formed Business Committee. I felt taken back in time with so much traditional process and surrounded by people who had given so much of their free time to foster the club. While this was quite humbling, the feeling was to grow much deeper when, on a quite moment, I sat in the Presidents' room looking at the pictures of our past Presidents, which of course includes many very famous people. Their eyes seemed to say, "If you intend coming on board here you better be committed and you better be good."

What this means to me is that what we may have achieved over recent years is only a small part of what has gone before us and therefore must contain a legacy for the future. I feel so fortunate to have made, together with others, in particular David Hodgkiss, Geoffrey Shindler and Jim Cumbes and the executive directors, a small contribution to the future of the club and to stand alongside those who have also contributed over the past 150 years. I am so sorry that former committee members like Murray Bernie and Colin Walker, who were both so supportive to me, are not with us to see what has been achieved.

The 12 years that it has taken to arrive at our current stage is a book in itself. Looking back over the minutes of the early meetings in 2001 I found the paper that set out our vision for the re-development, which was, at the time, extremely ambitious and considered by some to be impossible. I still can't believe that we have achieved more that 90% of what is set out in that paper and there are still areas we can improve and develop. We must not stand still in order to remain a pillar in our community and at the forefront of domestic and international cricket. It is for others to consider the contribution we have made, but for my part this is arguably the most satisfying venture I have ever been involved in.

Michael Cairns
Chairman, Lancashire CCC

Jack Bond

I FIRST came to Lancashire in 1948 as a youngster to watch Australia, who had players like Lindsay Hassett and Don Bradman. Lancashire County Cricket Club meant something to me before I ever joined. As a player growing up in Bolton and playing in league cricket you were always aware of its status. When I joined the club there were players like Cyril Washbrook, Brian Statham, Ken Grieves and Geoff Edrich who I learnt a lot from.

I had a good grounding and grew up with players in the second XI before coming into the first team and, although Lancashire had gone through a lean spell, I was proud to be appointed captain in 1968, which was seen as a caretaker role. It lasted for five seasons and we enjoyed a very successful time, winning three Gillette Cups and the Sunday League twice.

I tried to instill some of my Methodist values of friendship and fellowship and players responded. We were a family club with players, their wives, girlfriends and children. Clive and Farokh were very much part of our club and settled and fitted in well; it shows in that they have both become adopted Lancastrians. We were happy both on and off the field and played for one another. I knew that if I made a mistake there would be ten other players trying to put it right.

I was asked by Peter Moores to put a motto in the new dressing room for the players and I put: 'The traditions of this great club are in your hands'. Also, the words 'Pride of County' have always been important to me and the pride of playing for this great club should never be taken for granted. I was so proud when we won the County Championship in 2011. It was something we looked to win every season and at last it has been achieved.

Jack Bond played for Lancashire between 1955-1972 and was captain for five seasons between 1968-1972. He is now a Lancashire vice-president.

Jack Simmons

I THANK my dad and grandad for my love of cricket, and two teachers, Bob Cunliffe and Derek Day, helped and encouraged me when I played with the under 14s at Old Trafford in a North v South game. I was playing with the 18 and 19-year-olds when I was 16 and was selected to play for the Lancashire second XI in 1960 with Roy Tattersall and Roy Collins. I found it a bit strange playing as an amateur and having to stay in a different hotel, but we did win the Minor Counties Championship in 1960.

I was working in a drawing office from when I was 16 and my mother was keen that I got a profession, and so I served my time until I was 21. I thought my chances with Lancashire were finished and I went to be a professional in the leagues with Baxenden and Barnoldswick and then with Blackpool. It was there that Buddy Oldfield watched me score 60 and take three wickets. By the way, I didn't tell him I had been to a trial ten years earlier! He asked me to come and play for the second XI and pick up another fellow player form Haslingden on the way – that was Clive Lloyd and we have been firm friends ever since. I was also playing football for Great Harwood and I believe Everton were interested in me, but after breaking my leg three times in ten months I decided it was cricket in the future for me.

I have always enjoyed my involvement with Lancashire as both a player and then later on the committee and then becoming Chairman. During those playing days we won many one-day competitions and the secret was we always played as a team and for one another. Everyone played for everyone else. We were a happy family led by Jack Bond and I was very pleased to be part of it.

I went to Tasmania in the winters and helped them win the Gillette Cup, the first trophy they had won. They had never won anything before. I made a lot of friends there and when they wanted me to stay for 12 months it was a very good job offer which I turned down because I wanted to continue playing for Lancashire. I was 40 at the time, so perhaps I was being optimistic! I couldn't think of anything better than playing for Lancashire and I continued to do so till I was 48. Becoming Chairman was a great honour and I always tried to be fair to the players and the staff.

I came to realise that we needed help with the Lodge and I brought in Michael Cairns, who played with me in the second XI. I renewed that friendship I had made in Australia. He was the right man and this can be seen in the ground developments over the last few years. This 150th celebration year is a great way of showing that this club is not just a first-class club, but that the ground can hold its own with the best in the world and I am proud of that.

Jack Simmons played 429 matches for the club and was chairman between 1998-2008 and is now a vice-president.

Clive Lloyd

WHEN I first arrived in Lancashire it was a real culture shock, with having to learn the dialect, put on warm clothes for the cold weather and adjust to different kinds of food. I always thought that English people spoke 'proper' until I discovered the Lancashire dialect and Harry Pilling! I couldn't have had a better baptism, and players like Harry, Peter Lever and Jack Bond made me feel so welcome. I felt I had something to prove as it was just at the beginning of overseas players and there were people who questioned the wisdom of the change.

I played for Lancashire for 19 years and we won the Gillette Cup and Sunday League many times and I remember the games when they had to close the gates two hours before play and the thrill of those Lord's finals. Playing under such a thoughtful and helpful Captain as Jack Bond helped me. I had such fun with characters like Harry Pilling and I am sure that because of our contrasting attributes, bowlers hated us being at the wicket together.

I have admired the way Lancashire have overcome so many difficulties and low spots over the years, and there have been many difficult times both on and off the field. It is now a world-class ground, one of the best in the world, and it has not always had the help that other grounds have enjoyed. Lancashire County Cricket Club is 150 years old and it has lasted the test of time and is stronger now to go into the next 150 years. I am proud to be part of such a great club.

Clive is now Advisor to the President of Guyana on Sport and also an ICC Ambassador.

Farokh Engineer

IT ALL started on the 1967 India tour of England. It was John Arlott and Syd Buller who first approached me to play county cricket for Hampshire. Soon after Somerset offered me a contract. Then it was Don Kenyon from Worcestershire who approached me.

At the fag-end of that 1967 tour, we were playing Lancashire at Southport and I kept smacking their opening bowler onto the railway lines. At tea someone pointed out that the bowler was the great Brian Statham (who, incidentally, became one of my closest friends later in life). I respected him so much that I was almost apologetic for hitting him – as in Indian tradition one always respected one's seniors. Anyway, Lancashire approached me to sign for them.

As two overseas cricketers were allowed to be signed by each county, the great Garry Sobers was also offered a contract by Lancashire; whereby he would play in 1968 and I would qualify for a year playing in the Lancashire League. Soon after, it was learnt that Garry Sobers and Lancashire couldn't agree terms, so I was invited to play from 1968 and I was asked who I thought Lancashire could approach to fill Garry Sobers' place. Without any hesitation I suggested the name of Clive Lloyd. Cyril Washbrook, our Cricket Chairman even suggested, "But doesn't he wear spectacles?" I said. "Sure he does, but our county will never regret signing him up," which they did and Clive had to qualify for Lancashire playing for a year in the Lancashire League – which he did by playing for Haslingden.

Both myself and Clive jelled in marvellously with the rest of our teammates; and it was a wonderful experience driving the length and breadth of the UK with him and, more importantly, sharing a room with him for almost ten years. We had a great guy, 'Bondie', who was a wonderful skipper who invariably got the best out of everyone. We had Peter Lever, the great JB Statham himself, Ken Shuttleworth, Ken Higgs and Peter Lee – what a formidable attack to pick from. Our spinners were the extraordinarily accurate Flat Jack Simmons, very ably supported by David Hughes. Our batting line-up was spearheaded by Clive Lloyd, David 'Bumble' Lloyd, Barry Wood, Harry Pilling, Frank Hayes and myself (opening the innings in later years). It was an absolute privilege keeping wicket to all the great Lancashire bowlers.

I was initially offered a three-year contract, but as we were all combining so well and enjoying each other's success, which automatically reflected in the team's success, both myself and Clive were offered repeated contracts. So much so that both of us eventually settled in Cheshire (very close to Old Trafford) and still continue to live here. I do not think any other overseas player(s) have done this and both of us are hugely honoured to be made lifelong Vice-Presidents of our elite club, a club we were so proud to represent over the years. Even now, the first thing I do every morning is to see how our players and our team are faring.

The appearance of Old Trafford has now completely changed for the better as Test cricket is restored back where it belongs. Thank you Lancashire for having given me that wonderful opportunity. I do hope I repaid them, even briefly, with some lusty blows and divine catches over the glorious years I enjoyed with Lancashire.

Farokh is now a vice-president of the club and a commentator on Indian Cricket.

David Hughes

MY LOVE for this great game started at an early age, I think I was seven or eight. My father Lloyd and my uncle Frank both played for Newton-le-Willows in the Manchester Association. Lloyd was an all-rounder, a fast-medium right-arm inswing bowler and a powerful right-hand batsman. He once took all ten wickets for 17 runs against Colwyn Bay and, if I recall correctly, was the professional for Walkden in the Bolton League, maybe either side of World War Two. Frank was a right-hand opening batsman who had trials with Worcester and Somerset.

So there was an inevitability that I should be drawn to cricket, although quite where my left-handedness arrived from I don't know. My son, James, a right-hand batsman and slow left-arm bowler, continues the cricket line, having played and captained Warrington Sports Club in the Cheshire County League.

My early cricket was at Newton-le-Willows CC and I was coached by Alan Wilson, the former Lancashire wicketkeeper. I then played at Farnworth in the Bolton League for two seasons in 1964 and 1966, along with the Lancashire Colts in 1965 and the Lancashire Federation under 19s. I joined Lancashire in 1967 but played only one game that year for the first team, against Oxford University. In delivering my first ball, I fell on my backside, very embarrassing, but some consolation was that I got a wicket second ball, caught by Jack Bond, who was captaining the side whilst Brian Statham had a rest.

Little did I realise at the time what lay in store in the next five years, just to be a small part of Jack Bond's team was fantastic. It also gave me the chance to play alongside my boyhood heroes, Brian Statham and Geoff Pullar. Jack started to assemble a great squad, mostly from the leagues of Lancashire coupled with the two best overseas players, in my opinion, in the domestic game. What a privilege to play with Clive Lloyd and Farokh Engineer. Success in the Sunday League and Gillette Cups followed quickly.

During the 1970s and 80s, I joined Jack Simmons for ten winters in Tasmania, playing and coaching. We were good mates, the 'spin twins' of Jack Bond's team, and spent a lot of time together. Back in Lancashire, it was a tough time to play but enjoyable for the most part. All the great overseas players were available to counties, who all had very strong squads and most matches were played on uncovered pitches and very much a lottery based on the toss of a coin and the vagaries of the English climate. All Lancashire supporters at that time would remember Buxton, June 1975. Lancashire scored approximately 480 for 5 declared on a warm Saturday on a good pitch. Snow fell on the second day and there was no play!! Prompt start day three, Derbyshire 42 and 87, thanks for the game! Pleased we won the toss. Today's first-class cricketer is unlikely ever to experience this type of pitch.

The 1987 season saw big personnel changes at the club. I was honoured to be given the captaincy of Lancashire and whatever else happened throughout my 22-year playing career, this was my proudest moment. I tried to model my captaincy on all the great values I had learnt from Jack Bond, who will always remain the man I have most respect for.

I mentioned Clive and Farokh earlier, but in this era, in my opinion, we had the greatest overseas player around in Wasim Akram, and with my partnership with Alan Ormrod, the Cricket Manager, we were able to build another formidable squad of players. Successful times as well, Sunday League and Cup victories followed. I am often asked which was the greatest side, the 70s or the 90s… Impossible to tell. What a great contest it would be, though, both in a four-day or a one-day match! However, neither of those great sides were able to achieve what the side of 2011 managed, and that was to win the County Championship. A fantastic moment, not only for those lads, but for all Lancastrians. I enjoyed that moment very much.

Many congratulations to Lancashire County Cricket Club on their 150th Year and for the magnificent refurbishment of the stadium. As a Lancastrian there is only one place to play your cricket… Old Trafford.

David Hughes played almost 900 matches for Lancashire in a career lasting from 1967 to 1991. He was captain from 1987 to 1991. He is now an Honorary Life Member of the club.

Warren Hegg

ONE OF my proudest possessions is my Lancashire Cap. It's old, faded and falling to bits, but this is one of my cherished belongings. I still feel the same pride as when I was given it in 1989 by Cyril Washbrook and it should never be taken for granted. I feel very fortunate and proud to have played for Lancashire CCC and have my name linked with some of LCCC's famous keepers, like George Duckworth and Farokh Engineer.

It was also a massive honour to captain the side and lead the team onto the field at Old Trafford. I particularly enjoyed the games against the old enemy Yorkshire, especially if there was a full house at Old Trafford. There is something about the roar from the crowd which is very special and never emulated at any other ground in the world.

I have now changed my gloves for the laptop and mobile, working on the business development side of the club. You now see things in a different way, how we can build for the future with this historic and great club.

I still enjoy having a cup of tea in the dressing room with the players prior to the start of play, but I don't have to worry about chasing eight or ten an over in a limited over match, or keeping to Wasim and Murali. I sleep easier at nights these days as my hands are no longer battered and bruised, but the task of finding new partners and sponsors throws up a whole new challenge!

Jim Cumbes

It hardly seems possible that two years after I joined Lancashire as a young professional fast bowler, we were celebrating the centenary of the club, and now here we are celebrating the 150th! I was a Lancashire supporter – though never a junior member – from around the age of 12, and like many of that era, my hero was Brian Statham and it was the lure of this great county that brought me back again in 1987 after experiencing life with three other counties, not to mention a football career embracing three football league clubs, and thoroughly enjoying the journey.

For five years after retiring from the game in 1982 I was the Commercial Manager of Warwickshire County Cricket Club, another fine club. After living for 20 years in the Midlands I never envisaged moving back to the county of my birth, but the opportunity to take up a similar post with Lancashire was intoxicating.

As Lancashire's first Commercial Manager it was my job to oversee growth in income and sponsorship from the commercial sector as well as all the other opportunities for raising revenue. As it turned out, the growth in income which I was able to exploit coincided with a great period of success on the field for the playing side of the club. Narrow misses in the quest for the Championship on several occasions were frustrating, and it soon became clear that if we were going to win that coveted trophy we not only had to perform at our very best, but also win matches in less time than others in order to beat the ever present frustrations of the Manchester weather!

The nineties was an amazing decade with nine one-day trophies won, including the double of the two major 50-over competitions twice – the first county side to achieve such distinction – with a side that largely comprised home-grown players. David Hughes had been a great stalwart for the county and in the first part of that decade led the side as captain with great distinction. Others such as Graeme Fowler, John Crawley, Mike Atherton, Paul Allott, Peter Martin, Neil Fairbrother, Ian Austin, Warren Hegg, Mike Watkinson, aided and abetted by Philip DeFreitas, and probably one of the finest fast bowlers of all time, Wasim Akram, roll off the tongue. There were many more who also played their part.

Chris Hassell had been the Club Secretary during those years, but in 1991 the club decided that the world was changing and decided to appoint a Chief Executive. John Bower was appointed and, despite his not infrequent spats with a committee that was now becoming an anachronism in modern sport, he succeeded in turning the club into a more professional set-up with good business practices. After one row too many with the committee, and increasing frustration, John left in 1998 and I was asked to look after the club's affairs until a new CEO was appointed. After six weeks of ruminating over their next appointment I was approached by Chairman Jack Simmons, and Vice-Chairman Edward Slinger and asked if I would like the job. After much thought and discussion with my wife, I accepted.

The next 14 years were a bit of a rollercoaster in many respects. The great team of the nineties was broken up as time caught up and a period of disappointment on the field added to problems off the field. We had an ageing stadium that had seen a long periods of neglect – to be fair, as many other Test match grounds had – but without any meaningful capital to put things right. We had patched up here and there, still spending considerable sums on maintenance each year.

Soon after the turn of the century, we embarked on what we hoped would be a programme of development following the success of the Old Trafford Lodge, opened in 1999. Michael Cairns had been invited to join the committee by Jack Simmons to help with the development of the Lodge and add more business acumen to the committee. In 2003, after a row with Trafford Council over a licence for a pop concert, we started in earnest and had invitations to re- locate, firstly to Manchester and then to Wigan. The wagon had started rolling, but it was clear people's hearts were still at Old Trafford, and in 2006 we had the severe shock of losing an Ashes Test match to Cardiff for the 2009 series.

Jack Simmons had now been succeeded as Chairman by Michael Cairns, and the plans gained momentum, but little did we know of the planning challenges that lay ahead. Suffice to say that after several planning challenges that finally ended up in the Court of Appeal in London, we were able to progress. However, the struggle had taken its toll and big losses at the club brought about by legal fees and expiry of grants brought us to the brink on more than one occasion. Finally, after much frustration, planning was obtained and the club won its Ashes Test match and Test match status back again, and as a bonus, after a 77 year wait, the team won the Championship. Hallelujah!

The club has moved on further. The committee was replaced with a Board, which will create a firm foundation for the future of the club, and a development that should see it through the next 50 years. It may be 150 years old but there's still life in the old dog yet!

Jim Cumbes retired from his position as chief executive at Old Trafford at the end of the 2012 season

Mike Watkinson

LANCASHIRE CCC and its iconic home, Emirates Old Trafford, has a special place in the cricket world. The aura of association that oozes from the club is powerful and it is this that inspired me (and many others!) as a young cricketer to hang on to the dream of one day representing the county.

I have been fortunate to have been employed by the club for over 30 years. There have been highs and lows, but my times are jam-packed with great memories and experiences. In 2011 we won the County Championship for the first time in 77 years, definitely about time, but the messages of congratulation we received demonstrated how many lives we are able to touch, both near home and across the world. When I switched my phone on after the memorable day at Taunton, the first call I received was from football World Cup hero Nobby Stiles, who said he always follows our progress and we had made his year!

Whenever we tour overseas, Lancashire CCC needs no introduction with cricket followers keen to share their memories of great games and past players. I certainly don't have to sell the club to potential overseas players! When you are involved with the club on a daily basis it is easy to forget that we are making history and creating great memories for future generations. Jack Bond's message on the dressing-room wall reinforces our responsibilities to the people that will follow us.

I am really lucky to have some great personal memories, such as, being awarded my county cap (1987) in the old committee room, captaining the club in a number of Lord's finals and making my Test debut at Old Trafford (1995). However, making my county debut (1982) was very special. I wasn't on the playing staff and hadn't played in a second team Championship game. Clive Lloyd was captain for the home game against Kent and I felt immensely proud to walk out onto the field behind the great man and alongside names that had previously only existed for me in newspaper reports and scorecards (Lloyd D, Simmons, Hayes, Hughes etc.) This moment wasn't just mine; it belonged to my family, my friends, my junior coach (Teddy Gerrard), my home club (Westhoughton) and Bolton cricket in general.

The club has probably changed more in the past few years than in any other period in recent history. Despite the stadium looking completely different (for the better!) and the diverse ways we create a sustainable future for our cricket, we will always be mindful of the history and heritage of our great club.

Mike Watkinson is the Cricket Director at Old Trafford.

Mike Atherton

WHEN I think of playing for Lancashire, I don't think of the great victories or the trophies won, although there were plenty of both in the time that I played, nor do I think of runs scored or wickets taken in a personal capacity, although there were a few of those as well. No, I think principally of friendship and fun.

Perhaps friendship and fun are not supposed to be keywords in a professional game. Professionalism in recent times has been typified by the Dave Brailsford view of sport where layers of 'marginal gains' eke out world-class performances. Every facet of sport analysed and re-analysed so that the differences between winning and losing become ever more infinitesimal.

Although we were paid to play cricket, I never really felt I was a professional sportsman in that sense of the word at Lancashire. I simply viewed my time there as an extension of my schoolboy days. I played for fun, alongside many of the friends I had grown up playing alongside. Of course, I practised hard, tried to improve and wanted badly to win. But, in the words of the rugby player, Willie John McBride, 'nothing mattered more during the game than the result; afterwards, nothing mattered less.'

So at the end of 1986, when Jack Bond offered me a summer contract, I signed terms with a number of friends from Lancashire schoolboy days: Warren Hegg, who became an outstanding wicketkeeper-batsman; Ian Austin, Dexer Fitton, Nick Speak, Graham Lloyd, Steve Titchard, Mark Crawley, Gary Yates and Peter Martin all signed around the same time. This was to become the nucleus of the most successful one-day team of the time.

It was no coincidence that a bunch of mates should become successful together. We were all good cricketers, of course, but there was a special bond I think that we felt in representing the county from which we came. There isn't that same bond nowadays in county cricket, with players able to move more freely than before. I think that is a shame; the only point of county cricket is to produce decent cricketers from within the county. Otherwise there is no point at all.

When, in 1996, we won the domestic one-day double, we did it with a virtually home-grown team. We had, of course, great overseas players throughout my time who added infinitely to the team – Wasim Akram and Muttiah Muralitharan chief amongst them – but in both finals of that year we decided against playing our overseas player, Steve Elworthy. Jason Gallian was from Sydney, and had learnt his cricket there, but his father hailed from Lancashire, so we counted him as one of our own. The rest were produced from within the boundaries, or just outside, if you count Neil Fairbrother coming from Cheshire.

So these were great times. Good mates, playing good cricket, representing a community from which they had sprung. Celebrations were great fun: a stolen semi-final at Worcestershire provoked an all-nighter in the away dressing room there; another victory at Lord's was celebrated in unique fashion with a magic show from messrs Lloyd and Speak in a humble bar in St John's Wood. Those are the memories now that have stayed with me. Special ones, too.

Mike Atherton is a popular commentator on Sky Sports and is cricket correspondent of the The Times.

David Lloyd

PEOPLE TALK about dreams. I prefer ambition. As a young cricketer at Accrington Cricket Club my ambition was to play for England. Lancashire CCC would get me there.

Trials at schoolboy level can be harrowing, but I saw this as my chance. Would I get a good crack at it? Where would I bat? Would I get to bowl? I must have been nervous but I can't recall it. I do remember going to the bus to get to venues, meeting up with the other lads who were total strangers... and assessing how good they were.

I got my chance and I performed at Old Trafford. I was invited to spend the summer at the ground as an amateur and was then taken on as an apprentice, working on the ground during the winter. It was tough, long hours and many sleeps on public transport, but the ambition was there.

I was taken on primarily as a bowler, but like many left-armers, I got the 'yips' and David Hughes was bowling well. My batting was improving and I got lots of help and understanding from senior players. Geoff Pullar, David Green, Tommy Greenhough, Ken Higgs, Brian Statham and then, most importantly, Jack Bond. Jack became captain and believed in young players. We were a 'rum lot' ... Pilling, Sullivan, Snellgrove, Hughes, Lever, Shuttleworth, Wood, et al. I think we all sort of clicked together and had a wonderful time, genuinely enjoying each other's success. We had a fantastic following too, particularly in one-day cricket. We mischievously said to Southerners that, "We will be down at Lord's to play a final for you in September."

Ambition drove me on. Captaincy came and so did England. Cricket is a fabulous game for discipline in life and we all make mistakes and we see that in the present day with great players making wrong judgements. That's life.

It was time to go as captain as the team broke up and new lads came on the scene to repeat the cycle. Then it's time to retire and reflect on what you have achieved... and what you could/should have achieved. Time away was important to me before I came back as county coach, new players, young lads. But doing all the same things, making the same mistakes but with the same ambition.

A different job, yes, but at the same wonderful place. And everyone who has been on the staff at Old Trafford will tell you about the 'feel', the 'smell' of the place. Very special. The players are the hub of Old Trafford, but the administrators have a massive obligation in upholding the traditions of the club and ensuring that cricket is the core business.

I may be some sort of 'geek' but anyone who works at Old Trafford should have a grasp of the history. The Tyldesleys, Washbrook, Paynter, McDonald, Statham. Fairbrother, Akram, Lloyd (the other one), Engineer, Hegg. All this should be paramount as we celebrate 150 years. The game changes and Old Trafford has changed. The facilities are now world class. The current players are the custodians of Old Trafford. Make sure you leave your little bit of history.

David Lloyd is now a very popular cricket commentator for Sky Sports.

Paul Allott

I WAS born in Cheshire, played for Cheshire Schools, and for Bowdon in the Cheshire County League, but the link with Lancashire could hardly have been stronger. I was taken to Old Trafford regularly by my father, who has been a member since 1934, and still is one of the few I would imagine who has witnessed Lancashire play as outright County Champions on two separate occasions, some 77 years apart! I may have watched little, always preferring to play on the practice ground, but the die was cast when I saw Brian Statham bowl in his last Roses encounter. I knew I would never be as good but I would give it a go!

Years later, when my dad used to ask, 'Do you think I will ever see Lancashire win the County Championship again?' my response was always that we were trying to, but deep down the lure of the one-day game instilled by the Bond years always seemed to prove too strong and that's where our efforts were at their strongest through the eighties and early nineties. This could hardly be deemed a fault, and I always sensed that everyone (players, supporters, and even the committee) connected to Old Trafford in that period felt the same. During those years I remember there being a feeling approaching invincibility about the team, demonstrated by being the first team to win both knockout competitions in the same season in 1990.

Despite our one-day dominance, one of the matches that sticks so vividly in the memory is not from that genre, but a County Championship game from 1989, a game in fact that we lost, at Old Trafford in July on one of Peter Marron's best pitches, fast, even-bouncing and bringing out the best from the best. Sixteen internationals contested the fixture between Lancashire and Worcestershire in a game where the bowlers held sway. Botham, Dilley and Radford for Worcester, Patterson, DeFreitas, Allott, and Watkinson for Lancashire. Four innings with no side making more than 230 in a contest of the highest quality with the final word going to Graham Dilley in taking 10-124. The general consensus from batsmen and bowlers alike was that this was one of the best of games on the best of surfaces.

A quarter of a century on the feeling is still the same and the high quality of pitches are just one continuing feature of the modern Emirates Old Trafford.

Paul Allott currently works as a commentator for Sky Sports and he is on the Board of Lancashire CCC.

Neil Fairbrother

FROM A very early age cricket was in my blood, dad and uncles all played league cricket and mum did the teas!! I was proud to be named after a great Australian cricketer, Neil Harvey. Cricket was my life and I always wanted to be a first-class cricketer. I was brought up watching and looking up to the great players and the legendary Lancashire teams of the 70s.

I played my early cricket at Grappenhall CC and then for Cheshire Schools. Both parties gave me great help and encouragement to realise my dream of becoming a first-class cricketer. My only real professional coach during those early days was Lancashire wicketkeeper Alan Wilson, who came down to Grappenhall and coached the juniors.

My first team debut for Lancashire was like a dream. It was a Saturday morning in 1982 and I was still in bed at 9.15 as I was expecting to play for Grappenhall in the afternoon. The phone rang and it was Jack Bond, who told me because of a couple of injuries they wanted me to play in the first team at Old Trafford later that morning against Kent. I shot down to the ground and all the other players were practising in the nets. Clive Lloyd, Graeme Fowler, Paul Allott, Frank Hayes, all legends who I had looked up to and now I was playing alongside them. I will always remember Clive Lloyd putting an arm around me in the dressing room to calm my nerves. We fielded all day and it wasn't until I was going home that I had to stop the car and be sick – my nerves had at last caught up! On the Sunday there was a Sunday League game and I caught a catch off Jack Simmons on the boundary. Monday and Tuesday I didn't bat and watched Bumble get a big century. Jack Bond offered me a two-year deal and he said to me, "I look upon myself as a chance-maker and it's now down to you." I think I took my chance; in my first knock at Edgbaston I reached 96 not out before the declaration!

I am very proud to have played for Lancashire and even be a tiny part of the club's great history. Having played for the Red Rose for over 20 years, I guess the highlights were the ten Lord's finals that I played in. Lord's is an even more special place when it is full with family, friends and thousands of Lancastrians. The special memories and bonds, with players and supporters alike, I hold very dear.

I was at Old Trafford on the first day of the Ashes in 2013 in the ISM box we have on the top floor of the Pavilion. With the amazing facilities and tremendous view it was unbelievable. To look around the ground there as the Test began, there was a lump in my throat. Old Trafford is now back as a major ground in world cricket.

150 years of tradition and history is a great achievement. So many players and occasions stand out and I am proud to be part of the great tradition of the Red Rose. Old Trafford is like a cathedral to cricket in the North-West of England and now built to last for the next generations of Lancashire and England cricketers to continue the tradition.

Neil played for Lancashire for 20 years and scored more runs for the county than any other player if you include first-class and one-day matches. He is now Director of Cricket at International Sports Management Ltd.

Peter Moores

MY FIRST memory of Lancashire was as an under 12 when I represented Macclesfield CC in an eight-a-side tournament on the nursery ground at Old Trafford. We were privileged to have lunch with the professional players in the Lancaster Suite at the top of the pavilion as there was a Sunday League game on that day. I still have the menu from that day signed by the likes of Farokh Engineer, Peter Lee and Jack Simmons.

My next memory was being invited to Old Trafford for nets when Jack Bond was the coach. Exactly how I was invited I can't remember, though I was playing at The King's School, Macclesfield at the time and had represented Cheshire schoolboys - the latter at the same time Neil Fairbrother was coming through. We used to train before the pros, and Jack said, 'If you do well, you might get the chance to stay on and train for an hour at the start of their session', which was a great incentive. Although I never played county cricket for Lancashire, I always felt it was a special club due to my connections growing up. Playing against Lancs was always exciting, especially at Old Trafford.

When I returned to the club as coach in 2009, it was the ideal challenge after the England job. If at the start of the interview process I was slightly unsure about going straight into another coaching job, by the time the second interview came I was desperate to get the opportunity. Honestly, it has been some of the most enjoyable coaching I've been involved in, and that is credit to the players and support staff I've been lucky enough to work with. When I started Glen Chapple became captain and Mike Watkinson became director of cricket. It was a fresh start and a clean slate and a great opportunity to move things forward.

Winning the Championship in 2011 was an obvious highlight, though realistically the whole journey has been the real fun. The first year I came in, we'd lost some senior players and this gave opportunities to some of our own youngsters, who grabbed them with both hands. That year we scrapped hard to get fourth, and though we finished fourth again the following year, we were in it until the penultimate game. More recently, we've had the challenges of relegation and the battle to get back into Division One. All these experiences have been great learning opportunities for all of us, and hopefully they will help us move forward in the coming seasons.

We made it clear that we see the development of our own players as crucial for the future success of the club. The emergence of several exciting young players over the last few seasons bodes well for the future, though we realise we still have work to do. The goal is to be competitive in all forms of the game all of the time. You can't guarantee you'll win something, though you want to be in the mix every season. It's about getting better year on year, and I think at the moment we're doing that.

Finally, I would like to take this opportunity to thank all the coaching and support staff who are fantastic at what they do and have had a huge influence over the last few seasons. The players under Glen have always given everything, and as a coach you can't ask for any more. It seems a fitting time to celebrate our 150th anniversary as the recent changes that have happened both on and off the field will hopefully lay the foundations for another 150 years of unbelievable memories.

Glen Chapple

I'VE SPENT my whole life on a cricket ground, from a toddler watching my dad playing in the Lancashire League for Nelson and then later in the Ribblesdale League for Earby.

I have many early memories, but two stand out for different reasons. The first was during the interval at Nelson where we were having the traditional game on the outfield in between innings. I was walking back to my fielding position when I heard a shout, turned round and copped it straight in the face. An early lesson in the pain a cricket ball can cause.

The second memory is of a game between Padiham and Earby in 1979. My dad scored 142 not out, dispatching the Padiham attack onto the adjacent football pitch. Our Cumbrian professional Alan Sharp made 49 not out and Earby ran out easy winners. I was desperate to become a good cricketer after this.

My first experience of Old Trafford came thanks to Jim Kenyon, a well known and hugely respected figure in Lancashire cricket and a great coach and mentor to young players. I had impressed Jim at our club nets, so much so that he decided I was good enough to attend the Lancashire under 13 winter nets that were held in the old indoor school at Old Trafford. Following this at the start of the season were the trials for the actual under 13s team, but being just 12 at the time, I didn't expect to make the team. Luckily, however, a cover drive caught the eye of the team manager and I was selected as a batsman.

I was lucky enough to have played in all the age group teams for Lancashire and developed a loyalty and desire to represent them on a professional basis. The Lancashire cricket team in my mind has always meant a team full of quality players who play the game in the right way.

My earliest memories of watching Lancashire were when the Roses games used to be televised. That was the era when the likes of Neil Fairbrother, Phil DeFreitas, Mike Watkinson and Wasim Akram were making their way in the game. Little did I realise that one day they would be my teammates.

At the age of 17, I received a phone call from Lancashire asking if I would be interested in signing a professional contract. To have the chance to follow in the footsteps of the legends of Lancashire CCC, it's the call that all young players dream of. I went with my parents to meet Geoff Ogden, the Cricket Chairman, and David Hughes, the first team manager, to talk things through.

There have been some tremendous teams down the years, but the one I came into in the early nineties must rank highly. I remember

thinking, 'How the heck am I going to get into this team with the likes of Akram, DeFreitas, Fairbrother, Allott, Fowler etc., and Crawley, Irani and Gallian waiting for their chance?' Thankfully a chance came and I was lucky enough to take it. There were the inevitable ups and downs along the way, and the burden I felt at not wanting to let these great players down did weigh heavily at times. But, ultimately, they helped to strengthen my character.

Six Lord's finals followed in quick succession, with the big players stepping up to make the difference - Austin's deadly accuracy and self belief, Fairbrother's competitive edge and one-day nous, Crawley's class and Wasim's brilliance. So to win a man of the match award in the 1996 NatWest Final remains my most memorable day on a cricket field.

The captaincy of Lancashire is an honour and one I certainly didn't think would come my way. In truth, it came out of my fortunate longevity and the experience I had accumulated over the years, and the lack of another obvious candidate as we had just lost most of our senior players. I have enjoyed the role more than I could have imagined.

2011 was an unbelievable season. Written off from the start as an inexperienced and limited team, this assessment proved to be totally inaccurate as this young Lancashire side, moulded by Peter Moores, went on to display skill, character and spirit that are rare in any team. To relieve the burden of 77 years without a Championship was a fantastic achievement never to be forgotten.

In the last few years the club has been through trying times financially and with the redevelopment of the ground. But thanks to the unshakeable will of all those involved, Lancashire County Cricket Club now has a state of the art facility and bright and exciting future ahead. Here's to the next 150 years.

LANCASHIRE COUNTY CRICKET CLUB LTD OLD TRAFFORD, MANCHESTER M16 0PX

Founded 12th January 1864

Patron: Her Majesty The Queen

THE BOARD

President: J Livingstone OBE
Honorary Treasurer: DMW Hodgkiss
Chairman: MA Cairns OBE
GA Shindler OBE (Non-Executive Member)
PJW Allott (Non-Executive Member)
EM Watkins CBE (Non-Executive Member)
LM Platts (Non-Executive Member)
In attendance at Board Meetings:
Chief Executive: Daniel Gidney
Cricket Director: Mike Watkinson
Commercial Director: Geoff Durbin
Finance Director & Secretary: Lee Morgan
Operations Director: Anthony Mundy

OFFICIALS

Head Coach: Peter Moores
Captain: Glen Chapple
Assistant Coach: Gary Yates
Academy Director: John Stanworth
Head Groundsman: Matthew Merchant

HONOURS

County Champions: 1879 (joint), 1881, 1882 (joint), 1889 (joint), 1897, 1904, 1926, 1927, 1928, 1930, 1934, 1950 (joint), 2011, Division 2 Champions: 2005, 2013
One-Day Trophy Winners: 1970, 1971, 1972, 1975, 1990, 1996, 1998
B&H Cup Winners: 1984, 1990, 1995, 1996
One-Day League Champions: 1969, 1970, 1989, 1998, 1999 Division 2 Champions: 2003
Refuge Cup Winners: 1988 Lambert & Butler Floodlit Cup Winners: 1981

**Lancashire County
Cricket Club**

1864 – 2014

150 Years of Lancashire Cricket

Written, compiled and edited by

Andrew Searle
1864-1914

Paul Edwards
1915-1962

Graham Hardcastle
1963-2013

Rev. Malcolm G Lorimer
150 LANCASHIRE GREATS

Mark Taylor
STATISTICAL SECTION

Historic meeting sees formation of county club

LANCASHIRE COUNTY Cricket Club was born on the 12th January 1864 at a gathering of representatives of 13 of the county's leading clubs at the Queen's Hotel on the corner of Portland Street and Piccadilly in central Manchester. The stated aim of the meeting was "to consider the propriety of forming a county cricket club, with the view to spreading a thorough knowledge and appreciation of the game throughout Lancashire".

The driving force behind the idea to form a county club was the Manchester Cricket Club, who had by far the most representatives at the meeting, and, in particular, their secretary Sam Swire (pictured), who was to become one of the major influences on the growth of the county club right up until his death in 1905. From their earliest recorded games in the 1820s, Manchester had not only hosted teams from other clubs in the county at their various grounds, but also teams from other parts of the country as well as the travelling All-England Elevens, with some notable success.

Teams representing counties had been playing for much of the first half of the 19th Century in various guises, but an official County Championship with formalised fixtures played between officially constituted county clubs was yet to take off, although by the time of the meeting at the Queen's Hotel, that situation was about to change.

Kent had become the first officially constituted county club as far back as 1806, and they were followed by Sussex, Nottinghamshire, Cambridgeshire and Surrey between 1839 and 1844. But it was the events of 1863 which were to spark the Manchester club into action, when firstly Yorkshire was formed in January, followed by Hampshire in August and then Middlesex in December. These county clubs began organising fixtures with each other, initially on a haphazard basis, but with the clear intention of forming a County Championship.

With one eye on this wider picture, Swire and his colleagues at the Manchester club could see that the future of major cricket in England would lie in competition between the traditional counties and that they would have to move quickly in order not to be left behind. At the same time they would have to appease the various vested interests of the clubs in the county. They did this by agreeing to rotate matches between Liverpool, Preston, Blackburn and Manchester's Old Trafford ground.

Swire himself was of the opinion that a county club should have one base and that base should be Old Trafford, the home of Manchester Cricket Club. Eventually he got his way and by the end of the 1860s Old Trafford became the venue of all Lancashire's home fixtures, but whilst this gave the county an identifiable national profile in the nascent county game, within Lancashire itself it would be many years before the county club would be recognised as anything other than an extension of the Manchester club.

Old Trafford – a home from home

BEFORE THE formation of Lancashire County Cricket Club, the Manchester club was forced to move on several occasions before finding its home from home at the current Old Trafford site. Up to 1832 most of the club's games were played at Salford Crescent in Broughton. They then moved to Moss Lane in Moss Side, which lasted until 1847 when the land was required by the Catholic church to build St Mary's church, which still stands on the site. From 1848 until 1856 Manchester played at the Botanical Gardens in Old Trafford, now the site of the White City shopping park and previously the White City stadium. Their move to the current Old Trafford site in 1856 was due to the fact that the Botanical Gardens were required for the Art Treasures Exhibition of 1856.

An artist's impression of Old Trafford in 1861.

1864

The year 1864 marks three momentous events in the history of cricket. The first was the formation of some kind of County Championship competition; the second was the legalisation of overarm bowling; and the third was the publication of the first edition of John Wisden's Cricketers' Almanack.

Two draws as Lancashire begin with Birkenhead Park

WHILST THE other eight constituted counties organised games with each other to decide what would be termed a 'Champion County', Lancashire's first two official matches would be against local opposition in the shape of the Birkenhead Park club on the Wirral, the oldest club in Cheshire, with both games finishing as draws.

The first 'home' game was played at the Arpley ground in Warrington on the 15th and 16th June. Lancashire made 169 all out in their first innings, with James Rowley top-scoring with 57 and Benjamin Lawrence making 45. Lawrence then took eight wickets as Birkenhead Park were bowled out for 143. Lancashire then had a disastrous second innings as they were shot out for just 78, George Grimshaw top-scoring with 16. Park were seemingly on the verge of victory at 90 for 1, just 15 runs short of their target when play ended.

In the return fixture at Park Drive in Birkenhead on the 15th and 16th July, Lancashire again batted first and rattled up 234, with William Hickton making 80 and Frank Wright 41. Park replied with 235, with Lawrence adding a further two wickets to the eight he took in the first match and Hickton showing what a fine all-rounder he was by claiming a five-wicket haul. Lancashire were all out for 174 in their second innings just before the close of play on the second day. Septimus Rowley top-scored with 46 and Arthur Appleby made 38.

Most of the players who appeared in these two games would never appear for the county again. However, William Hickton, Arthur Appleby and Frank Wynyard Wright would go on to play major roles in the early years of the Lancashire county team, and Edmund Butler Rowley, who scored 29 in the first innings of the first match, was to be one of the cornerstones of the Lancashire team as its captain from 1866 until 1879.

It would be a rather different story for the two other Rowley brothers, who had performed so creditably in Lancashire's first two games. James Campbell Rowley, who scored Lancashire's first half century in the game at Arpley, had a distinguished career for the Manchester club stretching back to 1849. The return fixture at Park Drive was to be his last major match and he died in 1870 at the age of just 40. Even more tragically, the promising Septimus Rowley, who was just 18 in 1864 and was the youngest of the Rowley brothers, died in 1874 aged just 28.

It was fitting that Sam Swire should play in the club's first ever game. A stalwart of the Manchester club, whose playing career for them began in 1859 and ended in 1880, it was Swire who did more than any other person to see the Lancashire county club come into existence. He played just five first-class games, but his name will always be associated with the club as its first secretary (initially alongside yet another Rowley brother, Alexander Butler), a post he filled with consummate professionalism until his death in 1905.

Benjamin Andrew James Lawrence was one of Liverpool's top players but he didn't play for Lancashire again despite his performances in these two matches, although he did appear for his native Scotland twice.

Another player worthy of note from Lancashire's first fixtures is Gideon Holgate. A professional who was a wicketkeeper, he played for both Lancashire and Yorkshire between 1865 and 1867. Whilst at Yorkshire, he was involved in various strikes and disputes which ravaged the county, and some reports suggest he was the ringleader. In 1867 he played in the very first Roses match at Whalley, but by the third match between the two sides that year, at Middlesbrough in September, he was playing for Yorkshire! In 1868 he played for the United All-England XI. Although born in Sawley in Yorkshire, he had moved to Accrington as a young boy and played for and captained the town's cricket team, as well running a business there and being heavily involved in community activities. His grandson, also called Gideon, was secretary of the Lancashire League from 1935 until his death in 1949.

VE Walker makes history at Old Trafford *1865*

LANCASHIRE'S FIRST first-class county match was played at Old Trafford over the three days of 21st, 22nd and 23rd July 1865. The opponents were Middlesex, with whom Lancashire had organised home and away fixtures. It was expected that this would be a stern test for the team as Middlesex had narrowly failed to be hailed as the 'Champion County' in the first year of county cricket the year before. A three-wicket reverse at the hands of Sussex in August had robbed them of a 100% record for the 1864 season.

Lancashire included a number of new players who would prove to be great acquisitions for the club. Roger Iddison was a superb all-rounder who was yet another who played for both the Red and White Rose counties, usually in the same season. He played for Lancashire from that very first county game against Middlesex until 1870, although when Lancashire faced Yorkshire he preferred to play for the opposition. Fred Reynolds was to have ten seasons at Old Trafford and take over 200 wickets and Alexander Butler Rowley, one of the famous Rowley brothers who had been appointed joint secretary with Sam Swire the year before, would play sporadically for the county until 1871 and eventually become President of the club from 1874 to 1879.

As regards the match itself, Lancashire recorded a famous victory. All but two of Lancashire's batsmen reached double figures as the Red Rose men notched up 243. Reynolds, Iddison and AB Rowley then shared the wickets as Middlesex were bowled out for the exact same score.

It was then that Old Trafford experienced its first piece of county cricket history. Vyell Edwards Walker, the Middlesex captain who bowled slow underarm lobs, became the first man to take all ten wickets in an innings in county cricket, and that despite not bowling a single ball in Lancashire's first innings. His figures were 44.2 overs, five maidens, 10 for 104 out of a Lancashire total of 178. This wasn't the first time he had taken all ten in an innings; he had done so for the All-England Eleven against Surrey in 1859 and he had come very close to the same feat the previous season in a match against Sussex when a run out robbed him of all ten.

Walker's remarkable performance

Lancashire second innings

SH Swire	b VE Walker	16
FJ Crooke	st Morley b VE Walker	20
JF Leese	c Haines b VE Walker	0
R Iddison	c and b VE Walker	6
J Makinson	st Morley b VE Walker	0
EJ Bousfield	c Wilkinson b VE Walker	15
E Whittaker	c RD Walker b VE Walker	39
AB Rowley	c RD Walker b VE Walker	60
R Blackstock	b VE Walker	5
+W Perry	c and b VE Walker	0
FR Reynolds	not out	13
Extras	(3 lb, 1 w)	4
Total	(all out, 102.2 overs)	178

Fall of wickets: 1-31, 2-33, 3-43, 4-43, 5-50, 6-67, 7-135, 8-145, 9-145, 10-178

Middlesex bowling

	O	M	R	W
T Hearne	8	6	6	0
Wilkinson	7	4	6	0
RD Walker	2	1	3	0
Howitt	36	14	49	0
Catling	5	2	6	0
VE Walker	44.2	5	104	10

Despite VE Walker's heroics, Roger Iddison became the first Lancashire player to take five wickets in an innings (5 for 45), and with the support of Fred Reynolds, Middlesex were bowled out for 116 to give Lancashire their first ever county victory by 62 runs in their first match.

This was to be a high point for Lancashire county cricket. In the return fixture at the Cattle Market Ground in Islington, they lost by 10 wickets after being forced to follow on. No Lancashire batsman made more than 25, with the damage done, not by VE Walker, who failed to take a single wicket in the first innings and didn't bowl in the second, but mostly by his brothers Russell and Isaac Donnithorne Walker, part of a dynasty of brothers at Middlesex which resembled that of the Rowleys at Lancashire.

The only plus point for the Red Rose county was the performance of Fred Reynolds, who took 6 for 92 in Middlesex's only innings. It was not until 1868 that Lancashire were to taste victory again.

150 LANCASHIRE GREATS
2. Roger Iddison

Yorkshire-born Roger Iddison was one of the great professional cricketers of the mid-19th Century. A stockily-built man, he was a batsman with a free style who could hit the ball very hard. Originally a fast round-arm bowler, he changed to under-arm lobs depending on flight and pitch variations. He scored Lancashire's first century, 106, at the Oval in 1866. He went on the first tour of Australia in 1861-2, played in the All-England and other representative sides and in the days before strict qualifications had been introduced, he played for Lancashire and Yorkshire in the same season. He played for Lancashire for the first five seasons and in 16 matches scored 621 runs, ave. 23.88, and took 56 wickets at 15.62, helping to steer Lancashire through those early days when the team, particularly for away days, was often desperately weak. He went on to play 72 matches for Yorkshire and retired to live in York where he sold cricket gear. An astute businessman, he was frequently at odds with the county committees as he tried to balance his numerous obligations.

Sport gains foothold in Lancashire

1866

LANCASHIRE SUCCEEDED in doubling their county fixture list in 1866. Two matches against their 1865 opponents Middlesex were supplemented by home and away fixtures with Surrey, who were the busiest county team in this period.

The three day match at Old Trafford against Middlesex began on 5th June and a familiar face was to be Lancashire's tormentor. VE Walker this time produced the goods with the bat, top-scoring with 41 in Middlesex's first innings total of 134. Lancashire replied with 181, which included 85 from Cornelius Coward batting at number eight, Lancashire's top individual score to date. VE Walker then added a half century, which, added to scores of 60 and 87 from AH Winter and T Hearne, left Lancashire needing 222 to win on the final day. They fell short by 54 runs.

In 1899, Fred Reynolds was to recall the following incident involving Coward: "In his later days Coward was somewhat lame, and had a runner. On one occasion at Old Trafford he hit a ball and himself started to run, forgetting for the moment the runner. The runner ran too, half way up the wicket. The other batsman met them (Coward and his runner) just half way. It was then that Coward saw that the run was no run, and he turned tail. So did the runner, but the batsman from the other end kept straight ahead, and was about level with them at the wicket. All three stormed in at one end together, and the

sight must have been comical. The wicket at the other derelict end was, of course, put down. Thoms, the umpire, was asked 'How's that?' and of course he said 'Out'. 'But who's out?' asked the three breathlessly. 'Why,' laughed Thoms, 'you're all out.' It was the last wicket."

The return match in Islington started on the 16th July but lasted less than two days. Despite AB Rowley's undefeated 63 and the now available Roger Iddison's 5 for 54, Lancashire trailed by 56 runs on first innings. Coward scored another half century in the second innings, but Middlesex were left with just 87 to get for victory, which they achieved for the loss of just four wickets. Coward's two half centuries against Middlesex were the only two he scored in 49 first-class matches.

The Lancashire team stayed in London and moved on to the Kennington Oval for their first ever match at the ground and against Surrey. Although he failed to take a wicket with the ball, Roger Iddison proved his worth with the bat, making 49 in Lancashire's first innings as opener and then becoming the club's first ever centurion in the second with 106. Gideon Holgate supported his fellow Yorkshireman in both innings with half centuries, but Lancashire had to settle for a draw after Surrey had led on first innings by 227 runs, having rattled up a very imposing 422 in their only innings. Henry Jupp, who was to play two Tests for England in Australia ten years later, made his highest first-class score of 165, which would remain the highest individual innings against the Red Rose for some time.

In the return match at the Wavertree Ground in Liverpool at the end of August,

Lancashire lost by the narrow margin of three wickets, despite Arthur Appleby's 6 for 31 in Surrey's first innings and Roger Iddison's 5 for 34 in the second. The Lancashire batting failed miserably, totalling just 125 and 86 in the two innings. Lancashire's top score in the match was 39 by opener Thomas Owen Potter, a keen cricketer for the Liverpool club for whom this would be his only outing for the county. He would become more famous later as one of the first members at the Royal Liverpool Golf Club in Hoylake, where he ruled the roost from 1882 to 1894 and became famous in golfing circles for founding the Amateur Championship.

150 LANCASHIRE GREATS
3. Arthur Appleby

He was born at Enfield, Clayton-le-Moors, Lancashire, in 1843, the son of mill owner Joseph Appleby. He began his playing days at Enfield Cricket Club, where he was coached by the Yorkshire professionals John Berry and WH Iddison. A left-arm round-arm medium pace bowler and left-handed batsman, he played 58 matches for Lancashire as an amateur between 1866 and 1887 and 81 first-class matches in total. Bowling was his strongest suit, with 9 for 25 against Sussex being his best innings analysis. He took five wickets in an innings on 24 occasions and ten wickets in a match three times. He never made a first-class century, falling just one run short against Yorkshire in a Roses Match. In later life he assumed control of the family firm and, amongst other directorships, sat on the board of the Leeds & Liverpool Canal. He was an Alderman of Lancashire County Council and Chairman of the County Bench, sitting at Church. He died at Mill House, Enfield, on 24 October 1902 and it was said the whole town paid its respects as 700 mourners led the funeral cortège in respect for a true Lancashire Gentleman.

It wasn't only cricket that was seeing a growth in the number of clubs in the 1860s. In 1862 the first football club was formed, Notts County, followed by Preston North End the year after and Nottingham Forest in 1865. The Manchester rugby club had been formed in 1860, and they were followed by Sale and Richmond in 1861, Bath and Bedford in 1865, Harlequins in 1866, along with Rochdale and Swinton, Wasps in 1867 and Preston Grasshoppers in 1869. In this unprecedented growth in organised sport, it was not only clubs involved in team sports that flourished. In 1868 The All-England Lawn Tennis and Croquet Club was founded and, in 1869, The Royal Liverpool Golf Club, for which Lancashire one-cap wonder Thomas Potter was to become such a prominent member, opened its doors for the first time.

Roses nightmare for Lancashire

1867

MIDDLESEX DROPPED their fixtures with the club for the 1867 season, but Lancashire still managed to increase their number of county games by one with the introduction of the first Roses matches. In 1867, Lancashire were to play Yorkshire on three occasions, but unfortunately for the Red Rose, they were to result in three heavy defeats.

Before that first Roses match at Whalley, which began on 20th June, Lancashire travelled to London at the end of May for the first of their home and away matches with Surrey at Kennington Oval, which was to be followed by a prestigious first-class friendly against the Marylebone Cricket Club at Lord's.

The game at the Oval was another high-scoring draw, but it saw one of the most remarkable debuts of any Lancashire player ever. Batting first, the Red Rose notched up their highest first-class score so far, 429, of which opener James Ricketts carried his bat for a mammoth 195. He was supported in a second wicket stand of 166 by skipper EB Rowley, who made 78. Surrey replied with 340 and 200 for 7, Arthur Appleby returning match figures of 9 for 173.

Ricketts was born in Manchester and played for the Manchester Clifford club, whose ground adjoined Old Trafford. His performances for his club, and a solid game for the Gentlemen of Lancashire against the Gentlemen of Yorkshire at York in September 1866, when he opened with AN Hornby, saw him given his chance in the county side. Unfortunately, he never really lived up to this early promise, even though he continued playing for Lancashire on and off for ten years. Although he gained a reputation as a somewhat dour opening bat, he only managed one more half century and his appearances became restricted with the emergence of RG Barlow in 1871. Eventually he became an umpire, officiating in several first-class matches. However, his 195 against Surrey was to remain Lancashire's highest individual score until Archie MacLaren produced one the greatest innings ever in county cricket at Taunton in 1895.

The first-class friendly with the MCC at Lord's was the antithesis of the game at the Oval. Lancashire were bundled out for just 79 and 66 and lost by 50 runs, Ricketts making a duck in the first innings to prove just what a fickle game cricket is. There were, however, two excellent performances with the ball for the Red Rose. William Hickton took 11 for 91 in the match, whilst Arthur Appleby was beginning to prove what a great performer he was to become for Lancashire with match figures of 7 for 60.

And so, on to the very first Roses match, played at Station Road in Whalley from the 20th to the 22nd June. It was the only time a first-class match has been played at the ground and was chosen for its geographical position near the border between the two counties.

The frailties of Lancashire's batting at Lord's were again in evidence at Whalley as they were dismissed for just 57 and 75 by George Freeman and Luke Greenwood in reply to Yorkshire's first innings of 188, to lose by an innings and 56 runs. Appleby was Lancashire's only outstanding performer in the match, with six Yorkshire wickets for 62 runs in 53.2 four-ball overs, which was the norm at this time.

Playing for Yorkshire, as he was to do in the two other Roses matches of 1867, was Roger Iddison, who had made such a fine contribution to Lancashire's 1866 campaign. It seems that Yorkshire had first call on his

---

The Yorkshire Connection

THE CUTTELLS were not the only familial anomaly amongst Lancashire and Yorkshire playing arrangements. Astonishingly, playing for Lancashire in the second and third Roses matches of 1867 was Roger Iddison's younger brother, William Houldsworth Iddison, who was also Yorkshire-born.

Perhaps even more startling was the role of Gideon Holgate in these first Roses matches and the 1867 season. He played for the Red Rose at Whalley and Old Trafford, only to then turn out for the White Rose in the third game at Middlesbrough. Indeed, he played in all four of Yorkshire's other first-class games that summer and both Lancashire's matches against Surrey, and the game at Lord's against the MCC. Such were the loyalties of cricketers in the 1860s!

Also making his debut for Lancashire at Whalley was Elisha Barker Rawlinson, yet another Lancashire player born in Yorkshire. Rawlinson batted at number ten and didn't bowl, so when Roger Iddison heard that he was Yorkshire-born, he promised to get him a game for his native county. Lo and behold, at Old Trafford one week later he was in the Yorkshire side and continued playing for them with mixed success until 1875.

services, a fact that he may have regretted as his performance in the only game he played for Lancashire in 1867, the return fixture

Lancashire v Yorkshire

At Station Road, Whalley
on 20th, 21st, 22nd June 1867 (3-day match)
Toss: Yorkshire won the toss and decided to bat
Result: Yorkshire won by an innings and 56 runs
Umpires: T Burlinson, J Wright

Yorkshire first innings

J Rowbotham	c Hornby b Appleby	7
J Thewlis	b Appleby	I
E Stephenson	b Leventon	54
R Iddison	b Appleby	14
JE Lee	b Appleby	0
E Dawson	b Hickton	11
G Anderson	b Leventon	6
G Freeman	c Rawlinson b Hickton	28
J Berry	c Hibberd b Appleby	27
L Greenwood	c and b Appleby	19
GR Atkinson	not out	14
Extras	(2 lb, 1 nb, 4 w)	7
Total	(all out, 145.2 overs)	188

Fall of wickets: 1-1, 2-24, 3-54, 4-54, 5-89, 6-98, 7-98, 8-137, 9-169, 10-188

	O	M	R	W
Appleby	53.2	27	62	6
Hibberd	22	6	37	0
Rowley	9	5	8	0
Hickton	47	26	50	2
Leventon	14	4	24	2

Lancashire first innings

AN Hornby	c Stephenson b Freeman	2
J Ricketts	b Greenwood	3
JF Leese	c Freeman b Greenwood	22
C Coward	b Greenwood	13
AB Rowley	b Freeman	0
G Holgate	c Anderson b Freeman	8
A Appleby	b Freeman	1
W Hickton	c Anderson b Freeman	2
EC Leventon	b Freeman	0
EB Rawlinson	not out	1
G Hibberd	b Freeman	2
Extras	(2 lb, 1 w)	3
Total	(all out, 45.1 overs)	57

Fall of wickets: 1-3, 2-5, 3-31, 4-34, 5-44, 6-45, 7-50, 8-50, 9-53, 10-57

	O	M	R	W
Greenwood	23	7	44	3
Freeman	22.1	14	10	7

Lancashire second innings (following on)

EB Rawlinson	b Greenwood	14
G Holgate	run out	21
JF Leese	b Freeman	4
J Ricketts	b Freeman	0
AN Hornby	b Freeman	3
C Coward	c Iddison b Greenwood	5
AB Rowley	b Freeman	0
A Appleby	b Greenwood	18
W Hickton	b Freeman	0
EC Leventon	c Iddison b Greenwood	6
G Hibberd	not out	2
Extras	(2 b)	2
Total	(all out, 61.1 overs)	75

Fall of wickets: 1-20, 2-27, 3-27, 4-41, 5-45, 6-46, 7-54, 8-57, 9-72, 10-75

	O	M	R	W
Freeman	31	5	41	5
Greenwood	30.1	16	32	4

against Surrey, far outweighed anything he produced for Yorkshire in the three Roses matches.

Before Lancashire hosted Surrey at Old Trafford, there was the second Roses game, which began soon after the first on the 27th June. Lancashire led on first innings by 10 runs thanks largely to a half century from skipper EB Rowley, who had missed the Whalley game. But Yorkshire then notched 273 and Lancashire were bundled out for just 98 to lose by 165 runs. The destroyer-in-chief for Yorkshire, with 9 for 84 in the match, was William Cuttell, for whom this was his best performance for the White Rose in a sporadic county career which amounted to just 14 games from 1864 to 1871. But, from a Lancashire point of view, his major claim to fame was that at home in Sheffield was his one-year-old son Willis Robert, who was to become one of Lancashire's greatest ever bowlers and part of one of the club's greatest eras in a county career that lasted from 1896 until 1906.

Lancashire were hanging on by the skin of their teeth at Old Trafford against Surrey when play ended on 24th August. That was largely thanks to Roger Iddison. He followed an undefeated 71 in Lancashire's first innings with 64 not out in the second, adding four Surrey wickets to cap a sublime all-round display. The next best score for the home side in either innings was James Ricketts' 42.

At the beginning of September, in the third Roses match of the year at the Swatter's Carr, Linthorpe East Ground in Middlesbrough, Ricketts was to get an opportunity to bowl. With Yorkshire strolling along at 143 for 2 in reply to Lancashire's 97 all out, he came on to bowl third change and claimed four wickets for 40 runs to help bowl Yorkshire out for 205. It was his best bowling performance for the county, but he rarely bowled again. At the other end Arthur Appleby took 6 for 87 to notch his third five-wicket haul of the summer and 30 wickets for the season, and to head the Lancashire bowling averages on 15.13.

However, Lancashire's frail batting line-up, exacerbated by the fact that skipper EB Rowley was unavailable for this match, saw them bowled out a second time for just 68 and to lose by an innings and 40 runs. The Yorkshire destroyers this time, with 19 Lancashire wickets between them (the other was a run out), were Freeman and Tom Emmett, who was at the beginning of a long and distinguished career for the White Rose which would see him take over 1500 first-class wickets and play seven times for England, including in the very first Ashes Test at Melbourne in March 1877. Roger Iddison bowled ten wicketless overs in

Albert Neilsen 'Monkey' Hornby, who made his debut in the first Roses match and was to become one of the legends of Lancashire cricket.

Lancashire's second innings, whilst brother William was unsuccessful in his five overs in Yorkshire's only innings.

So, it had been a humbling experience for Lancashire's cricketers on the field of play in 1867. Three resounding defeats at the hands of Yorkshire, a defeat at the hands of the MCC at Lord's and two draws with Surrey, one of which they were lucky to achieve. However, there were some plus points. It was no disgrace to lose to the Yorkshire side of 1867, who had been arguably the strongest line-up in county cricket so far, winning all seven of their first-class county games, whilst being invited to play the MCC at Lord's, a fixture that they would repeat in 1868 and 1869, was a feather in the cap for Sam Swire and the administrators at Old Trafford and their quest to put Lancashire on the cricketing map. Moreover, in Arthur Appleby and William Hickton, Lancashire had two bowlers who were amongst the best in the land.

It was, however, the batting that was Lancashire's problem. But unbeknownst to anyone at the time, the future of Lancashire's batting, and the club's rise to prominence in English cricket, was to be seen in a quiet and inauspicious debut in that first Roses match at Whalley. Twenty-year-old Albert Neilsen Hornby, the son of William Henry Hornby, the MP for Blackburn, made just 2 and 3 in his first match, and may have owed his debut to the absence of skipper EB Rowley, but he was to become Lancashire's first great batsman as well as the captain, chairman and president who would turn Lancashire into one of the great clubs of world cricket.

Batting woes continue *1868*

LANCASHIRE FARED little better in 1868 than they had done in 1867, despite achieving their first victory since their very first game against Middlesex in 1865. The sole success was against Surrey at Old Trafford, but this was mitigated by heavy defeats to Nottinghamshire at Trent Bridge, Yorkshire at Holbeck and in the return match against Surrey at the Oval, all by an innings. There was also a much narrower defeat to the MCC at Lord's and a 16-run reverse to Nottinghamshire at Old Trafford when victory seemed Lancashire's for the taking.

There was no surprise in the Red Rose's defeat in the opening match of 1868 against Nottinghamshire, whom they were playing for the first time. They travelled to Trent Bridge at the end of May more in hope than expectation as their opposition was laden with members of the various All-England elevens. James Ricketts top-scored in both innings with 35 and 47 respectively as the Lancashire batsmen failed to get to grips with the fast left-hand round-arm bowling of James Shaw and George Wootton, who collected all but two of the wickets between them as Lancashire subsided to an innings and 74-run defeat.

William Hickton and Roger Iddison were the stars for Lancashire in their only win of the summer. Hickton's match figures of 10 for 96 and Iddison's of 8 for 71 saw the Red Rose men victorious by eight wickets. In fact, Surrey had led by 49 on first innings, which would have been much more but for Hickton's unbeaten 41. The pair then got to work on the Surrey batting line-up, dismissing them for just 42, the lowest team total at Old Trafford so far, before Iddison partnered Ricketts in a 24-run stand to see the home side past their target.

The only Roses match of 1868, which began on 9th July, saw humiliation for Lancashire at the Recreation Ground in Holbeck. They were bowled out twice for 30 and 34, their lowest totals until another infamous match in 1871, by Tom Emmett and George Freeman, who garnered all 20 wickets between them. Only two Lancashire players got into double figures and no fewer than 11 made ducks! Iddison made 57 in Yorkshire's 250.

It was with some relief that the team headed down to London the following week for the return with Surrey and the game with the MCC at Lord's. That relief was to last no longer than the first morning at the Oval. Despite having Hickton and Iddison in tandem once again, Surrey reached 125 before a wicket fell, with Henry Jupp going on to post another century against the Red Rose men and Surrey to make 351. Lancashire then capitulated for 120 and 89, losing by an innings again

mainly due to the slow round-arm bowling of James Southerton, who took 14 wickets in the match. Southerton would, along with Jupp and Yorkshire's Tom Emmett, play in the very first Test match at Melbourne in 1877.

The game at Lord's against the MCC provided only a little relief for the Red Rose men. It was completed within two days, with Lancashire bowled out for 74 on the first morning. Hickton and Fred Reynolds then bowled unchanged to limit the home side's advantage to 38. However, they could only set the MCC a target of 90, and despite the best efforts of Hickton, Reynolds, Iddison and Ricketts, they crept over the line with four wickets to spare.

A busy month was completed by the Red Rose with the return home game against the formidable Nottinghamshire outfit, who were buoyed by a convincing victory over Yorkshire at Dewsbury the day before the game at Old Trafford.

Until the final throes of the match on the second day, it looked like Lancashire were going to cause a major upset. A 60-run second wicket partnership between Cornelius Coward and Ricketts, who went on to make his only other score past 50 other than the 195 he made on debut, ensured a Lancashire first innings lead of 41. Roger Iddison, who had remained wicketless against the same opposition in the game at Dewsbury, had grabbed 6 for 29 in Notts' first innings total of 127. He and Reynolds then took four wickets apiece as Lancashire were set the fairly simple task of making 70 runs for victory.

But Lancashire reckoned without the redoubtable right-arm medium pace of Alfred Shaw, who would bowl the very first ball in Test cricket ten years later. He cleaned bowled the first five batsman and finished with 6 for 29 as Lancashire folded for 53. Once again the Red Rose's bowlers had been let down by their batsmen.

The pavilion at Old Trafford, where for the forseeable future all Lancashire's home games would be played.

Century for Rev Wright

1869

LANCASHIRE'S FIXTURES against Nottinghamshire and Yorkshire were suspended in 1869, with the county down to five games, including the first-class friendly with the MCC and with Sussex as new opposition. They finished with two victories at Old Trafford and three defeats on their travels. It was a marginal improvement, but there were signs that the batsmen were about to get their act together.

Roger Iddison's bowling fell away in 1869; he managed just three wickets in three games as opposed to the 26 he took in five matches the previous season, but this was more than compensated for by the return of Arthur Appleby, who made an immediate impact in the first game against Surrey at Old Trafford. He followed three wickets in the first innings with 8 for 68 in the second, to finish with match figures of 94.1 overs, 36 maidens, 11 wickets for 144 runs.

On top of this he was one of five players who averaged more than 20 with the bat; in

1868 there had been just one, James Ricketts. Iddison steered Lancashire home with an undefeated 38 against Surrey and he finished in fourth place in the batting averages, just above Appleby. Above him was EB Rowley, who was only able to play in two of the matches, but his half century in the game against Surrey was a telling contribution in Lancashire's comfortable victory.

Above EB Rowley was the Reverend Frank Wynyard Wright. Wright had played in Lancashire's second ever game against Birkenhead Park in 1864, during the summer after his second year at Oxford. He gained his BA in 1866 and took Holy Orders. His cousin was Teddy Wynyard, who played for Hampshire for 30 years between 1878 and 1908, was capped three times by England, against Australia at the Oval in 1896 and two on the 1905/6 tour of South Africa when he was 44 years old, won an FA Cup winners' medal for Old Carthusians in 1881 and was an exceptional winter sportsman.

Settled in Broughton, where he became the Curate of All Souls from 1868 until 1870, his father's parish, Wright was able to play in all but two of Lancashire's nine first-class fixtures in 1869 and 1870. His undefeated 120 in the match against Sussex, only the third century by a Lancastrian so far and the first by a Lancashire player at Old Trafford, was largely responsible for the Red Rose men's second victory of the summer.

With Wright that day, in a century partnership for the third wicket, was the man who was to top the averages for the first time and dominate Lancashire's batting for much of the next 20 years. His name was Albert Neilson Hornby.

This, of course, wasn't his first game for the Red Rose. He had made his debut in the first Roses match at Whalley two years previously, scoring just 2 and 3 in Lancashire's heavy defeat. Then he appeared in the final match of 1868 against Nottinghamshire at Old Trafford, where he made just 8 and 7. In 1869, however, he managed a level of consistency at the top of the order which Lancashire had not yet seen and which was a portent for the future.

After defeat by two wickets in a remarkable game with the MCC at Lord's on Lancashire's third annual tour of London

in July, Hornby's runs and Appleby's 7 for 69 in Surrey's first innings were not enough to stop the Londoners gaining revenge by eight wickets at the Oval for their early season defeat at Old Trafford. Then, in August, a weakened side went down by five wickets at the Royal Brunswick Ground in Hove against Sussex.

Hickton finished 1869 with 39 wickets, including five 5-wicket hauls and 10 wickets in a match twice, at an average of 11.12. With bowling palpably the team's strongest suit, this was the best season's return yet, but it was merely a prelude to the greatest ever bowling performance by a Lancashire bowler.

Mr Grace comes of age

LANCASHIRE'S TWO-WICKET defeat by the MCC at Lord's on the 19th and 20th July was notable for two reasons. Firstly, it finished in great excitement with all four innings within nine runs of each other and Lancashire's first innings of 67 all out being the highest. Secondly, it marked Lancashire's first meeting with WG Grace, who was to become, arguably, the most famous figure in cricket history and certainly the most eminent sportsman of the late Victorian era.

Grace had celebrated his 21st birthday the day before the game and was beginning to make a real name for himself with the bat. Indeed, in July he scored four first-class centuries. But in this game he was to fall cheaply twice, for 6 and 0, to the bowling of William Hickton, who was one of the few bowlers to have the measure of Grace, getting him out cheaply on many occasions.

Hickton returned match figures of 11 for 49, but Grace, an accomplished bowler in his own right, responded with nine wickets of his own for just 34 runs. His analysis in Lancashire's second innings was 27.3 overs, 19 maidens, 6 wickets for 10 runs.

All ten for Hickton *1870*

LANCASHIRE'S FIXTURE list for 1870 dropped back down to just four games. The annual game against the MCC at Lord's was dropped and didn't take place again until 1875 and the home and away matches with Sussex had lasted just one season. Instead, the Red Rose men were to have another long trip to the south coast, with Hampshire as their new opponents. Hampshire had not competed against any county club since 1867, and wouldn't again after their two matches with Lancashire until 1875 even though they had been part of the original rump of eight county teams in 1864. For the second season running, Surrey were the first opponents at Old Trafford at the end of May. Their usually strong batting proved a disappointment as they were bowled out for 103 and 95 and lost by eight wickets, Appleby taking 6 for 37 in their first innings and Hickton 6 for 17 in the second.

And so to Lancashire's first ever game with Hampshire, an historic occasion producing a county record which still stands today. It was not often during the career of AN Hornby that he was upstaged, but at Old Trafford between the 21st and 23rd of July, this was certainly the case.

On the opening day, Hornby ran up the first of his 16 first-class centuries, 132 out of 262 all out. Hickton was then again into his stride, taking 4 for 27 in 30 economical overs as Hampshire were dismissed for 138. Following on, Hampshire were bowled out second time around for 129, with Hickton claiming all ten of the visitors' wickets for just 46 runs. It was, and remains, the best bowling performance by a Lancashire player in a single innings.

Incidentally, making his debut as Hickton's opening partner at Old Trafford against Hampshire in the absence of Arthur Appleby was an interesting character by the name of Fred Birley. He was born in Chorlton in 1850 and played just four times for the county, three in 1870 and once two years later. He went up to University College, Oxford, and although he played in the freshers' match he didn't get a game for the University. He did, however, play Association Football for the University, and was a member of the Oxford side that won the FA Cup in 1874. Later, as a member of the Wanderers Football Club, he was on the winning side in two more Cup finals in 1876 and 1877. He also played twice for England and became a well-known ornithologist.

After Hickton's performance in the ten-wicket demolition of Hampshire, it was definitely the case of after the Lord Mayor's Show for the Red Rose men in their trip to the Oval in mid-August. Despite the presence of Hornby, Ricketts, Appleby, EB Rowley and Hickton, Lancashire fell to an innings defeat as the old batting frailties resurfaced. In their two innings of 81 and 103, Hornby's 36 was the highest score.

So, instead of the short trip to Lord's, the team headed for Day's (Antelope)

Ground in Southampton. Hornby, skippering for the first of what would be many times in the absence of EB Rowley, won the toss and batted, but Ricketts' 47 was the only major contribution as the Red Rose men were skittled for 115. Fred Reynolds' 5 for 21 ensured a narrow first innings lead, and after Ricketts had again top-scored in Lancashire's second innings of 113, Appleby made sure that the team would not be going home from their trip down south empty-handed. His 7 for 37 were his best bowling figures of the season.

Hickton's Lancashire record

Hampshire second innings (following on)

EL Ede	c Birley b Hickton	25
G Carter	b Hickton	14
J May	not out	14
A Seymour	b Hickton	0
H Holmes	c Reynolds b Hickton	14
CV Eccles	c AB Rowley b Hickton	23
AH Wood	c AB Rowley b Hickton	3
G Ubsdell	b Hickton	9
C Martin	b Hickton	1
TH Wilson	b Hickton	2
F Tate	b Hickton	12
Extras	(7 b, 4 lb, 1 w)	12
Total	(all out, 83.2 overs)	129

Fall of wickets: 1-3, 2-5, 3-29, 4-69, 5-86, 6-87, 7-102, 8-113, 9-117, 10-129

Lancashire bowling

	O	M	R	W
Birley	7	3	12	0
Hickton	36.2	19	46	10
AB Rowley	40	21	59	0

150 LANCASHIRE GREATS
7. Rev. Frank W Wright

Rev. Frank Wynyard Wright was a dashing batsman who made hundreds for Rossall, Oxford University and Lancashire. He showed great promise as a cricketer at Rossall School. In 1861 he appeared for the Gentlemen of Lancashire and also for the North v South. He gained a Blue at Oxford for three consecutive years and scored 142 against Midland Counties, and in 1863 was chosen for the Gentlemen of England against the Free Foresters, giving a brilliant display of attacking batsmanship with 64 in 30 minutes. When he was curate at his father's parish at Broughton he made the first of his 15 appearances for Lancashire in 1869 and his highest score was an unbeaten 120 against Sussex at Old Trafford. His clerical duties left little time for cricket and his appearances were only occasional. A brilliant fielder at point, he was also a fine wicketkeeper. He played for Cheshire and was also very prominent in club cricket. After serving as curate at Bradford and Broughton he was appointed Rector of Hedsor in Buckinghamshire in 1870. He then became a teacher in Eastbourne for over 40 years, dying there in 1924 aged 80.

All Out for 25 *1871*

NEITHER SURREY nor Hampshire were to be Lancashire's opponents in 1871. Instead, the fixture list increased up to six with the inclusion of home and away games against the oldest county, Kent, the newest, Derbyshire, who had been formed the previous November, and a return of the Roses matches, the last of which had been played in 1868.

For William Hickton, this was to be his final season for the Red Rose. He was a Derbyshire man through and through and, being a proven bowler at this level, was called upon by his native county. He did, however, make one last hurrah for the club in the games against Kent and Yorkshire before throwing his lot in completely with his home county from 1872 to 1878. He is immortalised, however, in Lancashire history for that performance against Hampshire at Old Trafford in 1870.

Indeed, Lancashire lined up against Hickton in Derbyshire's very first county match, at Old Trafford on 26th May. He was to play a major role in yet another Lancashire record, as, on the opening morning of the match, the Red Rose men were bowled out for what was, and still remains, their lowest ever innings total of 25. In a day that will go down in infamy in the annals of Lancashire cricket, just one man, the wicketkeeper Alfort Smith, attained double figures and Hickton, who was instrumental in reducing the home side to 5 for 6, finished with 4 for 16, whilst his partner, Dove Gregory, who was to play in just four county matches, all against Lancashire in 1871 and 1872, finished with the remarkable figures of 12.3 overs, 9 maidens, 6 for 9

Derbyshire then made 147, skipper Fred Reynolds taking 5 for 54, before Lancashire's humiliation was completed when they were bowled out a second time for 111 to lose by an innings and 11 runs.

Hickton was back in the fold for the county's trip to Gravesend and the Bat and Ball Ground on 19th June for their first ever game against Kent, but their poor start to the season continued as they went down by five wickets. Then it was back to Old Trafford for the resumption of the Roses contest, but there was a familiar outcome as Tom Emmett and George Freeman once again tormented Lancashire's batsmen with 18 of the wickets to fall in a 222-run defeat.

So, halfway through the season and Lancashire's batting had reverted to type with a highest individual score of 36 in six completed innings and a record low – something had to change! And it did.

The scorecard for the game in which Lancashire recorded their lowest ever innings total.

150 LANCASHIRE GREATS
8. Albert Neilson Hornby

AN Hornby was the most influential person in the long history of Lancashire CCC. Born in Blackburn the son of a wealthy cotton merchant, he was given the nickname 'Monkey' because of his small stature. At 17 he was opening the innings at Harrow and went to Oxford purely to play cricket, but when he heard that study might be required he returned to his family business. He played 292 matches for the county over 33 seasons, scoring over 10,000 runs, and along with opening partner RG Barlow was immortalised in the stained-glass window at Old Trafford and Francis Thompson's poem. He was appointed captain in 1880, winning the County Championship the following year and also in 1897, and also sharing two further Championships. He led the county with determination and got the best out of his players. He captained England twice against Australia, including in 1882 at the Oval when the Ashes were born. He was President of the club for 23 years and known as the Squire of Lancashire. For decades he was the very soul of the club.

The debut of RG Barlow

IT WAS perhaps no coincidence that Lancashire's first ever Roses victory, and the turning around of what so far had been a fretful season, should be marked by the debut of one of the Red Rose's greatest ever players. Richard Gorton 'RG' Barlow had learnt his early cricket in Bolton, the place of his birth, and Staveley in Derbyshire, where his family had moved in 1865. It was William Hickton, who, on finding out he was born in Lancashire, suggested he ask his home county for a trial. He must also have put in a good word for the 20-year-old because a few days after the trial he was making his debut for Lancashire in their return fixture against Yorkshire at Bramall Lane.

Fred Reynolds won the toss and elected to bat and rather than the clatter of wickets that had become the norm from the top order that season, they actually got off to a good start. Tom Emmett and Luke Greenwood, who had so bamboozled Lancashire's batsmen

in previous Roses matches, were rendered ineffective as Ricketts and Hornby took the side to 94 for 1 before both fell to Iddison, who had played his final match for Lancashire at Old Trafford against Surrey the previous season, and Emmett respectively. There were useful contributions from Cornelius Coward and George Hartley, who was also making his debut and whose son Charles would be a stalwart of the great Lancashire era of the late 1890s and 1900s.

Barlow entered the fray at 149 for 5. He finished the first day 18 not out, but with a broken little finger on his right hand, which

had forced him to retire hurt. Meanwhile, Arthur Appleby had stroked his way to his highest first-class score of 99. William Hickton made his second highest first-class score of 55 batting at number 11 and with his finger bound up, Barlow had continued the following morning, taking his score to 28 not out. It was the sort of performance that was to become synonymous with the great RG.

Appleby and Hickton then shared nine wickets apiece as Yorkshire were bowled out 152 runs adrift of Lancashire's 343. Barlow bowled three overs, taking one wicket for eight runs. He added another three in the follow on as the home side only just managed to make the Red Rose men bat again. Ricketts and Hornby duly completed an historic ten-wicket victory and RG Barlow had made his mark.

In the return match with Kent at Old Trafford in early August, Appleby and Hickton were again on top form, taking 16 of the 20 wickets to fall in an innings and 14-run win. Barlow did not play in this game, but he returned for the re-match with Derbyshire at the County Ground in Derby, where no doubt he was watched by his large and enthusiastic cricket-loving family. He opened the innings but scored just eight in Lancashire's 116. He did, however, bowl in the home side's second innings when they needed 121 for victory, taking 3 wickets for 31 as Derbyshire were shot out for just 58. Appleby, with 7 for 21, had his best return of his best season and for the third time in a row it was sweet revenge for the Red Rose.

Stumper's folly

Before the arrival of Richard Pilling, Lancashire tried several wicketkeepers with varying degrees of success. One such was Edward Jackson, who made his debut in the famous victory at Bramall Lane, making two stumpings in Yorkshire's second innings, and playing 15 times for the county between 1871 and 1885.

He was a wicketkeeper of the type called by W.G. Grace 'ambidextrous', that is, he could take the ball one-handed on both sides of the wicket and he related the following incident in an article in The Liverpool Courier of 26th June 1921:

"The first time I played against WG Grace was at Eaton Hall, Chester. It is many years ago, but still has an interest for me, as I think I made an impression upon WG which he never forgot. We were 18 in the field, and when he came in to bat I had him out before you could say 'knife'. It was a one-handed stump, wide on the leg side. Old Perry (the Liverpool groundsman) was umpiring, and promptly shook his head, and WG looked at me as much as to say, 'Don't you do that again.' But I did, and had him out several times. Still the umpires were obdurate. After the fourth appeal I sent the ball back to the bowler in rather a temper, and WG looked round at me and said, whisperingly, 'What do you think the crowd's here for?' And before I had time to collect my thoughts, he added, smilingly, 'To see me bat.' 'Oh,' I said!"

The Gentlemen of Lancashire

SOME COMMENTATORS have cited the existence of a Gentlemen of Lancashire team as a reason for debating whether a Lancashire cricketing entity existed before the formation of the county club in 1864 and to cite these games as of a good enough standard to be regarded as first-class. However, before 1864 the only Gentlemen of Lancashire fixtures for which there are records consisted of games against the Players of Lancashire, effectively amateur versus professional. These games went on an almost annual basis from the first recorded game in 1858 until 1869 and were briefly revived in 1880.

Whilst some of these Gentlemen teams did include individuals who would go on to play for the county to varying degrees, such as EB and AB Rowley, Sam Swire and Arthur Appleby, they were nothing more than glorified trials games. Most participants on both sides were merely average club players seconded to duty for a team that was really just the equivalent of a touring side. Moreover, as we have already seen, many of Lancashire's star professionals were recruited from outside the county, so the opposition Players teams were also of dubious quality.

In 1864, the Gentlemen of Lancashire began playing fixtures with Gentlemen sides from other parts of the country. However, most of these fixtures were against sides whose counties were not first-class, for example Cheshire, Shropshire and Warwickshire, whilst other games, for example against Oxford and Cambridge Universities, were against teams of a negligible standard. And, whilst Lancashire did at least have a sprinkling of stardust, those fixtures with the Gentlemen of Yorkshire tended to be played against Yorkshireman who were a long way short of county standard.

The touring side ambience of the Gentlemen games is no better exemplified than in early June of 1871, when the Gentlemen of Lancashire travelled south

to play Cambridge at Fenners and Oxford at the Magdalen Ground. A fairly strong Lancashire team were beaten by Cambridge but defeated Oxford. The opposition included few players who either played or were to go on to play first-class cricket. It's worth running through the side that played those games at Cambridge and Oxford, which gives a good indication of the nature of Gentlemen cricket.

Arthur Appleby and AN Hornby, of

The Gentlemen of Lancashire who played Oxford University at the Magdalen Ground in Oxford on 8th and 9th June, 1871: Back row: Harris (Umpire), J Leach, R Walker, R Stubbs, HW Gardner, A Appleby, JR Hillkirk; Front row seated: WH Potter, EH Porter, JF Leese, J Makinson; Seated on ground: AN Hornby.

course, need no introduction. Appleby was Lancashire's leading bowler in 1871, whilst Hornby was the leading batsmen. Both appeared on a regular basis for the Gentlemen of Lancashire when it did not clash with other fixtures. On the other hand 19-year-old Herbert Gardner had just left Rugby School and was to play most of his cricket for Staffordshire in the Minor Counties Championship and managed just one first-class game, for the MCC in 1882, whilst RH Stubbs was a club cricketer at Birkenhead Park who played no first-class cricket.

James Makinson played in Lancashire's first county match against Middlesex in 1865, and sporadically for the next eight years, eventually becoming the club's chairman, whilst Joseph Francis Leese also played against Middlesex in 1865 and appeared for Lancashire 23 times between 1865 and 1881. His major claim to fame, however, was in the field of politics. He married Mary Constance, the daughter of William Hargreaves, whose family were great friends with Cobden and Bright of Corn Laws fame. A firm advocate of home rule for Ireland, Lees stood unsuccessfully for Parliament in Preston in 1868 and Accrington in 1886 before becoming MP for the latter in 1892, where he remained until retirement in 1910.

William Henry Potter played his only first-class game at the Oval for Lancashire in 1870, whilst at eight, John Leach played three times for Lancashire in 1866, and then again against Kent in 1876 and the MCC in 1877. All four of his brothers also turned out for the county.

Edward Horatio Porter played for Birkenhead Park in Lancashire's first game at Warrington ten years before he was to make his debut for the county against Yorkshire at Bradford, where he scored 61, his highest innings in 17 first-class games for the county between then and 1882.

John Ritson Hillkirk made his debut for Lancashire in the notorious game with Derbyshire at Old Trafford the same year, scoring just a single in the 25 all out. During the next six years he appeared for the county fairly often, making a top score of 56 not out against Yorkshire at Sheffield in 1873. He was a renown gymnast and athlete who could throw a cricket ball 115 yards.

Roger Walker, like Hornby, with whom he was great friends, was a noted rugby player who was good enough to play for England five times. He made his debut for Lancashire in the game against Derbyshire at Old Trafford in 1874 and played just one more time, at Lord's against the MCC the following year.

McIntyre and Watson give Lancs clean sweep

1872

THE PROGRESS Lancashire had made at the end of the 1871 season was continued into 1872. They won all four of their county matches, two by an innings, beating both Yorkshire and Derbyshire home and away, to complete a winning streak of seven consecutive matches.

Whilst RG Barlow had a relatively quiet time in the three games he played, it was two other Lancashire new boys, who were also to become Lancashire legends, who stole the show. They were Scotsman Alec Watson, who had made his debut at Derby the previous season, making 0 and 4 not out and not bowling, and William McIntyre, who

sounded like a Scotsman but was, in fact, born in Eastwood in Nottinghamshire, for whom he played from 1869 to 1871. In 1870 he took up the professional's job at Bolton Cricket Club and by 1872 he was qualified to play for Lancashire. They took 61 wickets between them at just 6.72 apiece. The pair were to be Lancashire's leading bowlers for the next six seasons and were to continue to be an integral part of a successful Red Rose outfit well into the 1880s.

Watson bowled just seven overs and took 2 for 5 in the second innings of the 43-run win over Yorkshire at the end of May, a game in which Arthur Appleby and McIntyre, on debut, shared 16 wickets between them. The first of three consecutive ten-wicket or more hauls in a match then came from McIntyre in the innings victory over Derbyshire at Old Trafford, Watson himself adding match figures of 6 for 41. In a low-scoring game at Bramall Lane in the middle of July, Yorkshire were routed for 55 and 68 (McIntyre 11 for 31, Watson 6 for 60).

At the County Ground in Derby in August, McIntyre did even better. Derbyshire were bowled out for just 42 and 69 with the Scottish-sounding Nottinghamshire man producing extraordinary match figures of 56 overs, 35 maidens, 12 wickets for 38 runs. Suffice to say, with that second mauling of the summer for Derbyshire, Lancashire's humiliation from Old Trafford at the beginning of 1871 was well and truly put to bed.

Alec Watson

McIntyre had taken 41 wickets in four games at an astonishing average of 5.65 and at just over a run an over. It was the best season's performance by a Lancashire bowler so far. Watson had chipped in with 20 at 8.9 and the only other bowler for Lancashire that season was Arthur Appleby. The man who had done so much to turn round Lancashire's fortunes the previous year had been reduced to a mere bit-part player!

150 LANCASHIRE GREATS
9. Fred Reynolds

Fred Reynolds was born in Cambridgeshire and played for Lancashire from 1865-1874. He was engaged by the Manchester club and lived at the cricket ground at Old Trafford. It was said of him: "As a batsman he does not excel, hitting at everything with but small defence. He is, however, a superior fast and straight round-arm bowler, with a break from the off, and with an easy delivery." He played for the United and All-England XIs as well as for Cambridgeshire. Playing at Hove for All-England in 1859 he took 9-40 and 6-15. He played 38 matches for Lancashire between 1865 and 1874, taking 94 wickets, ave. 19.39. He first became manager of the Old Trafford ground in 1870, a position he held till 1908 when he retired on a pension of £100 a year. In 1875 in a friendly match at Old Trafford he cleaned bowled all nine batsmen in an innings (one was absent). In addition to his work at Old Trafford, he produced three volumes of scores of all Lancashire matches from 1864-1883. He was, in fact, the first historian of the county club.

Death by misadventure

MAKING HIS debut in the defeat of Yorkshire at Old Trafford in the opening game of 1872 was Robert Dewhurst, whose family were amongst the founders of Clitheroe Cricket Club. He scored 24 in each innings, the second being the highest score out of 79. He went on to play 13 times for Lancashire between 1872 and 1875 with a top score of 59 against Derbyshire at Derby in 1875.

In later years he became a prominent member of the Manchester Stock Exchange, commuting into Manchester from Lytham on the Blackpool breakfast train. He was living at 33 Cleveland Road, Lytham, when, on Monday 13th October 1924, he was found in the first-class compartment of the 9.35am train from Lytham at Blackpool Central station, having collapsed from heart failure, and had died before he reached the Victoria Hospital. The train had come from Manchester, having originated from Blackpool earlier in the morning, stopping at Lytham. It was conjectured at the time that he might have done the round trip, but he was said to be alive when the train arrived back at Blackpool.

Ton up for McIntyre and Watson

1873

SURREY RETURNED to the Lancashire fixture list in 1873 after a gap of two seasons and home and away games with Yorkshire and Derbyshire were retained. Added to this was a single fixture at the Bat and Ball ground in Gravesend against Kent, which would be part of the resumed mid-July sojourn down south to play them and then Surrey at the Oval. It made for seven games in total, the highest so far as the Red Rose men celebrated ten years of county cricket.

Unfortunately, the seven-game winning streak came to an end in the first Roses match at Old Trafford at the end of May. Lancashire were bowled out for 58 and 82, Fred Reynolds being the top scorer in either innings with 20, as the Red Rose men went down by nine wickets. Watson, McIntyre and Appleby had bowled well in Yorkshire's first innings to restrict the visitors to 98, but there was little they could do after such a woeful batting display. The architects of the Yorkshire victory were the familiar Tom Emmett, who had match figures of 11 for 82, and Allen Hill. A little under four years later Hill was to open the bowling in the first ever Test match.

Relief was to come, however, in the form of the visit of Surrey to Old Trafford in the middle of June. McIntyre and Watson achieved identical bowling figure of 5 for 22 as Surrey managed just 44 in their first innings. Hornby then raced to his second Lancashire century, giving the Red Rose an unassailable 218-run first innings lead. McIntyre then wrapped up an innings and 113-run victory with 6 for 48 well before the end of the second day.

It looked very much like Lancashire were heading for revenge in the return Roses match at Bramall Lane as McIntyre and Watson shared five wickets apiece to shoot the home side out for a mere 63. Lancashire's first innings was rescued by James Hillkirk. He made 56 not out, his highest score in 30 matches for the Red Rose, as they established a 31-run lead. McIntyre then managed another five-for as Yorkshire set an eminently gettable target of 112. But Lancashire subsided to 47 all out against Emmett and Robert Clayton, the former finishing with match figures of 11 for 64, even better than in the game at Old Trafford. Only Arthur Appleby got into

double figures; batting at four he ran out of partners on 13. Making his debut in this game was Vernon Peter Fanshawe Archer Royle, who was to become an integral part of the great Lancashire side of the late 1870s and early 1880s.

The trip down to Gravesend in the middle of July ended in a narrow three-wicket defeat to Kent. It was a weakened Lancashire team on the batting front: no Hornby, no EB Rowley, no Leese. Set just 82 to win, Kent almost blew it at 50 for 7, including two run outs, one of whom was their skipper, Lord Harris, showing the distinct lack of judgment he was to display as one of the major arbiters of the game.

After a season and half of unparalleled success, Lancashire had now lost three out of four games, but they were not to be defeated again that summer. Three days later at the Oval they did the double over Surrey. They didn't bat well, making just 100 and 115, with James Southerton (Remember him!) round-arming his way to 6 for 52 in both innings. RG Barlow, who had had a quiet introduction to county cricket after the euphoria of that debut Roses victory, was Lancashire's highest scorer with 40. Willie McIntyre, however, who had added nine more victims to his growing ledger against Kent, took 11 for 54 in the match and Alec Watson 8 for 47 as the Red Rose came out on top by 106 runs.

All that remained were home and away fixtures against the might of a Hicktonless Derbyshire. Oh, how long ago and far away must that first county game have seemed to them. They were hammered by eight wickets at Derby and an innings and 82 runs at Old Trafford, their fourth and fifth consecutive defeats to the Red Rose.

Again Lancashire did not bat well until the first innings of the return fixture at Old Trafford, but they didn't need to. McIntyre took 16 wickets and Watson 18. Barlow took 2 for 19 in the first innings of the first game, whilst Fred Reynolds took the final two wickets to fall in the match, his last for Lancashire in a distinguished career that brought over 200 first-class wickets. He played just once more for the county the following season, at

Saltergate in Chesterfield against the same opposition, making a duck at number 11 and not bowling.

Hornby finished top of the batting averages by a wide margin, but his figures were somewhat skewed by his century against Surrey at Old Trafford. There were, however, no doubts as to who the stars of the season had been, as there had been the previous year. Of the 128 opposition wickets to fall in 1873, Willie McIntyre and Alec Watson had taken 107 of them. They had established themselves as the most lethal pair of opening bowlers on the county circuit.

150 LANCASHIRE GREATS
10. William McIntyre

McIntyre was born in Eastwood, Nottinghamshire and first played for his home county without much success. A fast round-arm bowler who bowled extremely straight, he was of great value to Lancashire. He shared the bowling attack with Alec Watson and they made a formidable pairing. The best testimony to their great efficiency is the comparatively low scores made against them. In his first four matches for Lancashire in 1872 he took 40 wickets, ave. 5.65. During his career for the county he played in 72 matches, taking 441 wickets, ave 11.65, and he took five or more wickets in an innings 49 times. For a few years he was one of the best bowlers in England and he was instrumental in Lancashire sharing the Championship with Nottinghamshire in 1879. He was awarded a benefit by the club, which was worth £1,000, a hefty sum in that year. He died at Prestwich Asylum in 1892 aged 48, leaving a widow and five children.

McIntyre's wickets wins Roses match

1874

ONE MATCH fewer was played in 1874, a home game with Kent being offset by the suspension once again after just one season of the games with Surrey. Lancashire finished with a worse record than at any time since 1868, a single victory accompanying two draws and three defeats. Part of the reason for the poor record for this season can be put down to the fact that there were no fewer than 14 debutants, more than any year since 1867, 12 of whom were to play a sum total of 26 first-class matches for the club, whilst five of those played just a single game.

It had always been notoriously difficult to put together an eleven for long trips to London and the south coast, and so club cricketers not up to the required standard, or gentlemen amateurs with the means to support themselves on the trip, would be selected. However, some home fixtures proved themselves unpopular too, and one of these was the first game of the 1874 season at Old Trafford against Derbyshire.

Whilst the Lancashire eleven included the now irreplaceable talents of Alec Watson and Willie McIntyre, there were also six debutants, four of whom would never play for the club again and the other two just once more. Of the other three, this would be Alfred Ollivant's last of two matches and R Roberts was a wicketkeeper who played ten times for the club and of whom little is known. Only John Hillkirk had any sort of a career with Lancashire, or could have any sort of pretension to be a batsman of the required standard.

Thus, against a team whom Lancashire had completely dominated, winning comfortably the last five times since the ignominious 25 all out, a nine-wicket defeat was the result. It was worse than that, however. After Watson had claimed his best bowling figures so far, 9 for 118 in Derbyshire's 190, the Red Rose men were bowled out for 38. Horace Mellor, who was one of the debutants who did get another chance, in the same fixture the following year, scored 17 of them.

McIntyre, who for the first time in his Lancashire career remained wicketless in a match, then top scored with 48 as the home side made a better fist of their second innings. But Derbyshire were left to score only 30 for victory, which they did for the loss of one wicket. Watson took that wicket to finish with his second ten-wicket haul for the club, a minor consolation.

For the Roses match at Old Trafford at the end of June, Lancashire were back to something like their strongest line-up, but there was an almost uncannily similar result. After his relative failure against Derbyshire, it was Arthur Appleby who opened the bowling with Watson in place of McIntyre, and they bowled unchanged to dismiss Yorkshire for 96. In reply, no Lancashire batsman reached double figures as they were dismissed for just 39. Yorkshire then left the Red Rose men 154 to win, but Hill and Emmett who bowled unchanged in both innings, finished Lancashire off for 87. Appleby top-scored with 33 and was, in fact, to finish the season as the club's leading batsman, while Watson took 10 wickets for the second consecutive match, yet another minor consolation.

McIntyre did not bowl in the first innings of this game and came on first change again in the second to take just a single wicket in 12 overs. After his magnificent successes of the two previous seasons, 100 wickets at 6.2 apiece, a return of one wicket for 91 runs in two games was very worrying. Were his powers in decline? After all, he had just turned 30. The answer was an unequivocal 'no'. For in the next four games, which Lancashire were to draw with Kent at Old Trafford and Derbyshire at Chesterfield, achieve a famous victory over Yorkshire at Bradford and, with a weakened side, lose to Kent at Maidstone, McIntyre would show that he was a tremendous performer at the peak of his powers.

The whole first day and the first part of the second was lost to the weather in the home game with Kent, but McIntyre, bowling first change to Watson and Appleby, still managed to take 6 for 37 in the visitors' first innings and 3 for 55 in the second. At Chesterfield in early August, the game was completely washed out at the end of the first day, but, back to his usual position taking the new ball, McIntyre took three wickets. He had warmed up nicely for the return Roses match at Bradford, and consequently he was to produce his most electric performance so far in his Lancashire career.

The Red Rose won the toss and batted and were indebted to debutant Edward Porter, whose 61, his highest first-class score in 17 matches for the county, was the top score in a total of 209. McIntyre then ensured the visitors did not have to bat again. His 5 for 31 in the first innings saw Yorkshire slump to 107 all out, but his 8 for 35 in the follow on, his best analysis so far, was an extraordinary performance. The White Rose were humiliated on their own ground by an innings and 33 runs and McIntyre had out-bowled future England men Tom Emmett and George Ulyett.

A similar team to the one that took on Derbyshire at Old Trafford at the beginning of the summer travelled to Mote Park in Maidstone for Lancashire's final game. They lost by 10 wickets, but not before McIntyre had put the seal on another splendid personal season with 7 for 72 in Kent's first innings.

150 LANCASHIRE GREATS
11. Alec Watson

Alec Watson was born in Coatbridge, Lanarkshire and was one of the first county professionals from Scotland. He was a wily and deadly-accurate off-spinner who, it was said, was so accurate that he went through one innings without the keeper handling the ball. In 23 seasons with Lancashire he seldom missed a match and never delivered a wide. He bowled a formidable off-break and could keep an accurate line and length, even bowling against a strong wind. Topping the Lancashire averages on numerous occasions and achieving 100 wickets in all matches in three seasons, it was strange that he was never picked to play for England. He took 1,308 wickets for Lancashire at 13.39, 98 times taking five or more wickets in an innings. Always a popular player, there was a hint of a suspect action, although he was never no-balled, nor was there ever a complaint against him. He was the first man to take a first-class hat-trick for Lancashire and after he retired he coached at various schools, including Marlborough. He lived in Manchester for the rest of his life, running a successful sports outfitters.

Hornby and Barlow open up in Roses stroll

1875

1875 SAW THE return of the fixture with the MCC at Lord's. It would not take place in 1876, but after then it would become an annual event. It was a chance to renew acquaintance with WG Grace. At the time of the last MCC game in 1869, Grace was something of a new kid on the block, but by 1875 he was the best cricketer in England. Despite the MCC's comfortable seven wicket victory, he didn't have it all his own way in this game. He was snared by Willie McIntyre for 9 and 27 whilst batting and was wicketless in Lancashire's first innings, but his game was saved by five wickets in the Red Rose's second knock.

Apart from an innings defeat to Yorkshire at Bramall Lane in the middle of July, that was the only defeat Lancashire were to suffer this season. Derbyshire were saved by the weather in the opening game at Old Trafford, but were beaten by an innings in the return at Derby at the beginning of July. And Kent were dispatched by 32 runs and five wickets home and away in the last two games.

Lancashire won the first Roses match at Old Trafford at the end of June by 10 wickets, having been set a tricky 146 to win on the final day. In previous seasons that target might have been the trigger for a collapse of monumental proportions, but this game was to see the start of an opening partnership which was to become a part of Lancashire folklore.

RG Barlow and AN Hornby had both opened before; indeed, Hornby usually opened when he played and Barlow usually opened when Hornby was missing, and they had, in fact, opened together once before, against Surrey at the Oval in 1873 when Barlow had been run out by Hornby for 0 in the first innings without a run on the board, an inauspicious start to what would be a truly great double act.

In the first innings of the game with Yorkshire, they put on 32 as Lancashire took a first innings lead of 71. In the second they tore apart a bowling attack consisting of Allen Hill, Tom Emmett and George Ulyett, all players who would appear for England in the first ever Test match two years hence.

Barlow was known as a stonewaller, but on this occasion he was no slouch and completed his half century as victory was achieved. Hornby was on 78. It was Lancashire's highest first-wicket partnership.

With McIntyre and Watson, and the rejuvenated Arthur Appleby, the bowling was in capable hands, as indeed it had been with the likes of Fred Reynolds, William

Mr. A. N. Hornby

R. G. Barlow

Hickton and Roger Iddison since the club's formation. Hornby scored 331 runs at 41.37 in 1875, whilst Barlow made 298 at 33.11. They were the best two batting returns of Lancashire's short history. The batting had always been something of a curate's egg, but in Hornby and Barlow the club had found the cornerstone of a team that would soon embark on its first great era.

150 LANCASHIRE GREATS
12. Rev. Vernon Royle

Vernon Royle played for Lancashire between 1873 and 1891 and was regarded as the finest cover point fielder English cricket had seen. It was said he was worth his place in a team for his fielding alone. He was awarded a blue at Oxford and won many athletic races while at Rossall School. Lord Hawke described him as a 'Terror' in the covers. He bowled round-arm and had a pleasant batting style with a powerful straight drive and a sound defence. Playing for the Gentlemen of Cheshire, he scored a magnificent 205 against Staffordshire Borderers at Chelford. Second in the Lancashire batting averages in 1874, he was invited to Australia with Lord Harris's team. He made one Test appearance and was Lancashire's first Test cricketer. He was schoolmaster at Elstree School for 20 years from 1879 and was ordained in 1881. In 1901 he leased Stanmore Park, founding one of the best-known preparatory schools in the country. He died in 1929 when he was Lancashire President, an appointment he described by saying that, "Nothing during my whole career had given me greater pleasure."

Another of Lancashire's one-cap wonders was Edward Kewley, who played in the game against Kent at Catford in 1875. Kewley was better known as a rugby player of some repute. Like AN Hornby, he played for England, appearing seven times for his country between 1874 and 1878. He was also appointed captain for the landmark game on 5th February 1877 against Ireland at the Oval, the first match that the playing strength of each side was reduced to 15-a-side.

County for hire

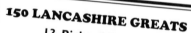

1876

ALTHOUGH THERE was no MCC game in 1876, the county fixtures increased to 10, the most so far, with the return of home and away matches with Nottinghamshire and Sussex, who Lancashire had last played in 1868 and 1869 respectively.

The season began well, with wins over Nottinghamshire by six wickets at Trent Bridge, an innings victory over Derbyshire at Old Trafford and a ten-wicket beating of Kent at Castleton Cricket Club in Rochdale, the first time a home game had taken place outside Old Trafford since the first Roses match at Whalley in 1867.

One may wonder why Lancashire, for the first time since 1867, took one of their home games away from Old Trafford, and in particular to the unlikely confines of Castleton Cricket Club in Rochdale, which has never hosted another game. The reason was simple: John Leach, his cousin Edmund Leach Chadwick and James Schofield had agreed to underwrite the profit from the match and were hoping to make a tidy sum. It was one of the first examples of sports sponsorship. Unfortunately, the crowd was small and the game over in two days and all three were asked

to make up the shortfall, a not inconsiderable sum. It was fortunate, therefore, that the Leach family was rich, owning a 500,000 acre estate in Jujuy, Argentina.

Other than a hefty bill at the end of the match, what did the trio get for their money? All three played for Lancashire on a number of occasions to no great effect, but in this game they took centre stage. Schofield kept wicket and Leach batted at four in his only innings. Chadwick could be said to have had the better of the deal as he made 33 not out in Lancashire's first innings, batting at number three, and 10 not out in the second as the Red Rose men strolled to a comfortable ten-wicket victory. It was his best performance in 13 first-class games for the county.

Against Yorkshire at Old Trafford, the Red Rose men never recovered from being bowled out on the first morning for 56, with Hornby carrying his bat for 23, and lost by nine wickets. And then, the completion of the double over Derbyshire was followed by three narrow defeats, by 18 runs at Bramall Lane against Yorkshire when Lancashire's last seven wickets fell for just eight runs, by one wicket against Nottinghamshire at Old Trafford,

when the result could have gone either way, and by three wickets against Sussex at Old Trafford, where, once again, they did not recover from a poor first innings performance.

Revenge was gained over Sussex by 12 runs at Hove when the home side were asked to make just 97 for victory, and this up and down season finished on a low note against Kent at Gravesend when only Barlow's 36 and 17 extras saved the Red Rose men from total humiliation as they were bowled out for 85 to lose by 129 runs.

The bowlers again performed above and beyond the call of duty. Willie McIntyre claimed 89 wickets, far and away the highest number of wickets in a season by any Lancashire bowler, with no fewer than nine five-wicket hauls and his best match figures to date of 14 for 72 in the win over Derbyshire at Old Trafford. Alec Watson passed 50 wickets in a season

for the first time and Arthur Appleby chipped in with 20.

Hornby, with 423 runs, and Barlow, with 344, both increased their aggregates from the previous season, but there was precious little consistent support. It did look like they had found someone in the game against Nottinghamshire at Old Trafford. On debut, Douglas Quintin Steel made 82 out of a first innings total of 158. He rather blotted his copybook, though, in the next match against Sussex when he made a pair. Although he did play for Lancashire on and off for the next eight years, he was not the answer to the Red Rose men's occasional batting lapses. His brother, however, Allan Gibson Steel, who was to make his debut the following season, was.

Playing twice for Lancashire in the 1876 season, in the matches with Sussex at Hove and Kent at Gravesend, was a man by the name of John Benjamin Barber. Originally a member of the Manchester club, he had moved to Mitcham in Surrey in 1872, where, with a few others, he was instrumental in re-forming the Mitcham Cricket Club. He tellingly described the rules of the club as "founded on those that govern the Manchester CC, though having a more democratic tendency!"

His debut for Lancashire had been at Maidstone in August 1874, although he was first asked to accompany the Lancashire team to Hove to play against Sussex in August 1869. He was left out of the team, but Cornelius Coward ricked his knee during the first innings and Barber "had the pleasure of fielding as substitute in both innings – and paying his own expenses."

He was no more than an above average club cricketer, but it was obviously useful to have a Lancastrian living in the South as it was usually difficult at that time to get a team together to fulfil the engagements for away matches, and particularly to get someone to fund their own trip. Barber himself was even more pointed. He said that he never received a penny from the Lancashire Club, "and I know that I can safely say that even at that period there were very few who could say the same."

Many cricketers of this and later periods purported to be Gentleman amateurs who played the sport for love at their own expense. The reality was that some, for example WG Grace and, as we shall see later in the Lancashire story, Archie MacLaren, were paid sums well in excess of any professional.

150 LANCASHIRE GREATS
13. Richard Barlow

RG Barlow was one of the most colourful characters to play for Lancashire, although he was a stonewalling opening batsman. He formed the famous opening partnership with AN Hornby and they opened together in the famous Ashes Test match at the Oval in 1882. He played in 17 Test matches, sharing in the first century opening partnership in Test cricket and he also took seven wickets in an innings twice during his England career. For Lancashire he carried his bat through an innings 11 times, scoring 11,217 runs and taking 951 wickets in a career spanning 20 years. Later he became a highly respected Test umpire and also played other sports, notably soccer, as a goalkeeper. He refereed the Preston v Hyde record FA Cup score of 26-0. He was one of the first cricketers to collect memorabilia and even designed his own headstone for his grave with a wicket and the words 'Bowled at last'. He also helped design the window, now at Old Trafford, immortalising his partnership with AN Hornby. He summed up his career with the words, "I don't think any cricketer has enjoyed his cricketing career better than I have done."

The arrival of Steel and Pilling

1877

IF THE definition of a genuine all-round cricketer is someone who would justify his place in a team as both a batsman and a bowler, then Lancashire's first great all-round cricketer was Allan Gibson Steel, who made his debut in the innings victory over Sussex at Old Trafford on 2nd August 1877 at the age of 18, a few weeks before he went up to Trinity Hall, Cambridge.

In many ways, it was an outstanding debut, not dissimilar to his brother's the year before. In Lancashire's first innings of 345, he top-scored with 87. He then bowled 15 overs of tidy right arm slow-medium for 25 runs as Sussex made 241 in reply. In the company of McIntyre, Watson and RG Barlow, he did not look out of place. He didn't get a chance in Sussex's second innings because Watson and McIntyre weaved their magic to bowl unchanged and shoot the visitors out for 73. Indeed, because of his university studies and his immediate elevation to the Cambridge side the following year, he didn't play again for his home county until the Roses match on 11th July, but in that Roses match we were to see a bowling performance which marked him out as a future star of the game..

Yet another man who was to make his debut in that Sussex match, and was to also become an integral part of Lancashire's first great era, was Dick Pilling. Finding a consistent wicketkeeper who was available on a regular basis had proved a difficult task for the Lancashire selectors, so the elevation of Pilling to the side shortly before his 18th birthday turned out to be a masterstroke. Pilling and Steel not only bestrode county cricket like colossi during the 1880s, they were also significant elements of the nascent international scene.

For the record, Lancashire played 11 matches in 1877, the same line-up as 1876 plus the resumed fixture with the MCC. They won six and lost five, with four of those five losses coming in the first five games, away to Derbyshire, the MCC and Nottinghamshire and at home to Kent. Their victory that interspersed those losses was in the return with Derbyshire at Old Trafford. They then had five consecutive successes, home and away to Yorkshire and Sussex and at Old Trafford against Nottinghamshire. They finished the season with a one-wicket reverse against Kent at Maidstone, where, not for the first time in their history, a poor first innings had all but sealed their fate. Of the six victories, only the Roses match at Old Trafford was by anything other than a significant margin.

McIntyre took 85 wickets, with 11 five-fors and three lots of ten wickets in a match. Watson had his best season yet with 68 victims. Neither, however, topped the bowling averages. That was done by the now 34-year-old Arthur Appleby, who astonished everyone with career best figures of 9 for 25 in Sussex's second innings of 68 in the victory at Hove. At the other end the otherwise prolific McIntyre had wheeled away for 26 overs without success. For good measure, Appleby topped the batting averages as well, thanks largely to a match-winning 69 not out in the Roses match at Fartown, Huddersfield.

Nor did McIntyre or Watson finish second in the bowling averages. That position belonged to William Seeds Patterson. He was about to finish at Cambridge, where he had starred for the 1st XI for three seasons, when he made his debut for his home county at Trent Bridge in June and had one of those games that are the stuff of dreams. In defeat he took 7 for 72 and 7 for 30 for a match analysis of 14 for 102. He played one more time for Lancashire that season, in the Roses victory at Old Trafford in August, when he took 5 for 90 and 5 for 40. In both games he did not just overshadow McIntyre and Watson, he blew them out of the water.

In the search for synchronicity for which cricket is famous, it's easy to see that AG Steel replaced him in the Cambridge team, and, what's more, it seemed Steel also put paid to any further ambitions he might have had at Lancashire. He played for the club just twice more in 1878, against Yorkshire and Gloucestershire at Old Trafford in July. Steel opened the bowling and took 23 wickets in the two games, one less than Patterson had done in his two games the previous season. Moreover, Patterson bowled not a single over.

He was, however, selected for the Gentlemen three times whilst still at University and in the 1877 match against the Players at Lord's in the second innings he went in last to join GF Grace with the Gentlemen on 97 for 9 having been set 143 to win. He contributed 24 runs in the famous last wicket stand of 46 which won the match.

A more pertinent reason for his absence from the Lancashire side was that on leaving University he entered the family business of corn merchants in Liverpool and North America. He played several recorded games of cricket on the East Coast and continued to play cricket in the Liverpool area on his return to this country. In addition to his business, he was a member of the Mersey Docks and Harbour Board for many years.

In his later years he was asked why he had never been President of his county. He replied: "Lancashire had rather a strong amateur representation, two or three Steels, two or three Hornbys, as well as Vernon Royle. The management was always jealously retained at Manchester. I lived in Liverpool!"

150 LANCASHIRE GREATS
14. Dick Pilling

Dick Pilling was known as 'The Prince of wicket-keepers' and richly deserved the tag as he was considered to be the outstanding professional wicketkeeper of his era, economical of movement, yet agile, brave and unobtrusive. He took all types of bowling with casual elegance and minimal fuss. His dexterity and courage in standing up to fast bowling was remarkable and he rarely missed a stumping. He played 177 matches for Lancashire, with 486 dismissals between 1877 and 1889. He shared in Lancashire's record 10th wicket partnership of 173 with Briggs at Liverpool in 1885. He was chosen for two tours to Australia and played in eight Tests. He was immortalised in the famous window at Old Trafford with Hornby and Barlow. He was at his peak and only 34 when inflammation of the lungs, contracted after playing soccer in 1889-90, forced his retirement. Although Lancashire paid for him to convalesce in Australia during the following winter, he died six days after returning home.

Old Trafford welcomes Australians

1878

LANCASHIRE'S FIXTURE list increased to 12 in 1878. Sussex were dropped after the two innings defeats of the previous season and in their place were WG Grace's Gloucestershire, who had been the leading county for three of the last four years and had not lost a game since 1875. Added to the usual home and away games with Notts, Kent, Derbyshire and Yorkshire, and the MCC match at Lord's, which would open the season, would be a game against the touring Australian team at Old Trafford in mid August. An enticing summer was in prospect.

In many ways 1878 was a watershed for Lancashire cricket. County cricket was becoming a serious business. Before this year Lancashire had been hampered by having to, on occasions and particularly in away matches, put out weakened teams. Never before had more than four players appeared in all the games for the county in a season, and since 1870 there had been no more than three. However, in 1878, no fewer than six players appeared in all 12 of Lancashire's games.

Two of those were AN Hornby and RG Barlow, who formed an irresistible opening partnership. Wisden described their partnership thus: "Mr Hornby all fire, dash and daring in scoring runs; Barlow all coolness, cautious, and defensive in biding his time for run making." Both increased their aggregate run tallies for a season, with Hornby making his third Lancashire century in the drawn game against Gloucestershire at Old Trafford at the end of July and becoming the first Lancashire player to top 500 runs in a season.

A. G. STEEL.

EB Rowley had been skipper since 1866 but had never played in every game in a season. In 1878, however, and at the age of 36, he also managed all the matches and gave solid support with the bat down the order, including a highest score of 30 not out batting at number eight in the first innings of the   73-run win over Derbyshire, at Old

Trafford, which prevented one of Lancashire's perennial batting disasters.

Rowley was nearing the end of his career, but wicketkeeper Richard Pilling was just beginning his. He was just 22 years of age at the start of the 1878 season, but having made such a good impression in four games in 1877, he also played in all the fixtures in 1878 and claimed an astonishing 16 catches and 17 stumpings. In the second innings of the innings victory over Yorkshire at Old Trafford, he stumped four, only to cap that with five in the second innings of the ten-wicket win over Nottinghamshire at Old Trafford in the middle of July. All nine of those stumpings were off AG Steel. He also managed a further five stumpings off the same bowler and three catches.

Willie McIntyre and Alec Watson also appeared in all the matches, and though their figures weren't as impressive as in previous seasons, they were still very good, with the only reason they did not take as many wickets as they had been accustomed to being the emergence of AG Steel and the growing influence with the ball of RG Barlow.

Steel played in the opening game of the season at Lord's against the MCC. Lancashire won by 59 runs, the first time they had been successful in this fixture, largely thanks to Steel's incredible match figures of 12 for 42. Because of his commitments with Cambridge, he was unable to play again until the Roses game at Old Trafford, when he trumped his performance against the MCC with match figures of 14 for 112, including 9 for 63 in the second innings, which would remain the best bowling performance of his career.

In the very next match, against Nottinghamshire, he had match figures of 13 for 72, and in the rain-affected draw with Gloucestershire, he took 5 for 59 in the first innings and was on 4 for 55 in the second, with the visitors hanging on at 125 for 5 chasing 235, when play ended. He was unavailable for the drawn Roses match with Yorkshire at Huddersfield and the innings victory over Kent, but returned for the game with Gloucestershire at Clifton College, where he took 5 for 85 in the first innings and the only two wickets to fall in the home side's second knock as Gloucestershire won convincingly by eight wickets. In total he had claimed 55 wickets in five games for the Red Rose at an average of 8.1 in his first season of county cricket.

150 LANCASHIRE GREATS
15. Ted Roper

He was born in 1851 in Richmond, Yorkshire and first played for the Gentlemen of Yorkshire and five matches for the Yorkshire county team between 1878 and 1880. As an amateur, though, he was not popular and he left Yorkshire to move to Liverpool. For many years he was secretary of Liverpool Cricket Club and also Sefton and later became a Vice-President of Lancashire. A very good organiser, he was instrumental in helping with the administration of the Lancashire club. He played 28 matches between 1876 and 1886, top-scoring with 65 v Kent at Old Trafford in 1884. He developed his batting and in good class matches made many high scores. An all-round sportsman, he was a leading amateur pedestrian walker in Yorkshire and became a great coursing enthusiast, attending the Waterloo Cup on 53 occasions. He was author of a book, *A Sportsman's Memories*, and his reminiscences were always interesting and often amusing. He died in Liverpool in 1921.

He missed one other Lancashire game in 1878, and that was the county's first ever game against a touring Australian side in mid August. However, for Cambridge at Lord's in July he scored 59 and took 5 for 106 in the match in an innings victory, and for the Gentlemen of England at Scarborough in September, he took 6 for 80 in the first innings. Although he managed just one half century for Lancashire, 78 out of 152 against Notts at Old Trafford, his performances this season for Lancashire, Cambridge and the Gentlemen of England had established him as one of the game's great all-rounders. He was still only 19 years of age.

With the success of McIntyre and Watson, RG Barlow had bowled only fleetingly in the five seasons since his debut in 1873 and taken a total of 17 wickets. In 1878, however, he, too, was to establish himself as a top class all-rounder. Although

he bowled a few overs at the start of the season, he had remained wicketless until a truly remarkable performance in Kent's second innings at Old Trafford on 21st June. Coming on to bowl to replace Watson with Kent having just wiped out a 52 run deficit, he proceeded to claim five wickets for three runs in 9.3 overs.

He had little success in the next game against Derbyshire, in which Lancashire were defeated by an innings and William Hickton played his final game against his old club, and he didn't bowl against Yorkshire, Notts and Gloucestershire at Old Trafford because of the presence of AG Steel, but in the Roses match at Huddersfield he produced another sensational performance of 8 for 22, to help bowl out a Yorkshire side brimming with current and future internationals for 47 in their first innings. He followed that with 5 for 47 in Australia's

first innings, and 3 for 16 and 7 for 35 in the innings victory over Kent at Malling.

Three other bowling performances deserve mention in games involving Lancashire that season. Barely five weeks after leaving Australia after playing in the first two Test matches, Alfred Shaw had match figures of 12 for 68 for the MCC and then 10 for 95 for Notts against the Red Rose. In the match against Derbyshire at Old Trafford in the middle of June, Enoch Storer, who had made his debut against Middlesex in Lancashire's second ever county game but played just six times in 13 years, took 5 for 12 and 3 for 25 in the 73-run victory. And, in the game against Australia, Fred 'The Demon' Spofforth, who become one of the first great Test match bowlers, took 9 for 53 and 4 for 81 in the drawn game at Old Trafford, where rain on the final day saved Lancashire from certain defeat.

O my Hornby and my Barlow long ago!

Lancashire's first ever game at Old Trafford against Gloucestershire, and the batting of Hornby and Barlow in that game, inspired one of the most famous poems ever written about cricket. The author, Francis Thompson, was born in Preston on 16th December 1859. At the time of the game he was 18 and had just moved to Owens College in Manchester to study medicine. There is no doubt that with WG Grace and his famous Gloucestershire team in town, this would have been one of the biggest sporting occasions that Manchester had witnessed.

Thompson was a tragic figure who gave up on his studies and moved to London in 1885 in order to attempt to become a writer. Unfortunately, he became addicted to opium and lived on the streets until 1888, when he was rescued by Wilfrid and Alice Meynell, who were the editors of the magazine 'Merrie England', and to whom Thompson had sent some poems. He published several well-received volumes of poetry, but his addiction took a huge toll and he was to die of tuberculosis at the age of 48 in November 1907.

Shortly before his death, he was invited to watch Lancashire's game with Middlesex at Lord's. Apparently, as the game approached he became increasingly nostalgic for the cricket and cricketers that he watched in his youth. In the end, he decided not to go to the game and instead penned the poem, _At Lord's_.

It is little I repair to the matches of the Southron folk,
Though my own red roses there may blow;
It is little I repair to the matches of the Southron folk,
Though the red roses crest the caps, I know.
For the field is full of shades as I near a shadowy coast,
And a ghostly batsman plays to the bowling of a ghost,
And I look through my tears on a soundless-clapping host
As the run stealers flicker to and fro,
To and fro:
O my Hornby and my Barlow long ago!

It's Glo'ster coming North, the irresistible,
The Shire of the Graces, long ago!
It's Gloucestershire up North, the irresistible,
And new-risen Lancashire the foe!
A Shire so young that has scarce impressed its traces,
Ah, how shall it stand before all-resistless Graces?
O, little red rose, their bats are as maces
To beat thee down, this summer long ago!
This day of seventy-eight they are come up north against thee
This day of seventy-eight long ago!

The champion of the centuries, he cometh up against thee,
With his brethren, every one a famous foe!
The long-whiskered Doctor, that laugheth the rules to scorn,
While the bowler, pitched against him, bans the day he was born;
And GF with his science makes the fairest length forlorn;
They are come from the West to work thee woe!
It is little I repair to the matches of the Southron folk,
Though my own red roses there may blow;
It is little I repair to the matches of the Southron folk,
Though the red roses crest the caps, I know.

For the field is full of shades as I near a shadowy coast,
And a ghostly batsman plays to the bowling of a ghost,
And I look through my tears on a soundless-clapping host
As the run stealers flicker to and fro,
To and fro:
O my Hornby and my Barlow long ago!

Title shared with Notts *1879*

THE CONCEPT of a 'County Championship' had been mooted since county cricket began in 1864, but many believe the first 'official' Championship was not until 1890, when the counties themselves agreed how the Championship would be decided, or even 1894, when the MCC were asked to take over this task. Between 1864 and 1890, however, a number of cricket publications put forward the county whom they considered to be 'Champion County'. Fred Lillywhite's *Guide* up to 1866, John and James Lillywhite's *Companion* from 1864 to 1884, *James Lillywhite's Annual* from 1871, and, of course, *Wisden Cricketers' Almanack* from 1864 all declared at the beginning of the following season who they believed to be the 'Champion County'.

For a good proportion of the period 1864 to 1890, these publications broadly agreed on who were the champions, but with there being a big difference in the number of matches each of the official counties played, and also the contrasting strengths of the opposition that the leading counties played against, it is difficult to make accurate judgments for some of the years between these dates.

Many years later, when Wisden had become the only annual cricket publication, respected cricket historian Roland Bowen wrote a definitive piece on the subject by examining not only the four publications in question, but also the official histories of the counties themselves. He came to the conclusion that but for 1868, when Nottinghamshire were probably champions, and 1878, when it was completely unclear who was placed first, a champion county or counties could be assessed.

The Lancashire team of 1879 that shared the title of 'Champion County' with Nottinghamshire.

Lancashire had never been amongst the counties vying for the title of champion. They had had a very good year in 1878. Of their 10 games against the counties, they had won five, drawn two and lost three, but with the periodicals of the time, and Roland Bowen later, placing a great emphasis on games lost, they were not amongst those considered to be the Champion County of that year.

In 1879, however, it was a different story. After a drawn game with Nottinghamshire at Trent Bridge, five consecutive fixtures were won; Derbyshire and Kent at Old Trafford, then the return match with Derbyshire, followed by home games with Yorkshire and Gloucestershire. After defeat in the annual match with the MCC at Lord's, the Red Rose men lost their only county match of the year, against Yorkshire at Bramall Lane by an innings. They finished the season with three draws; against Notts at Old Trafford and then on the southern tour at Canterbury and Clifton College against Kent and Gloucestershire respectively.

With Nottinghamshire's record reading played 12, won five, drawn six and lost one, and the two counties having fought out inconclusive drawn games which had been ruined by the weather, it was widely concluded that the two clubs would share the mantle of champion county. It was the beginning of Lancashire's first great era.

150 LANCASHIRE GREATS
16. Allan Steel

Allan Steel was considered second only to WG Grace as the country's finest all-rounder in a career which spanned 19 seasons from 1877. He was an outstanding cricketer and captain at Marlborough and later on at Cambridge University. Although he was only slightly built, he was quick-footed with a fine array of strokes as well as being a slow bowler who could spin the ball both ways. In 1878, his first full season, he took 164 wickets and topped the national batting averages. He only played 47 games for Lancashire because of his work as a barrister and scored only one century. He played in 13 Test Matches and was an inspired captain who led England to a 3-0 victory over Australia in 1886. He scored two Test centuries, including 148 against Australia at Lord's in 1884. He was elected MCC President in 1902.

Changing of the guard 1880

AFTER A gap of seven years, Surrey returned to the Lancashire fixture list in 1880. It meant that the club were now playing all the official counties, with the exception of the weakest two in Sussex and Hampshire. They slipped to fourth in the unofficial table, after losing both home and away to Nottinghamshire and in the final game against Gloucestershire at Clifton College, but in many ways 1880 can be seen as a changing of the guard of two generations of Lancashire cricketers, which would, arguably, make the team stronger.

Although EB Rowley played in all the games in 1879, as he had done in 1878, and was to play all but three in 1880, this was his last year as a player. He handed on the baton of captaincy after 15 seasons at the beginning of 1880 to AN Hornby, who had captained in his absence occasionally in the 1870s.

Although Alec Watson had an average season by his own standards in 1879, claiming just 23 victims, in 1880 he had his best yet at the age of 35, with 79 wickets at 11.48 and was to go from strength to strength. However, for his partner Willie McIntyre, who was just a few months older and who had been back to something like his best in 1879, being the Red Rose's leading wicket-taker with 46, including four five-wicket hauls and 10 for 64 in the innings defeat of Gloucestershire at Old Trafford at the end of July, this would be his final full season and he would play just three times in 1880 before retiring from county cricket.

Despite losing McIntyre, and the fact that AG Steel's appearances for Lancashire would become even more limited after leaving Cambridge, the Lancashire bowling was even stronger from 1880 onwards. This was not only because of the renaissance of Watson, but also the continuing progress of RG Barlow as a bowler, the replacement of McIntyre with two ready-made substitutions in John Crossland and George Nash, and the emergence of the man who would become Lancashire's greatest ever all-rounder, Johnny Briggs.

Watson would show that age was no barrier to success at this level with a prolific decade, culminating in topping 100 wickets in a season at the grand old age of 42 in 1887. Over the next five seasons Barlow, who was regularly called upon to open the bowling, was to increase his haul of wickets inexorably until, in 1884, he topped the averages with 93 victims at 12.79. And Crossland, who had made his debut in the Old Trafford Roses match of 1878, and Nash, who debuted a year later in the game with Notts at Trent Bridge, were models of consistency in the early 1880s until both of their bowling actions were questioned and they were forced to leave county cricket at the end of the 1885 season.

Briggs made his debut in the same match as Nash at the age of just 16. He was born in the same place as Crossland, Sutton-in-Ashfield in Nottinghamshire, and qualified for Lancashire because he was the professional at Northern CC in Liverpool. The club picked him at such an early age because he "looked something like a cricketer". In a team that boasted all-rounders of the calibre of AG Steel and RG Barlow, it was certainly no exaggeration to say that Briggs would become the best of them all.

Dick Pilling, Alec Watson, AN Hornby and RG Barlow, four of the players who were to make Lancashire one of the strongest teams of the early 1880s.

150 LANCASHIRE GREATS
17. Jack Crossland

John 'Jack' Crossland's obituary in Wisden describes him as one of the most talked-of cricketers in England because of the controversies about his bowling action. He was born in Sutton-in-Ashfield in Nottinghamshire and came from mining stock. He is fabled for throwing a cricket ball over 100 yards from a seated position in a bath! He was also a hard-hitting tail-end batsman. His bowling was very fast and straight, but many considered he threw when striving for extra pace. He took 1,002 wickets for Lancashire at 11.38, taking five or more wickets in an innings 17 times and 10 wickets in a match four times. The doubts about his action dogged his career and led to Nottinghamshire and Kent refusing to play Lancashire in 1884 and a rift developing between the counties. MCC solved the problem by deciding that Crossland did not have the correct residential qualification and therefore could not play for Lancashire. After leaving Lancashire, he played in the leagues and also returned to working down the mines at Clayton-le-Moors.

The first Championship *1881*

IT'S FAIR to say that the 18-year-old Johnny Briggs did not have the best of starts in the opening game of the 1881 season at Lord's against a strong MCC side. He didn't bowl a ball in the MCC's first innings as Barlow and Nash dismissed the MCC for 84 on the opening day, and then made a duck as MCC's bowlers, led by Alfred Shaw, reduced Lancashire to 17 for 6.

The Red Rose recovered to 82 all out, but looked to be facing a stiff run chase when Briggs was introduced into the attack with the score on 73 for 1. He bowled two overs, took two wickets for no runs, was replaced in favour of Barlow and Nash and barely bowled again that season. Indeed, they were the only wickets he took that season and the only ones he had taken in the 34 overs he had bowled since his debut in 1879.

Whilst his major impact with the ball had to wait for another few years, his batting was about to create the momentum from which Lancashire would go on to have "a series of brilliant successes almost unparalleled in the history of County Cricket" as Wisden put it. Entering the fray at 71 for 5, with MCC having set a tricky target of 129, he proceeded to pass his previous highest first-class score and guide Lancashire home by two wickets with an undefeated 40. It was the one and only game this MCC side lost to a county team all season, and Lancashire had done it without their skipper, AN Hornby, or AG Steel.

It was, in fact, the only game that Hornby was to miss that season. In the other 14, he was to become the first Lancashire player to score more than 1,000 first-class runs in a season. In a purple patch between 26th May and 27th June, he was to double his tally of centuries to six. It began with a career best 188 in the innings victory over Derbyshire at Old Trafford. That was followed by 102 in another innings victory over Kent at the same venue, and then it was 145 in yet another innings victory at Derby. Of Lancashire's seven centuries in first-class cricket so far, Hornby now had six of them.

Needless to say, he led his team throughout the season with aplomb. There were no fewer than six innings victories in the county games, three further wins by ten, eight and seven wickets, and a 216-run hammering of Surrey at the Oval. The nearest any other county got to beating the Red Rose was Yorkshire at Bramall Lane in early July, when, on 116 for 5 and needing a further 80 runs for victory, Barlow and Nash rolled over the last five wickets for 29 runs. Even in the three drawn games in August, against Notts at Trent Bridge, Middlesex at Old Trafford and Gloucestershire at Clifton College,

THE LANCASHIRE COUNTY ELEVEN.

NASH.   CROSSLAND.   J. SMITH (*Umpire*).   PILLING.   WATSON.
Mr. A. G. STEEL.   Rev. V. K. ROYLE.   Mr. A. N. HORNBY.   Mr. A. APPLEBY.
ROBINSON.   BARLOW.   Mr. O. P. LANCASHIRE.   BRIGGS.
From a Photograph by MR. C. VOSS BARK, *of Clifton.*

Lancashire were out of sight and would surely have won but for the intervention of the weather.

They did, however, lose one match in that season of incredible domination, and that was their first ever University game, against Cambridge at Aigburth. This was the very first first-class fixture on this ground, which continues as a popular outground to this very day. Lancashire lost by seven wickets, but who was it who took 11 for 91 in the match and was there to score the winning runs at the end? None other than Liverpool and Lancashire's finest, Mr AG Steel.

Steel played just five first-class matches for Lancashire in 1881, and the first of those was not until the game against Gloucestershire at Old Trafford on 21st July, but it was enough for him to cement his burgeoning reputation as one of the great all-rounders in world cricket. He scored 353 runs at 50.42 to top the averages, and added 42 wickets at 10.78, including seven 5-wicket hauls in an innings and ten wickets or more in a match twice, 12 for 123 against Gloucestershire in that match at Old Trafford, with WG Grace bowled twice for 14 and 1, and 13 for 146 in the Roses match that followed.

So what of the other cast members in that season to remember? Barlow passed 500 runs and 50 wickets for the first time. He made four half centuries in his 591 aggregate, including a best of 96 against Surrey at the Oval and an invaluable 69 in the 50-run win over Yorkshire at Bramall Lane. When Hornby was caressing his way to 188 against Derbyshire, he made 35 in his own inimitable style in a partnership of 157, which finally eclipsed the 148 he and Hornby had put on in the Roses match at Old Trafford in 1875. His 63 wickets included five 5-wicket hauls and two of ten or more in a match; 10 for 84 against the MCC at Lord's and 11 for 76 against Kent at Old Trafford. And do you remember that 5 for 3 in 9.3 overs against Kent at Old Trafford in 1878. Well, against Derbyshire at the County Ground, he bowled 10.3 overs, nine of which were maidens and took 6 for 3. Astonishing!

Alec Watson was to prove that 1880 was no swansong. He played in all the games again and was Lancashire's leading wicket-taker in this Championship season with 69. He matched Barlow with five 5-wicket hauls and two tens in a match, his being 11 for 86 against Notts and 10 for 64 against Surrey, both at Old Trafford. He also proved he could bat, with his first half century, an undefeated 60 in that same match with Surrey at Old Trafford, and a total of 304 runs with an average above 20.

George Nash passed 50 wickets for the first time. He lost nothing in comparison to Steel, Barlow and Watson and himself claimed four 5-wicket hauls and the stunning match figures of 12 for 47 in the final match at Maidstone against Kent.

John Crossland played just seven times in 1881, and his chances to bowl in those game were few and far between because of the success of Steel, Barlow, Nash and Watson. That all changed at the Oval in mid August when he blew away Surrey with match figures of 10 for 39. Although he managed only 13 wickets in 1881, he topped the averages with 7.15. As a consequence, his year in the sun was to come the following season.

Johnny Briggs gained confidence after that match-winning knock against the MCC in the opening game. He was the model of efficiency and consistency and belied his years. He finished as Lancashire's fourth highest run-scorer with 367 at 18.35, which included his first half century against Surrey at Old Trafford.

So, Hornby, Barlow, Steel, Watson, Nash, Crossland and Briggs were the main cast. But what of the supporting act? Well, they were impressive too. Yorkshire-born Walter Robinson had begun his first-class career with his home county in 1876, but played two seasons without success. In those two seasons he was the professional at Bacup in the Lancashire League, before moving to Littleborough, where he remained until 1885. He qualified for Lancashire and made his debut in 1880, finishing as the Red Rose's second highest run scorer with 391, with one half century. In this Championship season he played in all the games, scoring two half centuries and increasing his tally to 417, the best after Hornby and Barlow. His highest knock was the 90 he made in the innings victory over Kent at Old Trafford, when he and Hornby added 119 for the second wicket. He played for Lancashire until 1888 and was to score three of Lancashire's next four centuries.

The appropriately named Oswald Philip Lancashire made his debut in 1878 and was to play for the club in 97 matches over 10 years. He was in the Cambridge team at the same time as AG Steel and consequently was in the side that inflicted the only defeat on his home county. In 1881, he played 11 games for the Red Rose and scored 197 runs, with a best of 47 not out in the drawn game with Notts at Trent Bridge.

Because of the success of the five main bowlers, few others got an opportunity in this season, but Henry Miller, who made his debut against Derbyshire at Old Trafford in 1880 and played just five times for the county, opened the bowling with Watson in the Roses match at Bramall Lane and took an impressive 5 for 46 in the first innings and 2 for 54 in the second. He also made his highest score of 27 in Lancashire's second innings, an all-round performance which contributed greatly to the victory. His final match for the county, in which he bowled 10 wicketless overs and made a duck, was the return Roses match at Old Trafford.

Arthur Appleby, who had performed so heroically for the county since its inception in 1864, played four times. In the game against Kent at Old Trafford he bowled 14 overs, six of which were maidens and finished with 1 for 19. He did not bowl at all in the

Lancashire's unlikeliest ever Test cricketer was Birkenhead-born Reginald Wood, who played for the county three times in 1881 but only six times in total between 1880 and 1884. He scored two half centuries in the games against Notts and Surrey at Old Trafford in June. His main claim to fame, however, was that he emigrated to Australia in 1885 and played a few games for Victoria. When England toured there in 1886/87, he replaced William Barnes when he was injured and played three tour games, including the second Test match at Sydney, scoring 6 and 0 batting at number 10. RG Barlow and Johnny Briggs also played in that match.

games in August against Notts at Trent Bridge, Gloucestershire at Clifton College and Kent at Maidstone. In his five innings he made a total of 30 runs. Although he did play twice more for Lancashire, at Lord's against the MCC in 1885 and against Nottinghamshire at Trent Bridge in 1887 when he was approaching his 44th birthday, 1881 was, in effect, his final season as a player and he would have been overjoyed at the outcome for his beloved county.

As an interesting footnote to the season, Appleby did play in one other first-class match in 1881, at the beginning of August for the Gentlemen against the Players at Hove, in one of the closest ever finishes to these contests. In the Players' first innings he out-bowled AG Steel with 6 for 95, including the wickets of George Ulyett, Arthur Shrewsbury, Willie Bates and Tom Emmett. In the second innings he also claimed the wickets of Shrewsbury and Barnes and finished with match figures of 8 for 127. But the 22-year-old tyro Steel was not going to let his fellow Lancastrian have the final word as he took 7 for 54 in the Players' second innings for an overall analysis of 9 for 108. Appleby was then caught and bowled by Shaw for three with the Gentlemen just two runs short of victory.

150 LANCASHIRE GREATS
18. Oswald Lancashire

He was educated at Lancing College, where he captained the college XI for three years. Going to down to Cambridge, he played against Oxford in 1880 and helped his side to victory. For Lancashire he played from 1878 to 1888 in 97 matches and scored almost 2,000 runs. Although a short man, Oswald Lancashire hit very hard and was a fine fieldsman in any position. He was a good footballer and won blues at Cambridge, captaining the side to three wins against Oxford. He captained the Lancashire side in Hornby's absence and many thought he would be his successor, but he retired too early. He was elected President of Lancashire in 1923-24 during Lancashire's Jubilee season.

Another tie with Notts *1882*

FRESH FROM the success of 1881, Lancashire's fixture list increased again in 1882. The number of county games increased to 16 with the addition of home and away matches with Somerset, who had just become the newest first-class county. After the traditional curtain-raiser at Lord's against the MCC, Lancashire would then travel to Fenner's for the first time to play Cambridge, as well as another fixture with them later in the summer at Old Trafford. There would also be a meeting with the touring Australians at the beginning of June, So, 20 matches in all.

In the non-county games the Red Rose fared poorly. They lost by eight wickets to the MCC and then by the narrow margin of 14 runs to Cambridge, who were without AG Steel, who had now left university and was training to be a barrister. In this match Johnny Briggs got his first bowl of the summer, taking 4 for 11 off 5.2 overs. He was to bowl 62 more overs this season and claim just two more wickets. The return match with Cambridge was drawn, the weather putting paid to a possible Lancashire victory after Barlow and Watson had bowled the students out for 31 runs in their first innings.

Against the Australians at Old Trafford, the county put up a great fight despite trailing by 141 runs on first innings. AG Steel followed his five wickets in the Aussies' first knock with a half century, and Barlow carried his bat for 66 out of 269. But it was that man Spofforth who had the last word again: match figures of 12 for 157 saw the tourists home by four wickets.

In between those four non-county games there was a comfortable ten-wicket win over Derbyshire and an innings and 157-run demolition of new boys Somerset, both at Old Trafford. Poor Somerset lost the return at Taunton by nine wickets and would be on the end of further humiliation from Lancashire in future years. In some lists these two games are not even regarded as first-class, and certainly in the calculation of the champion county of 1882 they were overlooked.

The Red Rose lost just one county game this season, at Trent Bridge at the beginning of July by 37 runs, when Alfred Shaw and Wilfred Flowers bowled them out for 52 and 69. It was with Nottinghamshire that

Lancashire vied for the title of champion county this season. The return at Aigburth a few weeks later was ruined by the weather, with Notts on 23 for 4 needing 69 for victory. A positive result for either side would have seen the winners as champions. Instead, the two counties shared the accolade for 1882.

Following the draw at Aigburth, Lancashire had a wonderful end to the season. They drew the Roses match at Bramall Lane, which was again spoilt by the unseasonal July weather, but then beat Gloucestershire by seven wickets and Yorkshire in the return by 16 runs. Embarking on the southern tour on 10th August, the double was done over Gloucestershire at Clifton College by 13 runs, when Barlow again batted through an innings for 55 out of 240, After Somerset were beaten, Kent were trounced by 204 runs at Maidstone, and then John Crossland completed his second ten-wicket haul of the season as Surrey went down at the Oval by an innings and 21 runs.

They finished the season at Old Trafford against Middlesex. Walter Robinson, who at Maidstone had scored Lancashire's first century by anyone other than AN Hornby since James Ricketts' 195 in 1869, made 101 in a huge total of 439. George Nash then grabbed 12 for 99 as the county completed its biggest victory of the summer by an innings and 271 runs.

On the batting side, three players made over 200 runs, four over 300 and one, Walter Robinson, over 600. Richard Pilling, whose extraordinary wicketkeeping had already seen him play all four Test matches on England's tour of Australia the previous winter, showed that he, too, could bat. Promoted to number five in the game with Somerset at Old Trafford, he proceeded to top score with 78 and finished the season with 301 runs at an average in double figures.

Barlow eclipsed Hornby for the first time with 856 runs to 852, even though he managed just four half centuries and a top score of 69. Hornby's seventh county century was scored at Lord's in the nine wicket win over Middlesex in the middle of July, when he and Barlow extended their first wicket partnership record to 180.

Watson and Barlow both increased their record aggregate totals of wickets, but AG Steel was not as effective as he had been previously in the seven matches he played, distracted no doubt by the difficulties of having to earn a proper living.

John Crossland needed just three wickets in the final game to be the first Lancastrian to pass 100 wickets in a summer, but didn't get an opportunity to bowl. Nash also passed his record total of wickets from the previous season, but all was to change for Crossland, Nash and Lancashire in the furore that exploded in the penultimate game against Surrey. It was that furore that was to contribute to the passing of the club's first great era.

150 LANCASHIRE GREATS
19. Johnny Briggs

Johnny Briggs was a lovable and cheerful cricketer, the idol of the Old Trafford crowds and one of the finest all-rounders in the history of the game. He was born in Sutton-in-Ashfield and was playing as a professional cricketer at the age of 14. He played for Lancashire at the age of 16, mainly due to his sharp fielding and fast scoring and it was not until 1885 that his left-arm slow-medium bowling became a major part of his game. He is the only player to score 10,000 runs and take 1,000 wickets for Lancashire. In all first-class cricket he made 14,092 runs and took 2,221 wickets. He took 100 wickets in a season 12 times and was the first bowler to reach 100 Test wickets. In 33 Tests, he took 118 wickets and is the only player to have scored a century and taken a hat-trick in Ashes Tests. He took 15 wickets in a day (a record) against South Africa in 1888-89. His career ended in tragedy when he suffered a violent epileptic fit during a Test match at Headingley thought to have been brought on by a blow over the heart. Although he seemed to recover, he died two years later in Cheadle Asylum, where he was constantly bowling imaginary bowling spells up and down the ward. His funeral was attended by over 16,000 people and his headstone in Stretford Cemetery shows a wicket broken.

The Crossland and Nash controversy

1883

THE 1883 EDITION of Wisden commented thus on the bowling of John Crossland:

"The widespread opinion that Crossland's delivery is not above the suspicion of being unfair culminated in a most unseemly exhibition of feeling in the Surrey v Lancashire match at the Oval. Certainly no first-class county bowler of the present day has so frequently been charged with throwing, but his great success may have had much to do with increasing the hostile criticism he has met with from the supporters of his opponents' cricket, and it seems impossible that so thorough a cricketer as Mr Hornby would countenance a style of bowling which he was convinced was not fair. Many independent critics, however, condemn Crossland's style, and take occasion to point out that the present unsatisfactory manner in which umpires are appointed is the real cause of the continuance of questionable bowling. May the coming season see these matters righted."

Crossland took 11 wickets, ten of which were clean bowled in the penultimate match of the 1882 season at the Oval as Lancashire coasted to an innings victory. Having read reports of Crossland's bowling in the national papers, the crowd at the Oval called out 'well thrown' and 'take him off' on a regular basis and, even though the umpires did not no-ball him and he had the support of his captain, Hornby did not bowl him in the final match against Middlesex at Old Trafford, thus denying him the chance to become the first Lancashire cricketer to take 100 wickets in a season. He was also denied the chance of playing for England in the sole Test match of that year against the Australians.

It was George Nash who took the glory in that final game, with 12 wickets in the match, but his action, too, soon came under suspicion. Both Nash and Crossland bowled far less in 1883 than in 1882 and were much less successful, which was largely responsible for the county's fall from equal first to fifth in the unofficial table. Bowling had been Lancashire's strong point since 1864, and particularly so during the exceptionally successful seasons they had had between 1879 and 1882, so to emasculate the wicket-taking power of Crossland and Nash was to handicap a side whose batting was also some way short of the effectiveness it had shown in the three previous years.

Lancashire played just 12 county matches in 1883, with Somerset dropped after just one season because of their perceived weakness and Middlesex refusing to play any county who played bowlers whose actions were suspicious. As well as the MCC game at Lord's, Cambridge were replaced by Oxford, whom Lancashire would play home and away for the first time.

The season had begun with seven straight victories, including the games with Oxford and the MCC. Three were won by an innings, one by 10 wickets, one by nine wickets, one by 151 runs and one by 70 runs. However, as the throwing controversy developed and confidence ebbed, five of the last eight games were lost.

Nottinghamshire, whose rivalry with Lancashire had reached epic proportions over the previous four seasons, reclaimed outright ownership of the unofficial Championship and were to dominate the county scene until 1886. Undoubtedly upset that they had merely lost and drawn with the Red Rose this season, and that Lancashire included several players born in other counties, most notably their own, they began to take the lead in the protests against unfair bowling and a fair amount of bickering began between the two counties. Responding to a provocative Christmas card from Old Trafford, they replied aggressively with the following note:

> **LANCASHIRE COUNTY CRICKET: The only rules necessary for players in the County Eleven are that they shall neither be born in, nor reside in, Lancashire. Sutton-in-Ashfield men will have the preference**

At the end of the 1883 season, Nottinghamshire joined Middlesex and refused to play Lancashire again until Crossland and Nash had been dismissed. Nash, stung by the criticism of his action, bowled very little in the following two years and left county cricket of his own accord at the end of the 1885 season. Crossland was also to leave at the end of the 1885 season, but on a residential qualification technicality. He played on in 1884 with the support of the Old Trafford committee and Hornby, but the clamour to get rid of him from the county game continued.

150 LANCASHIRE GREATS
20. George Nash

It was said that only George Nash's lack of pace ensured there was not as much fuss made about the legality of his action as that of his colleague John Crossland. Lord Harris felt his action suspect after he was dismissed twice for 0 in the same match and called him "a real Lancashire chucker", but no action was taken during his career. George Nash was a very effective bowler for a few seasons in the early 1880s with some fine performances to his credit. In 1882, Somerset in their first ever county match were dismissed for 29 with Nash taking four wickets in four balls and five wickets in seven balls. In 1881 and 1882 he took 52 and 62 wickets at a cost of just over 10 runs apiece. He helped Lancashire to the Championship in 1881 when they went through the season undefeated. On soft wickets he was one of the most difficult of bowlers. He also played for Buckinghamshire, Worcestershire and five seasons for Accrington, where he took a remarkable 541 wickets at just 5.1 runs each. He subsequently kept a pub and was known as "Jolly Nash" after a well-known comic singer.

Briggs comes of age *1884*

THE POOR form which characterised the end of the 1883 season continued into 1884. Of the first 10 first-class games, two were won, two drawn and six lost. It meant that from 5th July 1883 until 25th July 1884, Lancashire had played 18 first-class fixtures and lost 11, drawn three and won just four. It was their worst run of form since entering county cricket in 1864.

The batting, which had been mediocre in 1883 to say the least, fell away even further in 1884. AN Hornby scored just two half centuries, a return that he had not equalled since 1879 when there were fewer games. The demise of RG Barlow's batting was even more marked. He scored just one half century and averaged a little over 12, his worst since 1872.

There were, however, some bright spots in the batting line-up. The Rev. Vernon Peter Fanshawe Archer Royle had been playing for Lancashire on and off since 1873 with moderate success. His appearances for the county were limited by, firstly, being a student at Oxford and then his job as an assistant master at Elstree School and his work as a curate in Watford after taking holy orders in 1881. He was well enough thought of to be part Lord Harris' team that toured Australia in 1878/79 and played in the only Test of that tour at the beginning of January in Melbourne. Known as a brilliant fielder at cover point, he topped the averages in 1884 with 199 runs at 49.75 from five games, including, on the southern tour in August, 66 not out at Clifton College against Gloucestershire, which narrowly failed to secure a victory, and an undefeated 79 at Maidstone, which contributed greatly to the seven-wicket win.

AG Steel's appearances for Lancashire were restricted to five also by the three Test matches against Australia he played in and various other representative games, but he was consistency personified with the bat, scoring 244 runs at 34.85 with a top score of 41. Steel's brother, Harold Banner, who had made his debut for the county at the Parks against Oxford the previous season, finished third in the averages with 393 runs from eight games at an average of 32.75, including exactly 100 in the first innings of the eight wicket victory over Surrey at the Oval in the middle of August. And yet another Steel brother, Ernest Eden, scored a half century in the Roses match at Old Trafford.

The performances of the Steel brothers and Royle turned Lancashire's season around. Five of the last six games were won and the other was a narrow seven-run defeat against Gloucestershire, and Lancashire finished third in the unofficial Championship.

Through the mayhem of the early part of the season, one player stood head and shoulders above all others on the Lancashire team: Johnny Briggs. Although his debut had been in 1879, he was still only 21 years of age. He had missed just a single first-class game in the previous three seasons but his progress had been steady rather than spectacular, with his place in the side down mostly to his superb fielding. In 1884, however, he made his great breakthrough, scoring more runs than any other Lancashire batsman, 569, and his first century. He did that in the second game of the season against Derbyshire at Old Trafford less than a week after taking 74 off an MCC attack at Lord's which included a very impressed WG Grace.

Briggs also bowled more in 1884, culminating in 6 for 54 in Somerset's first innings in the opening game of the southern tour. Alec Watson, who was the only player other than Briggs to play in all the first-class matches, had his most prolific season with the ball with 86 wickets at 16.29. He also contributed more than 300 runs with the bat. But Lancashire's main bowler in this year was RG Barlow. Putting aside his batting woes, he had his best season yet, with the ball, and what indeed would be the best season of his career, with 93 victims at 12.79 to top the averages.

John Crossland finished second in the averages with 44 wickets at 15.93. His performances in the early part of the season had seen him bowl himself into contention for the first Test match against Australia at Old Trafford. Lord Harris, who was Kent and England captain in 1884, refused to play if Crossland was selected as Test teams were chosen by the home venue at this time. In the end, neither Crossland nor Harris played. Crossland played his last match of the season in the innings defeat of Derbyshire at the County Ground. He was omitted from the southern tour where Lancashire's fortunes took a turn for the better.

Barlow and Briggs shine *1885*

LANCASHIRE PLAYED just 14 first-class games in 1885, the fewest since 1880. It should have been 15, but the final match of the season at the Angel ground in Tonbridge against Kent was cancelled. At the end of May Lancashire played Kent at Old Trafford in their second fixture of the season and John Crossland and George Nash were both in the team. Lord Harris was unhappy with this and promptly cancelled the return fixture, so Kent became the third county after Middlesex and Nottinghamshire to cancel matches with the Red Rose.

This was, however, to be George Nash's final game for the club. He had taken seven wickets in the opener at the Parks against Oxford, but Harris's criticisms proved too much for him and his county career was over. Crossland, on the other hand, who had himself taken seven wickets in the Kent game, played four more times in 1885, with his final appearance being against Sussex at Hove towards the end of June before the MCC decided he had breached his residency qualification by returning to Nottinghamshire during the winter.

But for the emergence of Johnny Briggs as a bowler of the highest class, Hornby and the Lancashire committee might have attempted to ride the storm. However, with three of the best counties having cancelled fixtures with the Red Rose because of the throwing issue, it was not in the club's interests to put up any sort of fight. As far as Lancashire was concerned, the great throwing debate was over. Or was it?

RG Barlow got his batting mojo back in 1885. He topped the averages with 698 runs at 30.34, including his only two centuries for the club, 117 at Lord's against the MCC and 108 against Gloucestershire at Old Trafford. His bowling was less successful than the previous year, but it was still mightily effective. Alec Watson managed just two victims less than his personal record in 1884, but at a lesser average.

While Barlow and Watson did the bulk of the bowling in 1885, and were the leading wicket-takers, the best strike rate was undoubtedly that of Johnny Briggs. He didn't bowl until the second game, and didn't get a wicket until the fourth, the return with Oxford at Old Trafford, when he took 5 for 11 in the first innings and 6 for 49 in the second. They were the first of eight 5-wickets or more in an innings haul and two ten-wickets or more match analyses. With Nash out of the picture, Crossland about to be and AG Steel only available for two games, he became the regular first change bowler.

His 12 for 99 in the match with the MCC at Lord's further impressed WG Grace. His pièce de résistance, however, was in the return match with Derbyshire at the County Ground when he helped Lancashire to a ten-wicket victory with 9 for 29 off 42 overs in the home side's second innings. His batting wasn't as consistent as in 1884, but he did score his second century for the club in the win against Kent and then topped that in the match at Aigburth against Surrey in the middle of July with a magnificent 186. Dick Pilling made 61 not out batting at 11, one of only two half centuries he made for the club, and the pair put on 173 for the 10th wicket, which remains to this day a Lancashire record.

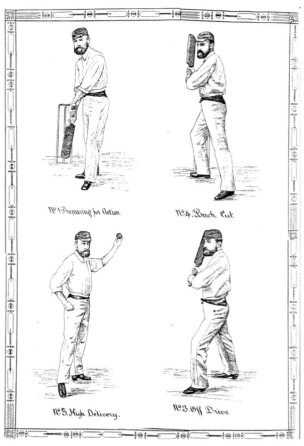

RG Barlow was so revered as an all-round cricketer that he even produced his own coaching manuals.

His form for Lancashire did not go unnoticed by the powers-that-be. He was chosen for Alfred Shaw's England team to go to Australia the following winter, where he played in all five Tests. After doing little in the first Test, he then scored his one and only Test century, 121, at Melbourne in the second in England's ten-wicket victory. It was the beginning of his 15-year Test career.

150 LANCASHIRE GREATS
22. Walter Robinson

He was born in Greetland and learnt his cricket in Yorkshire, but it was as professional at Haslingden that he came to the notice of the Yorkshire committee and played seven matches for them in 1876-77. He was then released and went back to league cricket before qualifying for Lancashire in 1880, and for whom he played 115 matches between 1880 and 1888, scoring 3,597 runs, ave. 20.43, with four centuries. He was slightly built but was a hard and often effective hitter described as having "the power of a steam engine". It was also said that there were few better hitters in his day and, referring to Lancashire, "He has deserved well, indeed, of a county which never fails to behave liberally to those who do it good service." Robinson was a good outfielder, a sure catcher and was, at a pinch, a useful medium-pace round-arm bowler. He went on to play league cricket for Haslingden, Littleborough and Bacup and died in 1919.

Indian Summer for Hornby

1886

DESPITE ONLY losing three county games in 1885, Lancashire slipped down a place in the unofficial table to fourth. It was a position they were to maintain in 1886 despite losing two more games. With the Crossland and Nash affair over, Nottinghamshire, and Kent were back in the fold, and with the games with the MCC, the touring Australians and home and away fixtures with Oxford, the Red Rose had a busy, and much more difficult, 1886 with 18 first-class matches.

Action from a Roses match of the 1880s.

150 LANCASHIRE GREATS
23. George Yates

Born in Haslingden, he moved to Derbyshire before playing for Colchester as professional and then Werneth from 1879 to 1886. He did not play for Lancashire until he was 29. He was an all-round cricketer, a quick run-getter, a good, fast round-arm bowler and also a first-class fielder. He played 92 matches for the county, scoring 1,632 runs and taking 30 wickets. He scored freely on the off-side and was a good cutter of the ball. He possessed a high easy delivery and at his best bowled at a good pace. He could also take up the gloves and keep wicket when the occasion demanded it. He died at Marple in 1925 aged 69.

One of the features of the successful period between 1879 and 1882 had been that the county had been able to field a settled side. In 1884, however, no fewer than 33 players were used in their 16 games, with 14 of them debutants. With two fewer fixtures in 1885, that total increased even further, with 37 players used, and 15 of them making their debuts. Given this situation, it was a surprise that results were not worse than they actually were!

Only seven players made their debuts in 1886, and one of those was a leg-break bowler from Broughton called Alfred Teggin, who was best known as a rugby forward who played six times for England. He played six times for Lancashire in 1886, taking just 16 wickets but topping the bowling averages. After relatively quiet games against Derbyshire at Old Trafford and Nottinghamshire at Trent Bridge, he came to life in the home match with Kent, with match figures of 10 for 87 in a five-wicket victory. He followed that immediately with 5 for 20 in the first innings of the innings defeat of Sussex at Old Trafford. In his final two games, he was used sparingly and, bizarrely, never played again for the county.

After his exertions in Australia during the winter, Briggs had more of a year of consolidation, playing in all Lancashire's games and scoring 586 runs and taking 59 wickets. Watson and Barlow, who, like Briggs, appeared in every first-class game, again bowled the bulk of the overs, with Watson, at the age of 41, increasing his personal record of wickets in a season once more to 90 and Barlow finishing with only six less. Unfortunately Barlow's batting was less reliable and he managed only 387 runs at an average of less than 15.

One player who did return to something like his old form was the skipper AN Hornby. After three poor seasons by his standards, he topped 800 runs, including two more centuries, 111 against Oxford at Old Trafford and 161 in the very next game at Aigburth against Surrey. Approaching 40 years of age, there was still life in the old dog yet.

Apart from Briggs, Watson and Barlow, three other players played in all the first-class matches for the county: Dick Pilling had established himself as the best wicketkeeper in England and claimed 47 dismissals, his best total since 1881, Oswald Lancashire was coming towards the end of a county career which had produced little of note, and all-rounder George Yates played for the county for ten seasons from 1885 without making any great shakes. The latter pair were perhaps a sign that selection wasn't as consistent as it might have been, but, to be fair to them, many of the better options, such as AG and HB Steel, and AN Hornby's brother Edward Christian, were not available on a regular basis.

In the match with the Australians in the middle of June, Lancashire fell victim to one of the great bowling performances of all time at Old Trafford as George Giffen bowled Australia to an innings victory with extraordinary match figures of 16 for 65. Briggs, Barlow and Pilling, who played in this fixture, and AG Steel, who did not, had the satisfaction of gaining revenge for this reverse by playing leading roles in England's 3-0 victory in the Test series.

Watson and Briggs top 100 wickets

1887

LANCASHIRE HAD their most successful season since 1881 in 1887. In any other season, they would have been declared the champion county. In all 17 first-class matches, 12 were won, two drawn and just three lost. Unfortunately, the three losses were all against other counties and all were by an innings, thus exposing a weakness in the county's bowling which had been absent for most of its 23-year history and which wasn't to be solved until 1889.

The first defeat came against eventual champions Surrey at Old Trafford in the middle of June after the Red Rose men had begun the season with three easy victories over Sussex, Kent and Derbyshire and a rain-affected draw with Oxford at The Parks. After Lancashire had made 205 in the first innings, the bowling attack, led by Barlow, Briggs, Watson and AG Steel, toiled against an onslaught from the Surrey batsmen over almost a day and a half. This onslaught was led by Walter Read as he made 247, the highest individual innings so far against the county, and Surrey amassed a mammoth 557. Despite a century from Steel, playing his only match of this summer, Lancashire went down by an innings and 134 runs.

After Lancashire had recovered from this with comfortable victories over Oxford at Aigburth and Kent at Gravesend, they travelled to Trent Bridge to play a Nottinghamshire side whose period of domination of the unofficial Championship was ending. The Notts batsmen piled up 375 runs to lead by 222 on first innings and duly completed an innings victory.

Then, in the final match of the season, the return Roses game at Old Trafford, after Lancashire had stormed to victory in seven of the previous eight games, including inflicting Surrey's only defeat of the season at the Oval in the middle of August with only the other Roses game at Bradford drawn, they conceded 414 after being bowled out for 129 and duly lost by an innings and 29 runs. Indeed, in that drawn Roses game at Bradford, the county had allowed Yorkshire to compile a massive 590, the highest innings score against the Red Rose so far in its history.

Although Watson and Briggs claimed more than 100 wickets each this year, the first time any Lancashire bowler had achieved the feat, Barlow's effectiveness was waning at 36 years of age and he took only 53 scalps. The next best bowler was George Yates, with 16 wickets at over 30, whilst a variety of other bowlers, including AG Steel, whose one wicket in the game with Surrey at Old Trafford cost 101 runs, failed to make any impact. In short, the lack of a fourth bowler of genuine county class was costing Lancashire dear in the games against the very best counties.

The batting, on the other hand, improved immeasurably. Although Hornby wasn't as successful as the previous season, he still managed 458 runs in 11 games, whilst Barlow's rollercoaster batting of the 1880s was on the upsurge this season with more than 500 runs accumulated. Walter Robinson had flattered to deceive most years since his debut in 1880, but he had one of his better seasons in 1887, scoring 604 runs and topping the averages at 35.52, and Johnny Briggs, now a fixture in the England team, had the highest aggregate number of runs with 736.

The real improvement in the batting came from the new men. Joseph Eccles had played five times in 1886 with moderate success, but he excelled in 1887 with 677 runs, including his first of only two centuries for the club in the defeat of Gloucestershire at Cheltenham and was only just pipped by Robinson for the batting prize. Ilkeston-born Frank Sugg had previously appeared for Yorkshire and his home county of Derbyshire before qualifying for Lancashire. In this, his first season for the club he would grace as a stalwart of the batting until 1899, he finished third in the averages with 417 runs at a little under 30, including a superb 98 in the defeat of champions Surrey at the Oval. In addition, Yates and George Jowett, who had both debuted in 1885, had what would be their best year with the bat, both topping 300 runs.

Yorkshire-born George Baker was another who debuted in 1887 and who would become another stalwart of the powerful batting line-up of the 1890s, whilst the great Arthur Appleby made his final appearance for Lancashire in the defeat at Trent Bridge. Approaching his 44th birthday and having been around since the club's inception, he laboured manfully against the skilled batting of Arthur Shrewsbury and William Gunn to take 2 for 58 in 34 overs and expose the paucity of Lancashire's support bowling.

150 LANCASHIRE GREATS
24. Frank Ward

Frank Ward was born in Cumbria and moved to Preston, becoming a promising junior with Leyland and topping their batting averages before being engaged by Lancashire in 1884 and playing 47 matches until 1896. A stylish batsman, his highest score was 145 v Kent at Old Trafford in 1890. He had the makings of a good all-round cricketer and was described thus: "He bats in good form with plenty of hitting power on occasion. His medium pace bowling was found to be useful." He coached at Rossall School and he was a convivial social companion with a liking for a strong drink and good food. He fell on hard times in 1909, being hauled up in front of the magistrates as a hopeless drunk. Lancashire CCC helped him out and also chipped in with £10 to ship him out to the 'colonies'. He ended up in New Zealand as a cricket coach. There were rumours of him becoming a centenarian but little is known of his death.

A HEARTY WELCOME HOME TO BRIGGS, *The famous Lancashire Cricketer, On his return from the Colonies, May, 1887.*

Lancs slip to fifth *1888*

FOR THE first time since 1876 there was to be no game with the MCC in 1888. However, the county still played the same number of matches, with that game being neatly replaced by what turned out to be an extraordinary match with the Australians at Old Trafford. In addition, Middlesex, whom Lancashire had not played since the Crossland and Nash affair blew up at the end of the 1882 season, returned to the fold at the expense of Derbyshire, who had lost all but one of their games in 1886 and 1887 and who were, midway through the 1888 season, demoted from first-class status by what was known at the time as the Cricket Reporting Agency. Thus the Red Rose would play all the other official first-class counties for the first time, but after the promise of 1887, 1888 became something of a damp squib. For the first time since 1874 the county lost more than they won and consequently slipped to fifth in the unofficial table.

There were several reasons for this. Firstly, the triumvirate of Barlow, Hornby and Watson, at 37, 41 and 43 years of age, were getting no younger and all had disappointing seasons. Barlow did take more wickets than in 1887 but made just 202 runs with a top score of 25, while Watson managed 39 fewer wickets than in the previous season and Hornby had his worst batting statistics for the club in 20 years.

Secondly, whilst Joseph Eccles and Frank Sugg came close to emulating their 1887 figures, George Jowett played just one match against another county, AG Steel none at all and Walter Robinson's form fell away to such an extent that he did not play again after this season.

Thirdly, they were genuinely unlucky with the weather. At the Spa Ground in Gloucester, Barlow and Briggs bowled the home side all out for 48 before Frank Sugg's maiden century for the club put them in a very strong position when rain washed out the last two days, and both games with Nottinghamshire might well have been won had the weather not intervened.

With the exception of a brief but entertaining two-match cameo from the Rev JR Napier, Lancashire still lacked that strike bowler who could make inroads into the quality batting of the very top sides. This missing link, however, was to appear in 1889 but was to set in motion a chain of events which would almost exactly mirror the Crossland and Nash affair of the early 1880s.

Four Wickets in Four Balls

J.R. Napier 1859-1939

The story of the Rev John Russell Napier's relationship with Lancashire County Cricket Club is both brief and exhilarating. Born in Preston on 5th January 1859, Napier went to Marlborough College, where he was captain of the cricket XI in 1878, and then on to Trinity College Cambridge, where he played twice for the university in 1881 under the leadership of AG Steel, including the game with Lancashire at Aigburth, where his only victim was Lancashire skipper AN Hornby and in which Cambridge inflicted upon the Red Rose their only defeat in the season they won their first Championship. Injury prevented him playing any more times for his university and obtaining a Blue.

He graduated with a BA in 1882 and attended Leeds Clergy School in 1882-83 before becoming curate of Leigh from 1883 to 1886. He moved to St Paul's in Preston from 1886 to 1890 and was vicar of Walsden from 1890 to 1906. While at Walsden he played for the local club and was the first President of the Central Lancashire League.

As a fast bowler who was also a hard-hitting batsmen, his first game for Lancashire in 1888 was the eagerly-awaited match with the visiting Australians at Old Trafford towards the end of May. Having contributed just seven batting at number eight in Lancashire's 98 all out, he proceeded to claim the wickets of the Aussie skipper Percy McDonnell, George Bonnor (both clean bowled) and John Worrall for 54 runs as Australia gained a seemingly decisive first innings advantage of 65.

Coming into bat with the home side six wickets down and just 30 ahead, he then smote an innings top score of 37, putting on a crucial 34 runs for the last wicket with Dick Pilling, to set the Aussies a mere 70 runs for victory. Then, bowling in partnership with Johnny Briggs who claimed 5 for 15, he added a further four wickets to his first innings tally as the visitors were blown away for 66 and Lancashire had achieved a famous victory by 23 runs.

He was not finished there. In his second and last match for the county, the Roses game at Bramall Lane at the beginning of July when the bad weather meant that play was restricted to just the final day, he took the last four wickets in Yorkshire's first innings in four consecutive balls for a remarkable analysis of 3.2 overs, three maidens, 4 for 0. Needless to say, he finished 1888 at the top of the Lancashire bowling averages!

150 LANCASHIRE GREATS
25. Sydney Crosfield

Originally a fast bowler, he played cricket for clubs in Surrey before moving back to his native Manchester where he changed to slow bowling to suit the slower wickets. He was a good fielder and a very useful batsman and made some good scores when they were needed for his side. In his early career with Lancashire he also played for Cheshire and played for both counties in 1885. He scored 1,909 runs for Lancashire, ave 15.03, but that does not reflect the value of those runs to his side. He scored 82* against Yorkshire at Bradford and also against Nottinghamshire a year later at Trent Bridge. His best innings was 57 on a difficult wicket at the Oval against Surrey in 1891. He was joint captain of the county in 1892-1893. He was also an excellent shot, winning the Grand Prix de Casino at Monte Carlo two years in succession, and was regarded as one of the best shots in the north of England.

Three-way tie _1889_

Lancashire, 1889.

LANCASHIRE HAD exactly the same county fixture list in 1889 as in 1888, with a markedly different outcome. Although three of the county games were lost, one was drawn and 10 were won. It was an identical record to Surrey, who had been awarded the title of champion county for the two previous seasons. Since 1887 a method of calculation of the champion county had been used that awarded one point for a win and half a point for a draw. With Nottinghamshire winning nine and drawing three in 1889, it was declared that all three of Lancashire, Surrey and Nottinghamshire should share the title.

It was, in fact, the last time that there would be anything unofficial about the destiny of the Championship, as from 1890 the counties themselves decided how the Championship should be decided, and then, in 1894, the job was handed over to the MCC. In truth, there had only been a few years in which the identity of the champion county had been disputed, but the very nature of the competition, with uneven numbers of games played by each county and their sometimes wildly different playing standards, making the award something of an anomaly.

Topping the batting averages in 1889 was debutant Albert Ward. Born in Leeds, he played for Yorkshire four times in 1886 with a conspicuous lack of success. He moved to Bolton and once he had qualified for Lancashire he became another of Lancashire's great batsmen of the 1890s. He made an immediate impact in the opening game of the season against the MCC at Lord's, compiling the highest score of the match, 62 not out, in Lancashire's second innings. He was also responsible for the club's only century of

the season, 114 not out in the innings victory over Middlesex, also at Lord's. He accumulated 673 runs at 33.65.

Fellow Yorkshireman Frank Sugg built on his first two seasons with the club and made over 600 runs too, whilst Barlow and Hornby made over 300 and Briggs and another debutant, Arthur Paul, made over 400. Despite the single century, the batting had a look of solidity and consistency about it, made all the more apparent by the county using only 17 players all season, the fewest since 1866.

Ward and Paul were two of only four players who made their debuts in 1889, the fewest since 1882. One of the other two was a character by the name of Josiah Mills from Oldham, whose only appearance for the county was in the game with Oxford at Old Trafford. He owed his one and only game for the club to the absence of wicketkeeper Dick Pilling. The last of the four debutants was to have not only the biggest impact on the fortunes of the county club, but also be at the centre of one of its biggest controversies. His name was Arthur Webb Mold.

Born in Northamptonshire, Mold had impressed two Lancashire players, who were more than aware of the county's lack of a fast bowler, while playing for his county, then of minor status, in a game against the Free Foresters in 1886. He moved to Lancashire and joined the Manchester club whilst serving the residency qualification period. After a slow start in 1889, he ended up with 92 first-class wickets at an average of 12.32 to finish second in the averages.

Top of the averages, and with over 100 wickets for the third season in a row, was Johnny Briggs. Briggs had owed his early appearances for Lancashire, and indeed the England side, to his outstanding fielding and more than useful batting in the middle order. He was now proving that not only was he of the highest calibre in all areas of the game, but also that bowling was his strongest suit in a very strong hand.

Many had feared that Alec Watson's days were numbered after taking so many fewer

wickets in 1888 than in 1887. However, Watson proved that age was no barrier to class in 1889 and 1890 by dismissing 171 batsmen in these two years. In 1889 he was only a few decimal points from besting both Briggs and Mold.

Between them, Briggs, Mold and Watson took 285 wickets, including 25 five-fors and seven hauls of ten wickets or more in a match. They also bowled well over 2,000 overs. Of only 126.1 overs bowled by other bowlers, RG Barlow bowled 113.1. His days of knocking over first-class batsmen, however, were almost over. He claimed just 13 wickets and but for his consistent batting, his glorious career might have been over sooner.

150 LANCASHIRE GREATS
26. Joseph Eccles

He was a stylish and successful batsman with a good defence and ability to hit all round the wicket. He was also a very good fielder and played for Lancashire between 1886 and 1889, performing very well in his brief career. In 1887 he scored 677 runs, ave. 33, his top score being 113 at Cheltenham. In 1888 he scored 184 v Surrey at the Oval and headed the Lancashire averages with 525 runs, ave. 27.00. He was chosen to play for the Gentlemen's XI at Lord's against the Players that year and in total he played 47 matches for Lancashire, scoring 1,787 runs, ave 25.52, with two centuries. He played league cricket for Lytham and Preston and when he retired returned to cotton manufacturing in Ashton-on-Ribble.

A star is born *1890*

THE FIRST official County Championship was overshadowed for the Lancashire club by the news that wicketkeeper Dick Pilling was seriously ill. During the winter he had caught a severe cold while playing football, and despite the fact that he had been almost an ever-present since his debut in 1877, he wasn't known for having the strongest constitution. His condition deteriorated to such an extent that the Lancashire club paid for him to convalesce in Australia during the winter of 1890/91. He died on 28th March 1891, just six days after returning home.

Widely regarded as the best stumper England had produced so far, and only rated behind Australia's Jack Blackham in world cricket, he had the phenomenal record of 459 catches and 208 stumpings in exactly 250 first-class matches. As it transpired, the last first-class match he played in was a game between his own invitation XI and that of Yorkshire batsman Louis Hall at the Recreation Ground in Holbeck in September 1889. True to form, he made four stumpings in the match, with his final victim being the prolific Surrey and England batsman Bob Abel off the Red Rose county's new fast bowler, Arthur Mold.

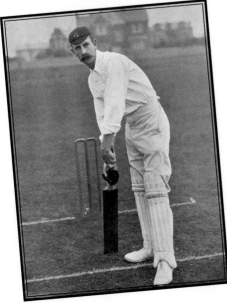

Lancashire, 1890.

Lancashire were lucky that they had a more than competent replacement for Pilling in Arthur Twiss Kemble. Born in Carlisle and a member of the Liverpool club, Kemble had filled in on most of those rare occasions that Pilling had been unavailable. He was to perform with distinction for the county for the next five seasons.

Arthur Mold's terrific debut season was to be replicated in 1890, and indeed in every season up to 1900. However, the seeds of what were to be yet another throwing controversy were laid bare in the pages of Wisden in its 1891 edition's review of the Red Rose's 1890 season and Mold's role in it. "We sincerely hope," it declared, "that the Lancashire professional, having obtained a prominent position, will make strenuous efforts to keep his delivery above the breath of suspicion."

Lancashire lost five first-class matches in 1890, two more than in 1889, but just three of them were in the Championship. They won seven of the Championship matches and drew the other four to finish in second position. Two of the three defeats were the home and away games against the eventual champions Surrey, who were to win the first three official Championships after coming top in the unofficial ones of 1887 and 1888 and tying with the Red Rose and Nottinghamshire in 1889.

In the first encounter, a low-scoring affair at Old Trafford near the beginning of June, Lancashire fell victim to an inspired George Lohmann. Already regarded as one of the best bowlers in the country and an England regular, he took 13 for 54 in the match in the visitors' 61-run win. In the return at the Oval in the middle of August, Lancashire were beaten out of sight by an innings and 76 runs, with Lohmann claiming a further eight scalps.

The only other defeat was a surprising 73-run reverse at Lord's against Middlesex. The home side finished joint bottom of the Championship this year with Sussex, and won only three games. The result was all the more of a shock as Lancashire seemed to be in full control of the game after gaining a first innings lead of 127.

The method that the counties had decided to operate in this first official Championship was the simple matter of subtracting the number of losses from the number of wins. Whilst Surrey also lost the same number of games as the Red Rose, they did win two more, and given the results between the sides, they were worthy champions.

Of the four drawn games which could have made a difference, the game at Trent Bridge against Notts at the end of June could have gone either way, Yorkshire were 2 for 2 chasing 261 for victory in the Roses match at Old Trafford, and the back-to-back games with Gloucestershire at the end of July and the beginning of August saw the visitors run out of time chasing a low total at Old Trafford and Lancashire do the same at Clifton. With honours even in these four drawn games, second position was the best that the Red Rose men could have hoped for, or deserved.

Incidentally, WG Grace, still captain of Gloucestershire and widely acknowledged as the best cricketer in England, had not had the greatest of success against Lancashire over the years. He had, on occasions, done some damage with the ball, but only rarely with bat. On these two occasions, however, he was to score 94 and take 6 for 68 at Old Trafford and make 90 and 31 at Clifton.

Of the seven Championship victories, four, at Old Trafford against Kent and Sussex, against Yorkshire at Huddersfield and Sussex at Hove were by an innings. The return game with Kent at Beckenham was won by 10 wickets, the return with Middlesex at Old Trafford by seven wickets and the final match of the season, at Old Trafford against Nottinghamshire, by 68 runs.

The four other first-class matches in 1890 were an interesting curate's egg of performances and results. A relatively poor MCC side was overwhelmed by seven wickets in the opening fixture of the season at Lord's, whilst the games with Oxford produced the statistical anomaly of an 11-wicket defeat for the Red Rose in the game at The Parks, when the home side were allowed to field 12 players, and an innings victory for Lancashire in the return at Old Trafford when they racked up a mammoth 475 in the first innings, with Frank Sugg making the county's highest individual score of the season of 171.

The touring Australians were scheduled to play no fewer than four matches at Old Trafford during 1890, the first of which was against the county at the end of May. It was, however, over in less than two days, with the Lancashire bowlers allowing the Australians off the hook on the first day when they had them 71 for 5. They went on to make 316 and bowl the Red Rose out for 78 and 83, Charlie Turner playing a lead role in the recovery with the bat and finishing with match figures of 11 for 63. The other three of Australia's games at Old Trafford were affected by the weather, with the Test match becoming the first ever to be abandoned without a ball being bowled; not, of course, to be repeated again until 1938 at… Old Trafford! Plus ça change, plus c'est la même-chose.

Alec Watson's bowling was holding up very well despite his advancing years and he claimed 81 wickets, including six five-wicket hauls. Mold added 90 to the 92 in his first season, with a career-best 9 for 41 in the innings defeat of Yorkshire at Huddersfield. Barlow managed just 13 again, but at a much higher average than in 1889, and the following season was to bowl very rarely, and George Baker gave an indication that he might make a useful all-rounder with 15 victims, including 4 for 43 against Notts at Trent Bridge and 5 for 29 against Gloucestershire at Old Trafford. And in the win over Oxford at Old Trafford, a bowler from Bolton called Joseph Hewitson took 6 for 57 in the second innings for match figures of 10 for 115, but he managed just four wickets in three subsequent games and never played again for the county.

Easily the most successful bowler, though, was Johnny Briggs. A strained thigh made him miss four games in the middle of the season, but he still took 78 wickets at 13.12 to top the averages. Lethal on the damp wickets of this season, he recorded nine hauls of five wickets or more and three times he collected more than ten wickets in a match. Ever reliable with the bat, he finished second in that list, with 534 runs, just .08 of a run behind Arthur Paul.

Paul's consistency was mirrored by most of the batting line-up. Although his average was just 26.78, no fewer than seven Lancastrians averaged above 20, two just below that figure and RG Barlow and George Baker just over 18 and 16 respectively. Even the new keeper Kemble proved adept with the bat, making 266 runs at 14.77.

One of those who averaged over 20 with the bat was an 18-year-old schoolboy from Whalley Range. His name was Archibald Campbell MacLaren. The step-son of AB Rowley, one of Lancashire's first great cricketers, he had skippered Harrow against Eton at Lord's in July. On 14th August he made his debut for the Red Rose at Hove against Sussex. Going in at number four with Lancashire reeling on 9 for 2, having dismissed Sussex for 86 in their first innings, he proceeded to stroke a sublime century. He did little in the three further games he played this year, but everyone knew that a star was born.

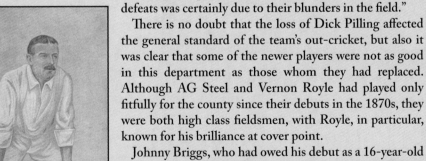

UP UNTIL 1890, Lancashire had been known as the finest fielding side in county cricket, but in Wisden's review of the club's season in its 1891 edition, it remarked the following: "On several occasions the fielding was far below the high standard which for years had been associated with the Lancashire eleven, and, though once or twice the play of the team in this respect left nothing to be desired, one of their defeats was certainly due to their blunders in the field."

There is no doubt that the loss of Dick Pilling affected the general standard of the team's out-cricket, but also it was clear that some of the newer players were not as good in this department as those whom they had replaced. Although AG Steel and Vernon Royle had played only fitfully for the county since their debuts in the 1870s, they were both high class fieldsmen, with Royle, in particular, known for his brilliance at cover point.

Johnny Briggs, who had owed his debut as a 16-year-old to his prowess in the field, was hampered by a thigh strain in 1890 and therefore not as effective. AN Hornby, who at school had acquired the nickname 'Monkey' because of his small stature and boundless energy and was a top class all-round sportsman, had been a magnificent cover point fieldsman, but in 1890 he was 43-years-old, whilst fitness fanatic RG Barlow was 39 during this season. Add to the mix the 45-year-old Alec Watson and the somewhat lumbering figure of Arthur Mold and it is easy to understand why the county were not as effective in this department.

RG 'Bowled at Last' *1891*

IN THE first seven years of the official County Championship, Lancashire were to finish runners-up on no fewer than five occasions. The two counties to whom they would cede the Championship on those five occasions were Surrey and Yorkshire. During this period, both the Red Rose's rivals could call upon almost a full team of internationals, so if they were going to win the Championship title they would have to build a team of similar quality and also acquire a competitive edge that would make a difference in the contests between themselves and their two main rivals.

The 19-year-old Archie MacLaren played just five games in 1891, but continued to enhance his burgeoning reputation. His first appearance of the season was in the first Championship match against the reigning champions at Old Trafford. George Lohmann and John Sharpe, who were at that time two of England's main strike bowlers, eased Surrey to a comfortable 207-run victory. MacLaren, however, remained defiant. He followed an undefeated half century in the first innings with 19 not out in the second as his team crumbled to 76 all out.

He didn't play again until the middle of August, when he made 18 in his only innings of a rain-affected match against Nottinghamshire. Then, in the very next game against Kent at the Bat and Ball Ground in Gravesend, he came into bat on the first morning with Lancashire

on 71 for 2 and stroked an elegant 89. In partnership with Albert Ward, who racked up 185 and with whom he would have many productive days over the next decade and more, he helped put on 215 for the third wicket, a new Lancashire record.

He was undone by George Lohmann in the first innings of the next match against Surrey at the Oval for a duck, but made 23 in the second, and then scored 22 in his only knock in the innings victory over Sussex at Hove in the final match of the season. His 222 runs in this season had come at an average of 44.40, and for the first of many occasions he was to top the county's averages.

Lancashire's batting continued to have a look of solidity about it. Seven players scored over 300 runs, one over 400, Frank Sugg managed 557 and Albert Ward was the main run-getter with 787, adding four half centuries to that huge hundred at Gravesend.

Arthur Mold put aside questions about his action for the time being to top the bowling averages with a new Lancashire record of 129 wickets, including 18 five-wicket hauls and 10 wickets in a match on five occasions. Johnny Briggs, incomparable Johnny, passed 100 wickets in a season again, although his batting was not as successful as in previous seasons, whilst Alec Watson's career looked to be winding down as he had his least productive year since 1879 with just 38 victims. He was, however, to have one last hurrah the following season.

One career that was over in 1891, however, was that of Richard Gorton Barlow. It was his 21st and last season with the club. On figures alone his batting looked passable, but his only innings of note was the 88 he scored against a weak Oxford side at Old Trafford in the middle of June. He was bowled very sparingly by Hornby and took just a single wicket.

When Lancashire dispensed with his services at the end of the season, it caused some bitterness as he still thought he had a few years left in him, and it was a few years before he and the club reconciled. He took up umpiring, which he continued to do until shortly before his death in 1919.

Joint captains *1892*

UP UNTIL 1892 the county had been fortunate to have just two captains. The first, EB Rowley, was a prominent member of the Manchester club and attended the meeting in January of 1864 when Lancashire were formed. He also played in that very first Lancashire game, against Birkenhead Park at Warrington that same year. When it was decided in 1866 that a captain of the side was needed, he was the natural choice.

Rowley captained the side with distinction for 14 seasons, culminating in the club's shared unofficial title in 1879 and the beginning of Lancashire's first great era. When he did step down, there was already a natural successor in the team in the shape of AN Hornby. In the 13 seasons from 1880, and indeed as chairman of the club from 1878, Hornby had led the side to a position where they were perennial challengers for the unofficial title at first, and then the official Championship from 1890. By 1892, however, Hornby was 45-years-old and the club needed a successor.

There were a number of problems in the appointment of a successor. Firstly, it had to be an amateur as, in tune with the social mores of the time, only amateurs were considered to have the acceptable standing to hold such a position, at any county club and indeed the national team, not just at Lancashire. It was a situation that was to prevail until well after the Second World War.

Secondly, with the club fielding predominantly a team of professionals, there was a limited number of candidates. AG Steel and Vernon Royle might have filled the role, but they, too, had aged under the captaincy of Hornby and, in any case, Royle had played his last game for the club in 1891, whilst Steel would play only twice more in 1893. Moreover, even though Rowley and Hornby had missed many games during their periods as captain, both Steel and Royle were available so infrequently, either of their appointments as captain would have been detrimental to the club. Therefore, in 1892 the club decided that, in order to make for a smooth transition, there would be joint captains, and the man chosen to be joint captain with Hornby was Sydney Morland Crosfield.

Crosfield had made his debut for the club in the game against Oxford at The Parks in 1883 and had made a good impression with 43 and 49 in his two innings. He played a further six matches that year with little success, but only one the year after and in 1885 before disappearing until 1888, when he played all but one of the county's games. His record was undistinguished until 1891, when he had his best season so far, scoring 320 runs in 11 matches at an average just below 30 and including two half centuries. It was this performance and Lancashire's strong finish to that season when Crosfield stood in as skipper, that persuaded the club that he might be the answer to the captaincy problem without unduly weakening what was becoming a very strong batting line-up.

In the two seasons he was joint captain with Hornby, he did, at times, look the part. In 1892 Lancashire slipped to fourth in the table and Crosfield played in all but two of the first-class games and scored more than 400 runs, including 82 not out in the first innings of his first game as skipper at Trent Bridge in the middle of June. This game was the club's third consecutive loss in the County Championship as they made their poorest start to the season for some time. That they recovered from this bad start to finish fourth reflects well on Crosfield's leadership. But even though the club finished second the year after, Crosfield's days in charge were numbered. The natural

Sydney Morland Crosfield, whose tenure as joint captain with AN Hornby was to last just two seasons.

successor to EB Rowley and AN Hornby, Archie MacLaren, was only 20-years-old in 1892 and establishing himself in the Lancashire team whilst becoming one of the great batting talents in the country.

150 LANCASHIRE GREATS
29. Frank Sugg

Frank Sugg was born in Derbyshire and first played eight matches for Yorkshire before playing two seasons for the county of his birth. He joined Lancashire in 1887 and was an immediate success, going on to play 235 matches and scoring almost 10,000 runs at 26.50. He was tall, strongly-built and a very hard-hitting batsman with a good eye and a variety of orthodox and unorthodox attacking strokes. In 1896 he scored 220 against Gloucestershire, moving from 60* to 204* before lunch on the second day. He was one of Wisden's nine batsmen of the year in 1890 and also played in two Tests for England. It was said of him that he was one of the safest catchers in the outfield. He was a well-known footballer for many league clubs, an excellent competition swimmer and shone at almost every sport he played. After he retired he was a sports outfitter.

Ward and Sugg dominate *1893*

THERE WERE 20 first-class matches for the Red Rose in 1893, as opposed to 19 the year before. It was the biggest number yet and included a visit from the Australian touring side towards the end of May. In this match George Giffen almost repeated what he had done to Lancashire in 1886, this time claiming a mere 11 wickets for 91 runs in the Aussies' innings victory.

The county's penchant for poor starts to the season was repeated in 1893 with interest. Of the first six games, four were lost and two drawn. Fortunately for the Red Rose, only three of these were in the County Championship. The club recovered to such an extent that of the next 11 Championship matches, they won nine, drew one and lost one and finished

second in the table. Even though the Championship had been conceded by then, they disappointed in the final two games of the season, losing to Middlesex at Lord's and Nottinghamshire at Old Trafford by seven and nine wickets respectively.

The champions this year, for the first time since they had been unofficially declared champion county in 1870, were Yorkshire, and from 1893 to 1912 they were to claim nine titles. What might have been, however, was reflected in the two games between the White and Red Rose: Yorkshire lost just three times in the season, and two of those were to Lancashire.

At Headingley in the middle of May, which two years previously had made its debut as one of Yorkshire's home venues, the home side were trounced by an innings after Johnny Briggs produced one of his regular spectacular bowling performances with 8 for 19 in Yorkshire's second innings of just 53. And it was a low-scoring affair at Old Trafford in August when Briggs again ensured victory by the narrow margin of five runs with 11 wickets in the match for only 60 runs.

Briggs topped the bowling averages with 128 first-class wickets at 13.71, but it was Arthur Mold who claimed the most victims, 142 at just over 15 each, a new Lancashire aggregate record. Both Briggs and Mold managed 14 five-wicket hauls and five times took ten or more in a match. The support bowling, however, was negligible. The next best aggregate of wickets was by debutant William Oakley with 31, but the following season he failed to make any impression and was jettisoned by the county.

This season saw the end of the career of Alec Watson barely more than a year shy of his 50th birthday. He took just a single wicket and played his last match against Sussex at Old Trafford at the beginning of June. In a career with the Red Rose of more than 20 years, he had become the club's first player to claim 1,000 wickets. Whilst other bowlers had fallen by the wayside after a few seasons in the sun, Watson had remained the rock on which Lancashire's successes had been built.

The batting was becoming truly formidable. Alfred Tinsley and George Baker scored 475 and 473 respectively, Johnny Briggs added 698 to his wickets, whilst Archie MacLaren made 617 in just 14 games, but the stars of the show

A. WARD

F. H. SUGG (Lancs.)

were Frank Sugg and Albert Ward. Sugg bludgeoned 926 runs in crowd-pleasing style, including three centuries, the best of which was an undefeated 169 in Alec Watson's last game against Sussex. Ward, however, broke the Lancashire run-scoring record, becoming the first batsman since AN Hornby in 1881 to pass 1,000 runs for the season. He finished with 1,185 runs at 35.9. He made two centuries, but his undoubted highlight was carrying his bat for 45 in the first innings of the game against Australia, a knock that contributed to his selection for England against Australia at the Oval in the middle of August. He and MacLaren were developing into a formidable opening partnership.

---

150 LANCASHIRE GREATS
30. Arthur Mold

Standing a full six feet tall with piercing eyes, square-chinned and with a full moustache, Arthur Mold was an imposing presence. Batsman feared his fast delivery and AC MacLaren said of him, "He has great command of the ball. He came off the pitch like lightning. He sent down at times a snorter that whipped back from the off to the leg stump." His figures for Lancashire were very impressive: 1,543 wickets, ave. 15.10, in 260 matches. He took 100 wickets in his first season in 1889 and his reputation went before him. At Huddersfield Yorkshire required 75 to win in their second innings and Mold took 7-35 to help Lancashire win by three runs. He took 100 wickets in a season nine times, going on to 200 wickets twice. He played three Tests, but in 1900 he was no-balled by umpire Jim Phillips. The following year Phillips no-balled him 16 times against Notts at Old Trafford and his career was finished. No other umpire judged his action unfair. He went on to play league cricket in his native Northamptonshire, enjoying shooting and running a pub. When he died in 1921 it was said of him, "Even his critics had to admit the fine grace of his action. He was a tall, supple, genial man."

MacLaren takes charge *1894*

IT WAS all change at Old Trafford for the 1894 season. Although the duopoly of AN Hornby and SM Crosfield continued to play on in a limited capacity after the 1893 season, the appointment of the 22-year-old Archie MacLaren to the position that seemed to be his birthright was confirmed. In truth, he had been groomed for the job over the previous two seasons, taking over the reins when both Hornby and Crosfield were unavailable, and was, with the exception of a two-year hiatus at the end of the decade, to remain at the helm until 1907.

Unfortunately for MacLaren, his first season as captain was the least successful the Red Rose had had since the formation of the official Championship and they slipped to equal fourth with Kent. This was mostly down to yet another poor start to the season, with no fewer than seven of the first eight county games lost. Once again, it was followed by a remarkable run of form which would see just one other match, the Roses encounter at Bradford, end in defeat. It was a Jekyll and Hyde performance that prompted Wisden to suggest: "…it might surely be worth the attention of the executive to insist upon their players having consistent and prolonged practice before the dates of the Championship fixtures."

The disappointing start to the season did not apply to the bowling. Johnny Briggs again increased his total of wickets in a season, this time claiming 137 in all first-class matches at a similar average to the season before, as well as 588 runs. His contribution to Lancashire cricket was recognised when he was given the Roses match at Old Trafford in the middle of May as a benefit. How must he have felt, therefore, with himself at the crease and the score reading 0 for 4! Even though the match ended in an innings defeat inside two days, it still raised over a thousand pounds.

Arthur Mold was on fire in 1894. He created a new Lancashire record of 189 wickets in the season at 11.84, claiming five wickets in an innings on 21 occasions and ten wickets in a match no less than nine times. He did not, however, finish top of the averages. That honour went to one Jeremy Ellis from Bury. He had made a fairly innocuous debut for the county against Oxford at Old Trafford in 1892. The following year he had played against the same opposition at The Parks and against Kent at Old Trafford and managed a total of six wickets. His only outing of 1894 was in the game with Leicestershire at Grace Road, where he produced the remarkable figures of 14.2 overs, five maidens, eight wickets for 21 runs in the home side's first

MOLD (Lancashire)

Yours faithfully
Arthur Mold

innings. He then played just twice more for the county, both against Essex, in 1897 and 1898 with little success.

The main problem appeared to be the batting, with several players, MacLaren included, taking time to get into their stride. Albert Ward was an exception, passing 1,000 runs for the second consecutive season, but Frank Sugg, even though he again bludgeoned the highest score of the season, 157 not out against Somerset at Taunton, which followed 105 in the home game against them at Old Trafford, his highest score in the first half of the season was just 24.

MacLaren himself epitomised the cavalier attitude of the batting in many ways. Although he played in all the first-class games and scored over 900 runs, he passed 50 on seven occasions without ever going on to three figures. It was an anomaly which would be put into further relief by the events of the following season. Nevertheless, he was selected for AE Stoddart's England touring party to Australia that winter, where he would begin a long and successful Test career opening the batting with his Lancashire colleague Albert Ward.

The County Championship was now growing and its control taken under the auspices of the MCC. Lancashire played 23 first-class games in total in 1894, although only 16 counted towards the Championship. The following season it would begin to take on the shape which would be more recognisable to followers in the 21st Century, with Leicestershire, Essex, Warwickshire, Derbyshire and Hampshire added to the list, the latter two returning after a gap of seven years. Before Derbyshire and Hampshire, the one other county club to be in and out of the county set up was Somerset. They appeared for three seasons from 1883 to 1885 and were included again in 1891. Oh, poor Somerset!

150 LANCASHIRE GREATS
31. Albert Ward

Albert Ward began his career with Yorkshire and played just four matches in 1886 before taking up a teaching post in Lancashire and, once qualified, came to the attention of his new county. A tall and very sound batsman, his defensive technique, straight and positive, and his driving ability made him an ideal opener and an automatic choice for his adopted county for 14 seasons. He employed the late-cut and leg-glance as his favourite shots. In his first season he topped the Lancashire averages as the county shared the Championship. He scored over 1,000 runs in nine seasons and in 1895 scored 1,790 runs, ave. 42, remarkable figures in his day. He was chosen to play for England, top-scoring at the Oval in 1893 and touring Australia, where he scored a century at Sydney. He played in seven Tests in total. He started bowling late in his career and took 65 wickets with his leg-breaks. He finished his career with over 15,000 runs for Lancashire, ave. 30.96, with 24 centuries. He had a determination and passion for cricket; honest and dependable, he was one of most popular professionals of his day.

MacLaren makes history *1895*

THE PERIOD from some time in the 1890s up until the outbreak of the First World War has been referred to by cricket historians as the Golden Age of Cricket. It was a period when great cricketers, who were also great characters, flourished in a high level of competition, both domestically and internationally, and in front of growing audiences. So, when did the Golden Age of Cricket actually begin? Many cricket historians put that date as the 15th July 1895 on a sunny summer's day at Taunton.

It seems that Lancashire's players had taken Wisden's words about their lack of preparation to heart in 1895 as the club had its best start to a season for some time. After beating the MCC by 10 wickets in the traditional curtain-raiser at Lord's, they reeled off four consecutive Championship victories by comfortable margins: Sussex and Leicestershire were beaten soundly by seven wickets and 177 runs respectively, the Roses match at Bramall Lane at the beginning of June was won by 145 runs and, back at Old Trafford, Kent, who had done the double over the Red Rose men in both the previous seasons and thus helped to scupper their chances of winning the Championship, were put to the sword to the tune of an innings and 291 runs.

The new pavilion at Old Trafford was opened in 1895 – it was to remain largely the same until the redevelopment which was completed in 2013.

In the Kent match the county's batting had fired on all cylinders to the tune of 487 runs, with Arthur Paul contributing 140. Paul, who was yet another Lancashire player since the arrival of Hornby who also excelled at rugby, had been the star of the batting in this first phase of the season, top-scoring in both the Leicestershire and Yorkshire games as well. Although he was to have just two seasons at the very top of his game, there is no doubt that Paul's early-season form was responsible for the significant upsurge in the ambitions of the county club and, later in the season, he was to produce another century which would have even more significance for Lancashire's history.

The other Lancastrian to have a spectacular start to the season was Arthur Mold. Carrying on where he left off in 1894, he took five wickets in both innings of the match against the MCC, 11 against Sussex, including 8 for 84 in the visitors' first innings, nine against Leicestershire and another 11 against Yorkshire. His 7 for 68 in the White Rose's second innings included the first six wickets to fall, all clean-bowled. Against Kent he surpassed anything he had done previously, following 7 for 49 in the first innings with 9 for 62 in the second, for both his best innings and match analysis of the season. He was to go on to eclipse even his prolific season of 1894 and claim a total of 192 first-class wickets this year.

Inexplicably, therefore, the Red Rose men lost their next match at Old Trafford, admittedly to the very strong Surrey side, by an innings and 39 runs. Both the batting and the bowling failed, but this was not the case in the next two games, at Trent Bridge, where Nottinghamshire were hammered by an innings and 188 runs, Albert Ward making his only century of the season and Mold 15 for 85 in the match, and in the return with Kent at Tonbridge, where Frank Sugg hit his only century of the season and Mold claimed another 11 victims.

Then Lancashire stumbled. A narrow three-wicket defeat to Middlesex at Old Trafford was followed by a humbling 116-run reverse to new boys Warwickshire at Aigburth, where the visitors' wicketkeeper Dick Lilley displayed the skills with the gloves and the bat which were to make him a fixture in the England team in the first decade of the 20th Century.

Travelling down to the West Country for games with Gloucestershire and Somerset towards the middle of July, the Red Rose men only just managed to beat the former by 12 runs at Bristol. Despite the presence still of an ageing WG Grace, they had finished bottom of the table in the two previous seasons and should not have provided such difficult opposition.

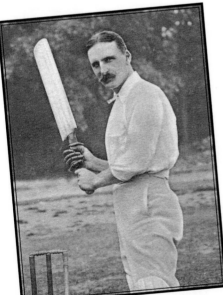

150 LANCASHIRE GREATS
32. Archie MacLaren

Archie MacLaren was a tall, majestic and powerfully built player epitomising cricket's Golden Age. His batting was often described as kingly and majestic. A brilliant schoolboy cricketer for Harrow, he scored a century in his first match for Lancashire at the age of 18. He played for over 25 years for Lancashire, scoring over 15,000 runs and captaining Lancashire to the County Championship in 1904. In 1895 Archie scored a mammoth 424 against Somerset at Taunton, establishing a world record individual score in first-class cricket. He captained England in 22 matches out of his 35 Test matches, scoring nearly 2,000 runs with five centuries, but had little success despite being highly regarded as a captain. When he was 51 he scored 200 for an MCC team against a full New Zealand XI at Wellington in his final first-class match. Neville Cardus described him as "The noblest Roman of them all".

It was clear that though the bowling was performing reasonably well, the batting was inconsistent, to say the least. One of the reasons for this was the unavailability of the captain, Archibald Campbell MacLaren. MacLaren had played just two of the county's first eleven first-class games of this season, and his last appearance had been the Roses match back at the beginning of June.

Despite having the title of 'gentleman amateur', MacLaren was not particularly wealthy. Even by modern standards he was not on the breadline, but he was forced, by dint of circumstance, to earn a living. After leaving Harrow, rather than following the normal path from public school to Oxbridge, he took a job at the District Bank, which inevitably meant his appearances for the county were limited in the first few years of his career. When he was appointed captain in 1894, he resigned from the bank and committed himself to a full season with the county and, subsequently, England's tour to Australia the following winter. It appears, however, that he returned from that tour in somewhat straightened circumstances and was forced to take a teaching job at a preparatory school in Harrow, much to the chagrin of the county club and its supporters.

The ill-feeling of the county and its supporters to its erstwhile captain would all be forgotten, for the time being at least, on the 15th July. With the prep school's summer term now over, he headed to Taunton to lead his men against Somerset. On a glorious day and a very good batting track, Lancashire ended play on 555 for 3. MacLaren was 289 not out, already the highest ever individual score by a Lancastrian in a first-class match, a record which had belonged to James Ricketts for almost 30 years. With Arthur Paul, who made 177 and was out shortly before the close of play, MacLaren had put on 363 for the second wicket, another record.

But MacLaren did not stop there. On the second day, he added another 135 runs to reach the astonishing individual total of 424. It remained the highest individual innings in first-class cricket until surpassed by Australian Bill Ponsford in 1923, and was to be the highest in county cricket for nearly 100 years, when West Indian Brian Lara made 501 not out for Warwickshire in 1994. It still remains the highest individual score for the county, and the eventual team total of 801 was not beaten until Lancashire made 863 at the Oval in 1990. In all, MacLaren's innings had taken just seven hours and 50 minutes and included 62 fours and one six.

After such an onslaught it was inevitable that Somerset buckled under the weight of runs. They were bowled out twice for 143 and 206, with Briggs and Mold sharing 18 of the wickets, and lost by the huge margin of an innings and 452 runs, which remains to this day a record margin of victory for Lancashire.

The team, and particularly MacLaren, returned to Old Trafford to a hero's welcome, but rather than building on such a magnificent performance, there was anti-climax. This time, however, it was not due to the fragilities of the batting, a risible concept after the events at Taunton, but to the vagaries of the Manchester weather. Four games in a row at Old Trafford were disrupted by the turbulent late July/early August weather, including, by one of those little ironies that only cricket can manufacture, the return game with Somerset, which was abandoned without a ball being bowled.

The sequence was only broken by the Red Rose's first visit to Edgbaston, where ample revenge was gained for the defeat earlier in the season in a comprehensive innings and 54-run mauling of Warwickshire. Arthur Mold added a further 12 wickets to his tally, but more importantly for Lancashire's future was the performance of John Thomas Tyldesley, Having made his debut in the rain-affected draw with Gloucestershire a week earlier, he stroked his maiden first-class century, an undefeated 152, in the Red Rose's first innings of 361. It was the first of 86 he was to make in first-class cricket.

Tyldesley's batting did not reach those dizzy heights again this season, but the rest of the batsmen's did. When the rain relented towards the middle of August, Lancashire won five of their last six games by ever-increasing margins, including against champions-elect Surrey at the Oval. The only reverse was another inexplicable one, at Derby, and despite a comfortable advantage on first innings.

After Taunton, MacLaren added a further three centuries to top 1,000 runs in a season for the first time, from only 13 games, and head the averages at 58.1. Albert Ward, after a slow start, smashed the county's aggregate record for a season with 1,486 runs at 43.7 and Arthur Paul and Frank Sugg both topped 800, whilst George Baker, who was to play a key role in the club's batting line-up over the next three seasons, made 699. Johnny Briggs had another superb season with the ball, with 124 victims in support of Mold, but his poorest with the bat since 1882, but he was to come again in this department.

Newcomer Johnny Tyldesley's average was boosted by that remarkable innings at Edgbaston, but he was to become one of the greatest players in Lancashire's history. There was, however, another newcomer who would make a significant contribution in the forthcoming seasons. Wicketkeeper Charles Smith had made his debut in 1893 and played a handful of games that year, and during the following season. In 1895, he finally replaced Arthur Kemble behind the stumps and played in every game, breaking Dick Pilling's record for dismissals in a season at the same time with 51 catches and 25 stumpings. In addition, he scored over 500 runs, with two half centuries, and would prove his real worth with the bat two years later.

But for the weather at the end of July and the beginning of August, and some unfathomably poor performances, there was no doubt that Lancashire would have been champions in 1895, and can certainly consider themselves unlucky not to have been. Instead, they had to settle for yet another second place, their fourth in six seasons. Surrey had won the title for the fifth time in six years since the inauguration of the official County Championship, but for most of the next decade it would be the Red Rose's rivals from across the Pennines with whom they would be vying for the title.

Lancashire, 1895.

E. Hawkins & Co., Photo, Brighton.

MOLD.   PAUL.   SUGG.   LANCASTER.   LUNT (SCORER).
BAKER.   BENTON.   A. C. MCLAREN (CAPT.).   BRIGGS.   WARD. A.
TYLDESLEY.   SMITH.   HALLAM.

Bowlers wanted *1896*

IT WAS becoming increasingly obvious that if Lancashire were ever to become the brides of the County Championship rather than the perennial bridesmaids, then they needed to find at least one bowler to support the heroic efforts of Arthur Mold and Johnny Briggs. Despite the fact that they were two of the best bowlers in the country, and had performed admirably together since Mold's debut in 1889, they had had little or no support since the retirement of Alec Watson. Indeed, the extent of their lack of support can be seen in the fact that in the three seasons up until 1896 they had easily bowled around three quarters of the overs, and claimed an even bigger fraction of the wickets.

Albert Hallam, who emerged in 1896 to add support to the bowling of Mold and Briggs.

One player for whom there were high hopes in the bowling department was Thomas Lancaster. Yet another exiled Yorkshireman who had come to Lancashire to earn a living as a cricketer, he had become professional at Enfield in the Lancashire League in 1892, where he was to remain for the rest of his life, playing with distinction for the club until the First World War and beyond, in the process becoming one of the greats of that competition. Having been brought to the attention of the county club after serving his qualification period, he made a spectacular debut for Lancashire in the final Championship match of the season against Nottinghamshire at Old Trafford, taking a splendid 7 for 54 with his slow left-arm orthodox deliveries in the visitors' first innings.

In 1895, however, he played in 15 matches, and although he added a little to the batting with over 300 runs, he managed just 27 victims. Given just two opportunities in 1896, he failed to take a single wicket in 58 overs. Although he was to play a few times in 1898 and 1899, and even trump his bowling figures from that Nottinghamshire game with 7 for 25 against Middlesex at Old Trafford in his first appearance in 1898, he never quite dispelled the impression that he wasn't quite of the requisite class and consistency.

The same, of course, was true of George Baker, who purported to be an all-rounder. He had a reasonable season with the ball in 1896 with 27 wickets, including two five-wicket or more hauls in an innings, but he was used sparingly and usually only give Mold and Briggs a break from their exertions. He was, however, a much better batsman and it was in this department he was now about to come into his own.

One of the answers to Lancashire's bowling problems was now to come in the shape of yet another Nottinghamshire-born bowler. His name was Albert William Hallam and he had debuted in 1895, but with a similar record to Lancaster, his 33 wickets coming in 15 games. In 1896, though, he was consistency itself, and although he managed just four 5-wicket hauls, he split Mold and Briggs in the averages with 70 victims at 18.62.

Lancashire's batting again proved formidable, with Frank Sugg having the best season of his career with 1,332 runs for the county, including three centuries, one a double. Archie MacLaren topped the averages but was again missing for half the season. He made only one century, but that was another big one, 226 not out as a match-saving effort against Kent at Canterbury at the beginning of August. Albert Ward was to have one of his least effective seasons of the 1890s but still topped 1,000 runs, George Baker was left just 22 runs short of that landmark, whilst Johnny Briggs had a batting renaissance with over 600 runs, a total also passed by Arthur Paul.

Despite not adding to that big century of the previous season against Gloucestershire, Johnny Tyldesley continued his cricketing education by making six half centuries in his 571 runs. And, in a connection with the early history of the club, there was a debut for Ernest Butler Rowley, son of Edmund Butler Rowley, the club's first captain. He played in 12 games, scoring 497 runs, which included four half centuries, to come fourth in the batting averages behind MacLaren, Sugg and Baker. Surprisingly, he never played again.

Unlike the previous season, when the battle with Surrey for the title was a close-run thing, Lancashire finished quite a way behind Yorkshire in 1896 and were beaten by them both home and away. Hallam's 70 wickets had been a welcome addition to the Mold/Briggs partnership, which had yielded a return of 282 wickets this season, but there was still a feeling that the county were a bowler light. Unbeknownst to them, he was already in their midst.

No longer the bridesmaids *1897*

BACK IN 1871, William Cuttell made the last of 15 appearances for Yorkshire against Lancashire at Old Trafford. Four years earlier he had taken nine wickets in the White Rose's easy victory in the first ever Roses match at Old Trafford. Ironically, 25 years later, his son Willis made his debut for Lancashire against Yorkshire at Old Trafford. It would be the first of more than 200 games for the county spanning a decade.

Willis Cuttell was one of a number of bowlers that the Red Rose were hoping would provide the support for Arthur Mold and Johnny Briggs that would propel Lancashire to their first official County Championship. They had found one the previous year in Nottinghamshire-born Albert Hallam, but there had also been disappointing returns from George Baker, the 17-year-old John I'Anson and, not least, Tom Lancaster.

Like Lancaster, Cuttell plied his trade in the Lancashire League, and had a similar return to Lancaster in the 1896 season, in that he played twice for the county and failed to take a wicket. But the Lancashire selectors must have seen more in the 33-year-old Cuttell than they did in the other three Yorkshire-born bowlers as, in 1897, he became part of a four-pronged bowling attack widely regarded as the very best in the country and which propelled Lancashire to their first official County Championship title.

Lancashire's Championship-winning team of 1897.
Standing: AW Hallam, J I'Anson, WR Cuttell, A Mold.
Seated: GR Baker, AC MacLaren, AN Hornby (capt), SM Tindall, A Ward.
Front row: JT Tyldesley, J Briggs, L Radcliffe.

Cuttell did not bowl a single ball in the opening game of the season in the middle of May as Mold and Hallam demolished Derbyshire twice at the County Ground to give the visitors an innings and 220-run victory. And he bowled 24 wicketless overs in the next match, the annual fixture with the MCC at Lord's, as the Red Rose went down by 174 runs. Indeed, in Lancashire's run of four wins and two draws in the next six county games, he managed just 12 victims. However, the county stuck with him and, after he had his first ten-wicket match

Yorkshire-born Willis Cuttell became the last piece in the jigsaw of the county's bowling attack in the Championship-winning season.

haul in the win over the Gentlemen of Philadelphia in the middle of June, he became a consistent and unstoppable force in support of Briggs, Mold and Hallam. He finished the season with 112 first-class wickets and second place in the averages.

Topping the bowling averages was Johnny Briggs. He once again improved his aggregate of wickets, claiming 155, including 14 five-wickets or more in an innings hauls and ten wickets in a match five times. With the bat, he managed just one half century, but was barely given a chance by the club's strong top order, although he did make more than 600 runs.

Both Cuttell and Briggs played in all Lancashire's first-class fixtures, as did Albert Hallam, who showed the previous year's success had not been a mere flash-in-the-pan as he garnered 94 victims. Sandwiched in between Cuttell and Hallam in the averages was Arthur Mold. He managed just 98 wickets in his least effective season since his debut in 1889. However, he missed seven games due to injury, something that was to become more of a problem for the 34-year-old fast bowler – along with doubts about his action – as the seasons rolled on. This magnificent quartet were responsible for more than 4,300 overs in the season; the 'also bowled' just 130.4!

So, with the bowling now the strongest it had ever been, what of the batting? This was also the most powerful it had ever been. For the first time four players, Ward, Baker, Tyldesley and Sugg, passed 1,000 first-class runs in a season. Archie MacLaren topped the averages with 879 at over 50 in his now annual truncated season, whilst wicketkeeper Charles Smith topped 500. There were also decent contributions when needed from Cuttell, Mold and Hallam, and several more chipped in too. With the fielding also back to its usual high standard, it was as complete an all-round performance as was possible.

A strong side, though, needs a good leader. The Lancashire selectors had grown tired of MacLaren missing half the season and in his stead was the second coming of AN 'Monkey' Hornby. Hornby

County Championship 1897

	M	W	L	D	Pts	FM	%
Lancashire	26	16	3	7	13	19	68.4
Surrey	26	17	4	5	13	21	61.9
Essex	16	7	2	7	5	9	55.5
Yorkshire	26	13	5	8	8	18	44.4
Gloucestershire	18	7	5	6	2	12	16.6
Sussex	20	5	6	9	-1	11	-9.0
Warwickshire	18	3	4	11	-1	7	-14.2
Middlesex	16	3	4	9	-1	7	-14.2
Hampshire	18	4	9	9	-3	11	-27.2
Nottinghamshire	16	2	5	9	-3	7	-42.8
Somerset	16	3	9	4	-6	12	-50.0
Kent	18	2	10	6	-8	12	-66.6
Leicestershire	14	1	10	3	-9	11	-81.8
Derbyshire	16	0	9	7	-9	9	-100.0

The 50-year-old AN Hornby was re-appointed as skipper for 1897 and captained the side on 18 occasions as they won the official County Championship for the first time.

had just passed his own personal half century in the February before the 1897 season began, but he could give many of those 20 years younger a run for their money. He had, in fact, never stopped playing, appearing a few times each season and occasionally giving glimpses of his glorious past. He did not play in all the games – he managed 18 – but his leadership skills, gained over years leading Lancashire to the top of the county tree, were invaluable. He was to captain the side for a further season – a season too far, unfortunately.

When Hornby was absent, others filled the breech. One was Sydney Crosfield, whose joint enterprise with the Lancashire patriarch earlier in the decade had been deemed, if not a failure, ultimately unsuccessful and unworkable. Another, of course, was MacLaren. In just his second game back, the drawn Roses match at Bradford in the middle of July, he plundered 152. He did even better in the game against Kent at Canterbury at the beginning of August: 244 out of 339, making him the proud owner of the three biggest individual innings in the county's 33-year history. Something needed to be done to allow this natural leader to take control of the team permanently all-season round. And it was, three years later.

For the first time, Lancashire played every other county in 1897, so there were 26 county fixtures. Only Surrey and Yorkshire did the same, and they had been the only ones with such a list since the Championship's expansion to 14 teams in 1895. It was, therefore, a level playing field for the big three, and it was the Red Rose that came out on top.

There were just three defeats: twice to Surrey, by an innings and 24 at Old Trafford in the middle of June and at the Oval in August by seven wickets when the batting failed to fire in all four innings; and at Leyton against Essex at the beginning of August by six wickets, when one Fred Bull claimed 14 Lancashire scalps, seven in each innings. A further irony: Bull drowned off the coast at St Anne's in September 1910.

Sixteen games were won and seven drawn. From the previous season the title was decided on a percentage basis, and although Surrey won one more game than Lancashire, one fewer defeat counted for more. It was a season of jubilation for the Red Rose, but turmoil was to follow.

150 LANCASHIRE GREATS
34. Charles Smith

He was born in Calverley, Leeds, and played one non first-class match for Yorkshire before playing for Darwen in 1890. He was a useful batsman and a very good and plucky wicketkeeper with his bubbling eagerness and almost hysterical appeal, which was heard in the remotest part of a ground. 'Charlie' as he was known had gnarled and twisted fingers which gave testimony to his earnest and successful endeavours behind the stumps. He was described as "Hard as pig-iron, he will, failing his impressionable hands, shoot some part of his body in the way of the ball." He played in 167 games for Lancashire between 1893 and 1902 and made 431 dismissals. In 1895 he caught 51 and stumped 25 victims. His highest score was 81 v Sussex at Old Trafford and he scored over 2,000 runs in total. In July 1903 Lancashire gave him and Willis Cuttell a match to share a benefit. In retirement he returned to Leeds to open a newsagent's business.

After the Lord Mayor's Show 1898

HAVING WAITED many years for a four-pronged bowling attack good enough to surmount the hegemony of Surrey and Yorkshire, its dismantling was both speedy and painful. Johnny Briggs, who had been so prolific, even by his own standards, in the Championship-winning season, had a poor tour to Australia with England during the winter and returned with his confidence, if not in tatters, then severely dented. When added to the fact that, at 35 years of age, he was no longer a spring chicken, it was obvious that sooner or later his powers would wane. Although he had some great days, these were few and far between and he ended the 1898 season with almost half the wickets he had garnered the previous year, and at a cost approaching 25 per victim.

Arthur Mold was just a few months younger than Briggs and the wear and tear on his body was also beginning to show. In his first eight seasons with the club, he missed just seven games, exactly the same number as in 1897 alone. Although statistically he seemed to have a season not too dissimilar to the previous year, he was, in fact, in scintillating form from the opening game against the MCC at Lord's. He broke down in the game with Kent at Canterbury at the beginning of August and didn't play again this season. It was no coincidence that his absence from the side coincided with a dismal run of form for the county.

The problems with Briggs and Mold, however, paled into insignificance when set against those the Red Rose encountered with Albert Hallam. He was unable to play a single game for the club in 1898 due to ill-health. He then played just two the following year before injuring himself and five in 1900, all with little success, before disappearing off to his home county of Nottinghamshire to give them sterling service throughout the first decade of the 20th Century.

Indeed, the only bowler to perform to anything like the standard of 1897 was Willis Cuttell, but he claimed three fewer wickets than in the previous year, and at a greater cost. Tom Lancaster was brought back for a few games, and George Baker attempted to rekindle hopes he might make an all-rounder, whilst a leg-break bowler from Liverpool called Wilfred Bowring Stoddart was also tried. They all had some decent spells, but the comparison with the potency of the attack from the previous season was more than evident, as can be seen in one stark statistic: 11 out of 26 games were drawn, more than at any time in the club's history so far. It was a figure that could not be put down to just the vagaries of the

Manchester weather; the bowling attack lacked bite, and it showed.

By the time of Mold's breakdown at Canterbury, the county was still in a reasonably strong position. The title was already lost and heading inexorably over the Pennines to Yorkshire, but there was still a chance to finish in a respectable position in the top two or three. Only two county games had been lost, nine had been won and eight drawn. Kent then easily held out for a draw and in the last six games, four resulted in heavy defeats, including the Roses match at Old Trafford, and the other two were drawn. August, a month in which the Red Rose had perennially shone brightly, was an unmitigated disaster. The county hosted Derbyshire at Old Trafford for the final game, and, having racked up an imposing 546, had the visitors reeling at 77 for 8 when rain washed out the rest of the match. It was a wholly appropriate way for the season to end.

The only bright spot for the county was the form of Johnny Tyldesley. He created a new Lancashire record with 1,868 first-class runs, capping a fine season with his first double hundred for the club in that final game with Derbyshire. Albert Ward and Frank Sugg were their usual selves, George Baker had another good season with the bat, whilst a newcomer, Charlie Hartley, whose father George had played for the county a few times in the early 1870s before emigrating to America, collected six half centuries and 843 runs in just 18 games. Moreover, Willis Cuttell proved that he was a fine all-round cricketer, finishing just 48 runs shy of what would have been the first double for Lancashire.

On the face of it, it seemed that all was well with the batting. But some crucial contributions were missing. Wicketkeeper Charles Smith broke down mid-way during the season and played just 12 times. Whilst his replacement, Lees Radcliffe, was competent behind the stumps, his batting was not in the same class. Then there was Archie MacLaren. The man who had bestridden Australia for England the previous winter – for the third time – was not quite as at home in the more prosaic surroundings of Leyton and Hove this season. He managed six appearances, all as captain in the catastrophic run in August, scored only one half century and made just 233 runs for the county. It was his worst ever contribution to the side.

And talking of MacLaren and captaincy; Lancashire's bowling woes were as nothing compared to what happened with the captaincy. There were, astonishingly, seven

of them. AN Hornby, the official skipper, appeared only seven times, the last in the Derbyshire game at the end of the season. Sydney Crosfield did it twice, Charles Benton from Glossop once, Sidney Tindall seven times and Alexander Eccles on four occasions. At least Eccles made some contribution with the bat, scoring a fine century against Leicestershire at Grace Road. The others, including MacLaren, contributed next to nothing.

So, Lancashire slumped to sixth in the table. It was their worst finishing position in any of the official County Championship seasons. Given the turmoil that multiple captains had brought to the county on the playing field at times in the 1890s, what did the club decide to do next?

Joint captains again *1899*

ONE NOTABLE feature of the 1897 Championship-winning Lancashire side was that only 20 players appeared for the club during the season. Of those 20, just two made their debuts that year, the fewest in any season in the club's history up to that point. Of those two, Charlie Hartley would make an impact the following season, whilst Lees Radcliffe was the reserve wicketkeeper. There were one or two anomalies amongst the 20; for example, Welshman Richard Thomas played 20 times for the club from 1894 until 1902 as a batsman and averaged just 3.52, but, by and large, it showed the wisdom of continuity in selection.

In 1899 the county used no fewer than 31 different players, and of them, ten were debutants. The difference in this year, however, was that of those ten, seven would go on to play important roles, to varying degrees, in the history of Lancashire cricket, and, indeed, international cricket.

One person who was not making a debut for the club in 1899 was Gerald Roscoe Bardswell. In only his third game for Oxford University, at The Parks in early June 1894, he claimed six Lancashire wickets for just 36 runs. It was to remain easily his best bowling performance in first-class cricket and impressed the county so much that, after finishing at Oxford for the summer, the Liverpool-born medium pacer would play six times for the Red Rose at the end of that season.

It's here that the fairytale goes awry. He took just eight wickets in those six matches. Two years later, he played eight times for the county, including the game with the touring Australians at Aigburth. This time his record was even more nondescript: he claimed not a single wicket in 40 overs, although he did score more than 200 runs. Bizarrely, for the start of the 1899 season, he was appointed joint captain with Archie MacLaren. He led the side on six occasions, including the games with the MCC at Lord's and the Australians at Old Trafford, did not bowl, scored 134 runs at 16.75 and never played another first-class game.

In truth, and despite another year of multiple captains, the repeated experiment with joint leaders did see a slight improvement on the year before. Three more games were won and four fewer drawn and Lancashire finished fourth. It could have been even better. From the 12th June until the 11th August, the Red Rose hit a purple patch which saw them win 11 times, draw three and lose just once to put themselves in with an outside chance of the title. But, in a near repeat of the previous season, they lost the next three games and were hanging on by the skin of their teeth in the final match of the season against Middlesex at Old Trafford when the rain came.

Arthur Mold was back to his rollicking best with 115 wickets, although his quicker ball was beginning to arouse some suspicion. Willis Cuttell was not quite as effective as in the previous two seasons, but still claimed 87 victims to add to his 983 runs, and a number of others,

including opening batsman Albert Ward, chipped in with a few wickets from time to time.

Ward was still the model of consistency with the bat and passed 1,000 runs for the seventh season in succession. Johnny Tyldesley was nearly as successful as the year before and had begun his England career the previous winter in South Africa. Charlie Hartley continued to impress and Archie MacLaren returned to something like his best form in the nine games he played. On the debit side, it was the end of the road for George Baker and Frank Sugg, and Arthur Paul was to play just twice more the following season. As the new millennium was approaching, the great batting line-up of the 1890s was finally breaking up.

AN Hornby played his final game for the county against Leicestershire at Grace Road in the middle of July. As Lancashire plundered 590 runs in their only innings, with Tyldesley making 249, Hornby, skippering the side and batting at number nine, made a clinical half century. He played two other games this season and topped the batting averages. It was an appropriate end to the Lancashire career of the club's great figurehead. Over 33 seasons as a player since his debut in the very first Roses match at Whalley, he had made 292 appearances for the club and scored more than 10,000 runs, with ten centuries. Appointed president in 1894, it was a position he was to hold until 1916.

In addition to all the various retirements, there was a worrying development in the life and career of Johnny Briggs. Even though he was now 36-years-old, it was hoped that he could hold out for a few more years to provide a cushion of experience to some of the new blood. Despite his difficulties in 1898, he seemed to recover his mojo in 1899. With half the season gone, he was hurtling towards 100 wickets for the season, looked like he was easily going to accrue his usual 500 runs with the bat and had regained his place in the England side for the third Test against Australia at Headingley. However, having bowled 30 overs on the first day and taken three wickets for 53 runs, he suffered an epileptic seizure whilst out with the team in Leeds that evening. He was confined to Cheadle Asylum and did not play again this season.

---

150 LANCASHIRE GREATS
36. Willis Cuttell

Willis Cuttell was the first Lancashire player to achieve the double of 1,000 runs and 100 wickets in a season. He helped Nelson win the Lancashire League title four times before joining Lancashire at the age of 32. A slow right-arm bowler, he had good command of length and turned the ball both ways. An excellent fielder and a sound batsman, his golden season was 1898 when he did that double. He helped Lancashire win the County Championship in 1897 and was selected by Wisden as one of its Cricketers of the Year. He became the first Lancashire League player to play Test cricket, playing twice for England against South Africa and taking six wickets at 12 runs each. He was appointed coach at Rugby School in 1907, where he remained for 20 years. He also acted as a first-class umpire for two seasons. His modest benefit for Lancashire allowed him to purchase a corner tobacconist shop in Nelson and he lived there for the rest of his life.

The Class of 1899

1899 SAW THE most number of debutants for the county since 1885, when no fewer than 15 players appeared for the club for the first time. Usually when so many new faces were seen in a season, they would be a motley collection of one-cap wonders, professionals from the Lancashire League who it was hoped might make the grade and gentlemen amateurs who were making up the numbers, particularly on the long treks down south which they could fund themselves. It was unusual to have more than one or two debutants go on to have any sort of longevity with the club, and very rare indeed to have a cluster of above average to great cricketers all turn up in one season. This is why 1899 must be considered truly special.

Three of the class of 1899 were from the standard cast: Charles Ingleby, a Yorkshireman from Leeds who ended up trying his luck with his home county without success, played just once for Lancashire, against Derbyshire at Old Trafford in the middle of June. William Silcock, whose figures suggest he might have made a decent county all-rounder but for the competition he faced at the time, played against Warwickshire at Edgbaston at the beginning of June and on five further occasions in 1902, whilst Jerry Ainsworth from Formby played in the first two matches of the season, against the Australians at Old Trafford at the end of May and in the Roses match at Bramall Lane at the end of June. The gentleman amateur Ainsworth also appeared in a number of games for various guest elevens, of whom there were a plethora at this time, including in the USA and India.

The seven who were to make an impact included Londoner Sidney Webb. The medium-pace bowler played a few games for Middlesex in 1897 and 1898 with limited success before moving north, and, although his time with Lancashire lasted just five seasons, he played a leading role in turning around the Red Rose's fortunes after the doldrums of 1898 and 1899 and was good enough to claim 112 wickets in 1901.

Another bowler with far more longevity was Bill Huddleston. He was to become an integral part of one of the club's great bowling attacks, which was to include Walter Brearley, Harry Dean, Willis Cuttell and the Aussie Alex Kermode, in the mid-1900s. He played in 183 games for Lancashire from 1899 up to the outbreak of the First World War and claimed 684

wickets. After the war, he was a stalwart of the Leigh club and helped them win the Manchester Association title in 1923 at the age of 50.

By far and away the most famous name on this list was the one with the shortest career for the club. Sydney Francis Barnes had had a handful of undistinguished games for Warwickshire in the mid-1890s, which also applied to his two appearances for Lancashire in 1899. One performance against Leicestershire at Old Trafford in the final match of the 1901 season redefined his career. MacLaren took him to Australia with his England party that winter and he became what many consider to be the greatest bowler of all time, and in 1963 he was named by Wisden as one of the five giants of the Wisden Century. His two years with Lancashire that followed his Test debut were fairly successful, but they were accompanied by acrimony and he preferred the less rigorous environments of minor counties and league cricket. His 189 Test wickets remained a record until well after the Second World War.

With the retirement of Albert Neilson Hornby came the first sighting of his son, Albert Henry Hornby. Somewhat unfairly compared to his father, he was no slouch with the bat and captained the county from 1908 until the start of the First World War. Unfortunately, this coincided with the club's eventual slump into mediocrity, but he did score over 9,000 runs for the club with eight centuries.

Liverpool-born Harold Gwyer Garnett's career mirrored that of AH Hornby. He did not, however, do quite as well with the bat as Hornby, making over 5,000 runs and with five centuries, but he had a spectacular first full season in 1901, which led MacLaren to take him to Australia along with SF Barnes. Although he excelled again in 1905, and had a very good season in 1914, he was regarded as something of an unfulfilled talent. He was killed at Cambrai in France in December 1917.

All-rounder Jack Sharp was no unfulfilled talent. He was still playing for the club in 1925, when he had been captain for three seasons, and was good enough to score over 20,000 runs and take more than 400 wickets for the club. In addition, he was selected for the final three Test matches of the 1909 series against Australia. He also played twice for England at football and had a long career as a right winger for Everton.

COUNTY CRICKETERS.

MR. A. H. HORNBY.

LANCASHIRE.

Last, but certainly not least, was Reginald Herbert Spooner. Still a schoolboy at Marlborough in 1899, he played five times at the end of the season, drawing praise for his classical style, particularly in a cultured innings of 83 against Middlesex at Lord's on his debut and two fine showings in the game with the Australians at Aigburth. He became one of the most admired batsmen of his generation and played ten times for England.

COUNTY CRICKETERS.

MR. R. H. SPOONER,

LANCASHIRE.

Incomparable Johnny *1900*

IN ANY other season Lancashire's performance in 1900 would have seen them crowned as champions. With Worcestershire now added to the Red Rose's fixture list and no game with the MCC, all 28 first-class matches this year were part of the County Championship. The first six were all won by convincing margins, and the first defeat did not come until the twenty-first match of the season, when Gloucestershire skipper Gilbert Jessop inspired his team to a narrow three-wicket victory.

Just one other match was lost, the game with Surrey at the Oval in the middle of August, when a last wicket partnership of 131 in the home side's first innings appeared to sap the confidence of the Lancashire side and they lost by an innings. By the end of the season, as well as the two defeats, there were 15 victories and 11 draws.

That the county did not win the Championship was down to the emergence of one of the truly great teams of county cricket history in the Yorkshire team of 1900 to 1902. It was the first of three titles in a row for this team and a period of three seasons when they lost just twice. In 1900, they didn't lose a single game, with the two Roses matches both ending in draws with the home side in the ascendancy in each case. Not for the first, nor the last, would the White Rose prove a thorn in the Red Rose's side.

The main reason for Lancashire's improvement was the final solution to the captaincy problem. Archie MacLaren was appointed "assistant secretary" and the salary he received for this post enabled him to give up his teaching job and play full-time for the club. Whether he actually performed any tasks in a secretarial capacity is a moot point, but it also enabled him to retain his status as a "gentleman amateur", although some at the time preferred to coin the phrase "shamateur".

Whatever the semantics of MacLaren's position, he had a wonderful year with the bat and was the club's leading run-scorer with 1,531, including five centuries. Moreover, he scored them at such a rate it enabled the Red Rose to win games that might otherwise have been drawn. It also meant his partner at the top of the order, Albert Ward, could play his natural game, and he topped the averages just above MacLaren with just 20 runs fewer than his skipper, his best ever season for the club. Johnny Tyldesley did not quite have the success of the previous year, but made 1,372 runs to place third, whilst Charlie Hartley, in fourth, passed 1,000 runs for the one and only time in his career.

Ward and Tyldesley played in every game and MacLaren missed just one through injury. Indeed, eight players missed just nine games between them, and one more, wicketkeeper Charles Smith, played in 20 and a further two others, Arthur Mold and newcomer Sidney Webb, played in 18. As had been proved a number of times in the history of the club so far, consistency in selection had been matched by results.

Amateur Alex Eccles, who had stood in as captain a number of times over the previous two seasons, added 799 precious runs to the 813 he scored in 1899, whilst all-rounders Willis Cuttell and Jack Sharp missed just two and one game respectively and garnered 787 and 508 runs.

Cuttell and Sharp were also key components of what was, in effect, a five-pronged attack every bit as effective as the four-pronged one that helped to win the 1897 Championship. Cuttell passed 100 wickets for the third time, whilst Sharp's 52 meant that he had performed the mini double in his first full season. Although Arthur Mold again missed plenty of matches through injury and other reasons, he only fell three short of another century of wickets, and Sidney Webb proved an able deputy when he was in the side and racked up 72 victims.

But the one player who was largely responsible for Lancashire's high standing this season was Johnny Briggs. After his seizure in Leeds the previous year, it was feared that his cricket-playing days were over. However, his miraculous recovery was completed to such an extent that he missed just one game, scored more runs, 761, than he had ever done in a season for the club before and claimed 120 wickets, his first century of wickets since Lancashire carried off the Championship in 1897.

On 24th May at Old Trafford, against new boys Worcester, he took all ten wickets in the first innings for 55 runs. It was his best ever bowling analysis. In the final game of the season at home to Leicestershire, he scythed through the visitors' second innings with 6 for 49 to bowl the Red Rose to a comprehensive 216-run victory. It would be his last ever game for the club.

The end of Briggs and Mold

1901

AS WAS the case at the beginning of the previous decade, a couple of seasons were overshadowed by the declining health and subsequent untimely death of a Lancashire Great. For Dick Pilling substitute Johnny Briggs. He had played in one more first-class game in 1900, for the North against the South at Lord's, where he took six wickets in the first innings, including those of WG Grace and Gilbert Jessop, and made a few runs. Soon after, however, it was obvious that there was something wrong and he was clearly mentally ill. He was confined to Cheadle asylum again, where he remained until his death on 11th January 1902.

He was the greatest all-round cricketer ever to play for the Red Rose. The only player to have scored more than 10,000 runs and taken over 1,000 wickets for the club, his final tally of 2,221 first-class wickets is second only to Brian Statham. Whereas some of the greats of the game at this time could be crotchety and aggressive – Grace and his skipper Archie MacLaren for example, and certainly a good number of the Yorkshire team of this period – Briggs was gregarious and popular. CB Fry summed up the man and his cricket best with these well-chosen words: *"This little animal is round and smiles, it bowls and bowls and bowls and it always gets wickets. Of course no one would call Johnny a beast, not even a disappointed batsman. Why, he beams upon you before and after your innings. The shorter your innings the happier he is towards you. He passes you a cheery time of day. He inquires with feeling about your health and form. He rubs the ball in the dust, takes two steps and serves you a fast yorker instead of the high tossed slow you expected. You retire, he smiles. What could be pleasanter?"*

Supplement to THE KING. July 20th, 1901.

THE NO-BALLING OF MOLD.
HOW THE LANCASHIRE BOWLER DELIVERS A BALL.

This series of photographs, taken on Tuesday last at Tunbridge Wells, shows Arthur Mold, the Lancashire bowler, whose bowling Phillips, the umpire, has declared to be illegal, in the act of delivering a ball. Those who hold opinions on what constitutes a throw and what constitutes a legal delivery, may have their theories strengthened by a study of these pictures.

The club slipped to third in 1901, behind Yorkshire and Middlesex, by virtue of winning four fewer games and losing three more. The only side to have a complete fixture list, they drew 12 games, a record. It wasn't the only record. Johnny Tyldesley amassed 2,633 runs for the club, including eight centuries and 13 scores of 50 or more. All were records. Having had a slightly stuttering start to his Test career, he would now be an England regular for the rest of the decade, often entering the fray from a separate gate than his batsmen teammates as the sole professional in a line-up of some of the classical names of the Golden Age of Cricket. He was amongst them by right.

Four others passed 1,000. MacLaren and Ward, of course, although they were not as prolific as in 1900, and James Hallows, from Little Lever in Bolton, for the first time, and, with 1,758 runs from all 30 first-class games, Harold Garnett. He would flatter to deceive right up to the First World War. Alex Eccles was consistency itself, whilst Jack Sharp continued to improve. Both topped 800. Others, however, declined: Charlie Hartley had peaked all too briefly and was soon to lose his place, Willis Cuttell's opportunity to become the first Lancastrian to do the double had gone and, although his wicketkeeping was still first rate, Charles Smith made no significant contribution with the bat from 29 appearances.

Cuttell only just made it to 50 wickets, although he did play in only 18 games. Sharp and Sidney Webb both topped 100 wickets, with the former now having taken over the mantle as the club's leading all-rounder from Briggs and Cuttell. Not far behind Sharp would be Hallows. Although he managed only 36 victims, his day would come when the Red Rose next won the Championship.

There was also a pleasing re-appearance for Ernest Eden Steel, brother of AG, DQ, and HB. Having played his last game for the club in 1888 before leaving for India, he had just turned 37 when he appeared in seven Championship matches at the height of summer. All those games for the Europeans against the Parsees had obviously kept him in shape as he topped the county's bowling averages with 44 scalps at 19.29.

Aside from Briggs, the biggest sadness was to be the fate of Arthur Mold. In the game against Nottinghamshire at the end of June the previous year, he had been no-balled for throwing for the first time by umpire Jim Phillips, who seemed to be on a one-man crusade to rid the sport of suspect actions. Mold continued to play that season, but not in any game umpired by Phillips.

In 1901, in the game with Somerset at Old Trafford on 11th July, Phillips no-balled Mold no fewer than fifteen times. Naturally, the Old Trafford crowd was incensed, and the club itself gave the player, and had given him in the past, unequivocal support. But with both the press and the other counties all being of the opinion that Mold's action was suspect, the writing was on the wall. The game against Middlesex at Lord's in the middle of August was his last for the club and he was drummed out of the sport, his reputation in tatters.

In one fell swoop, Johnny Briggs and Arthur Mold, who had laboured together for 12 years in the Red Rose cause, were gone.

Beaten by the weather *1902*

The weather was the determining factor in 1902, resulting in a season for the Red Rose every bit as disappointing as the one that followed the Championship victory of 1897. Only seven games were won, five ended in defeat and 11 were drawn, six of them in the space of seven games in a spell of horrendous weather between 30th June and 9th August. The game against Middlesex at Lord's just over a week later was abandoned without a ball being bowled.

The poverty of the season's cricket was reflected in both the batting and bowling statistics. Some careers were at an end, some stalled and others were in decline. Johnny Tydesley managed only half the total of runs he had achieved in 1901, whilst Archie MacLaren was the only other to reach four figures. He would surely have done much better were it not for his captaincy of the England side in a truly great Test series in which he and the Yorkshire oligarch Lord Martin Hawke were often seen in cahoots to destroy any chance the home side had of victory.

These spats centred some of the time around the somewhat curmudgeonly figure of Sydney Francis Barnes. With MacLaren having followed a hunch to take Barnes to Australia during the previous winter, and having seen his protégé take 19 wickets in the first two Tests before breaking down, he and Hawke conspired to give the one England bowler to put the fear of God into the Australians just a single Test match, at Bramall Lane, in which he claimed 6 for 39 in Australia's first innings. Barnes fared a little better in what would be the first of only two full seasons in county cricket, being the Red Rose's leading wicket-taker with 84.

For the first time since 1890, therefore, no Lancashire bowler reached the 100-wicket marker. Sidney Webb, blighted as much by his fielding as his bowling, had the worst fall from grace, managing 84 fewer victims than in the previous year, with Jack Sharp just three behind that figure. Whilst Sharp's form (with the bat too) would be a mere setback, Webb's career with the Red Rose would end the following year.

It looked like Willis Cuttell's days were numbered. Like Sharp, he had a poor all-round season, but he would have one last hurrah. Not so Albert Ward. The great opener failed to make 1,000 in a season for the first time for ten years and played unproductively in five more games the following season and once in 1904. And although EE Steel played more often, he managed just three more wickets than in 1902 and his Lancashire career, too, would end in 1904.

James Hallows reached 50 wickets for the first time, but his batting went backwards. Other than Hallows and Barnes, the only other bowler to reach 50 wickets was John I'Anson. The

Albert Ward with WG Grace. Ward's long and illustrious career was winding to a close in 1902.

Yorkshireman, who had made a promising debut as a 17-year-old all-rounder in 1896 but played little in between, took exactly 50 wickets and made a century. It looked like he had made a breakthrough, but, apart from minor contributions in 1904 and 1905, his career with the Red Rose was a major disappointment.

Three men who were to have a major part to play in the county's successes in the middle of the decade did make their debuts, however. Walter Brearley made two appearances, with his two wickets coming at a cost of 60 apiece. He would make a famous double act with MacLaren and go on to play four times for England. The Oxford University keeper William Findlay, who played three times, would become a more than reliable replacement with gloves and bat for Charles Smith, albeit for just four seasons; and Aussie Alexander Kermode, who took five wickets on his debut for the county against the Australians in the final match of the season at Aigburth, would prove an admirable foil for Brearley, although only for a handful of seasons as well.

Having lost the first fixture with Australia at Old Trafford to the weather in early June, the one at Aigburth was a cracker, the visitors just getting home by 18 runs. Slow left-armer George Littlewood, only 21-years-old and from Friarmere over the border into Yorkshire, had claimed nine wickets on debut in the previous game against Leicester at Old Trafford. Against this extremely powerful Aussie batting line-up, which included the likes of Victor Trumper, Joe Darling, Monty Noble and Clem Hill in their pomp, he produced the outstanding match figures of 12 for 98. It looked like a new star was born, but true to the dismal nature of this season, he was yet another who flattered to deceive. The following year he played 11 first-class games and accumulated just 35 wickets. He appeared only once more, the first match of the 1904 season at Leicester, before disappearing back to league cricket.

150 LANCASHIRE GREATS
39. Walter Brearley

Walter Brearley was a heftily-built amateur fast bowler who, from a short run, generated a very lively pace. He took 690 wickets for Lancashire at an average of 18.70 and he was very successful in Roses matches, taking 125 wickets at a cost of 16 runs each in only 14 games. He played in only four Test matches but took 17 wickets and in 1905 he claimed Victor Trumper's wicket six times. An individual character who spoke his mind, he kept having differences of opinion with the Lancashire committee which kept him out of the side on occasions. It was said that at Old Trafford when Walter Brearley hurried to the wicket to bat at no. 11 the horse which was used to roll the wicket, immediately walked between the shafts, such was his reputation as a batsman. In 1912, while playing for Cheshire, he was selected to play for England. He lived in London when he retired and often coached young cricketers at Lord's. A big-hearted cricketer, Brearley was a larger than life character in every way.

War over for Spooner *1903*

REGGIE SPOONER returned to Old Trafford in 1903. Having created such a good impression in his short spell with the club whilst still a schoolboy at the end of the 1899 season, he had then gone off to do his military service, some of it spent in South Africa during the Second Boer War. If anything, his cultured style, which would have many commentators purring with admiration throughout the next ten seasons, had been enhanced by this enforced break in his career.

He played all but one of the county's first-class matches and made 1,283 runs. Against Nottinghamshire at Trent Bridge at the beginning of July, he made a wonderful 247, putting on over 200 with Johnny Tydesley for the second wicket. At the end of that month, he and Archie MacLaren opened the batting together at Aigburth against Gloucestershire and plundered 368. It was a Lancashire record for the first wicket that remains to this day.

MacLaren's double century in that match was the highest of the three three-figure scores he made this season and he was back to his imperious best. Without the cares of the captaincy of the England team, he appeared in all Lancashire's games and racked up 1,628 runs, the highest aggregate he would achieve for the club in his 20-year career.

The only other player to play in every game was AH Hornby. Not quite in the class of his fellow amateurs MacLaren and Spooner, or indeed his father, he nevertheless made seven half centuries and 838 runs in total. He had not played for the club since making his debut in 1899, but he was now to become a consistent, if not prolific, run-scorer in the middle order. More importantly, like his father before him, he was to be groomed to become the club's next captain.

Others of the class of 1899 also made decent contributions with the bat. Although he now bowled only rarely, Jack Sharp added 755 runs to significantly improve on his poor 1902 season, whilst Harold Garnett played just over half the matches and netted 687, including a match-saving century in the Roses match at Old Trafford at the beginning of June.

Topping the averages and the aggregate number of runs for the third season in a row was Johnny Tyldesley. A formidable and consistent accumulator at number three or four, he was the rock around which the more prosaic talents of MacLaren, Spooner, Garnett and Alex Eccles, who passed 500 runs for the sixth season in a row, could flourish.

Sydney Barnes had a much more successful season with the ball, claiming 131 wickets, the highest total for the club

The great SF Barnes took 131 wickets but left the club before the end of the season.

since Johnny Briggs had taken 155 in the Championship-winning season of 1897. On his day, as he was to prove time and again for England later in the decade and beyond, he was virtually unplayable, but there remained a feeling amongst the Lancashire committee that he didn't fit in. Before the end of the season he departed, ostensibly over a dispute about winter payments, but many at the club – dressing room included – were glad to see the back of him.

The man who was to benefit the most from Barnes's departure was James Hallows. This season he played just eight times, as opposed to being the only ever-present in 1902. He easily topped the bowling averages, his 26 wickets costing a mere 11.69. In the absence of Barnes in the penultimate match of the season against Notts at Old Trafford, he claimed match figures of 12 for 95. In his first game of the season, against London County, the newly-formed vehicle for the dotage of WG Grace, he had made an unbeaten century, which had helped him nestle into third place in the batting averages behind Tyldesley and MacLaren. His all-round talents were to come to their ultimate fruition the following season.

Although his batting seemed to be in terminal decline, Willis Cuttell had something of a revival with the ball, often benefitting from being in partnership with Barnes, and garnering the second highest number of wickets with 73. Walter Brearley, in his first full season, added 69 victims, but Sidney Webb and Ernest Steel had bowled their last balls for the club.

A purple patch at the end of the season, when four games were won and two drawn, enabled the Red Rose to climb a place to fourth in the county pecking order, just behind a faltering Yorkshire. It was the start of a run that would see the county not lose again in the Championship until July 1905.

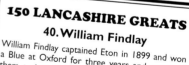

150 LANCASHIRE GREATS

40. William Findlay

William Findlay captained Eton in 1899 and won a Blue at Oxford for three years and captained them against Cambridge in 1903. He played for Lancashire between 1902 and 1906 in 58 matches, scoring 1,223 runs and taking 113 dismissals behind the stumps. He was a very capable wicketkeeper and more than useful batsman and was a member of the Lancashire team which won the County Championship in 1904. He then became secretary of Surrey CCC before transferring to Lord's as Assistant Secretary in 1919. He became Secretary in 1936, a position he held for ten years and for which his genial, diplomatic manner and never-failing courtesy suited him admirably. He was a shrewd counsellor and highly-valued member of any committee lucky enough to secure his services. He served on the committees of MCC, Lancashire, Surrey and Kent and was President of Lancashire 1947-48. He was elected President of MCC in 1951-52. He died at his home in Kent in 1953 aged 72.

The Invincibles *1904*

IN THE 40 years since the formation of the county club, the received wisdom had always been that the most successful seasons had been when there had been a settled side with around 20 players used in total and only a few debutants. For example, in the last year in which Lancashire won the Championship, 1897, just 20 individuals appeared that season and only two were making their debuts. This theory seems to have been blown out of the water in 1904. As the Red Rose revelled in a season in which they remained unbeaten and wrapped up the Championship by the end of July, no fewer than 29 names appeared on the county scorecards, with six of these making their debuts.

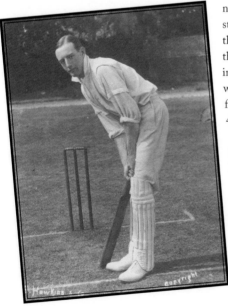

On closer inspection, however, the Lancashire team selection of 1904 was, in many ways, as consistent as that of 1897. Four players, Johnny Tyldesley, Reggie Spooner, Jack Sharp and AH Hornby, missed only one of the 27 first-class fixtures this season, James Hallows and Willis Cuttell missed three, Archie MacLaren five, and debutant Leslie Poidevin seven, with two other players, Harold Garnett and Alex Kermode, each making 15 appearances. William Findlay and newcomer William Worsley shared the wicketkeeping duties in all but two games, Conversely, no fewer than fourteen players filled in on one or two occasions.

The team began the season with six wins out of the first seven games. It was the manner and size of those victories that stood out: four were won by an innings and the other two by ten and nine wickets respectively. The only drawn game was the Roses match at Old Trafford when the visitors were reeling on 34 for 3 in their second innings when rain washed out the whole of the final day's play.

Two drawn games in the middle of June, against Warwickshire at Edgbaston, when the Red Rose men easily held out for a draw after a disappointing first innings, and against Sussex at Old Trafford, when England internationals CB Fry and KS Ranjitsinhji held the home side at bay on a very good wicket, were followed by a run of nine wins in ten matches. Once again, it was the emphatic nature of these victories that was most startling, with three won by an innings and the narrowest margin being by 70 runs at the Oval against Surrey. The only draw in this period was on another very good wicket at Trent Bridge, where Lancashire followed Nottinghamshire's huge total of 447 with a mammoth 586.

Thus, by the time of the Roses match at Headingley at the beginning of August, Lancashire had won 15 games and drawn four. It mattered little that this game and the following five were drawn as some inclement August weather, coupled with some fine pitches, saw the county fail to force a win from 1st to the 25th August. With nearest rivals Yorkshire's obdurate but slow batting, epitomised by their crawl to just over 400 in over 150 overs

in this game, giving them a Championship record of 16 drawn games, the race for the title was all but over.

The 131-run victory over Derbyshire in the final Championship match of the season at Old Trafford was the icing on the cake of the club's best ever season. Two weeks later, the county played the best of the rest at the Oval, but this game ended with an exciting finish in prospect after much of the first day had been washed out by rain.

In the drawn game at Trent Bridge, both Tyldesley and MacLaren produced their highest scores of the season. Tyldesley's 225 was one of eight centuries as he passed 2,000 runs for the second time in his career. MacLaren made two further centuries, although he only slipped past 1,000 runs in the final game against The Rest. Reggie Spooner, who had delighted everyone the year before, did even better in 1904 with 1,699 runs and five centuries, including his first double. And Jack Sharp had his best season so far with the bat, making 938 runs and two centuries. His maturing strokeplay was to see him pass 1,000 runs in every season but one up to the First World War and help him gain England recognition.

J. T. TYLDESLEY (THE LANCASHIRE ROSE).
Drawn by Fred. L. Jones.

The real architects of this triumphant season, however, were four players who one can easily class together in pairs. Firstly, there were all-rounders Willis Cuttell and James Hallows. It had looked as though the 40-year-old Cuttell's career was coming to its conclusion, certainly as a batsman.

HEAP.   CUTTELL.   KERMODE.   TYLDESLEY.   HALLOWS.   SLADEN.   SHARP.

LANCASHIRE CRICKET TEAM. (Professional)

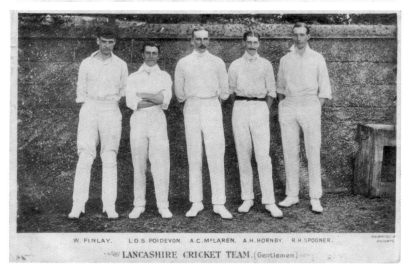

W. FINLAY.   L.O.S. POIDEVON.   A.C. McLAREN.   A.H. HORNBY.   R.H. SPOONER.

LANCASHIRE CRICKET TEAM. (Gentlemen)

The less experienced Kermode had actually made a successful debut for Lancashire as a fast-medium bowler against the touring Australians at Aigburth at the end of the 1902 season. He played twice for the county in 1903, against London County and the Gentlemen of Philadelphia, and when he joined up with the team at the end of June in 1904, he proved irresistible and claimed 77 wickets in only 15 games.

Another parallel with the 1897 team was in the bowling attack. With Hallows, Cuttell and Kermode all amongst the wickets, the other member of the four-pronged attack was Walter Brearley. He did not improve much on his showing in 1903, largely due to the success of the other three main bowlers, but his 77 wickets in 18 games was an invaluable contribution to the side's overall invincibility.

There were also 23 wickets from eight games for John I'Anson, but a glimpse into the county's future was to be shown by the performances of two players who were to become leading lights in the county's line-up right up until the First World War. Twenty-one-year-old James Sutcliffe Heap, an all-rounder from Lowerhouse in Burnley, had made an unremarkable debut in 1903, but in five matches in 1904 averaged above 30 with the bat and claimed two five-wicket hauls with the ball. And Bill Huddleston, who had made his debut as part of that class of 1899 but who hadn't played since 1901, appeared for the first of two games in 1904 in the match with Surrey at the Oval at the end of June, and, in the absence of Cuttell and Kermode, had match figures of 11 for 108. As well as going on to be a successful wicket-taker for the county, he would become a more than useful late order batsman.

It was an outstanding performance from the Red Rose, and arguably even better than Yorkshire's unbeaten season in 1900 considering the size of some of the victories. It also bore comparison to the county's first unofficial Championship title-winning season of 1881, when that team went unbeaten throughout the whole season. The task now was to do it again.

But in 1904 he made 660 runs, his highest total since 1900. In the drawn game against Warwickshire at Edgbaston, pressed into service as a makeshift opener, and with the Red Rose following on after trailing by 270 runs on first innings, he made 128, the highest of two centuries he scored this season. And, for the first time since 1900, he also topped 100 wickets. With a best of 6 for 58, he was a model of consistency as he bowled the most overs for the county and claimed nine 5-wicket hauls.

Astonishingly, Cuttell was not even the best all-rounder in the team. That mantle passed to James Hallows, who became the first player in Lancashire's history to claim the magical double of 1,000 runs and 100 wickets. Having played little the previous year, he made three centuries in his 1,071 runs and his 108 wickets included ten wickets in a match on three occasions. Although Hallows and Cuttell's careers with the Red Rose were not to last much longer, they could be rightly proud of their leading role in this magnificent season.

The other pair who had a leading hand in this Championship-winning season were two Australians, Leslie Oswald Sheridan Poidevin and Alexander Kermode. Both were born in New South Wales and had played for their state side but had come to England in 1903 to play for WG Grace's ill-fated London County experiment. Poidevin began his Lancashire career at Old Trafford in the match against Surrey at the beginning of June by top-scoring with 55 in the home side's first innings. He went on to muster 871 runs in 21 games, with two centuries, the best being 153 against Sussex at Hove towards the middle of August.

	P	W	L	D	Pts	FM	%
County Championship 1904							
Lancashire	26	16	0	10	16	16	100.0
Yorkshire	27	9	2	16	7	11	63.6
Kent	21	10	4	7	6	14	42.9
Middlesex	18	9	4	5	5	13	38.5
Nottinghamshire	20	7	4	9	3	11	27.3
Sussex	24	5	4	15	1	9	11.1
Leicestershire	20	6	6	8	0	12	0.0
Warwickshire	16	5	5	6	0	10	0.0
Gloucestershire	18	5	6	7	-1	11	-9.1
Derbyshire	18	5	8	5	-3	13	-23.1
Surrey	28	6	12	10	-6	18	-33.3
Somerset	18	5	11	2	-6	16	-37.5
Worcestershire	18	3	8	7	-5	11	-45.5
Essex	20	3	10	7	-7	13	-53.8
Hampshire	18	2	12	4	-10	14	-71.4

Unbeaten run ends *1905*

WALTER BREARLEY.

WHILST NOT quite the implosion that occurred following the Championship triumph in 1897, 1905 did, to some extent, follow a similar pattern. Up until the return match with eventual champions Yorkshire at Bramall Lane, the Red Rose men were still in with a chance of the title. Indeed, they began 1905 with an almost identical start to 1904, with eight wins, a draw and one game, against Surrey at the Oval, abandoned without a ball being bowled. This run included the Roses match at Old Trafford, which was won by an innings after centuries from Spooner and Tyldesley and some terrific bowling from Brearley and Kermode. It was Lancashire's first Roses victory since June 1899.

After the brilliant start, however, there followed a run of six drawn games, punctuated by an innings victory over Somerset at Old Trafford, which was followed by a ten-wicket reverse against Surrey at Aigburth. It was the county's first taste of defeat in the Championship since 5th August 1903. Despite winning three of the last eight county games, the two defeats proved crucial. The defeat in the Roses match at Bramall Lane was particularly galling as Walter Brearley had succeeded in bowling the White Rose men all out for 76 in the first innings of the match.

So what went wrong? On the face of it, the batting seemed to be as powerful, if not even more powerful, as in 1904. For the first time six players passed 1,000 runs. Leslie Poidevin continued where he had left off the previous season and topped the averages with 1,407 at a little over 40 and scored five centuries. Jack Sharp's growing maturity saw him pass 1,000 for the first time, whilst Harold Garnett, who had been the only player to disappoint in 1904, had his best season since 1901. Archie MacLaren played just 18 games, but he, too, topped four figures, whilst AH Hornby had his best season yet with 885 runs.

The two main disappointments with the bat were Reggie Spooner and Johnny Tyldesley. Both scored heavily, with Tyldesley managing yet another double century and the pair adding six further scores over 100 between them. But Spooner was down more than 400 runs on 1904, and Tyldesley almost 1,000. It was a different story for Spooner and Tyldesley in the Test series against Australia this summer, however, as both enjoyed their best ever returns in Test cricket.

Not for the first time, nor the last, had Lancashire's challenge in the County Championship been distracted by a visiting Australian side. As well as the Test calls, the inevitable result of such a brilliant season as 1904, the county lost both games with the tourists heavily. The first at Old Trafford at the end of May was their first defeat in any first-class fixture since the one in the Roses match at Bradford at the beginning of August in 1903, which had marked the start of their long unbeaten run in the Championship, and the second, a thrashing by an innings at Aigburth in August, confirmed the county's loss of form.

As in 1898, just as the Red Rose had found four bowlers capable of claiming wickets at the rate required to win the Championship, so the quartet was no more. Walter Brearley had a wonderful season and topped the bowling averages with 133 wickets at just over 19, and made his debut for England in the fourth Test at Old Trafford, whilst Alex Kermode claimed more than 100 wickets for the first time. But the two bowling centurions of the Championship-winning year fell from grace to such an extent that the pair's future tenure with the club was to be brief.

Willis Cuttell was now approaching his 42nd birthday, so it was little wonder that he played just eight times and managed only eight victims, although he was to have an Indian summer the following year. The imminent end of the career of James Hallows, the hero of 1904, was more startling. He managed a mere 30 wickets from 19 games at a cost of more than 40 and, but for his batting, he would surely have lost his place in the side.

There were some minor bowling contributions from newcomers James Heap and William Cook, whose brother Lol would soon arrive on the scene and become a Lancashire Great with the ball. Jack Sharp garnered 42 wickets, his best return since his century in 1901, and John I'Anson claimed another 21, whilst even Les Poidevin was pressed into action and added 23. All in all, however, the bowling failed to match that of the great Yorkshire quartet of Jackson, Haigh, Rhodes and Hirst and the county were forced to settle for second place.

150 LANCASHIRE GREATS
42. Harold Garnett

Born in 1879 at Aigburth, Liverpool, he was killed during the First World War. He played twice in 1900 and jumped to fame the following year, playing so finely that he seemed likely to become the best left-handed bat in England. His style was attractive and his hitting very strong. Against Sussex at Old Trafford he scored 110 and 89 and in the season he scored 1,758 runs ave. 35.87 and was second in the Lancashire averages. On the strength of this performance he was chosen to go to Australia with A.C.MacLaren's England team but he was not successful. He continued to play for Lancashire for several seasons and even though business took him to Argentina he came to renew his connection with Lancashire in 1911 and 1914. He developed into a first rate wicket-keeper and was chosen to play for the Gentlemen at Lord's and his performance helped win the match. He played in 144 matches for Lancashire scoring 5,599 runs ave 26.16 with five centuries. He volunteered at the outbreak of the War and soon obtained a commission. He was killed in action at Marcoing, Cambrai in France.

Tyldesley on the money 1906

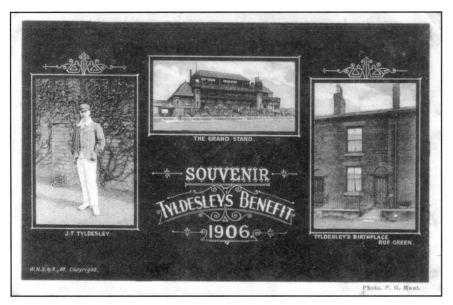

It was a monumental innings, only ended when he ran out of partners and witnessed by Kent debutant and later cricket legend Frank Woolley, who captured the spirit of the Golden Age when he later wrote: "All we wanted was to see Tyldesley get 300."

After 12 outstanding seasons for the club, Tyldesley was given a benefit, the Roses match at Old Trafford starting on 6th August. Fortunately the sun shone, as it did for most of this season, and although the match result did not go the way he wanted, Tyldesley would no doubt have been mollified and gratified by the size of the take: 3,111 pounds sterling. It was not to be surpassed until Cyril Washbrook's benefit raised 14,000 in 1948.

THE LAST two years of the captaincy of Archie MacLaren were marked by a gradual decline as older players retired, those that briefly shone departed and new recruits were blooded. Amongst the latter in 1906 were the two Harrys: Joseph William Henry 'Harry' Makepeace and Harry Dean.

In a career lasting up until 1930, Makepeace would score more than 25,000 runs for the county, and then return for two decades as coach. His deeds would forever be linked with those of Jack Sharp, as not only did Makepeace play cricket for England, like Sharp, he also played for Everton and England at football. Harry Dean burst on the scene in 1906, claiming 60 wickets as a versatile left-arm bowler. He took more than 1,200 in just 12 seasons for the county, which would have been many more but for the years lost to the First World War.

After a memorable opening fixture away to Leicestershire, which was won by one run as Willis Cuttell revived memories of the Championship season with five wickets in the home side's second innings, Lancashire had another good start to the season. Indeed, by the time they faced Middlesex at Lord's on 23rd July, they were still in with a chance of the title, having lost only two and won 11 of their 17 matches. However, defeat at Lord's and in the return with Middlesex in the penultimate game of the season, and further losses to Yorkshire in the Roses match at Old Trafford and at Canterbury against eventual champions Kent, saw them slide to fourth place.

Although Sharp had another great season with the bat, and Reggie Spooner and Leslie Poidevin adequate ones, MacLaren himself had easily his poorest return of the decade so far, as did captain-in-waiting AH Hornby. Cuttell made sure that the disappointments of 1905 did not stretch into his final season and he added over 400 runs to his 67 wickets. There also appeared to be a new find in all-rounder Frank Harry from Devon, who had made his debut in 1903, but for whom 1906 was his best year of only two at the top of his game. He played in all the games and made 767 runs and accumulated the second highest number of wickets, 87, two behind Alex Kermode.

Unfortunately, having become the best and most hostile fast bowler in world cricket, highly unusual for an amateur, Walter Brearley played only five times for the county in 1906. In dispute with the Lancashire committee, he managed 39 wickets in those five matches and then didn't play at all the following year, announcing that he had gone into business. He would, however, return again, for Lancashire and England.

The star of 1906, though, was undoubtedly Johnny Tyldesley. He fell just eight runs short of 2,000 runs for the season, although he made it easily in all matches. His total included what would turn out as his highest first-class score, 295 not out against champions Kent at Old Trafford on 7th June, and second only to MacLaren's 424 as the highest individual innings for the county at that time.

MacLaren reign ends on low *1907*

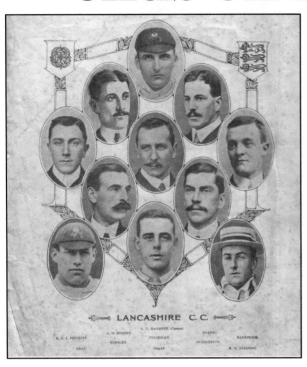

LANCASHIRE C.C.

A. C. MacLAREN (Captain).
L. O. S. POIDEVIN   A. H. HORNBY   HARRY.
WORSLEY   TYLDESLEY   HUDDLESTON   MAKEPEACE
DEAN   SHARP   H. D. STANNING

IT WAS unfortunate that Archie MacLaren's final season as skipper of Lancashire ended with the worst placing since he first took charge in 1894. Indeed, given the fact that during this period he often seemed distracted by the cares of the captaincy of the England team, had toured Australia three times and had missed many games through a variety of reasons, in many respects it was surprising that the county had enjoyed the success they had during his tenure.

County cricket was also changing; it was becoming more competitive. Whilst from the formation of the official Championship in 1890 (the year, of course of MacLaren's debut) until 1906, Surrey and Yorkshire had shared the title, with Lancashire, twice, and Middlesex, in 1903, considered mere interlopers, from 1906 new names and powerhouses emerged to challenge for honours. Kent, the 1906 winners, were to win the title twice more before the First World War. Nottinghamshire, who had dominated the unofficial Championship in the early 1870s and 1880s, won the official version for the first time in 1907, and Warwickshire became the seventh county to win a Championship in 1911.

As for Lancashire in 1907, the batting suffered from the absence of Reggie Spooner. He went into business and appeared only five times for the county and was unable to play anything like a full season until 1911. Tyldesley and Sharp again topped the run-getters table, whilst there was a welcome return to form for both the incoming and outgoing captains, with Hornby and MacLaren making a century apiece and over 800 and 700 runs respectively. Harry Makepeace topped 500 runs in only his second season and Henry Stanning from Leyland made 762 in his one and only full season with the club.

On the bowling side, Harry Dean showed that his first season was not a flash in the pan and flew past 100 wickets, the first of seven consecutive seasons of centuries, and Bill Huddleston provided solid support to top the bowling averages for the second time in a row with 76 wickets at 14.36. Frank Harry claimed 84 victims to add to his 87 of the previous year, and debutant Lol Cook, brother of William, showed the promise with 47 wickets that would see him become one of the leading bowlers in England in the early 1920s.

There was another very interesting debut in 1907 as well. Liverpool-born 19-year-old Morice Carlos Bird was an all-rounder who, earlier in the year, made two centuries as captain of Harrow against Eton in the annual match at Lord's. On the back of that, he was selected to play for Lancashire against Essex at Leyton in the middle of August and made 0 and 2. He then appeared in the final four county games, making a grand total of 36 runs in ten innings to finish rock bottom of Lancashire's batting averages, although he did claim four wickets as well.

Bird flew south, where he had an altogether better time of it. He played for the MCC in 1908 and the following year he pitched up at Surrey, scoring more than 1,000 runs in a season three times and becoming captain for two years in 1910. He also made ten appearances for England on two tours to South Africa, including the one in 1913/14 when former Lancashire man SF Barnes would create a record for wickets in a Test series which has not been broken to this day. Bird was a valuable member of that team with both bat and ball. Barnes and Bird; not the one, but the two that got away!

150 LANCASHIRE GREATS
44. Jack Sharp

Jack Sharp was one of the most enthusiastic and valuable of all Lancashire's cricketers. He was a double International, representing his country at cricket and football, scoring a Test century and winning an FA Cup final medal with Everton. Starting his career as a bowler, he had some success, taking 112 Championship wickets in 1901 before concentrating on his batting, scoring 22,015 runs, ave. 31.18, in 518 matches with 36 centuries. He played in all the matches of Lancashire's Championship-winning season in 1904 when they were unbeaten. He played three times for England and scored a Test century against Australia at the Oval in 1909. A very sound and brave batsman, he was strong on the offside with good cuts and drives. After the First World War he reverted to amateur status and in 1923 was appointed captain. In 1924 he became the first Test selector who was formerly a professional cricketer. He retired in 1925 after suffering abuse from the crowd because of his fielding. He played outside-right for Everton and Aston Villa and later became a director at Goodison Park and owned a sports shop in Liverpool. He died in 1938.

Aussies bow out *1908*

IT ALL started so very well for the captaincy of AH Hornby. Walter Brearley declared himself available and began firing on all cylinders from the off. He was supported in the bowling department by Harry Dean, Frank Harry and Bill Huddleston, all now proven performers at county level. Johnny Tyldesley and Jack Sharp were amongst the finest professional batsmen in England, and, at the top of the order, Hornby and new boy Alfred Hartley, whilst not in the same class as an opening pair as Hornby senior and RG Barlow, or MacLaren and Ward, would surely be solid and dependable. Then there was Les Poidevin, Harry Makepeace and Archie MacLaren in support. What could go wrong?

Indeed, nothing did go wrong to start with. The opening two games, against Somerset at Bath and Northamptonshire at Old Trafford were won by an innings, with Brearley claiming 11 wickets in both, and a rain-ruined second day meant that Lancashire were unable to close out a victory against Derbyshire at Old Trafford in the third county match.

It all began to go wrong in the next match, the return with Northants at the end of May. The Red Rose's opponents had been admitted as the sixteenth member of the county set-up in 1905, but had occupied the lower reaches of the table since then, and were to finish second bottom in 1908. Unfortunately for Lancashire, Tyldesley failed in both innings and they went down in a tense finish by a single wicket. Despite then beating Nottinghamshire, three games were lost in a row by ever increasing margins: to Yorkshire in the Roses match at Bramall Lane, and then Kent and Surrey at Old Trafford, the latter by an innings and 117 runs.

After beating Warwickshire at Edgbaston, there was another innings defeat, to Essex at Leyton, and even though there was a recovery of sorts, a run of four defeats in five games at the end of July and the beginning of August meant that, in terms of results, it was a dismal season. Nine defeats and seventh place were both records for the county and AH Hornby's reign had begun very inauspiciously.

Although Brearley and Dean had magnificent seasons, claiming 154 and 129 wickets respectively, the support bowling was generally inadequate. Harry started well but got injured and only returned for the final game, after which he never played for the county again. Huddleston was the next highest wicket-taker with 59, but he played in just half the games, and Lol Cook and James Heap appeared in only 14 games between them and were not quite the finished articles.

Tyldesley, who topped the batting averages again, had a good season, but not a great one, and when he failed the team tended to fail. Jack Sharp scored more than 1,500 runs for the first time and pitched in with a few wickets when needed, and Alex Hartley topped 1,000 runs in his first full season, but the rest

The two Australians, Leslie Poidevin and Alex Kermode, played their last games for Lancashire in 1908.

of the batting was middling to poor and too often the team were skittled out easily.

It was the end of the road for the two Australians. Poidevin and Kermode, who had been so integral to the 1904 Championship victory, were no longer the forces of old. Poidevin played just 11 times and Kermode only twice this season. Poidevin was also a fine tennis player who was good enough to play in the Davis Cup for his native country. In 1908, he was supposed to represent Australia at the London Olympics, but administrative bungling caused him to lose his place. Kermode stayed in England and played for Bacup in the Lancashire League up until the First World War. Both had contributed much in a few short years, and their partnership of 142 for the ninth wicket against Sussex at Eastbourne the previous season remains a Lancashire record. They had opened the committee's eyes to the value of overseas players. It was a lesson which would stand the county in good stead in the future.

Consistency the key *1909*

WHILST THE Red Rose had not hit rock bottom in 1908, there was a general feeling that the only way was up. And up it was; to second in the Championship and a finish above Yorkshire for the first time since 1904, even though both Roses matches were lost. The only team to best Lancashire were Kent, who were going through a purple patch having been runners-up to Yorkshire in 1908 and then going on to win the title again in 1910.

Of Lancashire's 24 county matches, 14 ended in victory and only four in defeat. Apart from the two Roses matches, the other losses were by an innings and 80 runs at Trent Bridge against Nottinghamshire at the end of June and by seven wickets against Worcestershire at Old Trafford in August. Both times the batting did not quite fire.

The loss against Worcestershire was the last of three consecutive reverses, starting at the beginning of August with the Roses match at Bradford and including a titanic tussle with the Australian tourists at Aigburth. Harry Dean took ten wickets in that match and no doubt this was in the memory of the selectors when the Aussies visited again for the Triangular Tournament in 1912, as he was to make his debut for England against Australia at Lord's.

So, what was so different in 1909 compared to 1908? In a word, consistency. Firstly, consistency in selection. Remember the old adage: Lancashire's best seasons are when there are the least amount of changes to the team and the fewest debutants. Well, in 1909 only 20 players represented the county and just one was making his debut, compared to 28 and four in the previous year. That one debutant was a good one as well: Ernest Tyldesley, brother of Johnny, and a batsman who would go on to at least equal the deeds of his sibling over the next 27 years.

Secondly, consistency in the batting. The same three players, Johnny Tyldesley, Jack Sharp and Alfred Hartley, passed 1,000 runs as in 1908, but even though Tyldesley had his poorest season since 1897, it was the support players that made the difference. Harry Makepeace, who had disappointed in 1908 after a promising 1907, failed by only 37 runs to pass the magical 1,000-run mark, skipper Hornby batted well at times and bowlers Bill Huddleston and Dean showed that they could both bat a bit by making useful contributions lower down the order. There was also a new man, Scot Kenneth Grant MacLeod, a batting all-rounder who was at Cambridge University and who would excel for the Red Rose over the next three seasons. He made over 500 runs, including a century, in 18 games after coming down from Cambridge.

There was also a welcome return to form for Archie MacLaren. In the doldrums the previous year, he made three half centuries and 466 runs at a little under 25 in 13 games for the county. At the age of 37 he was also to captain England, albeit unsuccessfully, in all five Tests against the Australians this summer.

An even more welcome returnee was Reggie Spooner. He had played just once in 1908, but in 1909 he appeared six times, scored two centuries and topped the batting averages with 421 runs at 46.77. It was a prelude to even greater contributions to the county's cause over the next three seasons.

E. TYLDESLEY
LANCASHIRE

Ernest Tyldesley, brother of Johnny, made his debut at Aigburth on 7th June. He was to have a career every bit the equal of his illustrious brother.

150 LANCASHIRE GREATS
46. Albert Henry Hornby

Born in Nantwich and educated at Harrow and Cambridge, he was the son of 'Monkey' Hornby and inherited his father's love of hunting, fishing and riding. A positive, hard-hitting and dashing opening batsman, his strokeplay was always tinged with daring. He made his mark as a determined and fearless captain, gallant and purposeful in his strong leadership and gaining respect from the professionals. During his time as captain the county had few top quality bowlers, but he did lead them to second place in 1909. During his career he scored almost 10,000 first-class runs, with a top score of 129. He scored a century in 43 minutes at Old Trafford against Somerset. In his final season he played for the Gentlemen against the Players at Lord's, opening the innings with CB Fry and top-scoring with 69. After military service in the First World War he bought an estate in Ireland to enjoy once more his hunting and salmon fishing.

End for Archie *1910*

A. C. MACLAREN

LANCASHIRE

BIZARRELY, THE Red Rose's batsmen and bowlers did even better in 1910 than they had in 1909, yet the county dropped to fourth in the table. Kent were runaway winners of the title for the second year in succession and won 19 of their matches, Surrey, who finished runners-up, won 16 and lost seven, whilst Middlesex, in third, won 11 and lost five. Lancashire lost two fewer games than Surrey and won three more than Middlesex, but the points system had changed so that instead of ignoring draws and taking the percentage of wins in non-drawn games, all games were included in the calculations and the best percentage of wins in all games played, including draws, won the day. Under the old system the county would have finished second to Kent, as in 1909, but instead the new system saw them in fourth. The irony of it was that the new system was proposed by Lancashire!

For the third year in succession the same three batsmen topped 1,000, but all of them improved significantly on their previous total. Moreover, this triumvirate also missed just two first-class fixtures all season. Johnny Tyldesley was back to his imperious best, scoring six centuries and ten other scores above 50 and failing to break the 2,000 run barrier by only 39, although in all matches he passed it comfortably. The consistent Jack Sharp easily passed 1,000 runs for the sixth season in a row, and Alex Hartley had what

would be the best year of his short career for the Red Rose, accumulating 1,415 runs, with three centuries. One of these was a massive 234 against Somerset at Old Trafford in late May when he added 295 for the second wicket with Tyldesley, who made his top score of the season with 158, followed by 175 with Sharp, who went on to make one of his three centuries.

Tyldesley, Sharp and Hartley occupied three of the top four places in the batting order, but sandwiched in between them was Reggie Spooner. Despite the performance of the three leading men against Somerset, it was Spooner who produced the innings of the season. In the Roses match at Old Trafford at the beginning of August, he made 200 not out in a little over six hours. It would be a Roses record that would stand for 90 years.

Harry Dean was the only bowler to pass 100 wickets, and indeed he had his best season so far with 133 wickets. Bill Huddleston, James Heap and Lol Cook also had their best seasons with the ball in terms of wickets taken, but Walter Brearley only managed four games and 19 victims.

There was also an eye-catching all-round display from Ralph Whitehead from Ashton-under-Lyne. He had made his mark with the bat in his debut season in 1908, when he scored 623 runs and two centuries in only 12 appearances. He played just once in 1909, but in 18 matches in 1910 he added 44 wickets to his 516 runs. He was to come more to prominence over the coming few years, but, sadly, he was yet another potentially outstanding cricketer to have his career curtailed by the First World War.

Another determining factor this season was the weather, in particular in the second half of August. Lancashire's last five games from 15th August were all at home and were to be played almost consecutively. The first, against Leicestershire at Old Trafford, resulted in a narrow three-wicket victory in fine weather. It meant that two wins in the last four games would secure the county second spot. In the following match against Middlesex at Old Trafford, the visitors were on the verge of victory when rain washed out the final day's play. The action – or inaction as the case was – then moved to Aigburth, when only 34.3 overs were possible in the whole three days. Only a little over ten overs more play was then possible

in the next game against Northamptonshire at Old Trafford, whilst play in the final match of the season, against Warwickshire at Whitegate Park in Blackpool was only possible on the final day of the season. Not for the first time, and certainly not the last, the Lancashire weather had blighted the county's chances.

There was added poignancy this season, and it came at the Oval on 20th June. In the absence of AH Hornby, the team were led out by Archie MacLaren. It would be his last game for the county as captain. Neville Cardus referred to him as "the noblest Roman of the all" and he had dominated Lancashire, and indeed English, cricket like a colossus for 20 years.

150 LANCASHIRE GREATS
47. James Heap

Born in Burnley, James Heap was a graceful left-arm slow bowler who played for Lancashire between 1903 and 1921. During his career he played in 210 matches and took 412 wickets, ave. 23.08. He also scored over 5,000 runs, with one century, and averaged 18.98. He was handicapped by periodical attacks of lumbago, otherwise his county record would have been more impressive. At Northampton in 1910 he took 14 wickets in the match for 93 (9-43 in the second innings). Twice he took 11 wickets in matches against Yorkshire, one of them at Old Trafford when he took 6-16 and 5-23. As a batsman he could defend stubbornly or hit hard as the occasion demanded. His benefit in 1921 realised £1,804. In retirement he went to coach at Lancing College and also Shrewsbury School.

Spooner slams Tykes

1911

SINCE THE advent of AN Hornby and RG Barlow, the Red Rose had been known for its batsmanship. In no season was this more evident than in 1911. No fewer than five batsman easily exceeded 1,000 runs, another came within a whisker and yet another within one decent innings. There were also eye-catching displays from one or two others. With the ball, there was a brilliant performance from Harry Dean, a sublime one from Lol Cook and a greater contribution from the peerless Walter Brearley.

Despite this, and winning two more games than champions Warwickshire, Lancashire remained in fourth place. In truth, as far as the title was concerned, it was all over for the county by 10th June. Five of the first eight games were lost, and, even though they then went on a run of eight wins in ten matches, all by huge margins, they were playing for the minor placings.

Reggie Spooner topped the batting averages. He made 1,743 runs for the county in only 18 games. In all the first-class fixtures he played, he passed 2,000 runs for the one and only time in his career. What might he have achieved had he been available more often? Jack Sharp also topped 2,000 runs in all matches for the only time in his career, with 1,959 of them for Lancashire. And Harry Makepeace, who would perform that feat twice in the 1920s, passed 1,000 runs, 1,623 to be exact, for the first of what would be 12 consecutive seasons either side of the First World War.

Johnny Tyldesley accumulated 1,307 despite missing a chunk of the season to injury, and the fifth past 1,000 was Ken MacLeod. He had impressed everyone with his mighty hitting during his debut season two years earlier, in particular with the 128 he made at Bath against Somerset, his first century for the county, which invited comparisons with the great Gilbert Jessop. Having missed the whole of the 1910 season, he played in every game and smote 1,353 runs, with 29 wickets to boot.

Alfred Hartley was the one that needed just a decent innings to pass 1,000 for the fourth consecutive year, but his days were numbered at the top of the order and he played on only eight further occasions before the outbreak of war. And there was new boy William

R. H. SPOONER
LANCASHIRE

Knowles Tyldesley who missed 1,000 by only nine runs. He was no relation to Johnny or Ernest, but he was to James Darbyshire Tyldesley, who made his debut the previous season and Harry Tyldesley, who played a handful of games for the county astride the war. There was a fourth Tyldesley brother here too, the youngest, Richard Knowles 'Dick' Tyldesley, who become a real Lancashire legend after the war.

Ernest Tyldesley continued his steady progress to stardom with exactly 500 runs, James Heap had his best season with the bat so far with 784 and six half centuries, and AH Hornby and Ralph Whitehead both produced occasional cameos. Last but not least, after a six-year hiatus Harold Garnett made a return – as wicketkeeper, because William Worsley's career behind the stumps was coming to an end – in 24 games. He passed 500 runs too, evoking memories of why he was once mentioned in the same breath as Reggie Spooner.

Harry Dean had a spectacular season with 179 wickets, the best return of his career, but he was relied upon too much. Lol Cook provided excellent support with 90 victims in what would be his best pre-war season, but too many of the others under-performed or succumbed to injury. It was only when Walter Brearley joined the side, bowling as fast as ever, that the bowling really fired. He collected 79 wickets in just ten matches. "Had fortune been kind and Walter Brearley able to play all through the season," remarked Wisden, "Lancashire might have come first among the counties." Sadly for the Red Rose, this would be his final season for the club.

150 LANCASHIRE GREATS
48. Alfred Hartley

He was born in New Orleans in 1879 and first played for Lancashire in 1907, when he excelled with his strong defence, which made him a worthy successor to Albert Ward. A steady accumulator of runs rather than a brilliant strokeplayer, he particularly good on the on-side. He scored 1,053 runs for the county in 1908 and 1,129 runs with an ave. of 36 in 1909. In 1910 he scored 234 against Somerset at Old Trafford and finished the season with 1,511 runs with an ave. of 38. On the strength of this he was chosen to play for the Gentlemen v Players at both Lord's and the Oval. On a difficult wicket at Lord's he performed well, scoring 24 and 35. In 1911 his batting fell away and the following year he retired. He was killed in action during the First World War near Maissemy in France in 1918.

Lancs prove international class in wet summer

1912

IN 1911 LANCASHIRE played 31 first-class games, the most that had been played in the county's history. Alongside playing home and away fixtures against all the other first-class counties, there was a game with the touring Indian team at Old Trafford in the middle of June which was accorded first-class status. Although soundly beaten by a weakened Red Rose side, for the Indians it would be the beginning of a road that would lead to the granting of Test match status in the 1930s.

Cricket, therefore, was becoming a more global game, and so, with South Africa having been part of the international cricket family for over two decades, the authorities decided to attempt in 1912 a concept which was to prove way ahead of its time. The Triangular Tournament of 1912 was a series of Test matches in England in which the hosts, Australia and South Africa played each other three times.

The concept failed for several reasons. Firstly, the Australians weren't as keen as the other two nations and sent a weakened team. Secondly, that weakened team was riven by dissension and created headlines for all the wrong reasons with constant in-fighting and even fisticuffs at times. Thirdly, the crowds were poor, in particular for the games between Australia and South Africa. It was the first time the public's appetite for a match where partisanship was not a key element was tested and the authorities had misjudged the appeal of it. Finally, the weather in 1912 was amongst the worst so far of the 20th Century and much of the cricket was spoilt.

Because of this tournament, Lancashire's own county fixture list was curtailed to 22 matches. However, they were the only county to be given two matches against both the Australians and the South Africans and their performance in winning three of these games, including both Australian fixtures, and drawing the other was outstanding. Indeed, they were the only county side to beat the South African tourists all season.

In the first match with the Australians in the middle of June, Harry Dean, who again sailed well past 100 wickets this season and was to make his Test debut, and James Heap bowled the visitors out twice to record an exciting 24-run victory. At Aigburth at the beginning of July, there were half centuries from Jack Sharp and Reggie

HUDDLESTON.
Lancashire.

Spooner and 11 wickets from Dean as Lancashire won more convincingly by nine wickets. At the same venue at the beginning of August, Sharp hit a century and Bill Huddleston managed ten wickets as South Africa were bowled out for 44 in their second innings to lose by a massive 225-run margin, and at Old Trafford at the end of August, that old favourite rain washed out both the second and third day's play of the return match.

Naturally, the Red Rose's chances in the County Championship were ruined by the weather, with, for the first time, two games at Old Trafford, against Essex at the beginning of June and Warwickshire in the middle of August, abandoned without a ball being bowled.

Reggie Spooner topped the batting averages again with four centuries in his 854 runs and Sharp, Johnny Tyldesley and Harry Makepeace all topped 1,000 runs. There was also a first century for Ernest Tyldesley, the first of more than 100 in first-class cricket, but the weather meant that the run feast of 1911 became a distant memory.

Dean, of course, was the top wicket-taker, and both Huddleston and Ralph Whitehead had their best seasons with the ball, the former only five victims short of his maiden century. The club finished a close fourth in the Championship, with Yorkshire champions for the first time since 1908 after two seasons in the doldrums. And it was the doldrums where Lancashire were heading.

Dean creates Roses history

1913

IN MANY ways it is hard to fathom what went wrong in 1913. With the sun shining again, many players, with both bat and ball, surpassed what they had achieved previously. Although Jack Sharp had his poorest season with the bat for a decade, Harry Makepeace topped what he achieved in 1911, James Heap had his most productive season, Johnny Tyldesley was back to his imperious best, even adding another double century, and Ernest Tyldesley passed 1,000 runs for the first of what would be 19 consecutive seasons. Skipper AH Hornby had what would be by far his best ever year, scoring 1,336 runs, well over 400 more than his previous best. There were even runs too for Bill Huddleston and Ralph Whitehead down the order, and Ken MacLeod returned having missed the whole of the 1912 season to exceed 400 runs.

Having threatened to do so on more than one occasion, Huddleston passed 100 wickets for the one and only time in a wicket-taking list headed, inevitably, by Harry Dean, who was only marginally less effective than in previous seasons. Both James Heap and Ralph Whitehead had their best seasons with the ball too, the latter what would be his best ever with 80 victims.

Nevertheless, despite these statistics, which seemed as good, if not better, than in any year the county had finished as runners-up, for example, the club slipped from fourth to eighth in the Championship, the lowest it had been since the official County Championship began. The seven games won was the fewest since the start of the official County Championship in 1890 and it would be 1962 before Lancashire would lose as many as the 11 games they were to lose this season.

So, what did go wrong? The season opened with a marvellous innings victory over champions Yorkshire at Old Trafford. Heap, Dean and Huddleston combined to bowl the White Rose all out for 74 and 53, with Heap recording incredible match figures of 11 for 39. It should have been a victory that shaped the rest of the season, but instead it presaged an innings defeat by Nottinghamshire, a draw with Essex and a four-wicket loss to Northamptonshire. It was a pattern that lasted throughout the season: a confidence-boosting win was followed by morale-sapping losses, with the losses out-scoring the wins.

They were unlucky in that they were on top on first innings in all the seven drawn games, and they came out on the wrong side of some close results, but double defeats to champions Kent, middling Sussex and lowly Worcestershire counted in the end.

J. S. HEAP.

There was one highlight, however. The only non-Championship first-class match began on 10th July at Aigburth. It was a special Roses match with Yorkshire to celebrate the club's 50th season. The Red Rose came out on top by three wickets thanks to a performance that remains to this day a Roses record. Harry Dean, whose splendid career would continue after the war, claimed 9 for 62 in Yorkshire's first innings of 177 and 8 for 29 in their second knock of 73 all out. The match figures of 17 for 91 are unlikely ever to be beaten in Roses history.

Red Rose slump to 11th as war looms

1914

THE FINAL year of the Hornby family's connection with the captaincy of Lancashire, although not, of course, with the club itself, proved an unmitigated disaster. The club slumped to eleventh in the County Championship table, its worst finishing position so far, and the total of just six wins would not be usurped until 1962.

As in previous seasons when results had not matched expectations, it was the number and quality of the players who appeared for the county that seemed to be the problem. In total, 28 players were used in 1914 and eight of them were debutants. Even though two of those debutants, Charlie Hallows and Cec Parkin, would go to greater things, there wasn't sufficient quality to arrest the county's obvious decline.

The six victories, however, hinted at what might have been for the Red Rose. Only one, the second match of the season against Derbyshire at Old Trafford was by a narrow margin and three of the others were by an innings. These innings victories included the one against defending champions Kent at Old Trafford in June, when the batting line-up fired on all cylinders against an international bowling attack including Colin Blythe, Arthur Fielder and Frank Woolley.

Indeed, the batting was not the problem in 1914. Johnny Tyldesley had his best season since 1910 and topped the averages with 1,754 runs at over 40, which was also his age, and Jack Sharp showed that his failure to pass 1,000 runs for the ninth time in succession the previous year was a mere aberration. Harry Makepeace and Ernest Tyldesley also easily passed four figures and Billy Tyldesley, James Heap, Bill Huddleston and Ralph Whitehead all made useful contributions from time to time. There was even a welcome return to the fold for Harold Garnett for the first time since 1911, and he accumulated 850 runs at an average of 20 with one century.

Garnett was perhaps the great tragedy of Lancashire cricket. Spoken of in the same breath as Reggie Spooner and Archie MacLaren on his debut in 1899, he was never available often enough to fulfil his obvious potential. More tragically, his life was cut short on the battlefield at Cambrai in December 1917.

It was, therefore, the bowling that was at fault in 1914. Only three players topped 50 wickets, and of these only Ralph Whitehead could look back on the season as a job well done. Bill Huddleston was effective only fleetingly and nothing like the force he was in the previous two seasons and managed just 61 victims. Harry Dean played just half the season because of injury and took 61 wickets as well, but it was the first time in eight seasons he had failed to pass the 100 mark. He showed what might have been in the Red Rose's one and only victory in eight games in August with 8 for 27 in Hampshire's first innings at Aigburth and 13 for 84 in the match as the county romped to an innings victory.

Dean lived to come again after the war, Huddleston and Whitehead's careers were cruelly cut short by it. Garnett, Billy Tyldesley and three more paid the ultimate price. By the end of August, with war now raging in continental Europe, all cricket was suspended. It was the end of the Golden Age.

150 LANCASHIRE GREATS
51. Bill Huddleston

A tall man with a high action, Bill Huddleston bowled medium-paced off-breaks. With an easy-going nature, he had a smooth, unlaboured action. Born at Earlestown, near Newton-le-Willows, he was an exceptional bowler in league cricket, making his living as a professional. He played 183 matches for Lancashire, taking 684 wickets, ave. 17.55, and was almost unplayable on 'sticky' wickets, taking 9-36 against Notts at Liverpool in 1906. He was a member of the side which in 1904 carried off the Championship without suffering defeat. Each season passed with continued success and impressive figures. In fair summers, when it was felt he was less effective, he played fewer games, as in 1911, but he still topped the bowling averages. As the First World War threatened, he had his best season with 110 Championship wickets and 500 runs. After the war, he played league cricket for many years and used his valued cricket skills to coach at Harrow school.

Old Trafford at war *1915-18*

IN COMMON with most sports clubs Lancashire contributed to the requirements of total war while making such preparations as were possible for the resumption of infinitely more civilised hostilities. In December 1914 The Times listed 12 players who were serving in the forces, and although that list did not include the names of JT Tyldesley or Jack Sharp, both these men did their bit for the war effort: Tyldesley, exempted from service because of age, helped the Red Cross by meeting the trains carrying wounded servicemen and taking the injured to hospital; Sharp, who had heart problems, raised money by arranging sporting events.

Old Trafford itself was turned into a hospital for sick and wounded servicemen, but by February 1919, when it resumed its original function, Lancashire supporters knew that five of the county's cricketers had died in the war. While Egerton Wright played just four games for the county and John Nelson only one, both Harold Garnett and Alfred Hartley made over a hundred appearances, and Billy Tyldesley, one of the Westhoughton Tyldesleys, scored over 3,000 runs for the Red Rose. It was Billy's brother, Harry, who reported on a match between Privates and NCOs which was played near the hostilities in 1915 and also wrote poignantly of the conflict in a letter home:

"To speak of the battle with the Germans I might say that it has been rather more exciting than the battle of the Roses, but this last day or two it has been very quiet. How long do you think this awful war will last? The sooner it closes, the better

The Old Trafford pavilion pictured in 1914 after it had become an auxiliary hospital.

for everybody, the Germans more than anybody."

Despite the encompassing demands of the conflict, odd games of cricket were played, such matches being seen as a means of maintaining national morale. In 1916 the club sent kit to the Ruhleben prisoner-of-war camp so that a Roses match could take place, and a Lancashire team of sorts also played their Yorkshire counterparts at Haslingden in the same year. This latter contest featured a century by Frank Woolley, an event to gladden the romantic heart of one Neville Cardus, who was then struggling to make a living as a music critic and collector of insurance payments.

By the time the armistice was signed, Lancashire's officials had made careful preparations for cricket's return: for one thing, the club had fulfilled its obligations to its professional staff during the war; for another, members had continued to pay their subscriptions and it seems clear that the total never fell below 1,100. Indeed, the official club report for 1915 states that 1,667 of 2,300 members had paid up. There were, however, changes among the club's officials. Although TJ Matthews remained as Secretary, AN Hornby, who had been President since 1894, retired from that post and was succeeded by Lord Ellesmere. The splendidly-named Talbot Fair resigned as Treasurer and was replaced by Sir Edwin Stockton.

A name on a war memorial

By Rev Malcolm G Lorimer

MOST LANCASHIRE members will have walked past the war memorial placed in the Pavilion next to the entrance to the dressing rooms. The five names on it are Lancashire Cricketers who were killed in the First World War. One of those was Egerton Lowndes Wright and an interesting discovery took place when a second-hand cricket book dealer offered in his lists a privately printed book which detailed the lives of the four Wright brothers who served in the First World War. The book was written by their father and it cannot have been an easy book to write as two of his sons were killed in France.

As soon as I saw it I thought the Lancashire Library must have it even though it was quite a price! It was printed for private circulation in 1933 and there is no record of how many copies were produced. The book details the lives of the four Wright brothers, the family home in Chorley, the education at Winchester, their cricket careers and also their involvement in the war. There is also a detailed account of the war in general and its causes and consequences. It is a worthy account of the brothers and makes a very unusual book.

EL Wright, known as 'Toddy' was a brilliant schoolboy batsman, scoring 113 against Eton in his first season at Winchester in 1901 and was second in the college batting averages with an average of 34. He captained the College in two of his four years and then at Oxford headed the batting with an average of 31, scoring 95 and 26 against Cambridge at Lord's. In 1907 and 1908 he captained Oxford and also won a football blue. He was described by a Master to his Father: "Your boy is everything to the College; he is the salt of the earth."

He played four matches for Lancashire between 1905 and 1910 and although showing great promise was not given a long run in the team. In 1911 he married Violet (a Major's daughter) and they had two children. Toddy had already started in a law partnership with his Father.

At the outbreak of the war all four brothers enlisted. They met once during the war and the photo shows all four in uniform. Toddy went to France early in 1915 in the Bucks & Oxford Light Infantry. His division went through the Somme battles and at the end of 1916 he was appointed Brigade Major. He was mentioned in despatches and won the Military Cross. Letters from the front testify to the universal esteem and affection in which he was held alike by officers and men throughout the brigade, and he is said to have known most of the men personally by name.

The book gives a detailed account of the manoeuvres of the brigade. They took great casualties on the Somme and on the 12th May Toddy was killed instantaneously by a chance shell. His Father relates how he learnt the news of his son's death in a very poignant few paragraphs.

"In France, not far from the place where he fell, there was a military funeral, a grave and a cross, the gift of his own Brigade and an old schoolfriend, already a Colonel; three Generals were at the grave side, and the Last Post was sounded. In a few days the Brigade was in the line again with another Brigade Major.

"Toddy was 32; he always had the reputation of being a born leader and captain, at his best when his side was in difficulties. I am sure that he had been at his best, and most full of encouragement for others, in those dark days of Bourlon Wood and the retreat which had just ended. He had lived long enough to see England through her greatest peril.

"At home soon came those awful telegrams. I wonder how many hundred thousand or million such telegrams had to be scattered by the War Office over Great Britain in those fifty-one months of War. A telegram for his wife. She was a soldier's daughter; every time when those few hurried days of short leave were over, every time for more than three years, she had known that their brave good-bye smiles might be the last; and wives could be as brave as their soldier husbands. James, their little boy, was not old enough yet to understand, but some day he would realise it all and in his heart be proud.

"A Telegram for his Father. How many scenes flashed upon my memory. A glorious summer morning on that lovely old cricket ground at Eton; Winchester had won the toss and the board showed 0-1-0; the boy only fifteen playing for the first time in the Match was going in; before noon he had scored a century. A June evening three years later, when the match was played at Winchester; one hundred and thirty runs wanted to win the match and no more time to get them; a hard hit innings of 53 not out, the match is won and the boy carried shoulder high through the town. His whole too short life came back to me."

The book is a worthy tribute to a very brave soldier and is a very sensitive family account of how the First World War decimated families and tore them apart. It is I believe a worthy addition to the Library. The next time you walk into the Pavilion, look at the Remembrance Plaque and remember not only the five cricketers whose names are on the board but also the members of the cricket club who also died.

The four Wright brothers in their military uniforms with Egerton seated on the right.

MacLaren and JT at war

WG Grace and AC MacLaren.
(photo courtesy of Bodyline Books)

THE PHOTOGRAPH left shows an old WG Grace and AC MacLaren in Army greatcoat. WG would die in 1915 and the Grace era would be over. The colossus who towered over the game for almost half a century was no more. AC MacLaren enlisted as a Lieutenant in the Royal Army Service Corps and embarked on a recruiting campaign with Captain Gilbert Jessop, the great Gloucestershire and England all-rounder.

Most of the players joined up. *The Times* of 11 December 1914, listed the following who were serving: Hornby, Brooke, Spooner, Garnett, Boddington, Musson, MacLeod, Bill Tyldesley, Harry Tyldesley, Dean, Blomley and MacLaren. JT Tyldesley was too old to serve and during the war he helped the Red Cross as they attended to the injured returning home. He would meet ambulance trains and in one 12-month period travelled 5,000 miles in his own car and 1,000 in the ambulance taking the wounded to hospital.

150 LANCASHIRE GREATS
53. Cec Parkin

One of the greatest and most colourful characters in the history of cricket, Cec Parkin played county cricket first with Yorkshire before they discovered he was born in Durham – by 20 yards! A versatile mainly off-break bowler, he could, by variation of flight and pace, bowl almost any ball. He took 1,000 first-class wickets at 17.58, taking 10 wickets or more in a match 27 times. He played just 10 Test matches, losing his place after criticising the captaincy of AER Gilligan in a newspaper. Two years later he had a dispute with Lancashire which resulted in his returning to league cricket. One of cricket's great eccentrics, he was a comic and a comedian. Parkin enlivened any game of cricket he played in. No-one loved cricket more and after he died in 1943 they scattered his ashes on the ground at Old Trafford during a match in 1944.

The Lancashire League and The Great War

With no county cricket during the war it was left for the Lancashire League to continue to play cricket but they themselves were bereft of players and had to resort to paying some amateur players and also compensate loss of earnings on match days. The impact of the war was felt by all the clubs in both losing players in the war but also the financial constraints felt by the clubs. Burnley almost went of existence and were only saved by public subscription. Cricket only just survived with Amateurs playing in 1916 but by 1917 crisis point had been reached and the season had to be abandoned. It cannot have been easy to start the League again in 1919 with the images and effects of war deeply etched in players and spectators.

Play resumes _1919_

THERE WAS a Janus-like character about Lancashire's first post-war season. Much of the optimism about the resumption of cricket was clouded by memories of the war just concluded and perhaps it was appropriate that the tablet honouring the county's war dead should be unveiled in June when Kent were the visitors to Old Trafford.

There were echoes of the golden age, too. JT Tyldesley returned to the side for a final season at the age of 46 and scored 1,338 runs; his 272 against Derbyshire at Chesterfield and his flaying of Gloucestershire's attack during an innings of 170 at Old Trafford offered wonderful proof that his rich seam of talent was not yet worked out. Reggie Spooner played one game late in the season and, as Eric Midwinter points out most felicitously, "his few games after the 1914-18 conflict were poignant reminders of a lost world." Or as Philip Larkin wrote in MCMXIV some forty years after the armistice was signed: "Never such innocence again."

There were even some misgivings about playing cricket at all in 1919. Some doubted that the game would arouse much interest and only in February did MCC's Advisory Committee agree to the resumption. Even then it was decided that two-day cricket would be played in the first post-war summer, an innovation proposed by Lancashire and passed 11-5 by the counties. However, the change was deeply unpopular both with cricketers, whose working days were lengthened, and with treasurers, whose income was reduced. Wisden dubbed the experiment "a sad blunder" and it was abandoned after only one season.

Not until 4th April was Myles Kenyon confirmed as Lancashire's captain and his first net practice was interrupted by a snowstorm. Kenyon, a good leader if an unremarkable cricketer, led a more than decent side which won eight of its matches and finished fifth in the County Championship. Harry Makepeace topped the batting averages with 1,814 runs at 44.24 but JT and Ernest Tyldesley were not so far behind him. The most significant addition to the top order, however, was 24-year-old Charlie Hallows, who made 1,242 runs and

offered evidence of rich potential which was soon to be fully realised.

The most successful bowlers were seamer Jim Tyldesley, who took 72 wickets, and left-arm spinner Jimmy Heap, who dismissed 66 batsmen. But perhaps the most remarkable – and tantalising – development in Lancashire's attack in 1919 was the re-emergence of Cecil Parkin, who took 28 wickets in only four games, including 14 for 123 in his team's victory in the Roses Match at Old Trafford, a game attended by 35,000 spectators over its two days.

That game against Yorkshire was one of only four played by the versatile Parkin, who opted to turn out for Rochdale, where he earned a weekly wage of £10, better money than he could get at Old Trafford, although he realised that an occasional appearance in a midweek high profile county game only enhanced his earning power in the leagues. Such material considerations were not far from anyone's mind in post-war England. Admission prices were doubled to a shilling and Lancashire also announced that seven players would be receiving £250 per year talent money. The Manchester Guardian proclaimed that county cricket had become dependent on professionalism.

WILLS'S CIGARETTES.

H. MAKEPEACE.

Harry Makepeace topped the batting averages in 1919 and his form this year and the next would see him earn a trip to Australia with the England team.

150 LANCASHIRE GREATS
54. Richard Tyldesley

A cheerful, red-faced Friar Tuck-like character, Dick Tyldesley was a very accurate leg-break bowler. He was the youngest, and most successful, of the four sons of a Westhoughton CC professional. In his third year at the county club he first claimed 100 first-class wickets, raising his season's record total to 184 in 1924 at an average of under 14. Rewarded with a Test call, he played against South Africa and then went on an unsuccessful tour of Australia. In all he played in seven Tests. He is the fourth highest wicket-taker for the county with 1,509 at an ave. of 17. He played 374 matches for Lancashire, taking five or more wickets in an innings 100 times. A useful lower-order batsman he could use his weight to crack a ball over the leg-side boundary and once scored a magnificent century in only two hours at Old Trafford. He scored over 6,000 runs for the club. A good slip fielder he took 328 catches. After helping Lancashire to four County Championships, he had a disagreement with the county committee over wages and finished his cricketing days happily playing for Accrington and then Nantwich. He died at the age of 46 in Bolton.

Last hurrah for Harry Dean

1920

ON THE final morning of the 1920 County Championship season it seemed that Lancashire's well-balanced, talented team was on the verge of glory. Having beaten Worcestershire by nine wickets, members and even some players began to celebrate at Old Trafford, secure in the knowledge that Middlesex, their only rivals, had begun the third day of their match against Surrey at Lord's 46 runs behind, albeit with all their second-innings wickets intact. Only stand-in captain Jack Sharp, who had seen it all and forgotten little of it, counselled caution.

Yet Lancastrians would have done well to listen to the man who was deputising for the regularly indisposed Myles Kenyon. Pelham Warner's batsmen enabled Middlesex to set Surrey 244 to win and Plum's bowlers and fielders backed their skipper up magnificently, dismissing their rivals from south of the river for 188 and winning by 55 runs with ten minutes to spare. It was a wonderful end to the season – although it took a decade or so for this view to be widely accepted in the Rossendale and Ribble valleys.

Yet if the summer ended in disappointment for Lancashire, it had also been studded with good things. A team which beguilingly blended youngsters establishing their places in the game with veterans enjoying a last hurrah, won 19 of their 28 matches and no one enjoyed themselves more than those tireless shire-horses Lol Cook and Harry Dean. Neither bowler had played anything like a full season in 1919, Cook because he was late being demobilised, but in 1920 the pair of 35-year-olds made up for their lost days in the sun, taking a total of 274 wickets, Cook claiming 150 at 14.96 apiece and littering almost every other page of the scorebook with his name.

Cook was to take over a hundred wickets in the next two campaigns but Dean never again reached that landmark after 1920 and, indeed, played only one more season for the county. But at least the Burnley-born left-arm bowler played a key role in one of Lancashire's most famous victories when he and Cook, so the story was told, kept Hampshire's nightwatchmen at the wicket until the rain-affected Liverpool wicket deteriorated and they could run through the top order. If true, this ruse was all the more remarkable because Lancashire's opponents needed just 66 to win and had reached 53-3 on the third morning before Cook and Dean went on the attack and dismissed Hampshire for 65. Slower bowlers also enjoyed themselves in 1920: Cecil Parkin took 39 wickets in his five matches and the seemingly permanently jovial leg-spinner Dick Tyldesley accounted for 61 batsmen in his first full season.

Three batsmen scored over a thousand runs apiece. Harry Makepeace led the table with 1,672 but Ernest Tyldesley assumed his brother's mantle, if not his gloire, and the rapidly-emerging Charlie Hallows managed to notch 1,129 first-class runs in 43 innings without reaching three figures once. Attendances and finances improved in 1920. The 68,000 attendance for the August Bank Holiday weekend Roses match was only 11,000 fewer than the aggregate for the whole 1919 season and receipts for the game were £3,321 15s 3d.

The county's cricketers were also in demand when the 1920-1 MCC touring party to Australia was selected. Reg Spooner was picked to skipper the side but fitness problems and business commitments prevented him making the trip. Sydney Barnes was chosen despite having not played county cricket for 17 seasons, but the old curmudgeon refused because MCC would not pay for his wife and child to accompany him. This allowed Parkin to go on his only overseas tour and he and Makepeace were the two Lancashire cricketers in the 16-man party.

Harry Dean claimed over 100 wickets in a season for the final time in 1920.

150 LANCASHIRE GREATS
55. Lol Cook

With 821 wickets for Lancashire, Lol Cook is 15th in the list of all-time wicket-takers for the county with his medium-pace bowling. He was born in Preston and first played for Lancashire in 1907, but had his best seasons after the First World War. In 1920 he took a season's best with 150 wickets at 14.96. His seven Derbyshire wickets for eight runs at Chesterfield in 1920 was one of his best bowling performances. He added 148 in 1921 and 142 in 1922 before being granted a £1,657 benefit in 1923. He was chosen to play for the Players at Lord's in 1921. Like his brother William, he played both football and cricket. Lol played football for Blackpool, who were then in the second division. He also played a lot of Lancashire League cricket during his career and helped Burnley win the league championship in three consecutive years and once took all ten wickets in an innings against Todmorden. After retiring from active cricket he became a blacksmith's assistant.

Batsmen shine in Australian summer

1921

THE FIRST post-war Australian summer provided weather to make the tourists feel very much at home, although Warwick Armstrong's powerful team scarcely needed such generosity. Australia retained the Ashes by winning the five-match series 3-0 and three Lancashire cricketers, Parkin, Hallows and Ernest Tyldesley were among the 16 England debutants in the first home Tests since 1912.

Lancashire's batsmen revelled in the glorious conditions, although the hard wickets exposed deficiencies in the side's bowling attack. Age finally overtook Harry Dean, who could take only 59 wickets, but Lol Cook collected 148 at just 22.91 runs apiece. As might be expected on the dry pitches, the spinners had plenty of work to do, 17-stone Dick Tyldesley confirming his importance to the side by taking 80 wickets and also proving himself to be a very

adept close-to-the-wicket fielder. Indeed, Tyldesley pouched four or five catches – the scorebook is inconclusive – in the second innings of the game against Hampshire, which Lancashire won by 27 runs. Parkin took six for 90 and eight for 90 in that match and finished the season with 50 wickets for the county from a mere six matches. (His 16 wickets from four Tests also made him England's leading wicket-taker in the Ashes series.) All of which prompted the Lancashire committee to take the overdue decision to open negotiations with Parkin and Rochdale in the hope of engaging the great bowler on a full-time contract.

However, Parkin's many skills – Charlie Hallows said that he could use the new ball, bowl off-spin, leg-spin and wrong 'uns – could not make up for the lack of cutting edge in the new-ball attack. (The remedy for that deficiency was foreshadowed when Ted McDonald played in the Australian side which beat Lancashire inside two days at Old Trafford.) Kenyon's team finished fifth in the County Championship, winning 15 of their 28 games and losing four, one of the defeats being inflicted by Middlesex, who retained the title.

The powerful triumvirate of Ernest Tyldesley, Hallows and Makepeace all scored over a thousand Championship runs, with Hallows' 227 against Warwickshire being acclaimed as an innings of particular mastery. Younger professional batsmen were also attracting favourable comment from the stern critics at Old Trafford. Frank Watson, who had played just one match the previous year, scored 485 runs and offered indications of the gritty resolve which would characterise his next 16 seasons with the club. By contrast, Walker Ellis made a century in only 105 minutes against Kent but never reproduced such free-scoring form and did not play for Lancashire after 1923.

Two amateur batsmen caught the eye. George Shelmerdine's 546 runs in 11 matches included a sparkling century against Kent at Maidstone and Jack Barnes reached three figures against Worcestershire, although those who saw the 98 he took off the stronger Surrey attack reckoned the latter to be the better innings. Barnes had a curious career with Lancashire. Although he scored 811 runs in 16 games in 1921, his work as a Liverpool cotton merchant restricted him to 89 matches for the county over 12 seasons. Like most batsmen, though, he made the most of 1921. Many treasurers enjoyed the year too. Lancashire's membership stood at 4,661 and, despite spending money on Old Trafford, the county returned a profit of £2,981.

150 LANCASHIRE GREATS
56. Myles Kenyon

After skippering the 2nd XI in 1914, Myles Kenyon became captain of the 1st XI on the resumption of cricket in 1919 when AH Hornby decided to retire to Ireland. An Etonian, he captained Lancashire for three seasons and had no pretensions about his playing ability but was well respected and, in the transitional Post War years helped lay the foundations of better things to come. He enjoyed his best season in 1921 when he scored 635 runs, ave. 22.67. He captained the side with vigour and zeal and in 1920 they narrowly missed winning the County Championship, finishing second. He officially retired at the end of the 1922 season, although he did play a couple more times. He went to live in Stow-on-the-Wold and on his estate created a beautiful cricket ground where he entertained many visiting sides. He was held in high esteem at Old Trafford, being elected President in 1936-37, and was also High Sheriff and Deputy Lieutenant of the county.

Red Rose bows to Yorkshire efficiency

1922

WITH PARKIN available to play regularly for a team which also contained three of the best batsmen on the county circuit, many Lancashire supporters expected their favourites to win the County Championship for the first time since 1904. In the event, though, Kenyon's side finished fifth for the third time in four post-war seasons and the inquests into this perceived underperformance began. Some critics, asserts Brian Bearshaw, said that Lancashire's cricketers had the reputation of being "over-serious" and that they had taken the "pursuit of efficiency to an extreme," as if either of these traits was a great handicap to winning titles.

The more credible explanation, though, is more prosaic and entails the examination of the team's specific deficiencies. Firstly, although Parkin was able to open the bowling, Lancashire still lacked a genuine fast bowler. Secondly, the team was in sore need of a competent wicketkeeper; four men were tried in 1922 but none of them was really up to the job of keeping to bowlers as testing as Parkin and Dick Tyldesley. Thirdly, although Parkin claimed 181

wickets at 16.44 runs apiece, the consensus was that the quality of his performances declined in the latter stages of the summer as the demands of playing a full season and sending down nearly 1200 overs told on the great bowler.

Finally, there was the simple fact that there were better

teams in England in 1922, notably Yorkshire, whose mighty side won the first of their four successive titles. And the dominance of Lancashire's Roses rivals surely nails the argument that "over-seriousness" was an obstacle to winning the County Championship: few of Geoffrey Wilson's players would have had music-hall audiences in Leeds rolling in the aisles.

No, as the table reveals, Lancashire were a good team in 1922, but they were by no means the best in the country. Seven successive wins at the start of the season raised their supporters' hopes, but Kenyon's men had lost the same number of matches by the season's end, and that record included a rather embarrassing two-day innings defeat to Hampshire at Bournemouth in the last match of the season.

All the same, the bowling attack remained powerful enough, even without a genuine spearhead. Cook took a hundred first-class wickets – 142 in fact – for the last time in his career and Dick Tyldesley reached the same landmark for the first time as a Lancashire bowler. Apart from the mighty Parkin, no one else dismissed as many as fifty batsmen.

The batting was again dominated by Makepeace (1,983 first-class runs), Hallows (1,765) and Ernest Tyldesley (2,070). All three players scored four centuries in the County Championship and Makepeace reached a thousand runs as early as June 8, although as Wisden noted: "against more skilful bowling on less easy wickets he could not keep up this success." Nonetheless, such early summer success did not harm the takings for Makepeace's benefit match against Surrey in July. One of the county's most loyal servants, the future coach received £2,110 10s 6d from the game.

In 1922 the Lancashire coach was AC MacLaren, whose lack of tact when dealing with Old Trafford's committees probably only increased his popularity among the

Archie MacLaren, left, was Lancashire's coach and 2nd XI captain in 1922. As in his heyday, disputes with the county's committee were part and parcel of his cricketing life.

H. MAKEPEACE
(Lancs)

younger players, many of whom he captained in the second team. At the end of the season Myles Kenyon resigned as captain and was succeeded by Jack Sharp, once a professional but now, crucially for his chances, an amateur. Sharp was appointed despite being 45 years of age and having played a mere five games in 1922. Some members objected to the side being led by a man who had ever received lucre for playing the game, but Sharp's appointment was supported by the county's ex-President and eminence grise AN Hornby, which probably helped to settle matters.

Wicketkeeping problem solved *1923*

LANCASHIRE LOST only two County Championship matches in 1923 but drew 13 and, despite finishing third in the final table, Jack Sharp's side never threatened to disturb Yorkshire's supremacy.

Nevertheless, it was a season in which the team's most pressing needs began to be addressed. Most significantly, perhaps, 22-year-old wicketkeeper George Duckworth made his debut and soon established himself as a gloveman of undoubted competence. It is tempting to say that Duckworth's emergence – he played 27 first-class matches in 1923 – settled the wicketkeeping question for the next 15 years, but that would do no justice at all to Bill Farrimond, who played his first game for the county the following summer and soon proved that he deserved far more than to be an understudy. Having waited years for a decent stumper to come along, Lancashire found that they had two wicketkeepers capable of playing Test cricket.

Jim Tyldesley's death under anaesthetic in January and the clear decline in Lol Cook's bowling placed an even greater responsibility on Parkin, who responded by taking 176 wickets in the County Championship, 15 of them against Glamorgan at Blackpool. Dick Tyldesley also dismissed a hundred batsmen in 1923, but Lancashire's need for a fast bowler led them to enquire about the possibility of playing Bolton-born left-arm seamer Alf Hall. It might be thought that

no enquiry was necessary, but Hall had come to Lancashire's notice by taking 27 wickets for South Africa in the previous winter's Tests. Since he had played for another country in the same calendar year, Hall was therefore barred by the MCC from playing Championship cricket until 1924. Lancashire contented themselves with selecting the bowler for the university and other games, but Hall eventually made only nine appearances for the county.

Ultimately far more fruitful were Lancashire's attempts to secure the services of Ted McDonald. Indeed, as Peter Wynne-Thomas points out, the county had attempted to have the rules changed partly in order that the Australian fast bowler could play for them in 1923. However, their proposal that the residential qualification be reduced from 24 months to 12 was voted down and Old Trafford spectators had to wait until the following summer before they could enjoy McDonald's lithe rhythm and exceptional pace. In 1923 he was confined to playing Lancashire League cricket for Nelson.

But if the county's bowling resources were a cause of concern, the top order batting offered compensating reassurance. Harry Makepeace reached two thousand runs for the first time in his career and finished third in the national averages behind Middlesex's Patsy Hendren and

G. DUCKWORTH. LANCS.

Hampshire's Phil Mead. Double hundreds against Worcestershire and Northamptonshire secured some headlines for Makepeace in 1923, but his 106 out of 208 against Nottinghamshire was probably the better knock. Ernest Tyldesley was the second heaviest run-scorer and his 236 to save the game against Surrey at the Oval was by general consent Lancashire's best innings of the summer. Despite injuring his hand and suffering from influenza, Charlie Hallows also made a thousand runs and Frank Watson reached the same landmark for the first time in his career.

There was no doubt about cricket's popularity in 1923. Spectators broke down the gates on the first day of the Roses match at Bradford and when the cricket got under way it was watched by an estimated 30,000 spectators inside the ground with another 10,000 frustrated fans locked outside. Given the dominance of their team, the enthusiasm of the Yorkshire public was unsurprising: a home win left Lancashire without a victory in nine Roses matches. In the corresponding match at Old Trafford in May Lancashire had been captained by the 49-year-old JT Tyldesley, who had succeeded MacLaren as coach and was deputising for the ill Sharp.

150 LANCASHIRE GREATS
58. Jack Barnes

If he had been able to play continuous first-class cricket, JR Barnes might easily have reached the highest class. He was a free and attractive batsman who captained the Marlborough XI successfully for three seasons, topping the batting and bowling averages. For Lancashire in 1921 he scored 831 runs, ave. 33.24. He played 89 matches for the club between 1919 and 1930, scoring 3,271 runs, ave. 28.69, with three centuries. In 1925 the county tried to persuade Barnes to succeed Jack Sharp as captain, but his work as a cotton merchant in Liverpool took precedence, although he did lead the side occasionally. He enjoyed great success in club cricket for Ormskirk and Liverpool. Unusually, he served in both World Wars and distinguished himself by winning the Military Cross with the Royal Flying Corps in World War One whilst serving in France. He attained the rank of Major and died at the age of 48 in Grange-over-Sands.

Weather stymies title challenge

1924

LANCASHIRE'S DIAMOND Jubilee season was notable for muddy pitches and memorable matches, and some would argue that the first gave rise to the second. Wickets were uncovered, of course, and rain, which permitted only two of Lancashire's 12 games at Old Trafford to be played to a finish, produced conditions in which Cecil Parkin and Dick Tyldesley often revelled.

The most glorious victory of the anniversary season was Lancashire's first win in a Roses match since 1919, and also their first victory at Headingley since 1889. Those facts alone would make June's 24-run success sufficiently notable, but the match's fame also derived from the fact that Yorkshire's all-professional side, skippered by Wilfred Rhodes, required just 58 to win but were bowled out by Tyldesley, who took six for 18 in the second innings and ten for 87 in the match, and Parkin, who finished the game with eight for 61.

The two fixtures against Glamorgan were also worthy of note. In the first, the Welsh visitors bowled out Lancashire for 49 at Aigburth, only to be skittled for 22 by Parkin and Tyldesley and eventually lose the game by 128 runs. But in August's return match at Swansea Johnnie Clay's men inflicted a 38-run defeat on one of the most powerful sides in the country. For a team which had only made its Championship debut three seasons previously this was an achievement to savour and the South Wales Daily News gave it the works: "Lancashire, proud County Palatine….has yielded to parvenu Glamorgan," it observed quietly.

The Jubilee was also celebrated with a formal dinner at the Midland Hotel, but Jack Sharp's players could not respond to the demands of their supporters and secure the title. Lancashire lost only two games but they drew 17, very many of them rain-affected affairs, and finished fourth in the table. Red Rose diehards probably make rather too much of the role of climatic vagaries in determining their side's fortunes. All the same, there was an irony in the fact that in Ted McDonald's first season – the Australian still played for Nelson at weekends and made only 13 first-class appearances – most of the pitches were hardly conducive to his raw pace. Nevertheless, McDonald was given a flavour of the workload which might be expected of him when he bowled a 35-over spell in his debut against Kent, taking six for 73, and the fast bowler

Over the next few seasons the bowling triumvirate of Cec Parkin, Dick Tyldesley and Ted McDonald was to terrorise county batsmen.

finished with 64 wickets at 18 apiece. His great seasons still lay ahead of him.

Parkin and Tyldesley, meanwhile, enjoyed themselves hugely on the rain-affected surfaces. Parkin collected 194 first-class wickets at 13.38 apiece and Tyldesley, who made his Test debut at Lord's against South Africa, 167 at 13.32. The exploits of the pair, added to the poor weather, helps to explain why Lancashire were undefeated until they lost to Glamorgan in their 23rd game of the season. The county's only other reverse came when they were defeated by Kent in the last match of the summer.

As was the norm in this era, Ernest Tyldesley, Makepeace and Hallows all reached a thousand runs, with Tyldesley celebrating his benefit season with four centuries and 11 fifties. The trio proved themselves capable on both good and bad pitches, a quality identified by John Kay as "the hallmark of class". But the development of Frank Watson was confirmed by his accumulating 1,512 first-class runs, albeit in a style which rarely drew favourable comparisons with Reggie Spooner. Two other young professionals began to make a modest impression, both of them right-handed batsmen and left-arm bowlers. Mawdesley's Jack Iddon made 339 runs and Newton Hyde's Len Hopwood, 419, including an unbeaten 105 against the South Africans.

Viewed separately, the development of Hopwood and Iddon, the effective if dour technique of Watson and the regular availability of McDonald over the next two seasons were useful. Taken together and added to the power the team already possessed, they suggested that Lancashire were building a team capable of displacing Yorkshire and winning county cricket's only trophy.

150 LANCASHIRE GREATS
59. Bill Farrimond

Born in Westhoughton, Bill Farrimond played for Lancashire between 1924 and 1945. He was a very fine wicketkeeper and was unlucky to be a contemporary of George Duckworth although he still managed to play for England. He played in 134 matches for Lancashire and was a valuable batsman and more than once saved his side after early collapses. His wicketkeeping was of such a standard that he played four times for England whilst still the county's reserve keeper. He toured West Indies and also South Africa. He claimed seven dismissals in an innings against Kent in 1930, which equalled the then world record. He completed 297 dismissals for Lancashire and hundreds more in the second XI. Refusing offers to qualify for other counties, Farrimond was a patient and loyal man who was willing to play in the second team as long as he could continue to live in Westhoughton. In retirement he returned to play for Westhoughton and helped them win the Bolton League four years on the run.

Sharp resigns *1925*

"LANCASHIRE CRICKET springs out of the soil that is as honest and rich as any in Yorkshire. Let us cultivate it like any honest gardeners."

The words of Neville Cardus after watching Jack Sharp's side play Derbyshire at Nelson reflect more than a romantic temperament and a talent for extended metaphor. The Lancashire team of 1925 was, indeed, growing into a strong, powerful unit and the vast majority of its players were home-grown. Nevertheless, there was a certain irony in the fact that Cardus wrote those words after watching a match played as part of the deal by which the Tasmanian Ted McDonald could play full-time for the county. (Lancashire had bought out the fast bowler's £500 contract with Nelson and had also agreed to play a Championship game at Seedhill in 1925 and 1926.) McDonald's presence in the team did not meet with the approval of all members. At December's Annual General Meeting there was a motion, later radically watered down, which stipulated that only Lancashire-born cricketers could represent the county.

Yet even those who disliked the idea of McDonald playing for Lancashire could not doubt the beauty of his action or the efficacy of his bowling. The Australian took 182 Championship wickets in his first full season and 198 in all matches. Along with Dick Tyldesley, who dismissed 137 batsmen in first-class games, and Parkin, who accounted for 150, Lancashire had a triumvirate of bowlers whose power matched that of Hallows, Makepeace and Tyldesley as batsmen.

Moreover, Frank Watson was becoming a considerable cricketer with either bat or ball in his hand. The Nottingham-born all-rounder was the second-heaviest scorer in first-class

matches with 1715 runs and also took 62 wickets with his medium-pace bowling. Add in the 44 wickets of Frank Sibbles, an Oldham-born cricketer who could cut or turn the ball as conditions demanded, and the 882 runs scored by Jack Barnes, and it is scarcely difficult to explain why Lancashire were once again bidding to win the title in 1925.

Yorkshire, though, were too strong. Although Lancashire lost only four of their 32 games, Arthur Lupton's men were undefeated and finished more than 10% ahead of their Roses rivals in the days when some counties played as few as 24 Championship matches and teams were therefore not ranked according to their points totals. However, supporters at Old Trafford might have offered a rather different interpretation of the campaign, pointing out that Ernest Tyldesley's appendicitis in mid-season

Jack Barnes, above, filled in as captain in the absence of Jack Sharp.

restricted their talisman to only 16 Championship games and that three of their heroes' four defeats occurred when the batsman was hors de combat. Those losses resulted in Lancashire finishing third, behind Yorkshire and Surrey.

Yet if the title remained elusive, the 1925 season still marked the beginning of a golden era for Lancashire. The team was playing very well, its excellence epitomised that summer by Hallows, who made 2185 runs at 52.02, hitting seven centuries and nine fifties, though even those statistics were to pale before the left-hander retired. Off the field, membership stood at a healthy 3831 and the club's finances remained in the black, even after the construction of a new press box, committee room, scorebox and covered stand had ensured that Old Trafford would be ready to welcome the 1926 Australians.

The saddest features of the season were the decline and eventual resignation of skipper Jack Sharp. Alf Pewtress or Jack Barnes deputised for the captain when he was incapacitated in 1925 but nothing could protect Sharp from the scorn of the more unforgiving Old Trafford spectators when he dropped an easy short-leg catch off the first ball of the match against Middlesex. It did not help matters that the bowler was Parkin, who was playing in his benefit match. The barracking of the admittedly overweight Sharp continued and at the end of the game the captain announced that he would never again play on the ground where he had served his county so well. He kept his word for the next two matches at Old Trafford but was persuaded to lead the team in the final home match of the season against Gloucestershire. He received frequent rounds of applause but still resigned, citing business commitments, in November. "After 25 years of cricket, I am beginning to get tired," he said. Sharp had led Lancashire to the threshold of glory.

Champions again *1926*

JULY 2ND 1926: Dover. The last day of Lancashire's match against Kent. Needing an improbable 426 to win, the home side are 361 for five. Wally Hardinge and Frank Woolley have both scored hundreds. Lancashire's effort has not been helped by the mercurial Ted McDonald's decision to bowl off-spin. In vain have his team mates asked him to bowl fast. Now his captain, Major Leonard Green, adopts a different approach: he orders McDonald a large whisky and suggests that he might produce his best cricket. The Australian takes a hat-trick and Lancashire win the game by 33 runs.

Not all Lancashire's 17 victories in the glorious summer of 1926 were achieved by such unconventional methods, but events on

Lancashire's Championship-winning team of 1926. Back row: George Duckworth, Jack Iddon, Frank Sibbles, Frank Watson, Dick Tyldesley, Charlie Hallows. Front row: Cec Parkin, Harry Makepeace, Leonard Green, Ernest Tyldesley, Ted McDonald.

the final afternoon at Dover at least illustrate MacDonald's vital importance to his team and Green's ability to manage his men.

Prior to the Second World War, first-class cricket was littered with amateur captains who were not worth a place in their sides and who did not understand either the game they were playing or the cricketers in their charge. Appointed because they were "decent chaps" who could be relied upon not to commit some social enormity or other, they invited the hearty contempt of professionals whose livelihoods they frequently endangered.

Leonard Green was not such a skipper. While he may not have been anything like as astute a tactician as, say, Makepeace or Duckworth, he understood the men under his command and he knew when to ask them for advice. For all that he was appointed at the age of 36 and was a batsman of modest ability when compared

with Hallows or Ernest Tyldesley, he was a good enough cricketer to have made a century against Gloucestershire in 1923 and his players respected him. "Skipper's aw reet," John Kay reports George Duckworth as saying, "He does his job and we do ours."

And how well Lancashire's players did their jobs under Green's firm but kindly command! Nine cricketers, Ernest Tyldesley, Makepeace, Hallows, Watson, Iddon, McDonald, Sibbles, Dick

County Championship 1926

	P	W	L	D	Pts	%
Lancashire	32	17	2	13	106	75.71
Yorkshire	31	14	0	17	104	74.28
Kent	28	15	2	11	92	65.71
Nottinghamshire	29	13	7	9	82	56.55
Surrey	26	7	4	15	62	56.36
Middlesex	24	9	4	11	51	53.68
Hampshire	28	10	5	13	70	51.85
Glamorgan	24	9	9	6	48	50.52
Essex	30	6	9	15	62.5	44.64
Sussex	27	6	10	11	53	39.25
Derbyshire	23	5	7	11	43	39.09
Warwickshire	28	2	9	17	39	32.50
Leicestershire	27	5	12	10	38	31.66
Somerset	26	3	9	14	32.5	29.54
Gloucestershire	30	5	17	8	38	26.20
Northamptonshire	25	3	13	9	32	25.60
Worcestershire	28	3	13	12	28	24.34

Tyldesley and Duckworth made up the substantial core of the side that won a trio of titles and lost only three County Championship games in the process. A name missing from that list, of course, is that of Cecil Parkin, and the treatment of one of Lancashire's finest bowlers illustrates the harder edge to Green's leadership and his insistence that the team mattered above any individual.

The 1926 season did not begin particularly well for the Old Trafford side. By June 1st Green's men were seventh in the table and had won only two games. Later that month they travelled to Ashby de la Zouch to play Leicestershire and lost by 144 runs. Parkin did not bowl well and Green dropped him for the next game. The temperamental maestro announced his intention to return

Action from Old Trafford during the 1926 Championship-winning season.

to league cricket and the skipper set his face firmly against any suggestion that the he should be recalled. Jack Iddon replaced Parkin in the eleven and Lancashire did not lose again that season. Indeed, Green's side won nine of their last 12 games and claimed the title by 1.43% from Yorkshire, who were undefeated in 1926.

At the mighty heart of the bowling attack were McDonald and Dick Tyldesley. For all that he could be a temperamental cricketer, McDonald's performance in 1926 was quite superb. Bowling with a rhythm, grace and balance which some critics did not witness again until they saw Michael Holding perform in the 1970s, the Australian took 163 County Championship wickets for Lancashire and 175 in all first-class matches. On 17 occasions McDonald took five wickets in an innings and four times he claimed ten or more in a match. Had a Player of the Season award been instituted in 1926 Ernest Tyldesley would have been the Australian's only rival for it, although one senses that Leonard Green would have prohibited such individual accolades.

"Grace" was rarely the first word to pass anyone's lips when they watched Tyldesley bowl, but the leg-spinner was again a vital component of Lancashire's attack in 1926, taking 125 Championship wickets at 15.2 apiece. Iddon and Frank Sibbles also provided useful support, thus minimising the impact of Parkin's absence.

At the heart of the batting effort were Ernest Tyldesley and Makepeace. The 37-year-old Tyldesley enjoyed a particularly memorable summer, scoring 2,365 runs in the Championship, averaging 69.55, and enjoying a eight-innings sequence when he never failed to pass fifty. Makepeace, although his batting was far less easy on the eye than Tyldesley's, also passed 2,000 runs and his rapid 180 against Nottinghamshire in the match which clinched the title was generally regarded as the best he ever played. In that game, having bowled out the visitors for 292, Lancashire made 454 in reply, with Makepeace and Tyldesley adding 279 for the third wicket. McDonald then took six for eighty on a rain-affected pitch as Notts were bowled out for 199. Makepeace and Tyldesley were then given the chance to secure the County Championship, a task they completed with little fuss, knocking off the 38 runs required in 6.4 overs.

Ironically Leonard Green was unfit for that memorable game, so it fell to Peter Eckersley to select his two senior professionals to complete the victory. It was a nice touch by the stand-in skipper and an appropriate one too. Lancashire's first title for 22 years may have been orchestrated by an amateur captain, but it was achieved by a team composed of skilled, experienced professionals who had watched Yorkshire dominate domestic cricket for four years. Now it was Lancashire's turn – and triumph made men like Makepeace and McDonald hungry for more.

Notts pipped for second title

1927

LANCASHIRE SUPPORTERS apart, few cricket lovers remembered the 1927 season with great fondness. The second half of the summer was particularly wet and less than half of the 240 County Championship fixtures were played to a conclusion; Leonard Green's side drew 16 of their 28 games and the match against Glamorgan at Blackpool was abandoned without a ball bowled. Yet Lancashire's ten wins, seven of them achieved in their first ten games, were just enough to ensure that the title returned to Old Trafford.

It was a close run thing, though. With Green's men having completed their programme, Nottinghamshire had only to avoid defeat in their final match against Glamorgan at Swansea to clinch the Championship. The Welsh side had not won a game all season, yet Yorkshireman Billy Bates made 163 to earn a first-innings lead of 142 and Jack Mercer then took six for 31 as Gunn, Whysall et al were skittled for 61 in their second innings. Lancashire's points percentage was 68.75, Nottinghamshire's 67.85. Green said that he was "sorry for Notts" but neither the narrow margin at the top of

F. WATSON. LANCASHIRE

the table nor the miserable weather diluted the pleasure of Lancashire's professionals.

Charlie Hallows had particular reason for satisfaction. The stylish left-hander plundered 2,119 first-class runs in 1927, 1889 of them in the Championship, and at one stage seemed set to match Wally Hammond's achievement that spring by scoring a thousand runs before the end of May. Having made 850 in his first ten innings, Hallows finished the month with 921, although he probably derived comparable satisfaction from his unbeaten 20 in the match at Trent Bridge in August when he blocked Nottinghamshire's attack into a coma as Lancashire made 76 for two in 70 overs to save the game. Even then, the visitors were grateful for the arrival of yet more rain.

Hallows was supported by Ernest Tyldesley, who scored 1432 Championship runs in 1927, and by Frank Watson, who ground his barely imitable way to 1395. Those contributions were particularly valuable because illness restricted Makepeace to only 19 Championship appearances (690 runs). Hallows partly excepted, it was a summer

County Championship 1927

	P	W	L	D	Pts	%
Lancashire	31	10	1	20	154	68.75
Nottinghamshire	30	12	3	15	152	67.85
Yorkshire	31	10	3	18	135	62.50
Kent	28	12	6	10	129	62.01
Derbyshire	24	8	3	13	99	61.87
Surrey	26	8	3	15	107	60.79
Leicestershire	28	7	3	18	104	59.09
Essex	30	8	8	14	106	50.96
Middlesex	24	5	5	14	81	50.62
Sussex	30	7	9	14	108	48.21
Warwickshire	28	3	4	21	88	47.82
Gloucestershire	29	6	7	16	92	44.23
Hampshire	27	5	9	13	78	42.39
Somerset	26	3	9	14	65	35.32
Glamorgan	24	1	8	15	59	35.11
Northamptonshire	25	4	12	9	59	30.72
Worcestershire	29	1	17	11	40	18.51

150 LANCASHIRE GREATS
62. Ted McDonald

Ted McDonald was born in Tasmania and played in 11 Tests for Australia, taking 43 wickets. He headed the bowling averages against England in 1921 with 27 wickets. He signed as professional for Nelson in 1922, where he became a legend, taking 293 wickets before signing for Lancashire in 1924. McDonald was a fast bowler of exceptional pace and ability, but also with much grace, beauty and rhythm. He blazed across the Lancashire sky for only six full seasons and two shortened ones, but took over 1,000 wickets, including 198 in 1925, a county record. For three successive years he helped Lancashire win the County Championship. He was tragically killed in a motor accident in 1937 when he was offering assistance to the victims of a collision. Over 2,500 attended his funeral and the spectators at the Old Trafford Test stood in silence to honour one of the greatest fast bowlers of all time.

in which Lancashire's batsmen were regularly criticised for under-achievement and slow play; the argument that this was part of a strategy by which attacks could be worn down in the first two thirds of a day, only to be torn apart in the evening session, was not universally accepted. And what was viewed as the pedestrian batting of Lancashire's top order was thrown into even sharper relief by some of the innings played against the Red Rose in 1927: Kent's Percy Chapman made 260 in not much more than three hours at Maidstone, and Hammond demolished the Lancashire attack at Old Trafford, scoring 187 at virtually a run-a-minute. In this latter match McDonald's analysis was 36-1-165-2.

But for all that he was occasionally taken apart, Lancashire's Australian fast bowler remained the heartbeat of the attack, taking 143 wickets at 23.62 apiece, this in a season when pitches rarely offered him the pace and bounce he relished. McDonald took at least five wickets in an innings on 14 occasions and collected at least ten in a match three times. His analysis of 11-135 in the first Roses match, which Lancashire won by eight wickets, was merely one example of his ability to wrest a game of cricket and fashion it into a shape of his own choosing: Yorkshire's openers in the game were Herbert Sutcliffe and Maurice Leyland; McDonald dismissed the pair of them in both innings.

No other Lancashire bowler took a hundred Championship wickets in 1927, although Dick Tyldesley proved himself as reliable as ever by dismissing 93 batsmen and Frank Sibbles' 84 wickets offered further evidence that he was becoming an important member of the attack. All bowlers were given steadfast support by Duckworth, who took 40 catches, made 14 stumpings and was near the peak of his considerable powers.

There is probably no such thing as a low-key title triumph; and if a county wins the Championship, it almost certainly deserves its glory. Yet critics pointed to the fact that Nottinghamshire won two more games than Lancashire in 1927 and argued that Green's men had hardly established themselves as the best cricketers in the country.

George Duckworth was in outstanding form behind the stumps for Lancashire's second Championship success of the 1920s.

It was a charge which the Old Trafford players took to heart; they resolved to answer it the following summer.

LEONARD GREEN made no apologies for his tactics when it came to Lancashire's batting in their Championship-winning season even if the county did win the title with a swagger. The Red Rose captain was often described as a man for a crisis, a fighter. And he wanted the rest of his batsmen to show similar traits in matches, especially early on in order to lay a platform.

In his book *A History of County Cricket – Lancashire*, published in 1972, former Manchester Evening News cricket correspondent John Kay wrote: "The captain neither condoned nor condemned slow scoring. He often instructed Makepeace and Watson to lay a solid foundation, and encouraged his later batsmen to build on it. He aimed at 400 runs a day as a minimum, and few today would complain on that score.

"He supported a Makepeace declaration that to show respect to bowlers before lunch was no sign of weakness, but merely a necessary prelude to a successful onslaught afterwards. And Lancashire often made the period between tea and close of play a batting paradise.

"There were times when visiting batsmen meted out similar treatment, and it was in 1926 that a young man came north with Gloucestershire and played an historic innings against McDonald. His name was Hammond. He tuned in at Old Trafford with a magnificent 187 hit in three hours of exquisite batsmanship.

"It speaks much for Leonard Green's sense of fair play that he led the applause as the young newcomer returned to the pavilion. At the height of their achievements, Lancashire were never averse to paying tribute to the opposition."

The best team in the kingdom

1928

150 LANCASHIRE GREATS
63. Leonard Green

Lancashire's most successful captain, he led the county to three successive County Championships in the three years between 1926 and 1928. Though not himself a great cricketer, he possessed the strength of will and tact to wield a team of individual talents into a title-winning combination. Born in Whalley in 1890, he played four matches in 1922 before becoming a Lancashire regular. A natural leader of men, he quickly assumed control when Jack Sharp was injured in 1923. A useful batsman and a reliable fieldsman, he scored 3,575 runs for the county. He retired at the end of the 1928 season because of business commitments, although he played a further 11 matches over the next seven seasons. His record as captain is unique and he went on to serve on the committee and was elected President in 1951/2. He was awarded the MC in 1917 and for his work as Commandant of the Lancashire Special Constabulary in the Second World War he was awarded an MBE. He was also High Sherrif of Lancashire in 1954 and played rugby union and hockey at county level.

WHEN THE rain is falling from a slate-grey Manchester sky, Lancashire members with a reasonable knowledge of cricket history occasionally tantalise themselves by wondering which of their county's long-gone summers they would most like to have witnessed. A fair proportion plump for 1928.

Lancashire were clearly the best county team in the land that sun-soaked season. Leonard Green's men won half their 30 Championship matches and took valuable first-innings points in nine of the other 15. By contrast to the previous year, they won the title with two games to spare. Until they lost their last match of an idyllic season to a Rest of England side which included Jack Hobbs, Herbert Sutcliffe, Frank Woolley, Wally Hammond, Maurice Tate, Harold Larwood and Tich Freeman, the cricketers wearing the red rose were invincible. Bliss, it surely was, in that summer to be alive, but to be Lancastrian was very heaven.

Batting was particular fun in 1928, although Harry Makepeace and Frank Watson would probably reject such a cavalier description of their craft. Nonetheless, Ernest Tyldesley, Hallows and Watson took three of the top 11 places in the season's first-class averages, Tyldesley being one of five batsmen in the country to score more than 3,000 runs. To Hallows fell the rather rarer honour of following W G Grace, Tom Hayward and Wally Hammond in scoring a thousand runs before the end of May. Three centuries against Warwickshire and hundreds against Northants and Glamorgan set the prolific Boltonian on his way but he still needed 232 runs to reach the landmark when the game against Sussex began on May 30th. At the end of the first day Hallows was unbeaten on 190 and he scored the 42 runs he needed on the following morning before being dismissed by Arthur Gilligan next ball.

Yet if the left-handed opener's individual achievement was never eclipsed in 1928, it was joined by other feats in a summer when batting records fell like parched leaves of grass before the mower. By happy chance Hallows' benefit match against Surrey began on June 2nd and Watson marked the occasion by making 300 not out, then the highest individual score at Old Trafford, in a total of 588 for four; he also put on

371 for the second wicket, at that time Lancashire's highest partnership, with Tyldesley, who contributed a mere 187. Green's batsmen were replying to Surrey's 567 all out, of which Andy Sandham had made 282 before retiring ill, perhaps with a surfeit of runs. It was an indisposition with which many batsmen were glad to be afflicted in 1928. Hallows made eleven first-class centuries, Watson nine and Tyldesley eight. The season was also significant in that it marked Jack Iddon's increasing importance to Green's team; the all-rounder made 1239 runs and took 56 wickets in the Championship. However, it was also noted that Makepeace's fires were finally beginning to burn low; a tally of 1351 runs was a modest return

C. HALLOWS (centre) after completing 1000 runs in May, 1928. with E. TYLDESLEY, F. WATSON, R. TYLDESLEY, H. MAKEPEACE.

County Championship 1928

	P	W	L	D	Pts	%
Lancashire	30	15	0	15	186	77.50
Kent	30	15	5	10	167	69.58
Nottinghamshire	31	13	3	15	168	67.74
Yorkshire	26	8	0	18	137	65.86
Gloucestershire	28	9	6	13	133	59.37
Surrey	25	5	3	17	112	56.00
Sussex	30	12	8	10	134	55.83
Middlesex	24	6	5	13	102	53.12
Leicestershire	28	6	4	18	115	51.33
Derbyshire	25	6	6	13	97	48.50
Warwickshire	28	3	6	19	103	45.98
Hampshire	28	5	7	16	98	43.75
Northamptonshire	28	7	13	8	86	38.39
Somerset	23	4	11	8	62	33.69
Glamorgan	24	2	9	13	59	30.72
Essex	28	2	13	13	67	29.91
Worcestershire	30	0	19	11	38	15.83

McDonald's bowling against Kent inspired Neville Cardus to the following tribute:

He runs along a sinister curve, lithe as a panther, his whole body moving like visible, dangerous music. A more beautiful action than McDonald's was never seen on a cricket field, or a more inimical. The man's whole being tells of the sinister, destructive forces of nature – he is a satanic bowler, menacing but princely. Yesterday he was at his best; he like a comet burnt, and from his wheeling arm shot pestilence and war.

from 42 innings and the old warrior was succeeded as Hallows' regular opening partner by Watson. The new pair's first-wicket stands reached three figures on 12 occasions in 1928, five of those partnerships exceeding the 200 mark. Truly, it was a summer to make batsmen drool with pleasure.

Yet for all that it was a season characterised by tall scores and rewritten records, Lancashire's outstanding player was Ted McDonald. Supporters of Hallows and Ernest Tyldesley might dispute such a judgement with rare passion but there's a fair case that the Australian fast bowler, who had celebrated his 37th birthday on Twelfth Night, did more than anyone to ensure that the title was won. Playing in every one of Lancashire's County Championship matches, McDonald bowled 1173 overs and took 178 wickets at 19.34 apiece. While purists argued that he bowled short too frequently, McDonald insisted that such tactics were part of his trade and that they were usually successful. It was rare to find his contention disproved by events.

The home match against Kent, Lancashire's chief rivals in 1928, provided a lot of evidence to vindicate McDonald's supporters and a little to comfort his detractors. The strategy of trying to bounce out Frank Woolley succeeded – but only after the great left-hander had scored 151 out of his side's first innings total of 277. That was a modest effort, though, given that Kent had been 262-3 before McDonald and Sibbles took charge. Centuries by Hallows and Tyldesley then proved the inadequacy of the visitors' total. Lancashire declared on 478 for five and Kent were then swept aside for 113, McDonald taking eight for 53 to finish with career-best match figures of 15 for 154. An eight-wicket victory over Sussex at Hove a week later sealed the title, Kent finishing 7.92% behind the champions in the final table.

McDonald was at the peak of his powers in 1928. He played in one of the most professional county teams there has ever been, a team filled to the brim with time-served craftsmen, yet his bowling could move the prose-poets who had little time for functionalist efficiency.

McDonald's efforts were all the more remarkable given that he had no new-ball partner of remotely comparable pace in 1928. Moreover, Dick Tyldesley was reckoned to have lost his nip off the pitch that summer and took 85 wickets in the Championship. There is a good case to be made that the second most effective member of the attack was the effervescent Duckworth, who was a perpetual irritation to the batsmen and who claimed 91 victims, 29 of them stumped. Like his team-mates, Lancashire's wicketkeeper derived deep pleasure from that third Championship season. If some players were nearing retirement, if the skipper was contemplating stepping down, these were all matters that could be dealt with in the winter or in a future summer. For the moment, Leonard Green's cricketers could savour the indisputable truth that they played for the best county team in the kingdom.

Neville Cardus waxed lyrical over the exploits of the great Lancashire team of the mid to late 1920s and, in particular, the exploits of Australian fast bowler Ted McDonald.

Eckersley reign begins

1929

LANCASHIRE REMAINED a power in the land during 1929, but they were nothing like as dominant as they had been the previous summer. The Old Trafford side finished joint second in the table, equal on points with Yorkshire but ten behind the new champions Nottinghamshire after a campaign in which all teams played 28 games. And for all that five of Lancashire's home matches had been badly affected by rain, no one could dispute the justice of the final outcome.

Important changes had taken place at the club in advance of the new season. Business commitments compelled Leonard Green to resign the captaincy and he had been succeeded by 24-year-old Peter Eckersley, who had decided to take on the job in preference to immediately pursuing a political career in the Conservative party. Like his predecessor, the new skipper's cricketing ability did not make him a first-choice member of the team, but neither was he a rabbit or, just as importantly perhaps, a stiff-backed autocrat of the old school. Eckersley led Lancashire to two Championships in his seven years at the helm and the club was thus fortunate that the most powerful team in its history was led by two men who understood the professional cricketers in their charge. One can think of other amateur captains whose imperious incompetence would have messed the job up.

24-year-old Peter Eckersley began a successful seven-year stint as Lancashire captain in 1929, which was only ended when he became an MP in November 1935.

The new captain took charge of a side which was in the process of gentle transition. At the start of the season Harry Makepeace succeeded JT Tyldesley as coach, although the old master eventually played 11 Championship games. Coaxed out of semi-retirement in August, a few weeks before his 48th birthday, he finished top of the county's averages. Makepeace was to make three further first-class appearances in 1930, but it is still tempting to view his centuries against Warwickshire and Sussex as poignant farewells from an old player to a game he had graced. Cardus would certainly have done so.

Makepeace himself, though, was no romantic and knew he was playing in a side some of whose batsmen were having a thin time of it. Of no one was this more true than Charlie Hallows, who lost form in the second half of the season and finished with 1,202 Championship runs, 1,051 fewer than he had amassed in 1928. In a damp summer Frank Watson was the only batsman to score more than 2,000 runs and Ernest Tyldesley contributed 1,506. However, the player to reinforce his importance to Lancashire's fortunes was Jack Iddon, whose 1599 runs in the Championship was a considerable effort, given that conditions were not so favourable for batting as they had been in 1928.

There were also problems with the bowling attack. Although Ted McDonald and a rejuvenated Dick Tyldesley both took well over a hundred wickets, Frank Sibbles was restricted by illness to just a dozen first-class games and many were the occasions when left-arm spinners Len Hopwood and Iddon were the only realistic options available to the skipper when he needed to rest his leading duo, both of whom bowled over a thousand overs in the season.

None of which made Lancashire a poor side in 1929. On the contrary, Eckersley's men won twelve of their 28 Championship games and lost only three. But those defeats, to Sussex, Gloucestershire and Nottinghamshire, were suffered in the first twelve matches and left the champions with rather too much ground to make up in their quest to retain their title.

150 LANCASHIRE GREATS
64. Frank Watson

Frank Watson was not the most attractive batsman to play for Lancashire, but for many years, he was invaluable in a 'sheet-anchor' role, waiting for the bad ball which was unerringly hooked or driven to the boundary. His batting was effective, but not graceful or artistic. His fellow professionals realised his worth and during his career Lancashire won the County Championship five times. He played 456 matches for Lancashire, scoring 22,833 runs with 49 centuries. In 1928 he shared a dozen century opening stands with Charlie Hallows. He scored an undefeated 300 at Old Trafford and shared in a record 2nd wicket partnership of 371 with Ernest Tyldesley. He scored over 2,000 runs in a season three times. A useful medium-pace change bowler, he captured over 400 wickets for the county. In his Wisden obituary it said, "Watson was a batsman whom spectators, unless they were fervent Lancashire supporters, remember as one of whom they wished to see as little as possible." His worth to Lancashire was immense and bowlers knew his wicket was a prize capture.

Tyldesleys shine with bat and ball

1930

LANCASHIRE'S FOURTH County Championship in five seasons was a curious affair. Although they were undefeated in their 28 games, Peter Eckersley's team won only ten matches compared to second-placed Gloucestershire's 15. However, with only eight points being awarded for an outright win and five for gaining a first

innings lead in a draw, Lancashire's 8-2 advantage in this respect helped them end the season a mere three points ahead of Bev Lyon's side, who also suffered four defeats. If you lived in Chorley, you might regard the final table as illustrating the value of professional pragmatism; if you resided in Cheltenham, the best team in the land had finished runners-up. The MCC's Advisory Committee seemed to side with the latter view: in 1931 the number of points for a victory was increased to 15.

Yet Lancashire's 18 draws can be explained partly by the long periods of wet weather in 1930; over half the season's County Championship matches did not produce an outright victor. And when play was possible, the eventual champions took excellent advantage of their opportunities,

winning five of their opening seven games and three of their last five, clinching the title with a 174-run victory over Essex at Blackpool in late August. Eckersley's players needed an outright win in that final match to secure the title and they responded in the manner of champions, quite outplaying their opponents. In May they had first beaten Gloucestershire at the Wagon Works ground and then had the best of a draw at Old Trafford, all in the space of a week. While the points system may have benefited Lancashire in 1930, it did not explain their success. For that, one must look to the quality of the cricket played by some battle-toughened professionals.

The Tyldesleys had a fine summer. Ernest scored 1,811 Championship runs at an average of 54.87 and his seven centuries included a career-best 256 not out against Warwickshire. Possessing both an assured technique and a serene temperament, his barely estimable value to his county was illustrated once again. Dick Tyldesley maintained his fine form of the previous summer, taking 121 Championship wickets at 14.73 runs apiece and twice being selected to play Test matches against Australia. Duckworth played in all five of the games against Bill Woodfull's powerful team, but it is interesting that even during Lancashire's most successful era relatively few of the county's players received regular England calls. Dick Tyldesley played seven Tests, Ernest a mere 14. Even Duckworth made only 24 appearances in the period 1924-1936. The availability of cricketers such as Hobbs, Sutcliffe, Hammond, Ames et al may go a long way towards explaining the matter, but some of the county's supporters still wondered why their favourites received so little recognition on cricket's greatest stage. The more parochial probably observed that England's loss was Lancashire's gain.

Test calls had an impact on one of Lancashire's most important victories in 1930, their innings and 56-run defeat of Kent at Old Trafford. The visitors went into the match leading the table by nine points but deprived of the services of Frank Woolley and Percy Chapman; Eckersley's team had drawn their previous five games and lay third but were lacking only Duckworth. The absence of the team's regular keeper was barely noticed; Farrimond proved himself a supremely competent, albeit vastly quieter, deputy and both Lancashire's wicketkeepers were to be selected for that winter's tour to South Africa.

150 LANCASHIRE GREATS
65. Frank Sibbles

Frank Sibbles helped Lancashire win the County Championship in three successive years from 1926-1928 and five times in all. Born in Oldham, he became a member of Werneth CC at the age of 7. In 1925 he joined the Old Trafford groundstaff as a batsman but soon developed into a natural off-break bowler. As a most courteous, well-mannered, gentle and mature cricketer, Sibbles was a popular team man. Altogether, until a painful and persistent elbow problem ended his playing career in 1937, he took 932 wickets at an ave. of 22. 43. Among his best performances were 8-24 against Somerset at Weston and 5-8 against Essex. In 1932 he took 131 wickets, ave.18.25, and headed the Lancashire bowling averages. After the Second World War, in which he rose from the ranks to Major, he did much service as an administrator to Lancashire. He was on the General Committee and Chairman of the Cricket Committee. Neville Cardus said of him, "There is nothing cheap or spectacular about Sibbles. A nicer mannered cricketer never wore flannels." He became a partner in a Lancashire sports business and died in 1973.

Opting to bat first, Kent were dismissed for 194, McDonald taking five for 77 and Tyldesley three for 61. By the close of the first day Lancashire had replied with 171 for one and both Watson and Ernest Tyldesley went on to make centuries in a total of 390. On a rain-affected pitch, the Championship leaders could muster only 147 in their second innings, McDonald taking six for 83 to finish with match figures of 11-160. All six of the Australian's wickets were caught by Farrimond, who also made a stumping off Dick Tyldelsey. The keeper's seven victims in the innings remains a Lancashire record and he also conceded no byes. The match offered another illustration of how Eckersley's players could raise their game for the important occasion. Unlike two years previously, Lancashire were not plainly the best county team in the land in 1930. They were, however, the most difficult to beat and they knew how to scrap for every fragment of advantage.

Not all Lancashire's players enjoyed good summers though. Hallows' form continued

Lancashire's Championship-winning team of 1930.

County Championship 1930

	P	W	L	D	Pts
Lancashire	28	10	0	18	155
Gloucestershire	28	15	4	9	152
Yorkshire	28	11	2	15	150
Nottinghamshire	28	9	1	18	149
Kent	28	12	7	9	133
Essex	28	7	5	16	121
Sussex	28	7	5	16	118
Surrey	28	3	4	21	116
Derbyshire	28	7	8	13	106
Worcestershire	28	5	9	14	99
Glamorgan	28	5	9	14	98
Leicestershire	28	4	10	14	89
Hampshire	28	5	8	15	87
Somerset	28	4	11	13	87
Warwickshire	28	2	9	17	85
Middlesex	28	3	9	16	81
Northamptonshire	28	4	12	12	78

to decline and he was eventually dropped, although his absence helped give more opportunities to 28-year-old Eddie Paynter. A pugnacious left-hander, endowed with both courage and a love of life, Paynter had made only 11 first-class appearances since his debut in 1926. Now he was able to establish his value to his beloved county: his 63 made out of a second-innings total of 176 in that final game against Essex was one of many occasions on which he was to prove his worth to both Lancashire and England.

The county's attack was not entirely dominated by Dick Tyldesley in 1930. For the sixth and last time Ted McDonald took a hundred wickets and there were matches in which the 39-year-old fast bowler gave his team the necessary cutting edge. His celebration when he bowled Don Bradman for nine in the first match against the Australian tourists at Aigburth was something to behold in those undemonstrative times. But there were also days when it was clear that time was gaining remorseless ground on this great bowler, so it was vital for Lancashire's title hopes that Len Hopwood and Frank Sibbles were fit and in form. Hopwood snared 63 batsmen with his twisters while Sibbles' medium pace was good enough for another 49 batsmen.

So perhaps more than any of Lancashire's previous three title wins, the triumph of 1930 was a true team effort. If Tyldesley or Watson didn't get runs, Iddon or Hopwood did; if McDonald and Dick Tyldesley were not in the wickets, Hopwood or Sibbles proved themselves able deputies; if Duckworth was piercing eardrums at a Test match, Farrimond took the gloves for Lancashire and went about his business quietly. Even Eckersley made four fifties and scored 672 runs in the Championship. When Cardus expressed the hope on the eve of the Essex match that Gloucestershire would win the title, he merely revealed a preference for means over ends; none of Lancashire's players, most of them professionals to their very marrow, shared his view. A few days later those players returned to the Stanley Park pavilion, drank champagne and reflected on a job well done.

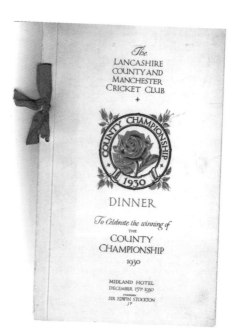

End for McDonald and Dick Tyldesley

1931

LANCASHIRE HAD won the title with all but nothing to spare in 1930; it was, therefore, not surprising that two hammer-blows to the playing strength of Eckersley's team should result in the county having its worst season since the war and finishing sixth in the County Championship. The most obvious of these reverses was suffered in early June when Frank Watson contracted pneumonia and could not play again that summer. Equally serious was the 40-year-old McDonald's precipitous decline in pace and penetration which saw him claim just 26 wickets in his final 12 matches for the county.

The Australian's contract still had a year to run but this was cancelled and the following season he returned to league cricket with Bacup.

Other players strove mightily sought to make good these losses. Eddie Paynter became a first-team regular and scored a thousand Championship runs for the first time; Jack Iddon also reached four figures and Len Hopwood took 67 wickets; Frank Sibbles bowled better than ever and claimed 82 wickets at a cost of 18.48 apiece.

The old and the new: The end of the career of the great Charlie Hallows signalled the start of that of Eddie Paynter.

Such steadfast efforts ensured that Lancashire's decline was moderate. Eckersley's team suffered only four defeats in their 28 games but two of these, to Sussex and lowly Worcestershire, were sustained very early in the season and they suggested that Lancashire were no longer to be numbered among the English cricket élite. Indeed, in the nine seasons until the outbreak of the Second World War the Old Trafford side only finished in the top three on one occasion; that, of course, was in 1934 when, against most odds, they won their eighth title. In the same period Yorkshire won the County Championship on seven occasions and lost only two of 18 Roses matches.

Some players' contributions were undiminished, even amid the team's adversities. Ernest Tyldesley scored over 1,400 Championship runs, including a century in June's innings win over Gloucestershire which was one of a damp summer's few highlights. In that game Dick Tyldesley took seven for 39 in the visitors' first innings before his namesake and Charlie Hallows made centuries to set up the victory. Even that success was tinged with sadness though: Hallows' hundred was his last in the Championship for Lancashire. The stylish left-hander batted 39 times in 1931 but did not amass a thousand runs. The following season he was to make only a handful of appearances before becoming a professional in the leagues and a well-respected coach.

No one knew it at the time but Dick Tyldesley's career at Old Trafford was ending too. His 116 Championship wickets proclaimed him the leader of his side's attack, but with the Depression beginning to bite Tyldesley's request for a guaranteed £400 salary whether he played or not was never likely to be favourably received by the county's committee. The jovial spinner announced that he had received decent offers from league clubs but he wanted to play county cricket. Lancashire's officials were unmoved and in 1932 Tyldesley turned out a few times for Haslingden. He later joined Accrington and Nantwich.

150 LANCASHIRE GREATS
66. George Duckworth

Born in Warrington in 1901, George Duckworth was probably the greatest wicketkeeper to play for Lancashire. A proud resident of Warrington, he was renowned for his piercing appeal of extraordinary volume for a small man. His skill behind the stumps contributed substantially to Lancashire's five inter-war Championships. For Lancashire he made a record 925 dismissals, with 97 captured in 1928. He played in 24 Test Matches and made 60 dismissals. George's character was blunt and honest, his knowledge of the game was vast and when he retired he became a broadcaster renowned for his humorous and forthright commentaries on cricket and rugby league. He was appointed tour manager of three Commonwealth tours to India and in later years he became one of the shrewdest observers of the game. His advice was available and eagerly sought by other cricketers, especially when he accompanied many England tours as baggage master and scorer.

Depression continues at Old Trafford

1932

OF THE chief architects of Lancashire's four Championships in the previous six years, only Ernest Tyldesley, Frank Watson and George Duckworth remained when April beckoned the cricketers back to Old Trafford in 1932. Peter Eckersley led a team with three players of Test quality: Tyldelsey, Duckworth and Eddie Paynter, who had made his debut against New Zealand the previous summer. True, Jack Iddon and Len Hopwood were to play for England in the 1930s, but the majority of the side was composed of good county professionals and amateurs of variable quality.

It was a tribute to the skill of such players that Lancashire retained their sixth place in the table and lost only half a dozen of their 28 games in 1932. Those losses included a defeat to Somerset at Weston-super-Mare, the first time the West Country county had won the fixture since 1903, but the Red Rose's eight victories included the innings and 50-run hammering of Yorkshire at Bradford in May. In that memorable match, Paynter produced one his greatest innings, making 152 out of 263 on a difficult pitch against an attack featuring Bill Bowes, Hedley Verity and George Macaulay. Frank Sibbles then took seven for 10 as Yorkshire were bowled out for a paltry 46 and followed this with five for 58 as pedigree batsmen such as Percy Holmes, Herbert Sutcliffe, Arthur Mitchell and Maurice Leyland sought in vain to repair the damage.

F. S. BOOTH — J. IDDON — W. HORROCKS — F. WATSON — W. FARRIMOND — L. PARKINSON — P. ECKERSLEY — G. DUCKWORTH — E. PAYNTER — J. HOPWOOD — F. SIBBLES — E. TYLDESLEY

LANCASHIRE CRICKET CLUB

Such morale-sustaining wins helped Lancashire lead the table at the beginning of June, but the familiar hierarchy was soon restored. Eckersley's men lost the return Roses match at Old Trafford by an innings and five runs and trailed Yorkshire by 136 points in the final table.

Yet the league tables of the 1930s are more a reflection of Yorkshire's undoubted excellence than anything else; Lancashire's inadequacies were only relative and rarely more so than in 1932. Sibbles rose to the challenge of replacing McDonald by taking 122 wickets at 17.44 runs apiece and Iddon established himself as an all-rounder by scoring 1,307 runs and dismissing 76 batsmen. Gordon Hodgson and Frank Booth, two right-arm seamers who had struggled for opportunities in the glory days of McDonald and Dick Tyldelsey, also passed 50 wickets.

The leading batsmen were Tyldelsey, who made 1,962 runs in the Championship and Paynter, who contributed 1,542. Frank Watson proved that he was back to full fitness by scoring 1,263 runs and it was cruel luck that the dogged right-hander's benefit match against Surrey was abandoned without a ball bowled. That left one of the county's most deserving and underrated cricketers with a sum of just £1,268, the lowest since 1918. However, unless one lived east of the Pennines – and even for thousands of Yorkshiremen, too – 1932 was a grim summer. Its cricket was frequently interrupted by rain and all sport in that era was played out against the background of severe economic hardship, particularly in the North, Clydeside and South Wales. Lancashire's own loss of £3,329 may have seemed serious at the time; compared to the struggles of the unemployed and their families, it barely mattered.

150 LANCASHIRE GREATS
67. Eddie Paynter

Eddie Paynter was born at Oswaldtwistle in 1901 and played for Lancashire from 1926 until 1945. He was a brilliant and consistent left-handed batsman who frequently opened the innings. He was also a superb fielder, especially in the covers. He scored over 20,000 runs in all with 45 centuries, including 322 in one day at Hove against Sussex in 1937. He played 20 Test Matches, scoring 1,500 runs, including 243 against South Africa at Durban in 1938-39 and 216 v Australia at Trent Bridge in 1938. He will always be remembered for his courageous innings at Brisbane on the 'Bodyline' tour when he left a nursing home sick-bed and batted four hours for an epic 83 in the second innings, hitting a six to win the match and regain the Ashes. His career was halted by the Second World War and afterwards he became an umpire. His own comment on his cricket career was, "It were grand fun while it lasted."

Washbrook debut mirrors that of JT

1933

IN AN attempt to stimulate interest in county cricket at a time of regional economic distress, it was decided to allow counties to play as few as 24 Championship games in 1933; the teams would again be ranked according to their percentages. Yet when attendances did improve that summer it was probably because the weather was the best England had enjoyed for a dozen years, and the reversion to the old system did nothing to alter the balance of power. Yorkshire (70%) won the title, with Sussex their only credible challengers. Lancashire (50%) finished fifth, having lost just one of their 28 matches but having won only nine.

Eckersley's team remained a power in the land, but its ability to pile up runs was rather greater than its prowess in bowling sides out. If such an assessment seems harsh on cricketers like Frank Booth, who claimed 82 Championship wickets, or the worthy Frank Sibbles, whose labours earned him 80 dismissals, it is borne out by an analysis of the scorecards: among the bowlers only Len Hopwood, whose 56 wickets cost 19.5 apiece, returned an average below 20; of the batsmen in the first-choice team, only Booth averaged fewer than 20. It was a neat statistical symmetry.

Yet 1933 was a significant season for Lancashire in that it saw the debuts of three professionals who were to render the Red Rose yeoman service and also the amateur who was to succeed Eckersley in 1936. The latter was Lionel Lister, who made a century against Middlesex in only his second game. The former were Eddie Phillipson, Dick Pollard and Cyril Washbrook. Phillipson played only two games in 1933 and distinguished himself in the first of them by helping Eckersley add 107 for the last wicket against Sussex. Pollard appeared in one game and took a single wicket. It would have needed the most percipient of critics to see that these fast bowlers were to provide the backbone of Lancashire's new-ball attack in the pre and immediate post-war years.

Washbrook's case was very different. While the first team were suffering their only defeat of the Championship season, an innings defeat to Yorkshire, the 18-year-old Barrow-born right-hander was making 202 not out against the White Rose's second team at Bradford. Selected for the same match in which Phillipson made his bow, Washbrook made seven and 40 not out; in his second he hit 152 against Surrey and shared a partnership of 191 with the 44-year-old Ernest Tyldesley. The knowledgeable romantics observed that Tyldesley's brother had also scored 152 in his second game for Lancashire in 1895. For some supporters, the signs could not have been clearer had Washbrook sported a purple band on his flannels. "For a lad of 18, this was cricket radiant with promise," wrote Cardus of the century against Surrey.

Washbrook finished the season with 419 runs from 19 innings. As he served his apprenticeship he was able to observe Iddon, Watson, Hopwood and Tyldesley all reach four figures in the Championship, with the under-estimated Hopwood adding 1,731 runs to his healthy haul of wickets. That leading quartet hit 15 centuries and 25 fifties in 1933, but Paynter, perhaps still jaded from his exertions in the Bodyline tour, made only 946 runs.

By contrast, Iddon and Booth enjoyed fine seasons. The pair

joined forces to take Lancashire to a three-wicket victory over Derbyshire at Buxton and Booth's medium-fast bowling was instrumental in the victories over Middlesex at Lord's, Hampshire at Bournemouth and Essex at Liverpool.

So when Lancashire's officials reviewed the summer of 1933 they were able to find more than a surplus of £2,438 to encourage them. Some veterans from the great team of the 1920s remained and a new side was very gradually taking shape. There was good reason to suppose that Lancashire would acquit themselves adequately the following summer – but almost none at all to foster a belief that they would win the title.

Hopwood at the *1934* double for title

WHEN LANCASHIRE supporters are asked to select the outstanding players from the club's most successful era the name of Len Hopwood is by no means the first to be mentioned. A couple of Tyldesleys, McDonald, Duckworth and Hallows are all more likely to be chosen. Yet when one seeks to explain why Peter Eckersley's team won Lancashire's fifth County Championship in nine seasons, the comparatively unlauded Hopwood's 1,583 runs and 110 wickets offer more than statistical assistance. His name appears frequently on the scorecards of vital matches, scoring important runs or taking crucial wickets. In 1934 he became the first Lancashire player since 1904 to do the double and, along with Jack Iddon, another of that summer's quiet heroes, he is one of only five cricketers to have taken 500 wickets and scored 10,000 runs for the county. The presence of men like Hopwood and Iddon, savvy, experienced professionals at the peak of their form, offers one of the most compelling, yet least identified, reasons why Eckersley's team were able to celebrate at the Oval in late August.

Lancashire also enjoyed some good fortune in 1934. Their skippers – Lister sometimes deputised for Eckersley – won 27 out of 30 tosses in Championship matches and batted first on 24 occasions. This gave the top order many chances to pile up tall scores and, so the strategy goes, control the game. Lancashire declared their first innings 18 times in 1934 and collected first innings points in ten

of their 14 draws. Tyldesley and Iddon, who both scored over 2,000 runs, and Hopwood, Watson and Paynter, who all garnered well in excess of a thousand, seized the proffered opportunities and exploited them. Good luck is one thing; making the most of that luck, quite another.

In 1934, Len Hopwood became the second Lancashire player to do the 'double' and played a crucial role in the title success.

The Old Trafford side remained relatively free of injuries and Test calls in 1934. Although Frank Booth missed some games with a shoulder injury and Frank Sibbles was laid low with synovitis, Lancashire called on only 18 players in their 30 County Championship matches and nine men played more than 25 games. Duckworth, Tyldesley and Iddon did not miss a fixture. Hopwood played his two Test matches that summer, but no other Lancashire cricketer was summoned to take on Bill Woodfull's Australians. One does not need to be a diehard Yorkshire supporter to see that the regular loss of Sutcliffe, Leyland, Verity and Bowes seriously

150 LANCASHIRE GREATS
69. Peter Eckersley

Lancashire's most charismatic captain, he gave up a possible political career to play for and captain Lancashire. Experience at Rugby and Cambridge University equipped him to captain the county at the age of only 24. He was a good judge of character and drew the best qualities out of his team and led Lancashire to the County Championship in 1930 and 1934. Known as the 'cricketer airman', he often flew his own plane to matches. He scored 4,588 runs for the county, ave. 18.50. A brave batsman and a risk-taker, he drove the ball hard and used his feet well against the slow bowlers. He was athletic in the field and instilled enthusiasm and a positive attitude into his players. He contested the Leigh by-election in 1931 before becoming the MP for Manchester Exchange in 1935. He joined the air arm of the RNVR when war broke out but was tragically killed in a flying accident in 1940 at the age of 36.

weakened even this most powerful of teams. Yorkshire finished the season in sixth place.

In the first month or so of the campaign it seemed that Lancashire's position would be similarly modest. One win in their first seven games left the county seriously off the pace and caused some writers to dismiss their chances. "None of us cares twopence about the Championship, certainly not this year, when it is obvious that Lancashire cannot win it," declared Cardus, and perhaps his words acted as something of a stimulus to the team whose prospects he had dismissed. In any event, 12 wins in the next 19 games put Lancashire top of the table – for the first time that summer – on August 14th. What followed was a classic illustration of the tough professionalism which helped earn the county at least a couple of their titles. Unable to win any of their final four matches, they collected first innings points in all of them, most notably in the vital game against the long-time leaders Sussex at Eastbourne. For their part, Alan Melville's side lost only their second match of the season when they were defeated by Gloucestershire at Cheltenham and Lancashire went to the Oval for their final game knowing that first innings points would be enough to settle matters. Hopwood made 151 out of 453 for eight declared and Surrey were then restricted to 294 and 172 for five. Reports relate that the new champions returned to the pavilion in virtual silence; even if so, one doubts it worried them very much.

In the aftermath of Lancashire's success, critics wondered how a team with admittedly powerful batting but seriously limited bowling could have secured the title. Indeed, the analysis continued for, perhaps, 77 years. What the detractors failed to see was that even though the Red Rose attack lacked a truly fast bowler like McDonald or a spinner with the mystery of Dick Tyldesley, Eckersley still had many options available to him, sufficient, indeed, to exploit any type of pitch. Hopwood's 15 wickets against Worcestershire at Blackpool, his 13 in the game against Derbyshire at Old Trafford and his dozen dismissals against Glamorgan at Aigburth were but three examples of his potency as a left-arm spinner on uncovered wickets. But Lancashire's attack was no one-man band: Booth took 89 wickets and Sibbles, 68; when the usual opening bowlers were unfit Dick Pollard's 38 successes established him as a seamer on whom the skipper could depend and Phillipson's 19 wickets also provided evidence of promise; leg-spinner Len Parkinson dismissed 46 batsmen and Iddon another 34; even Frank Watson claimed 35 wickets with his medium pacers. What the Lancashire attack lacked in apparent "star quality" in 1934, it made up for in variety. And when the bowlers needed some support they could always rely on Duckworth to provide it, whether by sharp glovework or vocal encouragement; the man judged by many to be the best wicketkeeper in the land took 53 catches and made 24 stumpings in 1934. Such sterling work made it particularly harsh that Duckworth's benefit earned him just £1,257, although that

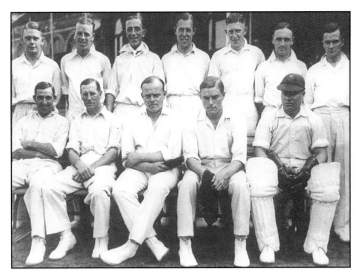

The 1934 Champions:
Back: Cyril Washbrook, Len Hopwood, Jack Iddon, Frank Booth, Dick Pollard, Len Parkinson, Buddy Oldfield. Seated: Eddie Paynter, Ernest Tyldesley, Peter Eckersley (capt.), Lionel Lister, George Duckworth.

total is explained more by the straitened economic climate in Lancashire than by any lack of appreciation for the keeper's efforts. Later in the thirties, Iddon, Sibbles, Hopwood and Farrimond were to suffer similarly modest returns.

Duckworth epitomised Lancashire's unyielding approach to their cricket in their five Championship seasons. When Iddon took the last Nottinghamshire wicket with three minutes to spare to win an acrimonious match at Trent Bridge by 101 runs, the effervescent wicketkeeper picked up the three stumps at his end of the pitch and sent them spinning skywards. Ernest Tyldesley's behaviour on the cricket field was much more reserved, which made his throwing of his cap into the air when that final batsman was dismissed all the more revealing of the importance he attached to the victory. Having conceded a lead of 147 on first innings, Lancashire had responded with 394 for seven declared in their second innings, Tyldesley making 109, before Hopwood's six for 58 completed the fightback. The game had featured plenty of Bodyline bowling from Harold Larwood and Bill Voce and the reaction of the Lancashire players indicated both their delight and, perhaps, a recognition that this was the sort of match potential champions should win. The game also carried a personal significance for Tyldesley: his century was the 99th of his first-class career and he was to collect his hundredth hundred at Peterborough in July. It was also in 1934 that Tyldesley overtook his brother and became Lancashire's leading run-scorer. His final tally of 34,222 has never been remotely threatened. This great cricketer did as much as anyone to bring five titles to Old Trafford.

County Championship 1934

	P	W	L	D	Pts	%
Lancashire	30	13	3	14	257	57.11
Sussex	30	12	2	16	243	54.00
Derbyshire	28	12	6	12	228	53.09
Warwickshire	24	10	4	10	190	52.77
Kent	30	12	7	11	225	50.00
Yorkshire	30	12	7	11	225	50.00
Gloucestershire	30	12	10	8	210	46.66
Essex	28	9	4	15	191	45.47
Nottinghamshire	28	8	7	13	173	41.19
Middlesex	28	8	9	11	169	40.23
Surrey	26	6	8	12	144	36.92
Leicestershire	24	6	9	9	123	34.16
Glamorgan	24	3	8	13	97	26.94
Hampshire	28	3	11	14	104	24.76
Somerset	24	3	10	11	78	21.66
Worcestershire	28	3	12	13	91	21.66
Northamptonshire	24	2	17	5	51	14.16

Double double for Hopwood *1935*

Dick Pollard, immortalised in cartoon form by Arthur Dooley left, was Lancashire's leading wicket-taker in 1935.

TOO MUCH was made of Lancashire's decline in 1935. In his final year as skipper, Peter Eckersley led his team to fourth place in a County Championship dominated by a tremendous battle between Yorkshire and Derbyshire. A very respectable 12 matches out of 28 were won, compared to 13 out of 30 the previous season. However, Lancashire lost six games and that was enough to reduce their final percentage from 57.11 to 54.04. Yorkshire, although still affected by Test calls, finished the season on 71.33% and Derbyshire on 63.33%.

The principal reason why Lancashire had won the title in 1934 was that all their leading players retained form and fitness. This situation did not obtain in the following season. Illness and injury restricted Ernest Tyldesley to ten matches in the County Championship and Jack Iddon to 18; their combined aggregate of runs toppled from 4488 to 1757. In addition, Frank Watson lost form for periods of the season and, although he was one of the six batsmen who amassed over a thousand runs, his consistently heavy scoring was missed.

Hopwood remained the most reliable of all-rounders and became the first Lancashire cricketer to do the double of 100 wickets and a thousand runs in two separate seasons.

Yet the summer was also notable in that it saw the full emergence of cricketers capable of replacing Watson, Tyldesley et al. in Lancashire's team. The most significant of these was probably Washbrook, who finished fifth in the national first-class averages with 1,724 runs at 45.36. Having played only half a dozen Championship games in 1934, the powerful young right-hander took a double hundred off the Oxford University attack before carrying his bat in both innings (49 and 87 not out) in the nine-wicket defeat of Worcestershire at Old Trafford. Originally selected to replace Iddon, Washbrook kept his place in the side.

Rather more surprising seemed the sudden blossoming of Norman 'Buddy' Oldfield, although this skilful, diminutive batsman had been on the Old Trafford staff since 1929. Six seasons later, having watched fine sides collect two titles, Oldfield made his debut at Lord's in the first game of the season and by the end of the campaign had scored over a thousand runs with two centuries and five fifties. The 24-year-old's batting was sufficiently pleasing on the eye to move Cardus to rhapsody: "If this young man does not go to the top of his calling there will be a scandalous interference with destiny," he wrote. Sadly, there was such a scandalous interference; it was called the Second World War. For five seasons, though, Oldfield enjoyed himself.

Joining Washbrook and Oldfield as members of Old Trafford's younger corps in 1935 were Dick Pollard and Eddie Phillipson. Pollard made the biggest impact, taking 93 Championship wickets and quickly establishing himself as a hard-working seamer, even if he was not the truly fast bowler some spectators believed the county needed. Phillipson, who offered more with the bat, took 62 wickets, and with Booth and Sibbles both dismissing well in excess of fifty batsmen, Lancashire's attack remained a reliable unit with which it was unwise to take liberties. However, the excellence of the wicketkeepers at Old Trafford in the 1930s was rivalled only by the quality of Kent's Les Ames and 'Hopper' Levett. Duckworth often stood down in 1935 to give Farrimond valuable experience and both men played a Test for England in the series against South Africa.

150 LANCASHIRE GREATS
70. Len Hopwood

Len Hopwood is the only Lancashire player to have achieved the double of 1,000 runs and 100 wickets in a season twice, in 1934 and 1935. He was an obdurate and valuable batsman whether opening or going in lower in the order and on occasions he could reveal a very wide range of strokes. He was also a very fine bowler, slow to medium left-arm, who was extremely accurate and in suitable conditions could be devastating. He played 397 times for the county, scoring 15,519 runs, ave. 30.01, and taking 672 wickets, ave. 22.18. He scored a century and took ten wickets in a match against Leicestershire and made a career top score of 220. He played in two Tests and was a member of three Championship-winning sides. In 1934 he took 110 wickets at 17 each and scored over 1,500 runs, ave 41. He became the first professional player to be appointed President of Lancashire in 1981-82.

Difficult start for Lister

1936

AT THE end of the 1935 season Peter Eckersley declared his intention to pursue his political ambitions and in November's General Election Lancashire's former captain was returned as the Conservative MP for Manchester Exchange. Although some consideration was given to the claims of the Rochdale amateur Harry Butterworth, the choice of Eckersley's successor finally rested between Formby's Lionel Lister and Ernest Tyldesley, who had declared his willingness to play as an amateur in the following summer. Whether influenced by tradition or age – Lister was 24, Tyldesley 47 – the Old Trafford committee finally voted by a clear majority in favour of Lister, who was to remain skipper during the four pre-war seasons.

The job of captaining Lancashire has never been one for the faint-hearted, but few skippers have had more difficult first years in the job than Lister. His task was not helped by Tyldesley's decision to retire after playing just two games. The great batsman had been talked out of ending his career following his glorious 1934 season, so it would be hard indeed to interpret his decision as evidence of resentment at being passed over. Rather, it simply showed that he realised it was time to stop playing first-class cricket.

Tyldesley's final game was Jack Iddon's benefit match against Surrey in early June, by which time it was already clear that Lancashire were to have a difficult season. Indeed, only two matches were won prior to August and at that stage Lister's team lay 15th in the table. Instead of battling for honours against the likes of Derbyshire and Yorkshire, they were scrapping with Glamorgan and Northamptonshire to avoid finishing bottom of the pile. In the event, Lancashire enjoyed a splendid final month of the season, winning five matches and finishing the campaign in eleventh position. That, though, was as low in the table as the county had ever been and, inevitably, there were many supporters ready to identify Lister as the chief culprit for the demise. He bore it all with sang-froid and courtesy.

There were, of course, many more convincing reasons for Lancashire's very mediocre season. Put simply, too many of the experienced players suffered dips in their form while most of the younger members of the squad were not yet equipped to take on the extra responsibility. Washbrook admitted later in his career that he had not yet developed the technique needed to bat on that damp summer's many wet wickets; neither he nor Oldfield scored a thousand Championship runs, although both reached the landmark in all first-class matches. Watson had a grim season, too, collecting just 621 runs from his 26 first-class innings; it became clear that this loyal servant's career was nearing its end.

By contrast, Iddon scored 1,639 runs, a tally which include five centuries, and Paynter's 1,930 runs in the Championship included 964 in August alone, when this courageous left-hander made three hundreds in successive innings. Hopwood again proved himself an effective all-rounder, but his 71 wickets represented a slight decline on his previous two seasons' returns. The bowler of the season was Pollard, whose 103 wickets in the Championship established him as the leader of the attack. Sibbles was

Jack Iddon, above, enjoyed a successful Benefit in 1936 and made five centuries in his 1,639 runs.

handicapped by an arm injury but still took 69 wickets, while Booth and Parkinson both claimed over 40 dismissals. Pollard and Paynter apart, the summer of 1936 was one which most players on Lancashire's staff were glad to see end. Their feelings were shared by the county's supporters.

150 LANCASHIRE GREATS
71. Dick Pollard

Dick Pollard was a red-haired fast bowler who played either side of World War Two and was known as 'Th' Owd Chainhorse' because of his ability and at times insistence on bowling for long periods. He was born in Westhoughton and joined Lancashire in 1933 and just two years later took 100 wickets in a season, continuing to do so every season up to the war. In 1938 he bowled more than 1,200 overs and took 149 wickets; he repeated that number of overs twice more after the war. He took over 1100 first-class wickets in all and it would have been much more if the war had not interrupted his career. For Lancashire he took 1,015 wickets at an ave. of 22.15, taking five or more wickets in an innings 55 times. He played in the Victory Tests in 1945 and subsequently played four Tests for England, dismissing Don Bradman twice in 1948. He retired from first-class cricket in the 1950 season and went to play league cricket. He was also an accomplished light pianist.

Paynter blasts 322 *1937*

ALTHOUGH LANCASHIRE improved their position in the table by only two places in 1937, the season was packed to bursting with incident and controversy. Perhaps the most unusual event occurred off the field when the committee issued a public rebuke to the team on May 22nd for their slow batting and demanded they play brighter cricket. "We have done no worse than follow the usual policy of Lancashire cricket for many years past," responded the aggrieved players, only for the committee to comment that while previous sides may have batted defensively, they had at least managed to win plenty of games. That was probably the nub of the issue: four draws in the first five County Championship games and a ten-wicket hammering in the first Roses match

were not the sort of performances the Old Trafford committee could tolerate.

Perhaps official discontent did have an impact. Lancashire's poor start to the season was followed by a 12-match unbeaten sequence. In late July and August five successive wins were achieved but, infuriatingly, none of the season's final five games were won. Lister's team dropped from a high-point of sixth to finish ninth, with nine wins balanced by five defeats and 18 draws.

Eddie Paynter enjoyed a summer to stimulate the fondest remembrance. The Oswaldtwistle left-hander scored 2,356 runs in the Championship and won a recall to the England side, although he was left out of the team for the third match against New Zealand at the Oval in August, when Washbrook played the first of his 37 Tests.

Probably more memorable for Paynter was his destruction of the Essex attack at Old Trafford, where he made 266; even more worthy of recall was his evisceration of Sussex's bowlers at Hove on July 28, when he made 322 in five hours. That innings is still Lancashire's third-highest individual score and the side's total of 640 for eight declared, scored in a day comprising 136.2 overs, is the county's eighth highest total. Two of the partnerships still make startling reading: Paynter and Washbrook put on 268 for the first wicket in 162 minutes and Paynter and Oldfield added 271 in 135 minutes for the third. Sussex responded with 340 and 295 to lose by an innings and 25 runs. Eddie Phillipson took five for 91 in the second innings, one of nine occasions in 1937 when he collected five or more wickets. The 26-year-old fast-medium bowler finished the campaign with 118 wickets, nine ahead of Pollard and 19 more than Sibbles, who was eventually compelled to retire with tennis elbow.

Lancashire completed their victory against Sussex on July 30th. The following morning they were in the field on the first morning of the Roses match at Sheffield. Pollard exhibited few signs of travel fatigue in taking five for 59 as Yorkshire were put out for 246. A competent display with the bat helped Lister's men establish a lead of 78 runs before Jack Iddon enjoyed one

EDDIE PAYNTER. 1938.

arthur Dooley

of those days which send slow bowlers into wistful reverie. The Lancashire spinner took nine for 42 in 18.5 overs as Yorkshire were dismissed for 168 and the visitors secured a five-wicket win, their first victory in a Roses match since 1932. For most Lancashire supporters the game was the highlight of their summer, but the White Rose fraternity had a rather different highlight to celebrate at the end of the summer: their fifth title in seven years.

There were significant debuts and departures in 1937. Watson was released at the end of the season, leaving Jack Iddon as the only man who had played in all the Championship sides. Rumours of Duckworth's retirement proved to be well-founded as this most loyal of wicketkeepers stepped down in the close season to pursue what would now be described as a media career. The availability of Farrimond in the following two summers ensured that Lancashire's gauntlets remained in the safest of hands.

The most notable newcomer was Winston Place. Born in Rawtenstall and coached by Harry Makepeace, this right-handed batsman's provenance was beyond suspicion. He made a century against Nottinghamshire and scored 515 runs in 20 innings. His arrival may not have made Lancashire's cricket that much brighter in the utterly destructive style of Paynter in his pomp, but Place's presence in Lancashire's top order was to be invaluable in post-war summers.

---

150 LANCASHIRE GREATS
72. Len Wilkinson

Len Wilkinson had a meteoric rise to fame as a leg-spinner. At the age of 20 he made his debut for Lancashire in 1937, and in 1938 took 151 first-class wickets, an outstanding performance, and he was regarded as the best young spin bowler in England. He was a wristy leg-spinner who delivered a deceptive 'wrong 'un' which brought him early success. He was chosen for the tour to South Africa in 1938-39, taking 44 wickets in all games and heading the bowling averages. He played in three Tests in total. A hand injury hindered him in 1939, but he still managed to take 63 wickets. The war years robbed him of continuing success. Playing only a handful of games in those barren years, he lost the rhythm and ability to spin the ball effectively. He only played a handful of matches for Lancashire after the war before returning to league cricket at Furness. He ran a newsagent's shop and then worked at the Vickers shipyard. He will be fondly remembered in the cricket world for his special guile and the way he bamboozled many great batsmen before the war interrupted his career.

Wilkinson shines briefly

1938

FOR ALL that Jack Iddon and Len Hopwood scored a thousand runs each, the season of 1938 was the one in which a predominantly fresh Lancashire side began to impose itself on English cricket. Given that six of the next seven summers were to be swallowed up in the fight against fascism, the team's flowering was brief indeed. The players' performance in 1939 was a little less impressive and by 1946 some men had retired, others were past their prime and a couple soon decided to leave the club.

For the first two thirds of the season Lancashire's County Championship ambitions seemed credible enough. Lister's team went into the second Roses match in late July with 12 wins from their 18 games, the same record as their keenest rivals. However, an innings and 200-run defeat completed Yorkshire's first double over their rivals since 1909 and it was followed by Lancastrian losses to Kent, Somerset and Gloucestershire. The Old Trafford team ended the season having won 14 and lost six of their 32 games. A fourth-place finish seemed a fair reflection of the side's merit.

Nobody enjoyed the season more than Eddie Paynter, who played in all the Tests against Australia, and Len Wilkinson, a leg-spinner of whom relatively few cricket lovers outside Lancashire had heard prior to 1938, yet who took 136 wickets in the Championship at an average 22.66. Wilkinson's record earned him selection for that winter's tour to South Africa and he played alongside Paynter in three of the Tests. Yet the 21-year-old never again approached the level of success he enjoyed in 1938. Injuries and his own striving for perfection were judged responsible for his decline and his county career ended in 1947. He made 34 of his 63 first-class appearances for Lancashire in 1938.

Both men enjoyed the hard, fast pitches which characterised the season. They helped Paynter's attacking style and they offered the tall, gangling Wilkinson plenty of bounce for his leggies, googlies and top-spinners. Placards were carried around Old Trafford telling spectators of Paynter's progress during his epic innings of 216 against Australia at Trent Bridge, but the cheery left-hander also registered seven centuries for Lancashire in the County Championship. His aggregate of 1,873 runs made him the county's heaviest run-scorer, albeit that he had played at least seven fewer innings than the other five Lancastrians who reached four figures. Cricket must have been the most tremendous fun for Eddie Paynter in the four seasons prior to the war.

Prior to 1938, there were no indications that Lancashire were about to unleash a most destructive leg-spinner on the English game. Wilkinson had made his debut in 1937, taking 22 first-class wickets in 190.4 overs; the next summer he bagged 145 in 1,192.2 overs. The Bolton-based spinner – he had played for Heaton before joining Lancashire – spun the ball hard and took five wickets in an innings on ten occasions in 1938. He thereby offered more than useful support to Pollard, who took 139 wickets in the Championship, and Phillipson, whose progress was hampered by an injury sustained when he collided with an opponent at Worcester. Fortunately, Lister was able to utilise the seam bowling skills of Albert Nutter to bowl the overs he might have expected Phillipson to deliver. Nutter, in reality a cricketer of most equable temperament, was regarded as a genuine all-rounder. His 1,128 runs and 84 wickets proved the case.

Eddie Phillipson's progress was hampered by injury.

Thus, despite their two defeats to Yorkshire, Lancashire could look back with some pride on the summer of 1938. Their batsmen had shrugged off the negative comments directed at them and scored 491 for eight in a day against Essex before piling up 564 for nine declared against Glamorgan. There was every reason for the county's cricketers to look forward to 1939; in Europe's non-cricketing circles such optimism was the merest fantasy.

150 LANCASHIRE GREATS
73. Norman Oldfield

Norman 'Buddy' Oldfield was a quick-footed and delightful stroke-maker whose blossoming career was interrupted by World War Two, and whose Lancashire days at the club were ended in 1946 when he decided that league cricket offered better pay and security. He later joined Northants and for seven seasons gave Lancashire supporters ample evidence of what they had missed. He made his debut in 1935 and made an immediate impact in a strong Lancashire side by scoring over 1,000 runs, a feat he repeated every season up to the war. Neville Cardus compared him with JT Tyldesley. In 1938 he helped set the county's 3rd wicket record of 306 with Eddie Paynter against Hampshire. His one and only Test was in 1939, against the West Indies, when he made a brilliant 80 in the first innings and a promising England career beckoned, but war broke out 12 days later. He played 151 matches for Lancashire, scoring 7,000 runs, ave 35.72. Altogether he scored 17,811 first-class runs at 37.89. He later became an umpire and returned to Old Trafford as coach. He always regretted leaving Lancashire: "I deemed it an honour to play at Old Trafford and for Lancashire. At Northants it was a job of work."

War curtails season *1939*

MOST CRICKET matches can be both enjoyed for themselves and viewed as part of a developing pattern. The late summer of 1939 was different. Spectators at Trent Bridge on August 15th savoured the enterprise of Lancashire's batting as they chased down a target of 323 to beat Nottinghamshire by six wickets, but only the purblind optimists among the visiting supporters could believe that it bolstered hopes that their team would mount a challenge for the title in 1940. There was to be no County Championship until 1946. The near certainty of a European war meant that the sport played in 1939 could be treasured only for what it was: a last hurrah before a descent into the dark unknown.

Cyril Washbrook in action against Yorkshire in 1939.

On August 24th Lionel Lister was padded up and waiting to go out to bat against Northamptonshire when he received a message saying that he should join his regiment. There was no question of the skipper waiting until he had played a final innings, no Charters or Caldicott to argue for cricket's pre-eminence. Jack Iddon took over the captaincy and Lancashire won by 95 runs. Five days earlier Buddy Oldfield had played his only Test, making a stylish 80 against the West Indies. He was told that he had a future with England. This was a nice touch of innocent bravado given that no one could be confident that either Oldfield or England had any future at all.

On the evening of August 29th Lancashire's players set off from Dover in the hope of getting to Manchester in time for the next day's game against Surrey. They arrived home at about 4am and some slept in the Old Trafford pavilion. Dick Pollard took ten wickets in the match and Lancashire were left needing 352 on the final day. In view of the "deteriorating international situation", to borrow Jim Ledbetter and Peter Wynne-Thomas's quaint phrase, no cricket was played on September 1st. The next day, Britain declared war on Germany.

Yet what could England's county cricketers do in the summer of 1939 except play the sport they loved and offer entertainment to those who had paid to watch them do so? Lancashire's players were no different to their counterparts in 16 other counties and several of Lister's men enjoyed successful seasons. Eddie Phillipson was the most successful bowler with 118 wickets, but Pollard, who bagged 98, was not far behind. However, neither Len Wilkinson nor Albert Nutter achieved the success they had managed in the previous season, Wilkinson being particularly handicapped by injury and a series of wet wickets. In consequence the Lancashire attack lacked balance, which was probably the most significant cause of the team dropping to sixth place in the final table.

Despite the rain, which frequently prevented matches achieving a positive result in 1939, four batsmen scored in excess of 1,500 runs, Washbrook's 1,547 including no centuries. But Paynter, Oldfield and Iddon all had higher aggregates and made 15 Championship hundreds between them. Two of Iddon's three-figure scores were made against Hampshire. The first came in an innings win at Old Trafford and the second seven days later when he put on 169 for the fourth wicket with Len Hopwood as Lancashire won by six wickets at Northlands Road, scoring 385 on the final day of the game. Hopwood made 135, his last hundred for Lancashire, although the abiding regard felt for this fine cricketer was shown over 40 years later when he became the first former professional to be elected President of the club.

Of the younger players Winston Place continued to make progress in 1939, milking the West Indies attack for 164 at Liverpool, and Jack Ikin, a left-handed batsman from Bignall End in Staffordshire, made his debut. Both players showed that they could play the incomparable game; whether they would have the opportunity to realise their promise was a different matter.

Howard keeps home fires burning

1940–45

former captain Peter Eckersley, who died in a flying accident at Eastleigh when serving with the Royal Naval Volunteer Reserve. He was 36.

The vast administrative requirements of a war even more total than its predecessor, added to the impact of bombing on the civilian population, ensured that very few people or sports clubs were left unaffected by the conflict. When the Royal Engineers had finished with the ground, it was used as a transit camp for soldiers who had escaped from Dunkirk. Then the Ministry of Supply used the old place as a dump for vehicles and other equipment. Even the heavy roller was called up and sent out to the Western Desert to aid the building of air-strips. In 1940 and 1941 the Luftwaffe inflicted serious damage on the ground when air raids damaged the top of the pavilion, two stands and the dining room. Bombs also left craters on the outfield, which some cricket lovers probably considered the greatest material injury of all.

But while Old Trafford remained out of commission until 1944, when three services games took place on the ground, a remarkable amount of cricket was played during the Second World War. Many leagues and clubs continued to function, rightly recognising that it was more important that some cricket happened than that the quality of the sport was always very high. This gave an opportunity for most of Lancashire's players to keep their skills in some sort of order. The most obvious exception was Len Wilkinson,

The Ladies' Pavilion also took a hit, whilst military vehicles are lined up by the main Pavilion.

SCARCELY HAD the war begun before Old Trafford was requisitioned by the army and occupied by the Royal Engineers. This action gives some indication of the many preparations that had already taken place in Britain in advance of Chamberlain's formal declaration of hostilities on September 2nd. Before long the vast majority of Lancashire's staff were in uniform and it was left to the Secretary, Captain, later Major, Rupert Howard to keep the home fires burning at Old Trafford. Howard spent his free time collecting half-subs from the many members willing to pay them and doing such administration as was necessary in preparation for the resumption of first-class cricket when the war ended. Such work was predicated on an Allied victory, an outcome that was by no means likely until, perhaps, 1942.

So for six years Lancashire County Cricket Club and its staff were put at the service of the war effort. Three second team players were killed during the hostilities, but the only first teamer to pass away was the

150 LANCASHIRE GREATS
75. Lionel Lister

Lionel Lister captained Lancashire from 1936 until the outbreak of war. He was born at Freshfield near Formby and was educated at Malvern. He went on to play cricket and football at Cambridge in 1933 and then was invited to play for Lancashire. In only his second match he scored a rapid century against Middlesex at Old Trafford and at Worcester he made 96 in an hour. The following year, a very brave innings against Notts against Larwood and Voce enabled Lancashire to win. He was appointed captain at the age of 24 in succession to Peter Eckersley and continued to impress with bursts of exuberance, scoring a century before lunch against Middlesex at Lord's. He showed defiance and strong leadership as a captain and they were a popular and happy side under Lister when war came. "I had my pads on when the Army telegram arrived. I took them off, said goodbye to the lads and was away." Wisden reads, 'Lister absent 0'. He was a natural leader of men, in peace and war. June 1944 saw him in Normandy as a brigade major. He was a friendly, gregarious man, always gentle and humorous and was elected Lancashire President in 1969–70.

whose postings gave him few chances to bowl leg-spin and who lost his control, although it could be argued that this had begun to happen before the war began. However, ensuring that first-team players had opportunities to practise was only one of the reasons why cricket was played as frequently as possible during the war. As in the Great War, sport entertained a public who had few opportunities for relaxation and some games also raised money for war charities.

By the time the conflict had ended, Old Trafford was more or less ready to host one of the Victory Tests against Australia. Eddie Phillipson, Dick Pollard and Cyril Washbrook all played in England's six-wicket victory, Pollard and Phillipson sharing 15 of the Australian wickets to fall. Despite the pretty spartan facilities, the three-day game was watched by some 72,463 spectators. Many of them may not have been able to believe that they had survived; many others probably thought of friends who had not made it through. So perhaps the most poignant match to take place before the resumption of a full County Championship schedule in 1946 was the first-class Roses match at Bradford, which was played in aid of the widow and children of Hedley Verity, who had died in Italy in 1943. Seven of the Lancashire team had played pretty regularly in 1939 and the drawn game was keenly contested, Washbrook making 97 and Albert Nutter taking five for 57. Nevertheless, insofar as it could ever be said of a Roses match, the result really didn't matter that much.

*Cyril Washbrook walks out to bat with Middlesex's Bill Edrich
in the Victory Test at Old Trafford in 1945.*

In 1942 AD Procter, well known in Manchester cricketing circles, found himself in charge of the Welfare Section of the Ministry of Labour in Manchester. His task involved raising funds for appropriate welfare schemes and he decided cricket was to be the method. With so many cricketers in the services or on war work in the north-west, and with a large population to provide the audiences, it was an astute stroke, and he organised some very interesting matches, not exhibition ones like the Empire XI. This resulted in his raising £3,500 for charity in 1942, with 125,000 attending the 20 or so games. At Aigburth they witnessed a 500-run thriller, with Lancashire, helped by a Cranston hundred, beating a full Army side (CS Dempster 89, Denis Compton 73) by four wickets. At Longsight, Manchester, EH Eytle's half-century just failed to bring the West Indies a win in a drawn match with Lancashire, for whom Cyril Washbrook (pictured left) scored 53. At Didsbury, Lancashire hung on to their last wicket to draw an exciting game with the strong RAF team. An Empire XI amassed 385 for 5. Eddie Paynter, Norman Oldfield and Winston Place, born and bred in the County Palatine, may have been startled to find they were members of the British Empire XI and they celebrated with 60 apiece. A North Wales XI could summon up only 151 in reply. Then, at Blackpool, an England XI beat the West Indies by 70 runs. This pattern of entertaining games, spread throughout Lancashire and into North Wales, was one of the most successful initiatives of the war.

Bomb crater discovered at Old Trafford

A PIECE of Old Trafford's history came back to life in 2008 as workmen laying the new outfield at the ground came across the remains of a Second World War bomb crater. Old Trafford was hit by several bombs during the War, with the Ladies Pavilion taking a direct hit and the rear of the main Pavilion badly damaged. A sentry on duty at the main gate on Talbot Road was killed by one of the blasts. The Australian Prime Minister Robert Menzies was photographed inspecting one of the craters on the outfield a few days later in 1941 (above left), and it was this crater that was uncovered in 2008.

The photograph above right shows the area of the bomb crater. Instead of continuing to extract soil, as the outfield was being dug down a few feet, the workers discovered a circular area that was a mixture of clay, pot, glass and shale. This was probably used as backfill and would have likely been the only material to hand at the time. This area is the darker coloured patch in the foreground in the photograph.

These two photographs record the location of a small, and unusual, part of the ground's history before it finally disappeared forever under the new outfield.

Part of a letter from A.C.MacLaren written in 1942 when he was asked to speak at Wellingborough School during the Second World War, it was one of his last letters. As you can see he was a good judge of character.

"I am still hoping to see plenty of cricket in spite of Hitler, who would hardly be able to play any game to give enjoyment to others and to get enjoyment out of it himself."

Grounds for optimism in first post-war season

1946

from across the globe. Plans for the rebuilding had to be adjusted, but Old Trafford proved itself perfectly capable of staging regular first-class cricket when it resumed in 1946. The facilities may not have been palatial but they were sufficient.

There was also a pressing need to recruit some new players in advance of the 1946 season. Ill-health had forced Len Hopwood to retire and neither Lionel Lister nor TA Higson jnr., who had shared the captaincy duties in 1939, would be able to continue in the role after the war. It was also made clear to 44-year-old Eddie Paynter that his playing days with Lancashire were at an end, although this may have been something that the cricketer

Despite the austerity of the immediate post-war years, crowds flocked in their thousands to Old Trafford.

IN 1945 Lancashire needed to rebuild a home ground which still exhibited signs of the Luftwaffe's attentions and put together a team capable of competing in the following

year's County Championship. The Old Trafford officials were not alone. Across the country sports clubs of all sizes were coming to terms with the effects of war and the price of victory. Money was short and luxury was not an option. To meet Lancashire's material need an appeal was launched aimed at raising £100,000 to construct a new stadium capable of accommodating 40,000 spectators, but it had raised only £42,236 when it was closed. Yet this in itself was a noble effort in the austere economic circumstances and money had come in

150 LANCASHIRE GREATS
77. Cyril Washbrook

By any standard, he was an outstanding cricketer. In only his second match for Lancashire he made a brilliant 152 against Surrey. His cap set at a rakish angle, sleeves folded at the elbow, his arms swinging in military precision, that was Cyril Washbrook as he marched on to the field. As a batsman he played to perfection the hook and square cut and excelled at driving the over-pitched ball. He was also a superb cover fielder. He played exactly 500 matches for Lancashire, scoring over 34,000 runs with 76 centuries in all first-class cricket. He held almost every role for Lancashire in a 60-year association as captain, manager, committee man and President. He played 37 Tests for England, scoring 2,569 runs with his most famous innings the 98 at Headingley when he was recalled at the age of 41 after a six-year absence. Washbrook and Hutton for England, and with Winston Place for Lancashire, have become woven into the fabric of cricket history. He was awarded a CBE in 1991 by the Queen and was President of Lancashire in 1989-90.

Winston Place, along with Cyril Washbrook, provided one of the best and most prolific opening partnerships in the immediate post-war years.

himself had come to accept. Nevertheless, the grant of £1,078 made to Paynter in lieu of a benefit was shamefully mean given his service to the county he loved. Washbrook's 1948 benefit raised £14,000.

Initially it had been thought that Buddy Oldfield and Albert Nutter were going to be available in the post-war era, but neither player could agree financial terms and both decided that league cricket was the better option for them. Subsequently both men joined Northamptonshire, although Oldfield always regretted his decision to leave Lancashire. Bill Farrimond opted to retire – he would have celebrated his 43rd birthday during the 1946 season – and, in a final tragic blow, Jack Iddon was killed in a car accident a few weeks before the new season was due to start.

That left a core of perhaps five players who could be relied upon to play first- team county cricket at the required standard: Cyril Washbrook, Dick Pollard, Eddie Phillipson, Winston Place and Len Wilkinson. (It was soon clear that Wilkinson had lost most of the control that had made his leg-spin such a threat in 1938, although it was evident in equally short order that Jack Ikin was a fine batsman, useful bowler and outstanding close fielder.) Lancashire officials therefore took advantage of the relaxed qualification rules in the post-war period to recruit a number of players. Phil King, a hard-hitting batsman, was signed from Worcestershire and Tom Brierley, a wicketkeeper who had previously played for Glamorgan, also agreed to join the Old Trafford staff. Batsmen Geoff and Eric Edrich were recruited from Norfolk, while Alan Wharton and slow left-armer Eric Price were signed from league cricket. Lancashire also hoped that medium-pace bowler Gordon Garlick and spinner Bill Roberts would be able to progress as first-team cricketers after making a few appearances in the pre-war side. To captain this somewhat experimental team, the Lancashire committee chose Jack Fallows,

the son of the county's treasurer and an amateur club cricketer who had skippered Manchester in the pre-war period.

The results of all this activity were far better than could have been anticipated. With Washbrook and Place in some of the best form of their careers and the reconstituted bowling attack proving itself a potent force, Lancashire led the table during the early months of the season before narrow defeats to Essex and Hampshire and a succession of lost tosses enabled both Yorkshire and Middlesex to overtake them. Nevertheless, a record of 15 wins from 26 matches was very creditable and it left Fallows' team just 16 points behind champions Yorkshire in the final table.

Perhaps the most pleasing aspect of the season was the form of the left-arm spin bowlers Bill Roberts and Eric Price. Although placed in the same cricketing category, they offered contrasting challenges to batsmen. Roberts' use of flight earned him 110 wickets in the County Championship, while Price's more attacking style snared 82 batsmen. With Phillipson collecting 80 wickets and Pollard a further 72, Lancashire possessed a well-balanced attack in 1946, especially when Garlick, who could double as an off-spinner, was used to back up the new-ball bowlers.

The most improved cricketer on Lancashire's staff in 1946 was probably Ikin; the most impressive was Washbrook. By scoring 1,095 first-class runs, taking 49 wickets and pouching a remarkable 45 catches, Ikin established himself as an all-rounder of whom his adopted county could expect much in the coming seasons. Most spectators at Old Trafford knew that they could count on Washbrook for hooks, courage and cuts, but he exceeded even their hopes with 1,475 Championship runs at an average of 73.75. In the national first-class list, his average was second only to Wally Hammond and his aggregate second only to Denis Compton. Washbrook was moving in exalted company and did not suffer by comparison. The opener's place on the boat for the winter tour to Australia was assured and he was joined on the voyage by both Ikin and Dick Pollard.

There remained problems with the side, of course, but that could be said of most counties in the immediate post-war period. Tom Brierley and Eric Edrich were both tried as wicketkeepers, but neither impressed spectators used to watching Duckworth and Farrimond. Fallows was a genial, engaging skipper who had the good sense to follow Washbrook and Pollard's advice on tactics, but his first-class batting average of 8.14 was something of an embarrassment. Nevertheless, Lancashire emerged from the slight chaos of the first post-war season, knowing that they had recruited fairly well. There were good reasons to hope that 1947 would be calmer but no less successful.

The County Championship resumed in 1946, and despite some bomb damage, the ground was in surprisingly good condition.

Runs galore in *1947* vintage season

NO SOONER had the 1946 season ended than Jack Fallows was sacked as captain and replaced by the highly-regarded Neston all-rounder Ken Cranston. The decision itself was controversial, but the means by which Fallows learned of it – through a press leak – was squalid and indefensible. Few people could make a case for the ex-skipper as a cricketer, but he had succeeded in blending some new players with some established professionals to produce a proper team. Off the field, his common sense and concern for his players was undoubted; he was yet another Lancashire captain who didn't manage to irritate the professionals beyond tolerance. Many historians have argued that his dismissal sowed seeds of distrust between the dressing room and the committee room, which grew into weeds of dissent and disharmony over the next decade or so. It seemed to some players that the decision had been taken without the least regard for their opinions.

On the other hand, no one could doubt that Cranston had the better credentials as a cricketer; if he had been brought into the side alongside Fallows there would only have been praise for the enterprise shown by the club. But there was the perception that the new skipper consulted committee members more frequently than he did the professionals in his team, although that is challenged by evidence suggesting that Washbrook and Cranston worked reasonably well together.

Whatever the merits of the decision, Cranston quickly showed himself to be worthy of a place in the side as an all-rounder. Indeed, after playing 13 first-class games for Lancashire in 1947, he was selected for the last three Tests against South Africa and did so well that he was also included in the party for the winter tour to the West Indies. All this from a man with film-star looks who had made it abundantly clear that he did not want a long first-class career. In fact, Cranston played full-time cricket for just two seasons and resisted all attempts to persuade him to revisit his decision. He scored 3099 first-class runs and took 178 wickets. A brief encounter, indeed.

Lancashire flourished under Cranston's leadership and retained their third place in the final table, although given the players in his charge, this was not surprising. As the captain pointed out later, his team's only deficiency was that it did not boast a truly fast bowler capable of finishing teams off. Some might have argued that neither did it possess a spinner of the quality of Dick Tyldesley.

What it did possess were a couple of very high-class opening batsmen in Washbrook and Place, two rapidly maturing middle-order batsmen in Ikin and Edrich, a veteran fast bowler capable of taking 131 Championship wickets – that was Dick Pollard, of course – and a left-arm spinner in Bill Roberts whose 74 wickets represented another fine season's work. Cranston himself scored 835 runs in the County Championship and took 57 wickets. Endowed with those riches, Lancashire won 13 of their 26 games in 1947, losing only to Somerset at Frome, when Washbrook and Cranston were playing for England and Place was 12th man.

Inevitably, there also was a winnowing of players as the post-war side assumed a more familiar shape. Neither Eric Price nor Gordon Garlick enjoyed anything like the success they had managed in 1946 and both left at the end of the season, Price to join Essex and Garlick to try his luck at Northamptonshire. Perhaps more surprisingly, Eddie Phillipson's form declined sharply – he took only 27 wickets at 37 runs apiece – and he remained on the staff for only one more season before becoming Littleborough's professional.

Yet even when Cranston's glamorous presence is taken into consideration, 1947 will be remembered as a season when Washbrook and Place bestrode Lancashire cricket. While Denis Compton and Bill Edrich dominated the national stage, Old Trafford's opening pair were also sharing a series of memorable partnerships, including one unbroken stand of 350 against Sussex at Old Trafford which was only 18 shy of Lancashire's first-wicket record, set by MacLaren and Spooner some 44 years previously.

In the return match Washbrook and Place put on 233 in a mere 113 minutes at Eastbourne to clinch a ten-wicket win with only ten minutes to spare. Place finished the season with 2,023 Championship runs, a tally that included nine centuries; Washbrook managed a mere 1,639 at an average of 78.04, although his full first-class tally of 2,662 was 151 more than Place and behind only Compton and Edrich in the national list. Lancashire even defeated the new champions Middlesex by 64 runs in the final game of the season. It was, indeed, a vintage summer.

Cranston era ends *1948*

AN OLD failing returned to bedevil Lancashire in 1948. Although difficult to beat, they found it hard to press home the advantage and win matches. No team in the country lost fewer Championship games, yet no county in the top half of the table won less frequently. A record which read: Played 26, Won 8, Lost 2, Drew 16 told of a side whose attack lacked penetration and whose captain probably did not possess the tactical nous to engineer a victory, albeit at the risk of defeat. Even more revealing is the statistic that on 14 occasions Cranston's team took first innings points in drawn games. A first innings lead was worth four points, whereas a win earned 12. Lancashire were a powerful side in 1948, but they finished fifth in the table, 20 points behind Glamorgan.

The team's most obvious deficiencies were the absence of a truly expert wicketkeeper and the lack of an opening bowler to partner Dick Pollard. Two medium-pacers, Roy Tattersall and Peter Greenwood, were tried in 1948 but neither quite fitted the bill, although Greenwood took 44 first-class wickets in the season. For his part, 36-year-old Pollard remained eager for work and removed 95 batsmen in the Championship. 'Th' Owd Chain-Horse', as he was known, laboured on, even when he was ploughing a lonely furrow. Lol Cook, Dick Pollard, Brian Statham, Glen Chapple: it is a noble lineage.

The wicketkeeping problem was particularly vexatious, given that Lancashire were to possess so many spin bowlers of high quality in the post-war era. Four men were tried behind the stumps in 1948: Tom Brierley, Eric Edrich, Alf Barlow and Alan Wilson.

Malcolm Hilton shows off one of the balls with which he dismissed the great Don Bradman twice in a match in May 1948.

Barlow had been signed for the previous season and had seemed to offer a solution to the problem, but he sustained injuries to his hands in 1948. Wilson was to play 171 games for Lancashire over 15 years but made only eight appearances in his first season. He was to prove himself one of his county's most steadfast servants. Yet as Roberts and Ikin deceived batsmen in 1948, it must have irritated Red Rose supporters that there was no Duckworth or Farrimond to make the absolute best of the chances offered. The rapid development of slow left-armers Malcolm Hilton and Bob Berry, added to the conversion of Tattersall from a seamer to a spinner who could bowl at medium pace, was to make the need for a regular keeper no less pressing over the next few years. (Hilton had grabbed the headlines in May by twice dismissing Don Bradman in Lancashire's first match against the Australian tourists.)

Batting remained Lancashire's strong suit in 1948. Place had one of his less impressive seasons, but still scored over a thousand Championship runs, a feat also achieved by Ikin. Neither Geoff Edrich nor Alan Wharton achieved that landmark, but both showed themselves capable of coping with the demands of county cricket. Nigel Howard, a young batsman who was the son of the Lancashire secretary, amassed over 900 runs in first-class games, as did Cranston. And towering over them all, when England calls and injury permitted, was Washbrook, who was awarded the second game against the Australian tourists as his benefit. In 17 Championship innings for Lancashire he made 1,391 runs at an average of 92.73. They are statistics which may even have satisfied the captain of Australia.

And so the brief Cranstonian adventure at Old Trafford ended. There had been great matches in 1948: a one-run defeat to Surrey at the Oval and a four-run victory over Leicestershire were just two that spectators might remember fondly. The skipper himself made 82 and 39 not out in his last game, clinching the seven-wicket win over Kent with a boundary. He then returned to his dental practice in Liverpool and club cricket with Neston, having satisfied himself that he could, indeed, play first-class cricket. What super fun it had all been! For their part, Lancashire officials had to appoint a new skipper and work out how to make a challenge for the title.

Grieves arrives *1949*

WRITERS INCLINED to be severely critical of Lancashire's performance in the 1949 season, when the side won only six games and finished 11th in the County Championship, should remember that pretty much the same side with the same captain shared the title with Surrey twelve months later. The change in fortunes – it really wasn't a transformation – may be explained by the dramatic improvement of a couple of bowlers, the avoidance of major injuries and the decision not to use the heavy roller in matches at Old Trafford. The lines between mediocrity and magnificence are sometimes very narrow. Such thoughts may have occurred to Lancashire supporters over 60 years ago, but it was probably little

comfort as they watched their side lose their first and last matches of the campaign and suffer three successive defeats to Warwickshire, Derbyshire and Middlesex in the middle of the season.

The reasons for Lancashire's poor showing in 1949 were fairly plain. A side containing a number of young and relatively inexperienced cricketers could not cope easily with injuries to their most seasoned warriors. Thus, when Washbrook pulled a leg muscle in the First Test against New Zealand and when Place's arm injury caused him to miss seven Championship games, their county felt the loss of their services very severely. Both men were among the six Lancashire cricketers to reach a thousand runs during the summer, but no one scored more than Jack Ikin's 1,318.

There were also deficiencies in the county's bowling attack. Not only was a satisfactory new-ball partner for Pollard not found, but it became plain that the 36-year-old Stakhanovite was finally running out of puff, albeit that he took his thousandth Championship wicket against Leicestershire at Blackpool. The underestimated Peter Greenwood led the county's end of season rankings with 69 dismissals, while Pollard bagged 68 and Bill Roberts, 50. Just above Roberts, however, was the 23-year-old Australian leg-spinner Ken Grieves, who had qualified by residence after coming to England in 1947 to keep goal for Bury and play cricket for Rawtenstall. Grieves, who had played for New South Wales in the Sheffield Shield, was undoubtedly the discovery of Lancashire's season and can be seen as one of the county's most important post-war recruits. Not only did he become only the fourth man to score a thousand runs in his debut season, but he quickly revealed himself to be a close catcher of rare ability. Even in a season when his side's fortunes were at their lowest ebb since 1936, Grieves took 29 catches. If one added the Australian's facility in this department to that of Ikin, who claimed 32 catches, and Geoff Edrich, who snaffled 13, it was

The newly-arrived Ken Grieves signs autographs for young Lancashire supporters.

clear that Lancashire had a predatory trio of close fielders to rival any in the country. All it needed was a couple of spin or slow-medium pace bowlers to find their very best form and the county would be a force in the land once again.

None of which was probably too much comfort to the new skipper, 23-year-old Nigel Howard, as he struggled with a team having the hardest season most of its members could remember. It had seemed plain to most Lancashire supporters that Washbrook should have been appointed, but the committee was not ready to appoint a professional captain, and for all his lordly gait, Washbrook was a professional to his marrow. So Howard, a fine batsman who might have developed into an even better one had he not been skipper, led the team. The new captain was suspected of listening too much to his father, who had only recently stepped down as club secretary, and also to Lancashire's autocratic chairman, the mighty T A Higson snr., The latter's death on August 3rd may have liberated Howard, albeit in a most unwelcome fashion. Some eight months later began a season which would have gladdened the old dictator's heart.

---

150 LANCASHIRE GREATS
80. Bob Berry

An orthodox left-arm slow bowler, Bob Berry utilised his diminutive stature (5ft 6in) to accentuate a full range of flight variations. He was unlucky only to have gained two Test caps, both in 1950 against the all-conquering West Indians. He made an impressive enough Test debut, taking nine wickets at Old Trafford and was selected for the tour to Australia in 1950/51 but only made a limited number of appearances. He played 93 matches for Lancashire, taking 259 wickets, ave 22.77. He took all ten wickets for Lancashire against Worcestershire at Blackpool in 1953 (10-102). That season he claimed 98 victims, his best seasonal haul. After losing his place in the Lancashire team, he moved to Worcestershire and played 94 matches for them before finishing his career at Derbyshire. He was capped by all three counties, the first player to achieve this feat. He was a good outfielder with a strong throw. When he retired he became a licensee and later married the widow of Malcolm Hilton. An enthusiastic and humorous character, he was appointed President of the Lancashire Players' Association.

Bowlers make hay as title is shared

1950

WHENEVER LANCASHIRE just fail to win the County Championship, there are no shortage of amateur meteorologists ready to argue that Mancunian rain is responsible for their side's misfortune; and on the two occasions since 1945 when the Old Trafford side has either shared or won the title there have been supporters of other counties eager to explain that the dice were loaded in favour of the Red Rose. In 2011 Lancashire played all their home games on outgrounds. "Foul!" cried the critics. In 1950 it was decided not to use the heavy roller at the team's home games and to limit watering. When that year's title was shared with Surrey, the finger was pointed at Old Trafford's officials and their decision to create bowler-friendly conditions. Even John Kay, writing in 1974, described the title success as having been achieved "without flair or dignity". So there.

To the disappointment of the dogmatists the truth is invariably more complex than they would wish. Lancashire's bowlers were undoubtedly helped by the pitches prepared at Old Trafford and elsewhere in 1950, and on no day was this more evident than 12th July when Sussex were defeated in a day, Peter Greenwood returning match figures of nine for 67 and Malcolm Hilton 11 for 50. Yet, as many writers have pointed out, nine of Lancashire's 16 victories in

1950 were achieved in away games. Moreover, Nigel Howard's men had to bat on the Old Trafford wickets too, and one of the architects of the win against Sussex was the redoubtable Geoff Edrich, who made 89 in his side's only innings.

It was only natural that when Lancashire's improvement was assessed in the autumn of 1950, the performances of Roy Tattersall and Malcolm Hilton should receive high praise. Slow left-armer Hilton took 125 wickets at 15.04 apiece, while Tattersall's 163 successes were achieved at a cost of just 12.19. The Bolton off-spinner enjoyed one of the summers of his life, probably, to some degree

because he was more than an off-spinner: imagine, if you will, a taller version of Derek Underwood, bowling right-arm and capable of getting the ball to bounce alarmingly as well as turn.

But Championships are not won by bowlers alone. Plenty of publicity was rightly given to Lancashire's close catchers in 1950. Ken Grieves took an astonishing 57 catches in Championship games, Edrich caught 35 and Jack Ikin, 30. All three fielders took more catches than the regular wicketkeeper Alf Barlow. Crouched in eager readiness as Tattersall or Hilton prepared to bowl, this trio didn't need to sledge opponents. Batsmen felt sufficiently intimidated by their very presence.

While the Lancashire attack was dominated by Tattersall and Hilton in 1950, it was not monopolised by it. Grieves took 51 wickets with his leg-spin and both Peter Greenwood and Bob Berry played valuable supporting roles as matches required. Even more

Roy Tattersall and Malcolm Hilton, the stars of Lancashire's shared Championship in 1950, flank the great Ernest Tyldesley.

LANCASHIRE—JOINT CHAMPIONS. 1950

Standing (left to right) : R. Tattersall, M. Hilton, P. Greenwood, A. Barlow, R. Berry, K. Grieves.
Seated : G. A. Edrich, W. Place, N. D. Howard (captain), C. Washbrook, J. T. Ikin. Inset : B. Statham

significantly for the future of the county's cricket, a replacement was finally found for Dick Pollard, who was dropped from the side in late May and who retired at the end of the season. If Lancashire members wept a little at the departure of a player with whom they could identify so closely, they also rejoiced when the many virtues of Brian Statham were revealed. The Gorton lad who made his debut against Kent on his 20th birthday bowled fast and accurately and revealed a capacity for hard work. Pollard had retired having taken 1,015 wickets for the county in a career which sandwiched the Second World War; Statham was to take 1,816, 36 of them in his first season of Championship matches. By the end of the summer the England selectors had begun to take notice. It was no surprise when he and Tattersall were flown out during the winter to join an Ashes tour party which already included Washbrook and Berry.

Rather contrary to cricketing lore, Lancashire's batsmen were the poor bloody infantry of 1950. Six of them made over a thousand runs in the Championship, but no one contributed more than Washbrook, who made 1,294. The competitive juices of players like Edrich and Grieves were probably stirred by the prospect of having to battle it

out on difficult wickets and, indeed, it was a summer when Lancashire's innings were full of hard-won forties and fifties. Howard's batsmen made only ten hundreds in the entire first-class season and the highest individual contribution was Edrich's 147 against Oxford University.

Given the many qualities that had been displayed by Howard and his players following the disappointment of 1949, it was certainly a bitter disappointment that the title was not won outright. It was not, however, any sort of injustice. Surrey were also a fine team, and under the gloriously intuitive and uncompromising leadership of Stuart Surridge they were to win the County Championship in seven of the next eight seasons. Like Lancashire, they enjoyed purple patches in 1950,

Brian Statham is congratulated by skipper Nigel Howard on his debut.

winning eight of their last nine games. The ninth match was against Howard's men in late August, when the Red Rose needed to take only four points from a drawn game to settle matters. However, Surridge bowled both Washbrook and Place in his first over and Peter May's 92 ensured that Surrey took a first-innings lead of 66. Lancashire spent their second innings making 203 for four off 119 overs, thus ensuring that their opponents could not win. That completed the Old Trafford side's programme and left Surrey needing to beat Leicestershire to take a share of the title. Despite some interruptions for rain, Surridge's men completed a ten-wicket victory upon which, so Wisden informed its readers, "enthusiastic scenes followed the game".

The mood was a trifle less euphoric in Manchester, but there was much for Howard and his players to be happy with as they settled into their varied close-season occupations. Plainly, Lancashire were a very good side and few of its members were near retirement. Surely to goodness, reasoned the mild optimists, it would not be long before an outright title returned to the club.

County Championship 1950

	P	W	L	D	Pts
Lancashire	28	16	2	10	220
Surrey	28	17	4	6	220
Yorkshire	28	14	2	10	200
Warwickshire	28	8	6	13	132
Derbyshire	28	8	9	9	124
Worcestershire	28	7	9	9	114
Gloucestershire	28	5	6	17	112
Somerset	28	8	8	10	112
Kent	28	6	12	8	108
Northamptonshire	28	6	4	15	104
Glamorgan	28	6	4	9	100
Hampshire	28	7	9	9	96
Sussex	28	5	11	11	92
Middlesex	28	5	12	8	84
Nottinghamshire	28	3	6	17	68
Leicestershire	28	3	13	11	64
Essex	28	4	12	11	60

Test calls take toll *1951*

LANCASHIRE BEGAN the 1951 season as if determined to establish their dominance before the trees had shed their blossom; they ended it a distant third in the table, meekly acknowledging the superiority of both Warwickshire and Yorkshire.

By some quirk of the fixture-makers' system, the campaign started with another visit to the Oval, where Howard's team had the very best of a draw against the joint champions. Yorkshire, too, were on the defensive at the conclusion of the first Roses match and when Surrey were beaten by nine wickets at Old Trafford, Statham taking five for 33 and four for 29, Lancashire supporters dared to hope that this would be another glorious summer. After all, the only thing that had changed since the previous summer, apart from the departure of Bill Roberts, was that young Statham had succeeded the venerable Pollard.

Well, not quite the only thing. The Old Trafford groundsman had been instructed to use the heavy roller once again, and while this no more fully explained Lancashire's comparative failure in 1951 than it had their success the previous year, it was a factor to be weighed in analysing both seasons. What was perhaps just as significant was that the England selectors had begun to notice the quality of Lancashire's cricket. Four players had been on the winter tour to Australia and Tattersall, Statham, Hilton and Ikin were all to receive Test calls in 1951. Again it is unwise to make too much of this factor in causing Lancashire's decline. After all, while three first-team players were on Test duty when Hampshire beat Lancashire at Portsmouth, five were absent at the Gentlemen v Players game when Washbrook led the side to an innings win in the return match at Liverpool less than a month later. Nevertheless, an indication of the impact of Test and other representative calls upon Lancashire's attack can be gauged from the fact that Roy Tattersall finished the season with 121 wickets but only 82 of those had been taken for Lancashire, 74 of them in the County Championship.

Supporters of Yorkshire's teams in the 1930s or 1960s and of Surrey in the 1950s will rightly point out that Test calls are, indeed, a test of the county, too. If so, Lancashire's squad – as it would be called in the 21st century – did not really pass that examination.

*Harry Makepeace leads a youthful Lancashire squad out to the practise nets.
1951 would be his final year as first-team coach.*

Howard's men won none of their last 12 games and their final place in the table was a fair reflection of their season.

It was also worth Lancashire supporters remembering that 13 counties finished below their favourites in 1951. Howard's team played some fine cricket in the first half of the summer and no individual innings was better than Washbrook's 103 on a drying pitch at Chesterfield. Edrich, ever the man for a fight, scored 77 in the second innings and Lancashire won by 15 runs, Hilton taking 11 wickets in the match. Indeed, the Oldham slow left-armer showed that his figures in 1950 had not been a fluke by bagging 112 Championship wickets at an average of 17.6.

There was one departure to report in 1951 and one piece of sad news with which the players had to come to terms. At the age of 70 Harry Makepeace finally retired as first team coach and was succeeded by Stan Worthington. Meanwhile, Bill Roberts's bid to make a living as a club professional with West Bromwich Dartmouth in the Birmingham League was cut short by the onset of cancer. After appearing to recover, he was readmitted to hospital in Bangor, where he died on 24th August. He was 36.

150 LANCASHIRE GREATS
82. Jack Ikin

Jack Ikin was born at Bignall End, Staffordshire, in 1918 and was an outstanding cricketer for Lancashire. He was a sound left-handed batsman who could open or bat lower down the order as well as a leg-break and googly bowler and a brilliant fielder close to the wicket. He made his debut for Lancashire in 1939 just before war broke out. His career with the county extended to 1957, covering 288 matches in which he scored 14,327 runs, ave. 28.79. He also took 419 catches in 365 first-class matches. A determined and courageous player, he played many brave innings in his 18 Test Matches, scoring 606 runs, ave.20.89. After leaving Lancashire he returned to Staffordshire, for whom he first played when he was 16 and in the same side as Sydney Barnes aged 61. He captained his native county until 1968. A very popular and charming man who was widely respected throughout the cricket world, in later years he gave much back to the game by coaching young cricketers. Whilst serving in the army during the World War Two he was in the siege of Tobruk. He died in 1984 aged 66.

Marner debuts at 16 *1952*

BY THE summer of 1952 Lancashire's place in English cricket's post-war hierarchy was about to become reasonably well-established. In the ten seasons between 1951 and 1960 the Old Trafford side finished in one of the top six positions on eight occasions and were twice runners-up. For most of the decade Lancashire were more or less among the élite, yet they rarely challenged Surrey for the top spot. Nigel Howard's fourth season in charge illustrated one reason why this was so: like the champions, Lancashire lost three games, but they won only 12 compared to Surrey's 20. As a result, Howard's men finished 68 points in arrears. It was the old story; they knew how to avoid defeat but not how to win.

In 1952 Lancashire's form was even more frustrating. How was it, asked Old Trafford's regular supporters, that a team could beat both Surrey and Warwickshire by an innings yet lose to Sussex, who finished 13th in the table, and Nottinghamshire, who were next to bottom? Neither of those defeats were the product of attacking captaincy which didn't quite work out. Lancashire lost fair and square.

Howard's team also took part in their share of close finishes in 1952. The game against Essex at Brentwood finished in a tie; Northamptonshire were beaten by two wickets when an overthrow allowed a second run to be scrambled off the last possible ball of the game; and last pair Frank Parr and Bob Berry batted out to secure a draw in the Roses match at Old Trafford.

The team itself had a relatively settled look. The five usual suspects, Edrich, Grieves, Ikin, Place and Washbrook, scored over a thousand runs, the latter despite being handicapped by a thumb injury. Nevertheless the Baron of Bridgnorth still scored

a memorable one-handed undefeated double-hundred against Somerset at Old Trafford. Alan Wharton and the Rochdale all-rounder Geoff Lomax offered the top order useful support.

Roy Tattersall was not required by England in 1952 and all his 146 first-class wickets were taken for Lancashire, 130 of them in the County Championship. He took 13 in the opening home game against Kent and proceeded to befuddle the majority of batsmen in England during the summer. His close fielders, to whom he felt a particular responsibility, were as alert as ever. Brian Statham, having taken 90 Championship wickets in 1951, now bagged a hundred for the first time in his career, this despite feeling the after-effects of a winter tour to India which also restricted Nigel Howard's appearances. Despite having his critics at Old Trafford – which Lancashire captain has not? – Howard had been skipper for the trip to the subcontinent.

Nigel Howard, who captained the MCC team to India 1951-52, chatting with DK Gaekwad (left) and N Choudhury (right) at the British Sportsmanship Club Luncheon given at the Savoy, London in April 1952.

This was an era when Lancashire had an embarrassment of spin bowling riches. Malcolm Hilton and Bob Berry were both high-class slow left-armers, yet they were so similar that it was nigh on impossible to play them in the same team alongside Tattersall. In 1952, Hilton played 18 first-class matches, taking 69 wickets, Berry 16, taking 36, yet the difference does not reflect the excellence of the Gorton spinner. Both men played a handful of Tests for England – it was the era of Tony Lock and Johnny Wardle – and some indication of Berry's accuracy can be gauged from the fact that he bowled 66 balls at Gloucestershire's batsmen without conceding a run in the first innings at Old Trafford. His final analysis read: 39-23-44-1. The choice between Berry and Hilton was not finally resolved until Berry moved to Worcestershire in 1955. He later played with distinction for Derbyshire and was the first man to be capped by three counties. Leaving Lancashire, however, was the last thing on Peter Marner's mind when, aged 16 years 150 days, he became the youngest man ever to represent Lancashire in a first-class match when he played in the game against Sussex at Hove.

150 LANCASHIRE GREATS

83. Geoff Edrich

Part of a strong Norfolk cricketing family, Geoff joined Lancashire with his older brother Eric after the war after suffering under the Japanese for over three years as a prisoner of war in Thailand. When he was released he weighed just six stones. A man of strong principles and incredible determination, he showed relentless courage when batting, scoring 1,000 runs in eight seasons with over 2,000 runs in 1952. He played in 322 matches for Lancashire, scoring 14,730 runs, ave 34.74, and 24 centuries. He was a magnificent slip-fielder and captained Lancashire when Cyril Washbrook was absent, never losing a match as captain. After coaching and captaining the second XI, he left to play league cricket and also to play for Cumberland. In 1962 he was appointed head groundsman at Cheltenham College ground, where he stayed until his retirement. It was a very moving moment when he attended a Former Players' Association function and received a long standing ovation as he took his seat. He earned respect from all who knew him with his steely courage and his warm and friendly smile.

All ten for Berry *1953*

Malcolm Hilton's place in the team was often taken by Bob Berry in 1953, but at least he had the consolation of being joined in the Lancashire squad by brother Jim, right. Jim, however, was to leave for Somerset at the end of the season.

THE FORMER Southampton FC manager Ted Bates used to say that one of the problems with a football club's directors and supporters was that they didn't realise that only one team could win the league. For eight years in the 1950s the dominant county in English cricket was Surrey; relatively rarely did other sides make a really significant challenge. For Lancashire followers, many of whom vividly remembered the club's five titles in nine years, this was difficult to stomach, yet it was a truth they had to accept.

In 1953, Stuart Surridge's team made light of the loss of Alec Bedser, Jim Laker, Tony Lock and Peter May to England's cause and retained their title, finishing 16 points clear of Sussex and 28 ahead of Lancashire. This represented an improvement for Nigel Howard's side, although it was a wet summer and the large number of drawn games tended to compress the points differences between the teams.

The same quintet of Lancashire batsmen scored over a thousand runs in the County Championship, although a mere 109 runs separated Place (1,019), the lowest of the five, from Grieves (1,128), the heaviest. Eight complete days were lost to the weather at Old Trafford and the top order's opportunities to make tall scores were further restricted by the number of wet pitches

they encountered. It was another summer when batsmen capable of grafting three hours for 60 were prized above rubies; in all first-class games Lancashire's cricketers scored just nine centuries. In Northamptonshire's one-wicket defeat of Howard's team at Old Trafford, their first victory in matches between the sides since 1914, George Tribe's innings of 73 and 37 were vital to the outcome.

It was, therefore, something of a bowler's summer and it was Bob Berry's summer in particular. While Roy Tattersall collected 122 wickets and Brian Statham 87, Berry profited from the opportunities he was given in preference to Malcolm Hilton to bamboozle 92 batsmen in the Championship. His best day was at Blackpool on July 31 when he became the first bowler since Johnny Briggs to take all ten wickets in an innings. Berry's 10 for 102 against Worcestershire captured a few headlines, but he also claimed 13 wickets in a two-day defeat of Somerset at Old Trafford and had at least five wickets in an innings on seven other occasions in first-class matches during the summer. As ever, he and Tattersall were superbly supported by Grieves, Ikin and Edrich, who took 110 catches between them in first-class games, 95 in the Championship.

Rarely were Lancashire's fielders more usefully occupied than on 6th June, when a combination of Roy Tattersall's bowling and a newly-laid pitch at Bath helped the visitors to an innings-and-24-run victory over Somerset, the entire game being completed before six o'clock on the first day. Tattersall took 13 wickets for 69 and thereby ruined Bertie Buse's benefit match. It is doubtful whether any bowler could have

been more regretful at his success than this deeply humane cricketer. However, the game also featured a vital contribution by Peter Marner, who whacked four huge sixes in his innings of 44.

At the end of the season Nigel Howard resigned the captaincy and retired from the first-class game at the age of 28. He had led the side capably for five seasons and had succeeded in promoting a number of younger players when more cautious skippers might have insisted on their serving a longer apprenticeship. Some people criticised his lack of flair, but here he suffered when compared to Stuart Surridge. One might argue that 15 other county captains were in a similar predicament.

150 LANCASHIRE GREATS
84. Roy Tattersall

Roy Tattersall began his career with Lancashire at the age of 25 as a seam bowler. After two seasons he was persuaded to try off-spin and was an immediate success, taking 193 wickets, ave. 13.59, to put him at the top of the national averages. He was 6ft 3in, slim and with a high action; his changes in flight and direction made him a difficult proposition for batsmen. He played in 16 Tests, taking 58 wickets at an ave. of 26.08 with a best return of 7-52 against South Africa at Lord's in 1951. In 277 matches for Lancashire he took 1,168 wickets, ave. 17.39, including 9-40 against Notts at Old Trafford, which included a hat-trick and four wickets in five balls. He was in and out of the Lancashire side at the end of the 1950s and this was a sad and unaccountable end to a most distinguished career. He was a superb bowler, courteous, always ready to help a younger player and someone who was always willing to bowl, even to the best batsman. He retired to Kidderminster where he was professional for many years and he died in 2012.

Damp squib of a season

1954

THE CONSENSUS among cricket historians seems to be that Lancashire should have appointed Cyril Washbrook captain in 1949 and given Nigel Howard the job in 1954. In that way, so the argument runs, Howard would have been able to learn from the side's most experienced professional for five years and would therefore have been better equipped to skipper the side when his time came. This view presupposes that Howard would have been willing to put his career in the family textile business on hold in 1954 and that Washbrook would have been content to give the job up at that time.

But when the counterfactuals have been put to one side, no one seriously doubts that the 39-year-old Washbrook was the right appointment in 1954. "Lancashire had no alternative… and would have looked silly if they had tried to find one," wrote Brian Bearshaw in the club's official history. Really? Given the gulf in temperament that developed between the club's first professional captain and many of the younger players on the staff during his six seasons in charge, it might have been worth exploring the credentials of Geoff Edrich, but that notion is perhaps best left for a rainy day in the press box or pavilion.

Cyril Washbrook was finally appointed captain in 1954, but it presaged more than a decade of internal strife at Old Trafford.

What is beyond debate is that the 1954 cricket season was very wet indeed. Three of Lancashire's matches were abandoned without a ball bowled and in four others there was insufficient time for even first-innings points to be decided. All counties were affected by the wretched weather, of course, but none so badly as Lancashire, who lost 19 full days' cricket, eleven of them at Old Trafford.

Of the county's 28 County Championship fixtures, 16 were drawn and, despite losing only three games, Lancashire finished a comparatively lowly tenth in the final table. The Red Rose batsmen had one of their worst seasons on record, with only Alan Wharton (1144) and Washbrook (1046) scoring over a thousand runs. Edrich gritted his way to 959 runs in typical fashion, but others had a desperate time, Winston Place making 697 runs in 33 innings at an average of 21.78 and Ken Grieves 376 in 23 visits to the crease at an average of 17.90. Jack Ikin's appearances were restricted by the ill-health which was to blight his later career. "In batting… fighting spirit was conspicuous mainly by its absence… with the exceptions of Washbrook and Wharton," concluded the 1955 Wisden.

Few Lancashire cricketers enjoyed the 1954 season very much, but the bowlers had a better time of it. Roy Tattersall again took a hundred Championship wickets, while Malcolm Hilton collected 87 and Brian Statham, 73. By now, Statham was clearly one of the very best bowlers in England, but his county still searched in vain for a fast bowler with whom he could share the new ball.

Perhaps the most encouraging aspect of the year was the emergence of a clutch of young players, all of whom showed signs of promise. Leg-spinner Tommy Greenhough had made his debut in 1951 and he managed to take 27 wickets, even on 1953's wet pitches. Two 18-year-old batsmen, Bob Barber and Geoff Pullar, both of whom were to take important roles in Lancashire cricket, made their first-class debuts in 1954. The 19-year-old Oldham all-rounder Jack Dyson made his bow against Glamorgan at Swansea. Peter Marner, however, had sustained a serious injury when playing football and missed the entire season. One or two of his colleagues may have commented that he hadn't missed much.

150 LANCASHIRE GREATS
85. Alan Wharton

Alan Wharton was a product of the Lancashire Leagues who served in the Navy during the war, joining Lancashire in 1946 and winning his county cap in that first season aged 23. He also played rugby league for Salford. He played 15 seasons for the county, scoring nearly 18,000 runs, ave. 33.55, with 25 centuries. A forceful left-handed batsman and right-arm medium pace bowler, he was also a very good fielder. He scored over 1,000 runs in a season nine times, including 2,157 in 1959. He played just one Test for England in 1949. Along with Jack Dyson, he achieved the only Championship win ever completed without losing a wicket. In his late 30s he was asked to captain the second XI but refused and moved to Leicestershire for three years, scoring a further 3,000 runs. He played for Colne after he retired and he was also a keen golfer. He was the longest serving magistrate in the country and was held in high regard by all who knew him.

Bond makes quiet debut

1955

FOR ALL that the weather was a huge improvement on the previous year's offering, few Lancashire players or supporters remembered the 1955 season with particular fondness. The drier conditions enabled four more matches to be won, but six more were lost and Lancashire finished ninth in the table. The county accumulated less than half the points amassed by champions Surrey.

Brian Statham, who was widely regarded as the best new-ball bowler in the country by the mid-1950s, hit a career best 62 with the bat in 1955.

The seam bowling was a particular problem. Test calls and injury restricted Brian Statham to only 14 County Championship appearances, and even when Statham was available, he lacked a regular new-ball partner. A number of bowlers were tried in the role, including Fred Goodwin, Ken Standring and Fred Moore, and 20-year-old Standring enjoyed a moment of fame in the Roses match at Old Trafford when he bowled Len Hutton for two. Yet the game itself was lost and the end of season first-class statistics revealed that seven Lancashire bowlers, albeit not all of them seamers, had taken between ten and 26 wickets. Statham himself finished sixth in the national list, but only 79 of his 108 wickets were taken for Lancashire and the

perceived dearth of high quality fast bowlers remained. It did not go unnoticed that the county had allowed Farnworth-born Frank Tyson to play just one second team game for Lancashire in 1949 before apparently deciding that he was injury-prone.

Fortunately, Washbrook still had his proven spinners to call on, although it still seems slightly misleading to categorise Roy Tattersall so simply. This gangling master of pace and cut, as well as turn, bowled over a thousand overs in the County Championship and took 105 wickets, while Malcolm Hilton dismissed 91 batsmen. Together with Statham, these two bowlers were the heart of the Lancashire attack. Curiously, the trio also had days to remember with the bat in 1955: Tattersall shared a last-wicket partnership of 73 with Washbrook, holding up an end while the skipper completed his 170 against Worcestershire at Old Trafford; Statham hit 62 in 31 minutes against Leicestershire and then took four for 34 as his side achieved a win by an innings and 59 runs; and Hilton hit the only century of his first-class career, making exactly 100 not out in a drawn match at Northampton.

Most of Lancashire's batsmen enjoyed a better season. Four players, Washbrook, Wharton, Grieves and Ikin scored over a thousand runs in the County Championship, but Edrich only managed 916 in 40 innings. The most noticeable slump in form was experienced by 40-year-old Winston Place, who made just 179 runs in 14 innings and retired from first-class cricket at the end of the season. Rather like Len Hopwood and Jack Iddon, Place's contribution to his county's cricket has been somewhat overlooked in recent years. One of the most technically accomplished batsmen in the post-war period, his quietly-accomplished method enabled him to deal with the best opening attacks in the country and it is revealing that most of his contemporaries considered him a better player than Washbrook on a bad wicket. Another player who lost six

of his best summers to the war, Place retired to his newsagent's shop secure in the knowledge that he had rendered his county yeoman service.

Other Lancashire batsmen were approaching the end of their careers, too. The youngest member of the top order in May's Roses match was Edrich, who was 36. Fortunately, Grieves and Wharton were still in their prime and Jack Dyson showed in 1955 that he was developing into a useful batsman. However, Pullar and Barber made only a dozen appearances between them; their time had not yet come, and neither had that of a 23-year-old batsman from Kearsley who made his debut against Surrey at Old Trafford in August. His name was Bond... Jack Bond.

Dyson and Wharton make history

1956

Jack Dyson pictured in his Manchester City kit. He had an outstanding 1956, with an FA Cup-winners medal followed by 1,000 runs in a season for the only time in his career, which helped Lancashire to second place in the County Championship.

LANCASHIRE'S FAILURE to win the County Championship outright for 77 years between 1934 and 2011 prompted private grief in the county itself and public mockery almost everywhere else. Yet it could be argued that the situation was even more embarrassing: not only did a succession of Old Trafford teams fail to win English cricket's major domestic prize; for long periods they did not even get particularly close to doing so. In 46 domestic seasons up to 1986 Lancashire shared the title once and finished as runners-up only in 1956 and 1960. And what exasperated supporters even more was that the teams led by Cyril Washbrook and Bob Barber had good opportunities to win the title in those years, only to falter in the final month or so of the campaign.

By the end of July 1956 Lancashire were level on points with Surrey at the top of the table, although Stuart Surridge's team had a game in hand. However, the decision had been taken to drop Roy Tattersall for the match against Nottinghamshire on 18th July and he was to remain out of favour for seven County Championship games. Victories against Gloucestershire and Hampshire had tended to justify the non-selection of

Tattersall, but only one of the next four matches was won and by the time Lancashire went to the Oval to play Surrey in the penultimate game of the season, they needed to beat the champions and then win their last match while hoping that Surridge's team of tough cricketers won none of their final three fixtures. As it turned out, rain prevented any play on the last two days of the game at the Oval, thus enabling Surrey to secure an unprecedented fifth title in succession.

Tattersall's omission "seemed a mistake" ventured the 1957 Wisden; the circumstances in which he was left out, both in 1956 and later seasons, were "mystifying" suggested Robert Brooke and David Goodyear 35 years later. The decision also caused a heap of contemporary public comment. "Have you been a bad lad?" Tattersall was asked in the streets of Manchester. As if….

What was beyond serious dispute in 1956 was that Lancashire's cricket showed a considerable improvement on the mediocrity on offer in the previous two seasons. Partly this was due to the development of the younger players on the staff. Greenhough, who, at 24-years-old, could still be classed an apprentice spinner, took 62 wickets and was one of the four Lancashire bowlers in the top 14 places in the national averages. (Hilton (158 wickets), Tattersall (117) and Statham (91) were in three of the top eight spots.) Geoff Pullar went a long way towards establishing himself in the first team and his 642 Championship runs included a maiden

century against Derbyshire at Buxton. Jack Dyson scored over a thousand first-class runs. Roy Collins, a hard-hitting left-handed batsman and a useful off-spinner, played 22 first-class games and was highly rated by as good a judge as Edrich. The experienced cricketers did their bit too. Alan Wharton's 1,389 runs in the Championship included three centuries and Ken Grieves made 1,213 runs in his benefit year without reaching three figures once. Washbrook, his value as a batsman never in doubt, added 861 runs in 27 innings and was second only to Wharton in the county's averages.

These personal achievements combined to produce some notable victories. In May, Grieves scored fifties in each innings and Tattersall returned match figures of 14-90 as Yorkshire were beaten by 153 runs at Headingley. It was only Lancashire's second victory in a Roses match since the war and you would have got decent odds on Tattersall not being selected for the return game. Less than two months later Edrich's side became the first team to win a first-class match without losing a wicket when they beat Leicestershire by ten wickets at Old Trafford. After bowling out the visitors for 108, the stand-in skipper then considered both the pitch conditions and the weather forecast before declaring his side first innings on 166 for no wicket. Leicestershire were dismissed for only 14 runs more than they had managed in their first effort leaving Wharton and Dyson to knock off the 66 runs needed to complete the match.

150 LANCASHIRE GREATS
87. Malcolm Hilton

At the age of only 19 Malcolm Hilton dismissed the mighty Don Bradman twice, a feat which gained him national prominence. A slim, fair-haired figure, Hilton bowled left-arm spin at a brisk pace. He relied on turn rather than variety of pace and on uncovered pitches he was very effective. In 1950 he took 135 wickets at 16.79 and played in his first of four Test matches. In India he had the unusual experience of opening the English attack with Lancashire teammate Roy Tattersall and took 11 wickets at 17 but never played for England again. In 1956 he took 158 wickets at less than 14. His career best in an innings was 8-39 and in a match 14-88 against Somerset at Weston-super-Mare. He took 926 wickets, ave. 18.80, for Lancashire and over 1,000 in total in first-class cricket. He was an outstanding fielder and once hit a century batting at no.9 at Northampton. He was selected as one of Wisden's Five Cricketers of the Year in 1957. He captained the second XI in his last two years and retired at the age of 33. With a distinctive sense of humour and ready smile, he had a great ability to perform Lancashire monologues.

But for all Lancashire's excellence in 1956, there were fault lines appearing in the team. More specifically, there was a gulf developing between the captain and many of his players. Although no one doubted Washbrook's batsmanship, or his commitment to his county's cricket, players were increasingly questioning his judgement – and they were beginning to do so openly. In Stephen Chalke's excellent book _A Long Half Hour_ he tells how Washbrook planned to leave Edrich out of the team for the final game of the season against Sussex at Hove. "If you leave Geoff out," said one senior player, "you'll be left with ten because I won't be playing." The comment also reveals the respect in which Edrich was held by his colleagues. In the appointed captain's absence he had led the side to six wins and four draws. Washbrook's courage and his achievements in the game could not be disputed; they had been epitomised only that summer by the 98 he had made against Australia when recalled to the England team. Yet the truth remained that Lancashire's first team captain was growing out of touch with many of his players.

Jack Dyson wasn't the only Lancashire player with a footballing pedigree. Fred Goodwin, who played 11 first-class matches for the county in 1955 and 1956, was a half-back for Manchester United and was part of the squad that won the League Championship in 1956. He also appeared in the 1958 FA Cup final. Australian Ken Grieves, pictured above, who was Lancashire's youngest ever beneficiary in 1956 at the age of 30, played in goal for Bolton Wanderers and several other North West football clubs.

Laker stuns cricket world at Old Trafford

JIM LAKER created history on July 31, 1956 when he took 19 wickets in the Test match at Old Trafford as England took an unassailable 2-1 lead in the summer's Ashes series. The Surrey bowler's match figures of 19-90, made up of hauls of 9-37 and 10-53, remain the best return by anyone in the history of first-class cricket.

In fact, only two other players have taken 18 wickets in a first-class match, and Indian Anil Kumble is the only other player to have taken ten wickets in a Test innings, which he did against Pakistan in 1999. Amazingly, Laker had taken 10-88 for Surrey in a tour match against the Australians at the Oval approximately two and a half months earlier.

There was controversy over the state of the Old Trafford pitch, which the Australians believed was deliberately underprepared

to suit spin. But England left-arm spinner Tony Lock only took 1-106 from 71.4 overs in the match to suggest it wasn't an obvious turner. England's 459 all out, which included centuries for opener Peter Richardson and number three David Sheppard, was followed by a steady start to Australia's reply as their openers put on 48 for the first wicket to take them to the cusp of tea on day two in reasonable health. But England captain Peter May opted to switch his spinners around, and that was when Laker ripped through the visitors from the Stretford End as they capitulated for 84 all out.

Heavy rain meant only 45 minutes play was possible on day three (Saturday) before more inclement weather on Sunday's rest day and Monday's fourth day prevented lengthy play. Going into Tuesday's fifth day, Australia were 84-2 and had to survive on a pitch which had changed significantly. Australia opener Colin McDonald said of the match: "It started on sand and it finished up on mud."

Australia collapsed again, although it was not quite as obvious as the first innings. This time they went from 114-2 to 205 all out, with England winning by an innings and 170 runs. The momentous moment for Laker came when he trapped number eleven batsman Len Maddocks lbw, and he said: "Odd as it may seem now, I did not even consider the possibility of taking all 10 wickets. How could I when Tony was fizzing the ball through against nine, ten and jack with venomous lift and spin."

The Australians accused England of doctoring the Old Trafford pitch to suit the bowling of the Surrey spin twins Jim Laker and Tony Lock, but a more significant factor was the heavy rain on the Saturday of the Test, left, which rendered the uncovered pitch almost unplayable.

Career best for Statham *1957*

BY THE summer of 1957 the excellence of Brian Statham was almost taken for granted, yet it never failed to amaze. Since announcing himself to English cricket followers in 1950 by taking five for 18 against Somerset at Bath and then five for 52 against Yorkshire at Old Trafford barely a month later, he had been an automatic selection for the Lancashire team when fit and he had already taken 110 Test wickets for England.

Statham's strengths as a fast bowler and his virtues as a man have been carefully chronicled by the game's essayists. If you have a bad word to say about him, there must be something wrong with you. He was as much a part of the Manchester scene as rain and a decent pint of mild at Tommy Ducks. Cyril Washbrook was unstinting in his praise, commenting that Statham

Jack Ikin's long and successful career at Old Trafford came to an end in 1957.

"carried the Lancashire attack for years and every other Lancashire bowler ought to have been grateful for his presence in the team."

In the first month of the 1957 season Statham excelled himself, taking 37 wickets in five matches. Lancashire won all these games and Statham collected what were to remain career-best figures when he took 15 wickets for 90 (eight for 34 and seven for 55) against Warwickshire at Coventry. The impact of the fast bowler's absence, often on England duty, can be gauged from the fact that Washbrook's side won only five of their remaining 23 games and finished sixth in the final table. No one pretended to be satisfied with it.

Statham took exactly 100 wickets in 21 Championship games in 1957 and Roy Tattersall, an ever-present in the side that summer, collected 122. However, while Tommy Greenhough remained a useful member of the attack, Malcolm Hilton had a poor season by his standards, taking 82 fewer wickets than in 1956 and finishing the campaign with 46 dismissals at 21.17 runs apiece.

The composition of Lancashire's top order underwent significant change at various stages of the 1957 season. Having been entrusted with the coaching and captaincy of the second team, Geoff Edrich played only ten first-class games, and Jack Ikin, his later career cursed by ill-health, decided to retire from first-class cricket at the end of the summer. The 39-year-old signed off by scoring 1,074 Championship runs, second only to Wharton (1,421), in the autumn list. Moreover, Ikin's first-class figures for Lancashire, 14,327 runs, 278 wickets and 329 catches, tell of a career characterised by excellence. As a cricketer, he was quietly loved for his graceful batting, his lightning catches close to the wicket and his understated devotion to the cause. Ikin's retirement left Washbrook as the only survivor of the pre-war team.

There were, however, fresh talents to applaud. Geoff Pullar became a first team

regular, scoring 814 Championship runs and hitting a couple of centuries. A lot of compliments also came the way of Jack Bond, more, perhaps, than his 446 runs in 19 matches would seem to warrant until one observed the enterprise of his six first-class fifties and the excellence of the 25-year-old's fielding.

In a way, then, 1957 was a summer in which the team's modest achievement was overshadowed by individual accomplishment. After their side's excellent start, Lancashire supporters had to take satisfaction from the scrambled draw in the first Roses match and the fact that the bowlers had Yorkshire very much on the defensive in the second game. Washbrook's players were probably pleased that a £70,000 redevelopment would see new dressing rooms and dining rooms built by the following summer, but neither cricketers nor spectators could be happy that the centenary of cricket at Old Trafford was celebrated with nothing more than a match against MCC and a dinner at the Manchester Town Hall.

150 LANCASHIRE GREATS
88. Brian Statham CBE

"If my son became a professional cricketer, I hope he would be like Brian Statham." The words are Colin Cowdrey's but sum up the affection and respect 'George', as he was known, is held in. He took more wickets (1,816) than any other Lancashire player. He played in 70 Tests and took 252 wickets at 24.84. An extremely accurate and skilful fast bowler, Brian, being lithe and wiry, had a beautiful rhythmic action with a nagging and persistent accuracy with the ball. He formed a lethal new ball partnership with both Frank Tyson and Fred Trueman at Test level but missed a regular partner with Lancashire until Ken Higgs came along. He took 100 wickets in a season 13 times and five or more wickets in an innings 123 times in a career spanning 19 seasons. His final total was 2,260 first-class wickets. He captained Lancashire for three seasons and was awarded the CBE by the Queen for his services to cricket. He served on the Lancashire committee for many years and was President in 1997-98.

Action from the 1957 Roses match at Old Trafford.

Low scores dominate soaking wet summer

1958

LANCASHIRE'S CRICKET showed no great improvement in the wet summer of 1958, but the development of a new, young team gathered a little pace. The most important arrival was that of Ken Higgs, a 21-year-old seamer from Stoke-on-Trent, who at last provided Brian Statham with the type of support he had needed for many seasons. That Higgs did not possess great pace through the air barely mattered; his pace off the wicket and the movement he extracted from most pitches were enough. He took 62 wickets in 19 Championship appearances – he also amassed 62 runs in 21 innings! – and was a very good catcher close to the wicket. Thus, just as Lancashire had bidden its farewells to Bignall End's Jack Ikin, another cricketer from Staffordshire had arrived, ready to give the Red Rose over a decade's service.

However, for much of his first summer Higgs had an excellent view of rain falling at Old Trafford and elsewhere. Thirteen full days of County Championship cricket were lost and the matches against Sussex and Kent at Liverpool and Manchester were washed out completely. On 22nd August a five-hour storm left Lancashire's home ground under more than a foot of water.

Playing on rain-affected pitches hardly seemed likely to boost the confidence of young batsmen, although the old professionals would argue that such experiences were vital to their development. In fact, it was the freshmen and the sophomores in Lancashire's top order who coped best with the conditions. Peter Marner, never one to fret much about the wicket when there was a ball to be dispatched into the next county at an alarming velocity, scored over a thousand runs, as did Geoff Pullar. Grieves and Wharton struggled rather. Washbrook managed 860 runs in his 39 innings, 24 more than the very classy left-hander Bob Barber, who made one of only four first-class centuries scored by Lancashire batsmen in 1958. Pullar made two and Marner bludgeoned the other.

There were many days in 1958 when batsmen struggled and bowlers licked their lips. The most humiliating experience for Lancashire's cricketers was being dismissed by Surrey for a mere 27 in the second innings of Alan Wharton's benefit match, but the game against Somerset at Weston-super-Mare saw 40 wickets fall for 385 runs on a rain-affected wicket. Roy Tattersall took ten wickets, but his fellow off-spinner Brian Langford bagged 15 as Washbrook's men were rolled over for 89 and 59.

There were also occasions when runs came from unexpected sources and the Red Rose attack was in the ascendant. While Lancashire supporters were not happy with their side's seventh place in the final Championship table, they hugely enjoyed the home game against Leicestershire when

The above sign had become a familiar sight at Old Trafford in the 1950s.

Tattersall and the ever-loyal wicketkeeper Alan Wilson combined in a last-wicket stand of 105, Tattersall making 58, his only first-class fifty, and Wilson scaling a Himalayan batting peak with 37 not out. The spectators' enjoyment was completed when Statham took seven for 44 to complete an innings win and finish with match-figures of 13 for 64.

But there may well have been times in 1958 when the 43-year-old Cyril Washbrook looked round the Old Trafford dressing-room and wondered what he was doing there. By now the skipper was a decade older than anyone else in the first team except Wharton and Wilson and his role at the club had been transformed from the immediate post-war era when he was the hero of Manchester schoolboys playing cricket in the city's parks. There are team photographs in the late 1950s when Washbrook looks like a housemaster skippering the boys' team in the Founder's Day match.

150 LANCASHIRE GREATS
89. Peter Marner

Peter Marner was the youngest player to represent Lancashire at only 16 years and five months when he made his debut at Hove in 1952. He went on to make 236 first-class appearances and scored 10,312 runs, ave. 29.21. A thick-set and powerful middle order right-handed batsman, he was one of the hardest hitters of the ball in the game and was a pugnacious batsman, scoring quickly in all forms of cricket. National Service interrupted his career and then on his return he suffered a serious knee injury playing rugby for Broughton Park. He recovered to become an exciting and entertaining player. He was the first player to win a man-of-the-match award in the Gillette Cup, scoring the first century and taking three wickets in the first ever game against Leicestershire. During that game he hit one of the biggest hits seen on the ground, over the stand into what is now the Indoor School. He was not always respectful of authority and after 13 years with Lancashire he was released and joined Leicestershire, playing over 165 matches for them. He retired at the age of 34 and played league cricket for Todmorden. A gifted all-round sportsman, he played centre for Oldham and turned down offers from many top rugby league clubs.

Washbrook retires *1959*

CYRIL WASHBROOK made his first-class debut for Lancashire some four months after Adolf Hitler had been appointed Chancellor of Germany. By the time he had completed his final game for the county, West Germany was taking a full part in the development of a European Economic Community designed to facilitate co-operation and harmony on the continent. In 21 seasons – six summers were lost to the war – Washbrook played 500 first-class matches for Lancashire, scoring 27,863 runs and taking 182 catches. If opinions remain divided on his qualities as a captain, no one disputes his excellence as a batsman. When Lancashire members while away their winter evenings selecting an all-time eleven to take on Yorkshire in a celestial Roses match, Washbrook's name is often one of the first on the team sheet. After all, who would want to tell Cyril he wasn't quite good enough?

The last few years or so of Washbrook's captaincy had not been an untrammelled idyll, but he could still leave the job in September 1959 reassured by clear indications that his beloved county's fortunes were improving. True, a rise from seventh to fifth place in the County Championship scarcely counts as a major renaissance – Washbrook could remember what it was like to win the title – but the batting of Geoff Pullar, the bowling of Tommy Greenhough and the wicketkeeping of the new man Geoff Clayton – 59 victims in his first season – could encourage hopes that Lancashire might soon make a challenge for domestic cricket's only honour. More significant than personal achievements was the fact that Lancashire had finished just 20 points behind champions Yorkshire in a tightly-packed top half of the table. Victories against the new title-holders, Warwickshire, Gloucestershire and Surrey (two ten-wicket wins, if you please) had been deeply encouraging for the loyalists at Old Trafford.

It had been a good season in which to bow out. Weeks of unbroken sunshine had given batsmen every reason to get out of bed in the morning and virtually no one in the country had taken greater advantage of the conditions than Geoff Pullar. The stylish Swinton left-hander scored 2,647 first-class runs in all matches in 1959, a tally which included eight centuries. Three of Pullar's hundreds were made against Yorkshire, two in the Roses matches and one for the Rest against the Champion County. In addition, the Lancashire opener had made his Test debut against India and scored 131 at Old Trafford in only his second innings at the top level.

Both Alan Wharton and Ken Grieves enjoyed a return to form in 1959. Wharton racked up 2,064 runs in the Championship and Grieves piled up 1,691 (2,253 in all first-class games). The latter batsman's three hundreds included 142 against Worcestershire when Lancashire visited Southport and Birkdale CC's Trafalgar Road ground for the first time. Grieves cleared the smallish boundaries on six occasions.

Statham, Higgs and Greenhough all took over a hundred first-class wickets in 1959, but none of the trio could reach three figures in the Championship. Statham's 97 wickets were taken in just 19 matches and his overall total of 139 dismissals at 15.01 runs apiece left him top of the national averages. But the

Geoff Clayton snares another victim. He made his debut in 1959 and capped a fine season with a club record nine dismissals in the match away at Gloucestershire.

year brought only deep disappointment and frustration for Roy Tattersall and Malcolm Hilton, both of whom lost form. Tattersall played the one Championship match and took five wickets against Worcestershire at Southport; Hilton claimed eight successes in five appearances. In 1961 the bowlers who, with Statham, had carried the Lancashire attack for most of the previous decade were granted a joint-benefit. Did they really not deserve one each?

Washbrook, meanwhile, retired with a testimonial of £1,502, a life-membership at Old Trafford and, later, a place on the Lancashire committee. Few supporters begrudged him any of it, but the more thoughtful ones might have pondered the contrasting fortunes of professional cricketers in the post-war era.

150 LANCASHIRE GREATS
90. Geoff Pullar

Geoff Pullar was a tall left-handed batsman who had a distinguished Test career. He played in 312 matches for Lancashire, scoring 16,853 with 32 centuries. He scored 1,000 runs in a season nine times (passing 2,000 once), topping the Lancashire averages in six of these seasons. In 1959 he was selected to play for England as an opener because of his temperament and sound defensive technique. In his second Test match against India he became the first Lancashire cricketer to score a Test century at Old Trafford. He played in 28 Tests, scoring 1,974 runs, ave. 43.86, with four centuries. He made his career best 175 against South Africa at the Oval in 1960, sharing in a first-wicket partnership of 290 with Colin Cowdrey. A knee injury ended his Test career and 'Noddy', as he was affectionately known, moved to Gloucestershire for two years in 1969. A warm, honest, friendly man, generous in his praise for good cricket, he is President of the Lancashire Former Players' Association.

Youthful Barber leads Lancashire to second

1960

WHEN CYRIL Washbrook announced that he was going to retire at the end of the 1959 season there was no shortage of suitable candidates to replace him. Geoff Edrich, Alan Wharton or Ken Grieves would all have done a decent job. Edrich's credentials seemed particularly strong: as second team skipper in 1958 he had prepared many players for the first-class game. The young cricketers liked and respected him. But Edrich was dismissed in 1959 when he refused to name the players who had engaged in a daft hotel prank during an away game in Birmingham.

The claims of Wharton and Grieves were also overlooked, the committee preferring instead to revert to appointing an amateur, namely the 24-year-old Cambridge graduate Bob Barber. Now Barber's cricket had many qualities: he was a very good batsman, a fine fielder and a useful leg-spin bowler. Yet the committee managed to handicap his chances of making a success of the job by insisting that he should travel separately from his team and stay in a different hotel on away trips. He met the players in the dressing room and on the field. Three years before the distinction between amateur and professional was abolished, Lancashire returned to a policy reminiscent of the 1930s. Given the strong characters among the county's professionals, it seemed

equivalent to the committee lighting the blue touch paper and retiring to the library for a glass of Dows and a Montecristo.

Yet those who expected immediate mutiny in the ranks were confounded. For most of the season Lancashire's cricketers were united by the badge on their caps and played some outstanding cricket. Going into the last six matches of the season Barber's team held a comfortable lead over Yorkshire. Supporters dared to hope. At which point, to adopt a Boltonian idiom, the wheels fell off big style. Four of the last six matches were lost and two drawn. Yorkshire won the title and Lancashire were left struggling to finish runners-up.

The resentments that had been building up all summer finally boiled over and the season ended in what John Kay described as something akin to "open warfare between the players and their captain". Jack Dyson was sacked for "a serious breach of discipline and an act of insubordination and insolence to the captain." Alan Wharton refused an offer to captain the second team and joined Leicestershire instead. Thus, Lancashire lost two of their best batting all-rounders. The committee was divided. It was no way to run a sweet shop.

The acrimony tended to obscure the memory of the good cricket played by Lancashire for much of the season. Yorkshire had been defeated in both Roses matches for the first time since 1893, the second victory being a tense two-wicket affair when Dyson edged Fred Trueman's last ball of the match to the boundary. Grieves, Marner, Barber, Wharton and Pullar had all scored over a thousand Championship runs, Pullar in only 21 matches after injuring his wrist playing for England. Greenhough and Higgs had both taken over a hundred wickets and Statham had bagged 97 in just 19 Championship games. Yet again the England fast bowler topped the national averages with 135 wickets at 12.31 apiece.

The year ended with Lancashire in the doldrums. Unable to support his family on the money the county were paying him, Roy Tattersall left Lancashire at the end of the season. Malcolm Hilton followed in 1961 after skippering the second team for two years. He was 33. It was true that Barber had not helped himself by publicly criticising Colin Cowdrey after Lancashire's match against Kent had meandered to a draw. The county's committee had publicly disassociated itself from their skipper's remarks on that occasion but they might have done better to consider why a team packed with talented cricketers was falling apart.

The old and the new: The retiring Lancashire great Cyril Washbrook welcomes the 16-year-old Harry Pilling to Old Trafford.

Cracks begin to show *1961*

THE SUPPORTERS who expected Lancashire to have a poor season in 1961 were guilty of nothing more than optimism. Barber's team, insofar as it can be labelled as such, won only nine of their 32 County Championship matches and finished an unprecedented 13th in the final table. At the end of the season the committee issued a statement saying that the responsibilities of captaincy and a disinclination to put himself on to bowl were holding up Barber's development as an England cricketer. They would, therefore, not be inviting the 26-year-old to skipper the team in 1961.

But, here's the thing. If you look at the statistics for Lancashire's cricketers in 1961 they don't make particularly gory reading. Five batsmen racked up over a thousand runs in the Championship. Jack Bond's 1,399 runs and Brian Booth's 1,289 more than made up for those lost with the departures of Wharton and Dyson. Both batsmen were making the most of their opportunities, while Pullar, Barber and Grieves continued to play well.

The bowling figures are a little more revealing. Ken Higgs' 95 Championship wickets cost a pricey 28.74 runs apiece and Statham claimed a mere 78 wickets in his 20 games. However, the Atherton-born seamer Colin Hilton took 65 wickets and spinners Barber and Roy Collins had over 40 apiece. Such statistics may be far removed from the glory days of Statham, Tattersall and Hilton but they are not disastrous.

In order to understand why Lancashire had such a bad time in 1961 it is necessary to reflect on the players who were unavailable and also the general approach of the side to its cricket. Firstly, both Statham and Pullar played in all five Tests against Australia that summer, and they thus missed around a third of the Championship games. It was nothing more than other counties, including Lancashire, had coped with in the past, but the absence of the team's best batsman and best bowler was keenly felt. In addition, Greenhough sustained finger and foot injuries and was limited to only 11 first-class games. The leg-spinner took 26 wickets in his nine Championship appearances, 85 fewer than he had managed in 1960. It was a shortfall that other bowlers could not make up.

But what caused spectators great concern in 1961 was the poor quality of some of Lancashire's fielding. Bond was excellent, of course, and the team was scarcely composed of portly veterans. Yet there still seemed a lack of enthusiasm, a disinclination to make the extra effort. Chances went down and opponents scored more runs than they should have done. Fielding can be a matter of individual excellence but it can also be a showcase for teamwork, and it was here, in the opinion of many critics, that Lancashire so often fell short.

Geoff Pullar gets in some much-needed practise in his back garden before the 1961 Ashes Test series with Australia.

There were good days, though. Hampshire, who won the County Championship in 1961, were defeated by eight wickets at Old Trafford in May. Barber's rapid hundred, aided by 89 from the Cambridge philosopher Eddie Craig and fifties by Bond and Grieves, helped Lancashire chase down 372 in five hours to beat Nottinghamshire by six wickets at Worksop. But such pleasant afternoons were outnumbered by many occasions on which the Red Rose failed to bloom. Few supporters argued that their team had finished in a false position.

The most poignant reflection on Bob Barber's two years as Lancashire captain was his own: "Leadership is a matter of vision, encouraging people, getting them to walk through walls. I should have been offered a friendly hand, a listening ear, given quiet advice. I didn't get any. There was an enormous void and I also wasn't close to probably any of the young players. But we had a good team and if they had been allowed to stick together… I believe we could have been winning the championship for several years. Players were allowed or forced to leave, we dispersed to several places, and Yorkshire went on to win championships that could have been ours."

150 LANCASHIRE GREATS
92. Bob Barber

Bob Barber was born in Withington, Manchester, and made his debut for Lancashire in 1954 when still only 18 and midway between Ruthin College and Cambridge University. In 1960 he became captain of Lancashire, getting off to a flying start with two victories over Yorkshire and finishing second in the Championship. He was a superb all-round cricketer, an attacking left-handed batsman, right-arm leg-break bowler and an excellent close to the wicket fielder. He captained Lancashire again in 1961 and then played one more season before joining Warwickshire. He played 155 matches in his nine seasons at Old Trafford, scoring 6,760 runs, ave. 28.28, and taking 152 wickets at 31.36 each. At Edgbaston, caution gave way to attack and he became one of the most attractive batsmen in the country. He played 28 times for England with a top score of 185 at Sydney, one of the greatest innings in Ashes history. An adventurous cricketer, highly intelligent and independent, he sacrificed cricket for a business career whilst still in his batting prime. He now lives in Switzerland.

New low for the Red Rose

1962

THE SALOON bar raconteur would not have believed it. In 1962 Lancashire were captained by 34-year-old Joe Blackledge, who played for Chorley in the Northern League. Crucially, as far as the committee seemed to be concerned, the new skipper was an amateur and was said to possess leadership qualities. Blackledge also had experience of Old Trafford: he had played 33 second XI matches, seven of them as captain, in the early fifties, scoring 1,323 runs, a tally which included a couple of hundreds. In 1962, though, he was simply a very good club cricketer and in the words of Bob Barber, "a hell of a nice man". While his appointment was anachronistic, he probably deserves more than to be remembered as the least successful captain in Lancashire's history.

Blackledge's time as skipper began badly and then went south very rapidly. It had been hoped that Ken Grieves would serve as a sort of lieutenant, but the Australian opted to go into business and play league cricket (Grieves was persuaded to return as captain for the 1963 and 1964 seasons). After being introduced to the players he was to lead, Blackledge skippered Lancashire to just two victories in 1962 and the side finished next to bottom of the County Championship, 0.09 of a point ahead of Leicestershire. The captain himself hit two fifties and scored 569 first-class runs in 41 innings at an average of 15.69.

The summer was littered with dismal statistics. In August Lancashire were dismissed for under a hundred on five occasions, both Gloucestershire and Somerset managing to inflict this humiliation twice in the same game. Yet such seasons allow the observant spectator to gauge the measure of a cricketer. While his team floundered, Jack Bond managed to score 2,125 first-class runs in 1962, hitting five centuries and nine fifties as he established himself ever more firmly

Jack Bond was the outstanding performer for the Red Rose in 1962 in the worst season in the county's history.

at Old Trafford. Geoff Pullar and Peter Marner also scored well, the latter venting his frustrations by hitting sixes at every opportunity. Southport's affluent environs took another pounding as Marner made 106 to set up his side's 146-run victory over Warwickshire. They were hardly dancing in the boulevards of Birkdale that night, but they came pretty close to it. To his credit, Bob Barber remained at Lancashire and scored 1,128 runs in 1962 before deciding that he "would not put up with any more of it" and moving to Edgbaston. Like a number of former Lancashire cricketers around this time, he did very well once he left Old Trafford.

The bowling was even more of a problem in 1962. No one took a hundred wickets for the county, although Statham finished the season with 102 in all first-class games. The great fast bowler's successes had been more expensive than usual, though; he was only 25th in the national averages. Colin Hilton took 87 wickets and Ken Higgs 60, but the county that once had slow bowlers to spare now lacked a truly reliable spinner. However, given the side's travails, it was to wicketkeeper Geoff Clayton's credit that he claimed 92 victims in the season.

At the end of the summer Blackledge was relieved to give up the captaincy; Pullar and Statham were relieved that they could go to Australia for an Ashes tour; and Lancashire supporters were simply relieved that they would not have to watch any more cricket for a while.

150 LANCASHIRE GREATS
93. Geoff Clayton

Geoff Clayton was a fine wicketkeeper, good enough to establish his place in the Lancashire team as soon as he returned from National Service in 1959. He was born in Mossley and played for Ashton and Werneth before joining the club. In only his sixth match he created a record, claiming nine dismissals in a match. In 1962 he claimed 92 victims, a figure only surpassed by George Duckworth, and he was considered one of the best wicketkeepers in England. A more than a capable batsman, he played many notable innings for the county. He was equally at home keeping wicket against the pace of Brian Statham or the spin of Tommy Greenhough. In 1964, whilst still only 26, he was sacked by Lancashire along with Peter Marner because they were thought to be disruptive to the team. The Lancashire committee did not take too kindly to his go-slow in a Gillette Cup match against Warwickshire after the opposition had put all the fielders on the boundary. He went on to play three seasons for Somerset and in his career scored over 6,000 runs and claimed 666 victims. A regular at the former player reunions, he remains a popular figure in Lancashire.

First Gillette Cup tie ends in victory

1963

"There were no major defensive decisions made until around the 50th over. There was no retreat onto the boundary like there is today."

Marner clinched the man-of-the-match award the following day with figures of 3-49 from 11.3 overs of medium pace. But it was new ball demon Statham who had the honour of taking the competition's first five-wicket haul. He finished with 5-28 from 12 accurate overs.

Lancashire went on to reach the semi-finals, but they were bowled out for just 59 at New Road in early July. Still, it was a competition that they would become very fond of in years to come.

LANCASHIRE COUNTY CRICKET CLUB. 1963.
Left to Right. Back Row : E. M. Dalton (Physiotherapist). K. Goodwin. B. Booth. J. D. Bond. I. Leath. C. Hilton. K. Higgs. J. Dyson. G. Houlton. R. Entwistle. J. Cumbes. K. Howard. R. Bennett.
Middle Row : P. Marner. J. B. Statham. K. Grieves (Capt.). T. Greenhough. G. Clayton. T. B. Reddick (Coach).
Front Row : J. Sullivan. K. Tebay. H. Pilling. R. E. Jones. P. Lever. M. Beddow. N. Wood.

WOULD YOU believe it! The first one-day match in county cricket history lasted two days. The Manchester weather had its say in delaying the start of the Gillette Cup preliminary round tie between Lancashire and Leicestershire at Old Trafford on 1st May until 3pm, a clash to be played over 65 overs per side.

Both wartime and club games had been played in one day, but a drop in attendances at the beginning of the 1960s sparked a rethink of the county structure, which needed new impetus. There were some trial limited overs matches between the Midland counties in 1962 before a sponsorship deal with American safety razor blade company Gillette was signed for the following season. And Lancashire's poor performances in the County Championship in 1962 – they finished second bottom – helped them make history by winning the first one-day match to be played against the Grace Road outfit.

With the need to reduce the 17 counties down to 16, a preliminary knockout match was played between the Championship's bottom two teams. Peter Marner, who went on to play for the Foxes, and Brian Statham were the standout performers for the hosts with a century and a five-wicket haul respectively. Lancashire, having been put in, batted on the first day and made an excellent 304-9, underpinned by Marner's 121. He was also helped out by half-centuries for Bob Booth and new captain Ken Grieves.

"We basically played a game of traditional first-class cricket with attacking fields," said Marner, quoted in Lancashire's 2013 yearbook six years after his death aged 77. "There were no tactics as such. Nobody really knew what they were doing!

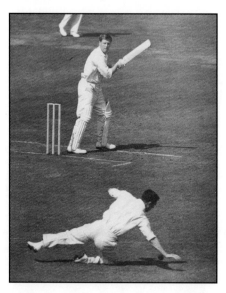

Peter Marner in action. He scored the first ever century in domestic one-day cricket.

Captain wanted in centenary season

1964

TO SAY that Lancashire celebrated their centenary year in style is quite true. Unfortunately, however, it was not the style the club would have wanted. A poor record in the County Championship – only four wins from 28 matches – led to prominent players such as Peter Marner, Jack Dyson and Geoff Clayton being shown the exit door from Old Trafford.

The club had called upon a survey from team manager Cyril Washbrook regarding player performance and dressing room harmony, and they said in a statement: "We intend to build up a new team who can be relied upon to conduct themselves well and pay a proper respect to the captain at all times.

"The committee are convinced they have such players and can now go ahead with confidence in the ability and determination of these young players to restore the standards of achievement and team spirit at all times, and in all conditions, which Lancastrians have the right to expect."

The intention was to build a team around the nucleus of Lancashire's first ever Second XI Championship-winning team in this summer. But that was not even the half of it. Ken Grieves was jettisoned as captain and an advertisement for a new captain was even placed in the Times newspaper.

Cedric Rhoades, a self-made Manchester businessman, also led a supporters revolt against the committee, half of which were ousted, and he became the club's new chairman. Six new committee members, including Manchester-based former Yorkshire left-arm spinner Arthur Booth, were elected in December.

"It was Lancashire's lowest spot in their history," said club historian Reverend Malcolm Lorimer. "To advertise for a new captain in the Times was quite unbelievable. The committee were just completely out of touch.

"It was just at the time of the crossover between amateur and professional captains. AC Smith, the Oxford University captain who played for England as a wicketkeeper, was a potential, but nobody came forward.

"Thankfully the club realised the error of their ways and appointed Brian Statham, a true and loyal Lancastrian."

Lancashire were at least boosted by 1,721 Championship runs from Geoff Pullar and 103 wickets for Statham.

Manchester businessman Cedric Rhoades is pictured standing left at the meeting in which he led a revolt against the club's committee and became the new chairman.

LANCASHIRE SEEK GOOD CAPTAIN

The Lancashire County Cricket Club chairman, Mr. T. E. Burrows, stated yesterday that the advertisement in *The Times* personal column yesterday seeking a first-class cricketer willing to take over the captaincy of a county club concerned Lancashire. Mr. Burrows said: "We are exploring every avenue in the hope of unearthing a good captain, and I do not think we can be criticized for advertising. It is not the first time this has been done and something good may come out of it."

The course taken by Lancashire follows the controversy within the county club in the autumn when some players were not re-engaged and the committee offered to resign.

Green in record-breaking season

1965

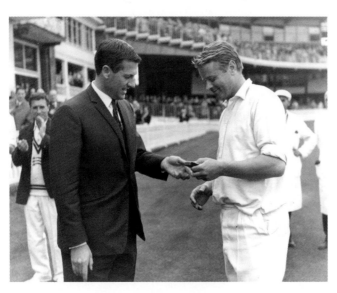

David Green picks up a man-of-the-match award in the Gillette Cup. In 1965 he scored more than 2,000 runs without hitting a single century. It is the one and only time this has been done.

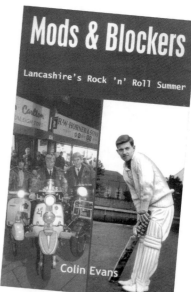

DAVID LLOYD described David Green as "the funniest man I have ever met in cricket". But the opening batsman did not leave opposition bowlers laughing in 1965 when he achieved the unique feat of becoming the only cricketer to score 2,000 runs in an English first-class season without posting a century.

Welsh-born and Timperley-raised, Green was the Red Rose county's standout performer in a disappointing County Championship season, in which they won only five of 28 matches. The right-hander, aged 25, scored 1,784 runs from 53 Championship innings at an average of 34.8, adding a further 253 runs in 10 first-class innings for Lancashire, the MCC and TN Pearce's XI. His highest score was 85 in a draw against Warwickshire at Blackpool in August.

Green, who was also a fine rugby player for Sale, was educated at Manchester Grammar School and Oxford University, and took up journalism with the Daily and Sunday Telegraph after his playing career with Lancashire and Gloucestershire finished in 1973. An attacking batsman, Green's sense of humour was also famous amongst his colleagues in dressing rooms and in press boxes.

He has been an integral part of two books. The first was written by former Manchester Evening News cricket correspondent Colin Evans. *Mods and Blockers* charts the early stages of Evans's career as a writer, life in

1965 and Lancashire's fortunes. The other, written by Green himself and published midway through 2012, is called *A Handful of Confetti*.

Lloyd, whose debut season was 1965, wrote the foreword for the latter: "There is no doubt to me that David Green is the funniest man I have met in cricket.

"Only one person has scored 2,000 first-class runs in a single English summer without making a ton, as he did in my debut season. He believed the ball was there to be hit, and his reckoning was that the first ball of the match might be the simplest to hit for six if the bowler was a bit stiff or tentative in getting it down the other end.

"In that respect, I suppose he was a sort of Lancastrian version of Chris Gayle!"

150 LANCASHIRE GREATS
96. Ken Higgs

Tall, fair-haired and strongly-built, Ken Higgs was a new ball bowler who relied on pace and movement from the pitch rather than speed through the air and gave Lancashire great service, taking over 1,000 wickets at an average of 22.90. He joined Lancashire in 1958 after a season with his native Staffordshire. For many years Brian Statham had lacked a regular partner to open the bowling with and his arrival at last put this right. He soon made his mark and was awarded his county cap in 1959 when he took 100 wickets in a season for the first of five times and he settled down as one of the mainstays of the side. In 1965 he made his debut for England and played in 15 Tests, taking 71 wickets, ave. 20.74. He shared in a record 10th wicket partnership with John Snow of 128 against the West Indies at the Oval in 1966. He was awarded a benefit in 1968, which raised £8,390. After leaving Lancashire he played for Rishton for two seasons before joining Leicestershire and becoming captain and then coach. He took three hat-tricks in his career, one of which was in a Lord's final for Leicestershire in the B & H Cup. He also played football for Port Vale.

Last ball Roses agony for Lancs

1966

While the country basked in the glow of a World Cup tournament which England were to win, another footballer was making waves at Old Trafford. He was no mean cricketer either! Here George Best strides out to bat with Jack Crompton in a charity match at Old Trafford.

LANCASHIRE AND Yorkshire were involved in an historic three days at Old Trafford in late July/early August. Unfortunately, however, it was the White Rose county who were smiling at the end of it thanks to a nail-biting victory. After Brian Close's side had completed a ten-wicket win at Headingley in late May, they travelled over the Pennines later in the summer to secure the double with a 12-run success on the way to the title. But it was by far from conventional means.

As the rest of the country were watching England beat West Germany 4-2 after extra time to win the football World Cup on Saturday 30th July, the Roses rivals were dodging the Manchester rain to fit in only 95 minutes of play on day one.

"Brian Statham always used to say that he felt more pressure in Lancashire v Yorkshire matches than he did actually playing for England," said middle order batsman Jack Bond. "For a lot of lads that had never played Test matches, their Test was the Lancashire v Yorkshire game.

"You weren't brought up to really hate Yorkshire, but there was a definite rivalry there. You were desperate to succeed in the Roses games. Whilst there were a lot of football fans in the dressing room who would have been interested in the score, I can't really imagine us concentrating on it too much with such a big game on our hands.

"You felt that if you succeeded in a Roses game, you were capable of succeeding in any of the other county matches."

A complete washout on day two forced Close to declare his side's first innings on 146-7 at lunch on day three. Lancashire responded by declaring their first innings on 1-0 after two balls before Close became the first captain to ever forfeit an innings, setting Lancashire 146 to win in 66 overs.

To make the match even more momentous, the visitors secured the 12 points off the last ball of the match when off-spinner Ray Illingworth trapped Tommy Greenhough lbw with Lancashire 13 short of their target. Illingworth took his 1,300th first-class wicket of 2,072 when he dismissed Barry Wood as Lancashire chased their target.

Ossett-born batsman Barry Wood made the move across the Pennines to Old Trafford ahead of the 1966 season following limited opportunities with his home county. Wood started off in the Red Rose middle order before making his way to the top of it in the ensuing summers.

He became the first native Yorkshireman to score two Roses hundreds in the same season against the White Rose county in the 1970 campaign, reaching three figures on both occasions with a six.

He went on to play 12 Test matches and 13 one-day internationals between 1972 and 1982. The right-hander scored a second-innings 90 on debut in the fifth Ashes Test of '72, which Australia won by five wickets to secure a 2-2 draw. England, however, retained the urn.

150 LANCASHIRE GREATS
97. Peter Lever

Peter Lever was born in Todmorden. He was a tall, determined right-arm, fast-medium bowler,. A thinking bowler who always gave 100 per cent, he could vary his pace and swing. He played in 17 Tests, taking 41 wickets, including 6-38 at Melbourne in 1974-75. He toured Australia twice with England and also played for England against the Rest of the World at the Oval in 1970, taking 7-83 on his International debut. An excellent fast-medium bowler and more than useful late-order batsman, he played 268 matches for Lancashire, taking 716 wickets, ave. 24.64. His highest score in first-class cricket was 88 not out at Old Trafford for England against India in a Test match in 1971. Back problems forced him into retirement and he was invited to coach the national team as well as giving time from his successful business to coach the Lancashire bowlers.

Hampshire Savaged *1967*

IT WAS a disappointing summer for Lancashire, who only moved up one position to eleventh in the Championship from the previous season's finish. But at least those who travelled to Blackpool's Stanley Park in early August were treated to something special and a little bit of history as the Red Rose clinched one of their four wins in the summer. Former Leicestershire off-spinner John Savage, who had joined his home county for the last three seasons of his 16-year career, was the star of the show in his debut campaign.

John Savage, who later became a respected coach, had the match of his life against Hampshire at Blackpool in his debut season.

Hampshire, the visitors, would have been pretty chuffed with their efforts after bowling the hosts out for just 197 following Brian Statham's decision to bat first upon winning the toss. However, their joy was short-lived – just like their first innings! Bowled out for just 39, Hampshire's total remains the lowest post war score in first-class cricket by a visiting team to a Lancashire home ground.

Five batsmen posted ducks and only one – Richard Gilliat with 12 – reached double figures as Savage returned incredible

figures of 5-1 from 5.4 overs, including five maidens. The only surprise was that he did not match the hat-trick taken by Ken Higgs against Essex on the same ground in 1960. Ken Shuttleworth, Peter Lever and Statham shared the other five wickets to fall.

Hampshire were invited to follow on, and fared better second time around. Still, they were bowled out for 148 to fall to an innings and ten-run defeat inside two days.

Ramsbottom-born Savage added 3-34 from 37 overs in the second innings to finish with match figures of 8-35 from 42.4 overs. One of three players to pass 50 Championship wickets in the season, he finished with 54 from 26 matches to complement 74 for Higgs and 89 for Statham.

Lancashire only lost three matches this season, but they drew no fewer than 17 of their 26 outings due to the weather and, strangely enough, the impotency of their bowling attack.

Gerald Knox, a batsman from Northumberland, was capped by Lancashire in 1967, but he ended up being one of four players released at the end of the season. He and all-rounder Duncan Worsley both pursued a career in teaching, while batsman David Green went to Gloucestershire.

Fast bowler Jim Cumbes, who went to Surrey, completed the quartet. But it would not be the last Lancashire fans would see of the Mancunian, who returned to the club briefly as a player in 1971 before making his mark as a successful administrator in the 1990s and 2000s.

In a three-day friendly between Lancashire and Pakistan at the end of August, the club experimented by turning the wicket from its usual east to west axis to north to south after lobbying from the members, who wanted to sit behind the bowler's arm.

It was an experiment that did not bear fruit, with it proving to be a one-off. However, in 2010 the idea was revisited, and it was decided to make the change permanent as part of the ground's multi-million pound redevelopment.

Jack Bond recalled the Pakistan game to the Backspin magazine in 2013, saying: "The background was that Lancashire wanted to appease the members who'd been on

about having the wicket turned round. They wanted to be able to sit behind the bowler's arm in the members' pavilion instead of having to move to another part of the ground.

"They'd been on about it at AGMs and lobbying committee men. So the committee decided to do something about it this particular season, and the match against the Pakistanis must have looked like a perfect opportunity."

Pakistan won a rain-affected match by 17 runs, with the two teams setting up a finish with three declarations following no play on day two. In a final day pursuit of 218, Lancashire were bowled out for 200.

150 LANCASHIRE GREATS
98. Ken Shuttleworth

A tall, strongly-built and fearsome right-arm bowler, Ken Shuttleworth was born in St Helens. He joined Lancashire in 1964 and captured the wicket of Geoff Boycott as his first victim. He was a genuine fast bowler with a long run and magnificent side-on action and provided good support for Brian Statham. In 1968 he took 65 first-class wickets. Two years later he took 74 wickets, averaging just over 21. He toured Pakistan with the Commonwealth Team in 1967/8 under the captaincy of Richie Benaud. He played for England v Rest of the World at Lord's and was chosen to go to Australia with Ray Illingworth's Ashes-winning side and took 5-47 at Brisbane. Lancashire's success in the one-day game in the 1970s was aided by his accurate short spells He took 5-13 at Trent Bridge in 1972, including the wicket of Gary Sobers. He also had some rewarding days as a flamboyant hard-hitting tail-end batsman before transferring via Leicestershire to league cricket in Staffordshire. He took 484 wickets for Lancashire, ave. 22.92, in 177 matches. After a few years in business he returned to the game as a first-class umpire for a number of years.

Statham ends career on high

1968

WHAT A way to go! It would have been the stuff of fairytales had Gentleman George bowed out with a Championship title to his name. But no, he had to settle for a six-wicket haul in his final match – against Yorkshire of all teams.

Brian Statham, otherwise known as George by those close to him, was a Lancashire icon. To this day, the right-arm fast bowler is the club's leading wicket-taker in first-class cricket with 1,816 at an incredible average of 15.12 and a mind-boggling 109 five-wicket hauls. Seven of those wickets came in his final Championship match for the county, including six in his penultimate innings against the White Rose at Old Trafford between 3rd and 5th August.

Former Manchester Evening News cricket correspondent John Kay, in his *History of Lancashire*, takes up the story:

"Statham, happily edging out of the game, marked his final appearance against Yorkshire with one of his most hostile spells in the last hour of the opening day at Old Trafford. Cheered to the echo as he went into bat, Statham expressed his appreciation by 'mowing down' the first five Yorkshire wickets for a mere 12 runs in a match set aside for (Ken) Higgs's benefit.

"Statham so whet the appetite that when play reopened on the Sunday afternoon, over 21,000 crammed into Old Trafford to see if he could complete the demolition. Alas he could not.

"Although the most popular Lancashire bowler in years had final figures of 6-34 in a Yorkshire (first innings) total of 61, he could not keep it up. With a stubborn 77 from Brian Close (second innings), Yorkshire saved the game. But the glory went for the very last to Statham."

In a piece for Wisden, Sir Neville Cardus also paid tribute to Statham, who retired at the age of 38: "He has been an adornment to the game, as a fast bowler of the classic mould and as a man and character of the rarest breed and likeableness."

Statham had been replaced as captain by Jack Bond for this summer. And while there would no doubt have been feelings of sadness at the great man's retirement, a celebratory mood was on the horizon with silverware not far away.

This summer saw the introduction of overseas players to county cricket, and Lancashire made Indian wicketkeeper-batsman Farokh Engineer their first such signing.

Although the Red Rose county had previously employed players such as Australian-born Ken Grieves, they had done so under residential qualification rules so they could feature as domestic players.

The year before, Engineer had come within six runs of scoring a century before lunch in a Test match against the West Indies, whose bowling attack consisted of Wes Hall, Charlie Griffiths, Garfield Sobers and Lance Gibbs.

There was a suggestion that Lancashire missed out on the signing of Sobers, who went to Nottinghamshire. But the capture of Engineer, who is still a regular attendee at Old Trafford to this day, proved to be a very astute signing.

Brian Statham is joined on the players' balcony during his final season by Peter Lever, Farokh Engineer and Ken Higgs.

First trophy for 35 years

1969

LANCASHIRE WON the race to sign much sought after West Indian all-rounder Clive Lloyd ahead of the 1969 season, and they followed it by winning the inaugural Player's County League 40-over competition at the end of the summer, their first major piece of silverware outright since winning the Championship 35 years previously

Lloyd arrived at Old Trafford on a contract worth £2,500, having enjoyed a spell playing Lancashire League cricket with Haslingden. He was also a target for Gloucestershire, Hampshire and Warwickshire, but he was loving life in the Red Rose county, and he realistically did not want to go anywhere else even if Warwickshire had offered him nearly twice as much money.

He would not be available all summer due to his country's international tour of England. But, having left in mid-May, he returned to Old Trafford in mid-July to help the county lift a trophy. Lloyd scored two half-centuries in nine 40-over matches, an unbeaten 59 in the opening fixture against Sussex at Hove in late April and 59 in the title clincher against Warwickshire at Nuneaton in late August.

Obviously, it was captain Jack Bond's first triumph – and he takes us through the two main events of the year: "I knew the county were interested in signing Clive, but the first time I saw him was when we were having net practice in April on a miserable morning at Old Trafford. This figure appeared in a raincoat with the collar up and glasses on, and he was stood at the back of the nets.

"We signed Clive, but we also had Farokh Engineer, who had played the year before and was a brilliant player for us. The West Indies were on tour in the early season. They weren't on tour for the full season, just until July.

"He played in a few matches early on. He got a good score against Sussex, and we won the game. Then he had to go and join the West Indies. We played a lot of matches without Clive, but we knew we'd get him back for the latter stages of the season.

"I said to the lads, 'It's great to have two world-class players in your side, but you've got to treat whatever they do as a bonus. You, yourselves, have got to try and win the games.'

"It couldn't have worked out better for us because when he came back we were still in the competition, and he came in and added that extra boost right at the end. We won it against Warwickshire at Nuneaton with a game to go after that at Worcester.

"We'd played against Warwickshire in the Championship at Birmingham on the Saturday and then went to play the 40-over game on the Sunday. We celebrated, but we had to put our toys away in the morning and finish off the Championship match on the Monday and Tuesday. There were one or two fuzzy heads having

Clive Lloyd, who arrived in 1969 after a spell as the overseas professional at Haslingden in the Lancashire League, and Farokh Engineer, who had come over from India to play for the county the previous year, played important roles in the club's first trophy success in 35 years.

The mood that had permeated the club for much of the 1960s began to change in 1969 with the success in the Player's County League. Here conductor Alex Mortimer leads an ensemble of Lancashire players, including Harry Pilling, Jack Simmons, John Savage, Jack Bond, David Lloyd and Graham Atkinson.

won it, and we ended up drawing the Championship game.

"That was the first year of 40-over cricket, the Sunday League. There were restricted run ups for the bowlers, and that to us was like a lifebelt because in 1968, we'd finished sixth in the County Championship, which was the highest finish we'd had for a good number of years.

"Everybody was looking forward so much to next season thinking, 'we're on the up'. But, for various reasons in 1969, we finished 15th again. It was quite a big drop for us.

"Luckily, the 40-over competition came in. We won the first game and then lost the second game badly against Essex. Then we got on a good winning run. We won nine on the trot after losing at Chelmsford in early May. A lot of the interest went into that with us out of the Championship and having been knocked out of the Gillette Cup early on in the second round against Yorkshire.

"The lads, having been brought up on one-day cricket in the leagues, adapted to it very quickly. It saved our bacon, and it probably saved my bacon as well because when I was appointed in 1968, it was only a temporary job whilst they looked for somebody else. I was a stand-in skipper. But because we did so well in 1968 and won something the following year, even though

we'd done badly in the Championship, I don't think the committee had the nerve to sack me.

"Thankfully, they didn't and the Gillette came along in 1970, 1971 and 1972. Also there was considerable improvement in our Championship form."

With their lowly finish in mind, it was somewhat of a surprise that Lancashire only lost one Championship match this summer. They went unbeaten at Old Trafford, where every match was drawn – rain was a significant factor – but lost to Derbyshire at Blackpool. Their two wins came against Middlesex at Lord's, secured with the last ball of the match, and against Somerset at Taunton.

150 LANCASHIRE GREATS
100. David Lloyd

David Lloyd has turned his hand to most things in the world of cricket. Born in Accrington, he learnt his trade in the competitive nursery of Lancashire League cricket. He joined Lancashire in 1965 and played 378 matches, scoring 17,877 runs, ave. 33.41. He captained the side from 1973-1977, reaching three Gillette Cup finals and winning in the competition in 1975. He was a competent left-handed opening or middle-order batsman with a sound technique, especially off the front foot. He scored 1,000 runs in a season ten times and was also prolific in one-day cricket, scoring over 7,000 runs and taking 200 wickets. He took 234 first-class wickets for the county with his slow left-arm spin, ave. 29.94. Invited to play for England in 1974, he scored 214* against India at Edgbaston and played in nine Tests. He managed both Lancashire and England and there were spells in marketing and also as an umpire. But it will be as sports commentator for Test Match Special and Sky, as well being an author and entertaining after dinner speaker, that many people will know him.

Player's County League 1969

	P	W	T	L	N/R	A	Pts	R/R
Lancashire	16	12	0	3	0	1	49	4.217
Hampshire	16	12	0	4	0	0	48	4.142
Essex	16	11	0	4	1	0	45	4.305
Kent	16	9	1	6	0	0	38	3.948
Surrey	16	9	0	6	1	0	37	3.762
Gloucestershire	16	8	0	8	0	0	32	3.690
Middlesex	16	7	0	7	0	2	30	4.181
Yorkshire	16	7	0	7	0	2	30	3.958
Warwickshire	16	6	0	6	0	4	28	3.959
Glamorgan	16	7	0	9	0	0	28	3.619
Leicestershire	16	6	0	7	0	3	27	4.086
Worcestershire	16	6	0	7	1	2	27	3.956
Nottinghamshire	16	5	1	9	0	1	23	4.142
Northamptonshire	16	5	0	9	1	1	22	3.988
Derbyshire	16	5	0	10	0	1	21	3.852
Somerset	16	5	0	10	0	1	21	3.635
Sussex	16	3	0	11	2	0	14	4.193

Lancashire at *1970* the double

A TRIO of team-mates in Jack Bond, David Lloyd and Farokh Engineer hailed Harry Pilling's influence on a superb year for Lancashire, which saw them win two one-day trophies, including their first Gillette Cup knockout triumph, and finish third in the County Championship. Pilling, then 27-years-old, became the first player to pass 1,000 runs across the two-year history of the 40-over Player's County League, re-branded the John Player League, which the Red Rose won for the second successive year.

He scored 1,313 runs in the Championship, including five hundreds, as they recorded their best finish in that competition since coming second in 1960, although the title eluded them as they failed to win any of their last six fixtures. And the 5ft 3ins right-hander also scored a superb unbeaten 70 as Lancashire beat Sussex in early September at Lord's to clinch the 60-over Gillette title by six wickets with 4.5 overs to spare after they had slipped into some trouble at 37-2 in pursuit of 185.

"That was very important because with Clive being our star and the type of man he was, he wanted to be successful not for himself, he wanted to be successful so that he could bring success to the club," recalled captain Bond.

"When we got into the final, he was desperate to win it. I'm sure he felt such a lot of pressure. He went in and got 29, and when he got out the score was 86-3. I can see him now sat in the dressing room looking very sad. I think he may have even had a tear in his eye, although I couldn't be sure.

Harry Pilling 1943-2012.

"But he certainly sat with his pads on for a long time probably thinking 'that's it'. That was certainly the impression I got because I knew it meant such a lot to him.

"And lo and behold, the little fella of 5ft 3ins managed to get 70 and win the game for us.

"I think if Harry had played for a southern county, he'd have got international honours. I reckon it's that simple. He was an amazing player, a brave player. He was top-class, even world-class really.

The expectant crowd at Lord's for the 1970 Gillette Cup final.

John Player League 1970

	P	W	L	N/R	A	Pts	R/R
Lancashire	16	13	2	1	0	53	5.14
Kent	16	12	4	0	0	48	4.78
Derbyshire	16	11	5	0	0	44	4.42
Essex	16	8	5	2	1	35	4.52
Warwickshire	16	8	6	1	1	34	4.43
Worcestershire	16	8	7	1	0	33	4.15
Leicestershire	16	7	7	0	2	30	4.59
Gloucestershire	16	7	7	0	2	30	4.34
Surrey	16	7	7	2	0	30	4.16
Nottinghamshire	16	7	9	0	0	28	4.04
Middlesex	16	6	8	1	1	26	4.44
Hampshire	16	6	10	0	0	24	4.64
Northamptonshire	16	6	10	0	0	24	4.18
Yorkshire	16	5	9	2	0	22	4.20
Somerset	16	5	9	1	1	22	4.10
Glamorgan	16	5	9	0	2	22	3.85
Sussex	16	3	10	1	2	15	4.30

Farokh Engineer leaps athletically, above, in Sussex's innings in the Gillette Cup final. Engineer later helped Harry Pilling steer the Red Rose to victory. Below, Barry Wood drives crisply through the covers on his way to 22.

"He was brought up on uncovered wickets. He was such a determined little devil who never wanted to give his wicket away. He always played for the side. He had such a great relationship with Clive, one being 6ft 2ins and the other being 5ft 3ins. One batted at three, the other at four. They batted a heck of a lot together.

"Sussex were favourites having won it before, and we'd been in a few semi-finals and never got through. We'd obviously done such a good job in restricting them. But, as I said, Clive thought it had gone at one stage during our chase.

"He was probably more delighted than anybody else at the end of the game when we won it. Everybody went daft in the dressing room where there had been a big bottle bin full of ice and champagne wheeled in for us."

Lloyd said: "Harry was such a dependable player. When you think that the number three position can be quite a problem position for some teams, he filled that position brilliantly. He was very much an on-side player. But being quite short, it was difficult to find a good length to bowl at him. The bouncer to Pilling, he used to just stand there and let it sail over his head. He never used to move!"

Even Indian Test star Engineer, one of Lancashire's two overseas players at the time, revealed to the Manchester Evening News: "He was one of the first people I met when I arrived at Lancashire from India, and he greeted me with a traditional 'alreet lad!'. I will never forget it, I didn't have a clue what he was saying.

"We used to call him Mr Reliable in the dressing room because we knew that whatever happened at one end, he would be at the other steadily going along making runs, whatever the wicket."

Six days prior to the Lord's final, which was on 5th September, Lancashire retained their 40-over title with a seven-wicket win over Yorkshire at a packed Old Trafford, where the official attendance of 27,559 remains the highest at the ground for a county one-day fixture. But guess who steered Lancashire home? Yes, you've got it, Pilling. He hit 55 not out in an unbroken fourth-wicket partnership of 72 with John Sullivan (56) in pursuit of 166. Pilling passed away aged 69 in September 2012.

The players celebrate their double success with BBC commentator and England legend Jim Laker.

Gillette Cup final 1970

Sussex 184-9 (60 overs)
(MA Buss 42, DP Hughes 3-31)

Lancashire 185-4 (55.1 overs)
(H Pilling 70 not out)

Hughes shines as darkness falls

1971

IT IS arguably the most famous match in Lancashire's history. The 'what were you doing when David Hughes hit 24 in an over?' match. The 'what time did it really finish?' match. Reigning Gillette Cup champions Lancashire were involved in a humdinger of a semi-final against Gloucestershire at Old Trafford on Wednesday 28th July in front of an official crowd of 24,079. Note the use of the word official!

Having been invited to bat, Gloucester made 229-6 from 60 overs, thanks in the main to South African all-rounder Mike Proctor's 65. An hour's break for rain meant that a match which started at 11am would last for ten hours, if not a little more. Three wickets through the middle of Lancashire's reply, including Clive Lloyd, rocked the hosts. But lower order contributions from Jack Simmons, who had earlier taken two wickets, and Hughes proved key. Lancashire needed 25 off the last five overs with the time approaching 9pm, and opening bowler Proctor still had two to bowl.

Gloucester captain Tony Brown took the decision to leave Proctor and Jack Davey to close out the innings with two overs each, bowling off-spinner John Mortimore, who had earlier picked up three wickets. It proved a costly move as Hughes smashed 24 off the over to leave Jack Bond with just one to get five balls into the 57th over.

Man-of-the-match Hughes takes us back to his day in the gloom:

"The thing I remember most is that it was a very long day. It was a rain-interrupted match, and I remember Proctor playing particularly well for them with the bat. It got to about 7.30pm and Tony Brown and Jack Bond got together with the umpires about the fading light. I think Jack said, 'There are 25-30,000 in the ground, and if Tony is in agreement, it should be played to a finish'.

"I don't exactly know the time it finished, but it must have been after nine. It probably was 8.45pm when I went out to bat. They even stopped the BBC nine o'clock news to take live coverage from Old Trafford!

David Hughes's long and eclectic career with Lancashire had many highlights. The innings against Gloucestershire in the semi-final of the 1971 Gillette Cup was one that will remain in the consciousness of Lancastrians of that vintage.

"There were five overs left and we wanted 25. I think Brown wanted to get Mortimore out of the way. Hindsight's a wonderful thing, but he'd actually bowled them into a winning position.

"Now, because of the darkness, it was virtually impossible to see the seamers. I faced Jack Davey, who wasn't of any great pace, but it was very difficult.

"When he decided to bowl Mortimore out, which then left Proctor and Davey with two overs each, we probably then decided that this was the over we had to get as near to 25 as we could.

"The fact was that when I hit those, the fielders struggled to see the ball too. It was that dark.

"From a personal point of view it was a nice moment for me then and still is to look back on.

"Jack's side was a great one to play in. But, as my career went on and towards the end, I got the captaincy. That was more the highlight, along with helping to turn around probably a decade where we had not really figured through the eighties apart from the Benson & Hedges final in 1984."

Lancashire went on to play Kent in the final on Saturday September 4, another thriller, which the Red Rose won by 24 runs with 3.4 overs to spare in front a 25,000-strong crowd.

After Kent captain Mike Denness opted to field first, David Lloyd's 38 and Clive Lloyd's 66 helped Lancashire recover from the early loss of Barry Wood to just the second ball of the match. Clive's effort, in particular, underpinned a score of 224-7.

Kent also had to recover from early strife in their chase as Peter Lever removed Brian Luckhurst, caught behind in the first over. He was one of the first four wickets to fall for 68 runs before a brilliant 89 from Pakistan international Asif Iqbal, who was eventually named as the man-of-the-match, looked to have turned the game on its head and put Kent on course for victory.

However, that was before a stunning one-handed catch from Jack Bond diving away to his right at extra cover to help Jack Simmons get rid of Iqbal left the score at 197-7. It was the first of four wickets to fall for three runs as Lancashire triumphed.

"I don't think I expected to bowl it as wide as I did," recalled Simmons, who had come back into the attack at his unfavoured

Bond catch fells Kent

Pavilion End after bowling the majority of his spell from the Nursery End.

"It was just outside off-stump, and I expected to bowl it on middle and off. He just clubbed it, and I thought 'another four' because I only had three fielders on that off-side.

"Then Bondy took off, and it was one of the best catches I'd ever seen. If you can ever turn around to youngsters and say 'catches win matches', that definitely won Lancashire the match on that occasion in a final."

Bond also recalled: "I caught well over 200 for Lancashire in the time that I played, but they weren't always in the outfield. A lot were at bat pad and things like that.

"The thing about it was.... our best bowler, the one I could always call on in a difficult situation, was Jack. At Lord's, I always preferred to bowl the spinners at the opposite ends. I didn't want my off-spinner bowling with the slope because I didn't want it to do a massive amount.

"I wanted them to bowl it straight virtually. And bowling it against the slope, that's what happened.

"Jack had been bowling at the Nursery End, as planned. But it got to the stage where I had to bring Jack back. It was desperate with the way that Asif was going, so I brought him on at the Pavilion End, the end I didn't want him bowling at.

"Thankfully, it worked out right because Asif ended up mistiming it because it ran back into him sharply. It wasn't an edge, but it wasn't in the middle of the bat. It looped to me. Thankfully, it all worked out well due to luck as much as anything."

Lever's 3-24 from 11.2 overs proved to be the pick of the Red Rose bowling figures, while new ball partner Ken Shuttleworth finished with 2-25 from ten. Wood and Hughes also struck to go alongside Simmons's strike.

LANCASHIRE

Standing: B. Wood, J. Simmons, D. Lloyd, D. P. Hughes, J. Sullivan, F. C. Hayes, K. Shuttleworth.
Seated: P. Lever, H. Pilling, J. D. Bond (Captain), F. M. Engineer, C. H. Lloyd.

Gillette Cup final 1971

Lancashire 224-7 (60 overs)
(CH Lloyd 66)

Kent 200 all out (55.1 overs)
(A Iqbal 89, P Lever 3-24)

150 LANCASHIRE GREATS
102. Farokh Engineer

Farokh Engineer was one of the first overseas signings by a county in 1968 and one of the most successful. Born in Bombay, he played 46 Tests for India, scoring 2,611 runs, including scoring 94 not out before lunch against the West Indies, and claiming 82 dismissals. A brilliant wicketkeeper-batsman, who often opened the innings, he played 175 matches for Lancashire between 1968 and 1976. He was a key figure in Lancashire's one-day successes in the early 1970s. A forcing batsman who was also a great improviser, he was a valuable asset to both India and Lancashire. In his career with Lancashire he completed 464 dismissals and was ranked as one of the world's leading wicketkeepers. After retirement he became a lively and amusing commentator and after-dinner speaker.

Hat-trick of Gillettes *1972*

A MAN-OF-THE-MATCH display from Clive Lloyd drove Lancashire to a special Gillette Cup treble and their fifth one-day trophy in four years. They beat Warwickshire at Lord's in early September in what proved to be Jack Bond's last success as Lancashire captain before he headed to Nottinghamshire. He was to return to Old Trafford as the county's first cricket manager in 1980.

Having lost the toss, Bond decided to bowl Lloyd's 12 overs of medium pace on the trot with the new ball, which "surprised Warwickshire" according to team-mate David Lloyd. He conceded 31 runs without taking a wicket. Warwickshire opener John Whitehouse laid a platform for his side with 68, built upon by 48 for captain MJK Smith

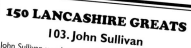

150 LANCASHIRE GREATS
103. John Sullivan

John Sullivan was born in Ashton-under-Lyne and came to Lancashire from the Saddleworth league. He played for Stalybridge from an early age, helping them to a league and cup double in 1963. That year he made his debut for Lancashire and went on play 153 first-class matches, scoring over 4,000 runs and taking 76 wickets. A forcing middle-order batsman and an occasional medium-pace change bowler, he showed himself particularly successful in the limited overs game. His record in limited overs cricket does not always tell the full story of his worth to the side. He was often asked to go in and retrieve a slow scoring rate with the power of his hitting. He played in 137 one-day matches, scoring 2,352 runs with 112 wickets. He was able to turn a match with an aggressive innings or an accurate bowling spell and helped Lancashire win the Gillette Cup in 1975. He was a junior amateur boxing lightweight champion at the age of 16. He later had a decorating business and then became landlord in a local pub. His final years were marked by personal problems and tragically died at the age of 61.

and 54 for Alvin Kallicharran, who shared 85 for the fourth wicket. Lancashire were able to limit the damage as they struck five times for only six runs, including three run outs, as the Edgbaston side slipped from 222-4 to 228-9 on the way to a still commanding total of 234-9 from their 60 overs.

It left Lancashire needing a target never previously achieved by the side batting second in any Gillette Cup match, let alone a final. But they had big Clive, who embarked upon a stunning 126, including three sixes and 14 fours, as the Red Rose won with four wickets and 20 balls to spare despite having been in early trouble at 26-2.

Mobbed by members of the crowd, who had run onto the square when Lloyd brought up his hundred, it was an innings

hailed by legendary commentator Richie Benaud, who was covering the game for BBC Television.

"What a magnificent innings," he said after Lloyd was trapped lbw by Bob Willis to leave the score at 219-5, and the Red Rose needing only 16 to win. "It must be one of the greatest innings seen on this ground in any type of cricket."

David Lloyd agreed: "235 was a big target in that sort of era, but Clive played one of the great one-day innings with Willis steaming in," he said.

"We always knew when Clive wanted to launch because his left foot used to tap the crease in his stance. It just meant he was itching to whack it, and he did it a lot that day!"

Gillette Cup final 1972

Warwickshire 234-9 (60 overs)
(J Whitehouse 68)

Lancashire 235-6 (56.4 overs)
(CH Lloyd 126)

Bond departs a hero

THERE WAS no doubt that Jack Bond was a great Lancashire leader. Aged 40, he relinquished the captaincy in 1972 and played his last first-team match for the Red Rose, a John Player League clash with Warwickshire at Old Trafford, eight days after the final. Lancashire won by four wickets – a fitting way to end for a captain who had steered his side to five limited overs titles, making the Farnworth-born batsman one of county cricket's most successful skippers in limited overs cricket.

There was quite some praise for Bond. In the Lives of Cricket book *Jack Bond – Lancashire Lad, Lancashire Leader*, written by Douglas Miller, wicketkeeper Farokh Engineer, the India Test player, said Bond was "the finest captain I ever played under".

Clive Lloyd also said in the same publication: "Jack's great strength was that he knew about teamwork. He was such a good man personally that you wanted to do well for him."

And his successor David Lloyd also had nothing but good to say about a special skipper: "Jack was honest and just genuinely wanted his young players to do well," he said, warmly. "When he was quite an older player, and his day had been, he used to slot himself in at number seven or eight and come in and bat accordingly himself.

"He would sacrifice himself and never ask anybody to do something that he wouldn't do. He was almost a father figure to all of us. He was very much character-forming for all of us. He formed our character both as a team and as individuals."

Bond, who became an England Test selector in his days at Trent Bridge, also graduated through to becoming an umpire in 1988.

This Lancashire legend finished his career with 12,125 first-class runs to his name, including 14 centuries and a best of 157. In his 99 List A matches, he scored 698 runs without a fifty or a hundred. His highest score was 43.

While Lancashire finished 15th in the County Championship, there was a respectable quarter-final finish in the first year of the Benson and Hedges Cup, the third one-day competition to be introduced to county cricket.

The Red Rose won three out of their four North Group matches, losing only to

Jack Bond shakes hands with teammates and staff before his final match for the club.

Yorkshire in their first outing at Bradford Park Avenue. They lost the quarter-final against Leicestershire at Grace Road.

The one-day season ended with winning a 40-over fixture against Kent at Old Trafford in mid-September, a friendly clash played out between the winners of the Gillette Cup and the John Player League.

Lancashire won by four runs as they successfully defended a target of 162. Opener Ken Snellgrove's 51 had underpinned the home side's 161-8 before Jack Simmons took 4-23 from his eight overs as the southern county slipped to 157 all out with three balls to spare having been well placed at 78-1.

In the midst of Lancashire's disappointing Championship performances, there was the highlight of beating the touring Australians by nine wickets inside two days of a three-day first-class match at Old Trafford just before the Gillette Cup final.

Opening bowler Peter Lee, in his debut season for the county, took three wickets in the first innings and two in the second as the tourists set Lancashire 163 to win.

David Lloyd (47 not out) and Harry Pilling (61 not out) shared an unbroken second-wicket partnership of 99 to help knock off the runs in only 29.5 overs. It was the county's fourth first-class victory over an Australian touring side. That would become five in 1993.

Hard act to follow *1973*

IT WAS not going to be the easiest task in the world to replace Jack Bond as the club's new captain, but David Lloyd didn't half make a cracking start. The batting all-rounder from Accrington, who had graduated through the second XI from 1963 onwards, had big shoes to fill, of that there was no doubt, following Bond's trophy-laden spell at the helm.

It was understandable that Red Rose followers headed into 1973 with plenty of doubts about the club's future due to Bond's departure following four years of silverware. But in Lloyd, they had another popular Lancastrian to get behind. And although he had skippered the side regularly in the John Player League through the previous season, he could not have asked for a better start to life as the full-time leader with a century in a Benson and Hedges Cup tie in late April.

Lancashire fell to 6-2 against the Minor Counties North side, with Barry Wood and Harry Pilling back in the pavilion. But Lloyd and Frank Hayes shared a third-wicket stand of 227 to get their side up to a 55-over total of 275-5. Lloyd finished with 113 and Hayes 102 before Peter Lever bowled seven overs 1-7 as the visitors were bowled out for 127.

Unfortunately for Lloyd and co, Lancashire could not add to their run of five one-day titles in four years. They reached the semi-finals of the Benson & Hedges Cup and quarter-finals of the Gillette Cup, the latter leaving Lancashire hands for those of Gloucestershire's. There was a three place improvement in the county's position in the Championship table, winning four of 20 matches on the way to 12th in the table.

Lloyd fell nine runs short of joining Wood with 1,000 Championship runs, but the skipper was hampered by a lack of bowling depth. Peter Lee led the way

David Lloyd had the unenviable task of taking over the captaincy from the legendary Jack Bond.

superbly with 96 wickets – he took 101 in all first-class cricket – but no other bowler topped Lever's total of 49. Out of sorts Ken Shuttleworth only took seven wickets from six matches.

150 LANCASHIRE GREATS
104. Peter Lee

Peter Lee was born in Northampton and made his debut for the county at the age of 22. He played 44 matches for Northants before joining Lancashire in 1972 and was awarded his county cap in the same season. In 1975 he became the last Lancashire bowler to take 100 wickets in a season, with 112 victims at 18.45. He had previously taken 101 wickets in 1973. He was chosen as one of Wisden's Cricketers of the Year. A fast-medium bowler with great pace and accuracy, he became one of the county's leading bowlers over the following seasons. He went to Lord's four times for Gillette Cup finals. A serious shoulder injury affected his form in 1978 and his last first-class wicket was Geoff Boycott in a Roses match. He took 496 wickets for the county, ave. 22.82 but missed out on a richly-deserved benefit after 11 seasons with the club. He became professional at Gateshead Fell and played with Durham in the minor counties championship.

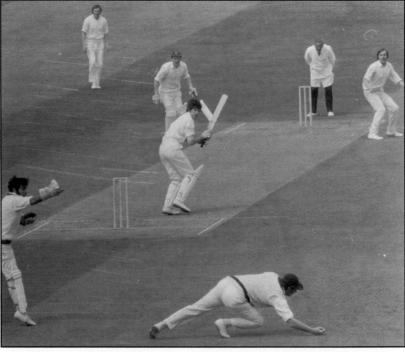

Peter Lee bowls to Richard Lumb in the Roses match at Old Trafford in 1973. Lee was Lancashire's outstanding performer in this year with 96 first-class wickets.

Clive leads Windies

1974

IT WAS late May when Clive Lloyd found out that he would become the next West Indies captain, replacing Rohan Kanhai. Lancashire were playing Yorkshire in a County Championship match at Headingley, which finished in a draw. Lloyd scored 69 and 84 not out. Incidentally, it was one of 15 draws out of 20 matches in the season, and the Red Rose were the only unbeaten county in the country.

It wasn't the way you would expect to find out that you had just landed the biggest job of your life – there was no phone call or telegram. Instead, the big man from Guyana was having a post-day pint with a writer from the Daily Mirror according to Lloyd's authorised biography *SuperCat*, written by Simon Lister.

"Congratulations," said the writer, who Lloyd thought was talking about his exploits with the bat. "Thanks," he replied. "It was a good pitch, but I was pleased with the way I got onto the front foot."

"No, not that. I meant congratulations on becoming the captain of the West Indies," said the writer.

"It was amazing really," reflected Lloyd, aged 29 at the time. "The most important piece of news in my life as a cricketer, and I hear it second hand! That's how it was in West Indies cricket. I was the last person to know.

"My first thought was 'well, this is a challenge'. But I don't recall being frightened or overawed. Since I was a kid there had always been challenges, and this was the next one. The captaincy was thrust upon me, and I had to make it work."

And make it work he did. Lloyd's first Test in charge was against India, who included Lancashire team-mate Farokh Engineer, at Bangalore in late November, which the visitors won by 267 runs. He scored 30 and 163.

In 1974, Clive Lloyd joined a select band of Lancashire players who have captained their country.

He secured 36 wins from 74 Tests in charge between 1974 and 1984, as well as winning 64 one-day internationals from 84 matches in charge, including two wins from three World Cup finals in 1975 and 1979. He remains one of the most successful international captains of all time.

While Lancashire finished eighth in the Championship with only five wins, they were beaten finalists in the Gillette Cup against Kent at Lord's. Rain forced the final into a Monday finish, and the Canterbury side won by four wickets. The Red Rose also finished in the bottom half of the John Player League for the first time and were knocked out of the Benson and Hedges Cup at the semi-final stage.

Players take strike action
1975

ANOTHER TROPHY-WINNING season it may have been, but things were not all calm on the Western Front at Old Trafford as England trio Frank Hayes, Peter Lever and Barry Wood became the first known players ever to go on strike in a move which split the Lancashire dressing room.

Hayes, Lever and Wood, who earned bans of two, two and six matches respectively, returned from England duty at the World Cup ahead of a home County Championship match against Derbyshire, starting on 21st June, to inform their team-mates they would take action against the

club's reluctance to tell them what their wages would be for the summer.

Make no mistake, all of Lancashire's players were keen to strike having previously discussed it. It was just that the trio's decision came at the wrong time, with the side going well and very much in the title race, having won four of the first seven matches, including the reverse fixture against Derby at Buxton when it snowed on the second day of the match on 2nd June.

Jack Simmons takes up the story: "We were playing Derbyshire at Old Trafford, starting on the Saturday, and Hayes, Wood

and Lever had been in the squad for the World Cup," he said. "The last game was on the Wednesday. They would then report back to Lancashire.

"We'd been asking and asking again, 'What are going to be our wages?' We didn't seem to be getting any further. After 1974, we'd been told there was likely to be a rise, but it never materialised. We all thought about striking, the entire staff.

"After that World Cup game on the Wednesday, they didn't come in on the Thursday or Friday (the last two days of a clash with Middlesex at Old Trafford).

"They arrived in at probably 9.30am on the Saturday morning, and they said, 'We are going on strike'. The rest of the players thought, 'hang on a minute'. We'd been

Snow stops play

UMPIRE DICKIE Bird admitted, "I've never known anything like it during my 50-year career" after snow stopped play during the Championship match between Derbyshire and Lancashire at Buxton in early June. The second day of the match on Monday 2nd had to be called off due to a one-inch blanket of snow covering The Park ground. The first day had taken place on the Saturday in glorious weather before the teams played a John Player League match on the Sunday. On the Saturday, Clive Lloyd's destructive unbeaten 167 underpinned the Red Rose's 477-5 before Derbyshire slipped to 25-2.

According to the Meteorological Office, a depression moving down from the Arctic, bringing very cold air with it, caused the snow to hit the East Midlands on the Monday. By the Tuesday, the snow had melted. Play was able to resume. Thankfully for Lancashire, the uncovered pitch had not dried out sufficiently and favoured the bowlers. Derbyshire were bowled out for 42 and 87 as Peter Lee and Peter Lever did the damage to secure an innings and 348-run win.

And in 2011, Bird told the Buxton Advertiser: "I've seen plenty of games affected by rain and bad light in my time, but never snow. When I woke up in my hotel room in Buxton and threw back the curtains, I couldn't believe my eyes. It was impossible to play and amazing to see. But then on the Tuesday, the sun shone, and we went on to have the best summer we had ever had."

150 LANCASHIRE GREATS
106. Clive Lloyd

Few players have made such an impact on Lancashire cricket as the bespectacled Guyanan. After joining Haslingden as a professional he was approached by Lancashire to join the staff. His massive presence and influence was immediate. In 1969 he contributed to Lancashire's success in the John Player League. He topped the Lancashire batting averages in 11 seasons. At Lord's he scored 126 in the Gillette Cup Final of 1972 and in 1975 scored 102 for the West Indies in the first World Cup final. Lloyd was one of the hardest-hitting left-handed batsmen in the world and during a long and distinguished career thrilled crowds with the power of his strokeplay. He was a useful medium-pace bowler and in his younger days one of the finest fielders in the game. He played in 110 Tests for the West Indies, scoring 7,515 runs and is regarded as one of the most successful captains of all time, leading the West Indies to 36 victories in the early 1970s. He was awarded the CBE and served on the Lancashire committee for over 15 years as well as being one of the cricket world's most respected statesmen.

doing well, and in those days it wasn't a matter of whether you'd beat Derby, but more by how many you'd win by. I turned round and said, 'I don't think we should be cutting our noses off to spite our faces'.

"We knew we'd get into trouble, and we would lose out because Derbyshire would probably be given the game. Seeing as we were in contention, I said I wouldn't do it. We needed to think about it after Derbyshire. They didn't agree. All this is going on within half an hour of starting the game, and David Lloyd as captain had to give a teamsheet.

"I had to have some treatment just before the game, and Harry Pilling was on the next bed to me having some treatment too. All I can remember is Bumble coming in in a right temper saying, 'Are you two playing?' Harry said, 'Are we picked?' He said 'yes'. So we played.

"We didn't know at that time that they had refused to play because they were apparently injured. Word got to the chairman and he ordered them to see the doctor to see what was wrong. Hayes and Lever agreed, but Woody didn't.

"We went out without eleven players and Bumble had to ring Bob Ratcliffe up. He was out shopping at the time. His dad brought him to the ground."

Lancashire won the game by ten wickets, with Ratcliffe taking three wickets and scoring 47 not out from number nine in the first innings. But they failed to win the title as they finished fourth. Lancashire's final match of the season against Sussex at Hove was heavily rain-affected, while their rivals Leicestershire, Yorkshire and Hampshire all played.

"I'm sure it worked out alright in the end," added Simmons. "I can't remember what increase we got, although we did get one. It was acceptable. I remember Harry Pilling said 'it's better than working down t'pit' a few times.

"There was a bit of friction in the dressing room at that stage, but it didn't take long for it to go away, especially with winning the Gillette Cup."

Fourth Gillette Cup in six years

LANCASHIRE WON the Gillette Cup for the fourth time in six years, providing David Lloyd with his only trophy as skipper, thanks to a seven-wicket win over Middlesex at Lord's in early September.

Hayes, Lever and Wood all played as the Red Rose restricted Middlesex to 180-8, including three wickets for Bob Ratcliffe, before Clive Lloyd underpinned the chase with an unbeaten 73 after opener Andrew Kennedy had scored 51.

"After losing in the final in 1974, I was itching for a win," admitted Lloyd. "It was a very proud moment."

Gillette Cup final 1975

Middlesex 180-8 (60 overs)
(HA Gomes 44, RW Ratcliffe 3-25)

Lancashire 182-3 (57 overs)
(CH Lloyd 73 not out, A Kennedy 51)

Gillette disappointment for Lancashire

1976

A DOMINANT force in the Gillette Cup through the seventies, Lancashire came a cropper at the final hurdle when trying to claim their fifth Gillette Cup in seven years at Lord's in early September. Instead, it was Northamptonshire's turn to celebrate a first piece of silverware in 98 years as, chasing a modest 196 in 60 overs, they won by four wickets with eleven balls to spare. Peter Willey took the man-of-the-match award for 65 from the top of the order.

Make no mistake, this was a disappointing year for Lancashire, who won only three matches in the County Championship as they finished next to bottom and also finished mid-table in the John Player League.

The absence of Clive Lloyd on West Indies duty for the entire summer hamstrung them, and the Gillette final proved to be a microcosm of their season i.e. nothing went right.

After David Lloyd elected to bat first, the Red Rose lost opener Barry Wood early on to a broken finger, while his opening partner, the Indian star Farokh Engineer, was bowled for a duck. With Harry Pilling also back in the pavilion without really troubling the scorers, Lancashire were effectively 17-3. A trio of middle order contributions from Lloyd with 48, South African-born John Abrahams with 46, both of whom were both bowled by Indian Test left-arm spinner Bishan Bedi, and 39 not out from David Hughes took Lancashire to respectability at 195-7. But, ultimately, it was not enough. Hughes even hit 26 off Bedi in the last over of the Lancashire innings a little over five years after hitting 24 off John Mortimore in that famous Gillette Cup quarter-final against Gloucestershire at Old Trafford. He hit three sixes, each of which Bedi applauded.

A 103-run opening stand between Willey and Roy Virgin, who made 53, set Northants up for the win, although Lancashire gave themselves a sniff of

pulling the game out of the fire with five wickets for 75 runs after Northants had targeted the bowling of David Hughes. The two Peters, Lever and Lee, and Bob Ratcliffe kept the Red Rose in the hunt. But, after the sixth wicket fell on 182, George Sharp and Sarfraz Nawaz took their side over the line.

Engineer, Lancashire's popular wicketkeeper-batsman, became the club's first overseas player to be granted a benefit year in 1976. This was the Bombay-born player's ninth season at Old Trafford, and he made a record £26,519 from the year.

In 1956, Australian-born Ken Grieves was also awarded a benefit. But, despite being born Down Under, he was playing for Lancashire as domestic qualified.

It ended up being Engineer's last campaign as a Lancashire player because he retired from the game altogether to concentrate on business commitments at the age of 38, although he did play a handful of exhibition matches in England through the early to mid-1980s.

Engineer, who earned 46 Test and five one-day caps, played 337 times in all forms of cricket for Lancashire. He finished with 8,892 runs, including 36 fifties and four hundreds. More importantly for a keeper, he took 587 catches and effected 65 stumpings. He would be replaced by John Lyon.

---

150 LANCASHIRE GREATS
107. Harry Pilling

At 5ft 3in tall Harry Pilling was one of the smallest first-class cricketers, but he was a true giant of Lancashire cricket, amassing 15,279 runs and 25 centuries in a first-class career spanning 18 years. He also scored 3,887 runs in 173 one-day matches, including 70 in the 1970 Gillette Cup final against Sussex which helped Lancashire to the trophy. He was born in Ashton-under-Lyne and lived in Mossley but spent the later years of his life at his home in Little Lever. He joined Lancashire as a 16-year-old and three years later made his debut in 1962, winning his county cap in 1965 and celebrating his benefit in 1974. He passed 1,000 first-class runs for Lancashire seven times in eight years between 1965 and 1972 and is one of a few Lancashire players who have scored two centuries in one match – a feat he achieved against Warwickshire at Old Trafford in 1970. He was great friends with Clive Lloyd, sharing several big partnerships. In a time when cricketers were only contracted during the season, Pilling had several jobs during the winter, including apprentice butcher, coalman and a coffin-maker. There have been many great players to play for Lancashire but few wore the Red Rose with more pride and his gritty determination won the admiration of the crowd.

Women's Test match at Old Trafford

Lancashire has played host to many a famous men's Test match down the years, but this year saw the county welcome England's women to headquarters for the first time as they took on Australia in a three-day match.

The contest, played between 19th-21st June, finished in a draw. Australia, invited to bat first, made 273-6 declared before the hosts replied with 254-6 during the third day. The Aussies finished on 128-6 in their second innings. England captain Rachael Heyhoe-Flint's first-innings 110 was the standout performance of the match. All three Tests in the series were drawn.

To date, it is the only women's Test to have been played at Old Trafford, although England drew with India at Blackpool in 1986. England have also played one Twenty20 and two one-day internationals at Old Trafford between 1999 and 2012.

34 off an over for Hayes 1977

Frank Hayes, who created a Lancashire record in 1976 with 34 off an over from Glamorgan seamer Malcolm Nash. He also took over as skipper at the end of the season.

FRANK HAYES created history by scoring 34 runs off an over in a drawn County Championship match against Glamorgan at Swansea in late August. But it was only a brief high during another forgettable summer for the county. The former England batsman, a stalwart of Lancashire's top order, fell short of Garfield Sobers's record of six sixes in an over, yet he still managed to score more runs than any other player in Red Rose history off a six-ball over.

There were a couple of glaring similarities between the feats of Sobers (1968) and Hayes – on the same ground and against the same bowler, left-arm seamer Malcolm Nash. Hayes hit 6,4,6,6,6,6 off Nash on the way to a first innings 119. The right-hander, aged 30, shared a third wicket stand of 202 with Barry Wood, who finished on 155 not out, as the visitors responded to 217 all out with 362-3 declared.

Hayes took two hours and ten minutes to score his first 50 runs, but raced from 50 to 100 in only 20 minutes. He hit seven sixes and 13 fours in all. Unfortunately, there was no play on the final day, robbing Lancashire of the chance to push for victory during a

season which saw them win only two of 22 matches and finish second bottom in the table again.

Hayes scored 1,152 runs during the campaign at an average of 50.08, his best average in a season. It was the fourth time he had completed 1,000 runs in a season. He went on to do it twice more in 1978 and 1980.

Ravi Shastri matched the feat of Sobers in 1985 whilst playing for Bombay against Baroda in India's Ranji Trophy, while Andrew Flintoff hit 34 in an Alex Tudor over for Lancashire against Surrey at Old Trafford in 1998. The difference was that Tudor's over included two no-balls. That sequence went 6,4,4,4,4,6,6,0.

Lancashire finished the summer of 1977 having also been knocked out of both one-day trophies at an early stage. They also finished 16th in the John Player League.

They were hurt by the absence through injury of Clive Lloyd, who ended up having cartilage removed from both knees, and David Lloyd resigned as captain. Hayes took over his job.

It would have been little consolation to Lancashire that two of their batsmen were amongst the most prolific run-scorers in the country.

Wood finished with 1,439 runs and an average of 51.39, the ninth best in the averages, and Hayes with his 1,152 runs and average of 50.08 was tenth best.

There was also cheer for Jack Simmons as the off-spinner claimed a hat-trick in the second innings of the rain-affected draw against Nottinghamshire at Liverpool in late July. Simmons claimed 5-8 from 8.3 overs, including four batsmen for ducks. It was the 31st hat-trick of Lancashire's first-class history. There have since been three more.

David Hughes claimed Lancashire's best ever one-day bowling figures in a John Player League win over Somerset at Old Trafford in late June.

The all-rounder, bowling his canny spinners, inspired the Red Rose to a 23-run win with 6-29 from 6.5 overs as the visitors were bowled out for 144 as they responded to 167-8 from their 40 overs.

Hughes was the fifth bowler used by captain David Lloyd, and his prized scalp was that of the dangerous Ian Botham, caught and bowled for 55. His record would not last long, however. Botham, meanwhile, made his Test debut for England a little over a month later.

150 LANCASHIRE GREATS
108. Jack Simmons

'Flat Jack' as he was known was one of the most popular Lancashire players and devoted to the club. He was a burly, accurate off-spinner and a useful right-hand batsman. He made his debut at the age of 27 and was capped in 1971. He played 429 first-class matches for the county and in total took 1,033 wickets, plus 464 in limited-overs wickets. He scored 9,417 runs, plus over 3,000 in limited overs cricket. In all types of cricket he became only the second player to score 10,000 runs and take 1,000 wickets after Johnny Briggs. He had the dexterity to dismiss batsmen and score runs at the right time. Altogether he played in nine cup finals at Lord's. Batting as nightwatchman at Hove in 1970, he made an excellent century with fluent strokes all around the wicket. During the winters he played for Tasmania and was a great influence on them as coach and captain. In his early years he played centre forward for Great Harwood FC for eight years. He had a record benefit in 1980 and topped the batting and bowling averages at the age of 41 and was chosen as one of Wisden's Cricketers of the Year. He was Chairman of Lancashire between 1998-2009 and he is now a Vice-President.

Another impressive season for Big Clive

1978

CLIVE LLOYD hammered a 91-minute century as Lancashire just missed out on beating the weather and Glamorgan in an entertaining County Championship draw at Liverpool in late June on the way to finishing 12th in the table. The West Indian overseas player recorded an unbeaten 110, but he missed out on the fastest century of the season to international team-mate Gordon Greenidge of Hampshire later in the summer.

The Wisden report of the match read: "With no play possible on the first day, Lancashire hurried for runs when they won the toss on Monday morning. Taking advantage of an easy-paced pitch, not one batsman failed as they raced to 401-5 in their 100 overs.

"(Andrew) Kennedy hit a solid century and David Lloyd contributed 51 to an opening partnership of 136. (Frank) Hayes followed with 40 and (John) Abrahams reached 66. But the highlight was a magnificent century in 91 minutes from Clive Lloyd, who hit two sixes and 12 fours.

"In reply, Glamorgan always struggled against (Colin) Croft, (Willie) Hogg and (Bob) Ratcliffe, and lost six wickets for 99 before totalling 195. (Gwyn) Richards scored 40 and (Malcolm) Nash hit out for a belated 29.

"Asked to follow on 206 runs behind, Glamorgan escaped when rain set in at tea of the last day, just as they were about to begin their second innings."

It was one of four centuries for Lloyd in another impressive Championship season, especially given he had the cartilage removed from both knees the previous year. He led Lancashire's batting with 1,116 runs from 21 matches at 37.20.

The two Lloyds, Clive and David, also shared the highest fourth-wicket partnership in one-day cricket for Lancashire, a record which still stands. They hit an unbroken 234 in a Gillette Cup match against Gloucestershire at Old Trafford in a second round win in mid-July. Chasing 267 to win in 60 overs, both players scored

hundreds to recover the innings from 33-3 following the losses of Kennedy, Abrahams and captain Hayes.

Lancashire were knocked out at the semi-final stage by Sussex at Hove, but the club's yearbook still has Kennedy's 131 in the last eight win over Middlesex at Old Trafford in early August as the highest score in one-day cricket by a Lancashire opener listed on the scorecard as coming in at number one.

Andrew Kennedy, who made the highest score for the club by an opening batsman taking strike in one-day cricket.

The pitches at Old Trafford had proved problematic for a couple of seasons now, but things started to improve under new groundsman Chris Hawkins. The club had suffered problems following the retirement of Hawkins' long-standing predecessor Bert Flack the previous summer and the shock resignation of successor Gordon Prosser on the eve of a June one-day international between England and Australia. Prosser had replaced Flack, having moved from Worcestershire.

Both batsmen and bowlers complained that they were struggling to come to terms with the changing nature of the pitches, and at the end of the 1977 season, the Red Rose opted to relay part of the square, and were grateful for Warwickshire's help in letting their head groundsman Bernard Flack supervise. Flack was the Inspector of Pitches to the Test and County Cricket Board.

Despite the wet weather of 1978, Hawkins did a good job in improving the quality of the pitches. Peter Marron would take on the role in 1983.

150 LANCASHIRE GREATS
109. David Hughes

Born in Newton-le-Willows, he made his Lancashire debut at the age of 19 in 1967 and was capped in 1970. He was a stalwart of the Lancashire side for the next two decades, scoring 10,126 runs and taking 637 wickets with his left-arm spin as well as snaring 325 catches. In 1970 and 1971 he took 82 wickets each season. He will be remembered for his astute leadership, captaining the side from 1987-91 and taking them from the bottom of the Championship table to second place. He always had a positive attitude, encouraging the best out of his colleagues, building confidence and achieving excellent results. His batting blossomed when his bowling declined and he scored 1,000 runs in 1981, repeating the feat the following year. An aggressive batsman, he could clear the field with clean hitting which he demonstrated best in that famous 24 in an over in the Gillette Cup match at Old Trafford against Gloucestershire in 1971. He was named as one of Wisden's Cricketers of the Year in 1988. After retirement he enjoyed a spell managing Lancashire and also became a pitch inspector.

Vote of no confidence fails to oust committee

1979

APPROXIMATELY 150 Lancashire members rebelled and forced a special general meeting to propose a vote of no confidence in the committee at the end of a disappointing season for the Red Rose county. There were a series of poor personal returns from senior players, with only Barry Wood and David Lloyd topping 1,000 runs in the County Championship and only off-spinner Jack Simmons topping 50 wickets.

"Lancashire frustrated and annoyed their supporters throughout the whole of the season," wrote John Kay in his Wisden review of the summer.

"It was not that the side dropped from 12th to 13th in the Championship table and from fifth to eleventh in the John Player League that caused concern. It was the very plain impression that several leading players did not play up to their potential."

In terms of the vote of no confidence, Kay continued, "They (the members) timed their move badly in view of the signing of Australian pace bowler Mick Malone and the engagement of former captain Jack Bond as the club's first cricket manager. The outcome was that the committee resisted the vote of no confidence by a substantial margin."

Lancashire had tried to bolster their bowling stocks prior to the season with unsuccessful moves for prolific Australian pace bowlers Dennis Lillee and Rodney Hogg, both of whom rejected the move to Old Trafford because of the demands of a hectic English summer.

No seamer took more Championship wickets than Bob Ratcliffe's 38 from 17 matches. Ratcliffe enjoyed a memorable summer in 1979, not just because of his exploits with the ball. In a draw against Warwickshire at Old Trafford in late July, the 27-year-old from Accrington helped Lancashire save the match with a second innings century, the only one of his 82-match career.

Wicketkeeper John Lyon also achieved the same feat during an eighth-wicket partnership of 158 in the second innings. It remains a club record stand for that wicket in first-class cricket. Warwickshire made 359-4 declared having elected to bat before Lancashire were bowled out for 208. Asked to follow on, they were reduced to 230-7 before Ratcliffe and Lyon united to post 101 not out and 123 respectively. The Red Rose finished on 469-9.

David Lloyd became the eighth player to score two hundreds in the same match for Lancashire when he did it in an eight-wicket win against Worcestershire at Southport in late June and early July.

In all, it was the eleventh occasion the feat had been achieved for Lancashire, and the first time since Harry Pilling did it in 1970 against Warwickshire. But Johnny Tyldesley, Ernest Tyldesley and Charlie Hallows all did it twice between 1897 and 1933.

Lloyd scored 116 in Lancashire's 303-7 declared as they replied to 342-9 declared. He then added an unbeaten 104 in pursuit of 188 after Worcester had been bowled out for 148 in their second innings.

Since Lloyd's two hundreds, Graeme Fowler, in 1982, Neil Fairbrother in 1991, John Crawley in 1995 and 1998 and Ashwell Prince in 2013 have all achieved the feat.

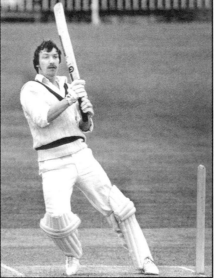

Bob Ratcliffe, left, and John Lyon, right, enjoyed a very good season in 1979, no more so than their club record eighth wicket partnership of 158 against Warwickshire.

Bond returns *1980*

FORMER LANCASHIRE captain Jack Bond was appointed as the county's first ever cricket manager ahead of the 1980 season. A hugely successful and popular skipper, Red Rose legend Bond returned to the county after a four-year spell as coach and groundsman at King William School on the Isle of Man.

"When I retired in 1972 and I came on to the coaching side, they wanted me to be head coach and have John Savage as my assistant. We actually operated as joint coaches in the end. I was really looking for a cricket manager's job. I wanted to be at the top of the pyramid and have responsibility for all cricket within the club and the county. I felt I had a bit more to offer.

"I think the TCCB asked Lancashire to put my name forward as a Test selector in 1973, but the committee chose not to because they felt I had enough to do with my duties. This is what I heard. To a certain degree that forced me to move to Notts.

"I had become friendly with Jack Baddiley, who I had played against in second-team cricket and was influential behind the scenes there. He rang me up and asked if I would be interested in going to Trent Bridge to do every job really. I was captain and coach, and Garfield Sobers was there as overseas player at the time."

Unfortunately, Bond could not wave a magic wand and turn Lancashire into trophy winners immediately in 1980. He would have to wait a few years for that to happen. The county finished 15th in the County Championship, two places worse than the previous summer. Their haul of 26 batting bonus points was the lowest in the country and hurt them badly.

Jack Bond returned to Old Trafford in 1980 with responsibility for all cricket within the county.

Bond had been joint-coach with John Savage immediately after his playing career at Old Trafford finished in 1972 before moving to Nottinghamshire as player-coach two years later. Whilst at Trent Bridge, he became an England selector. He has since revealed that being handed the cricket manager's job at Lancashire in 1980 was the realisation of a long-term goal: "People had suggested it for a while beforehand because of the problems the club had," he explained.

Action from the disappointing 1980 season: Left, Bernard Reidy's edge narrowly avoids Chris Old's safe hands at slip in the Roses match at Old Trafford. Right, Willie Hogg celebrates taking the wicket of Sussex's John Barclay.

Floodlit success *1981*

CLIVE LLOYD led Lancashire to their first trophy in six years with some stunning batting. Winning the Lambert and Butler Floodlit Trophy may not have gained the Red Rose county the kudos of their quartet of Gillette Cup triumphs had through the seventies, but any piece of silverware should not be sniffed at. An end of season experiment in September, which actually lasted just the one year, this competition was played as ten overs per side, with seven players on each team and was hosted at football grounds around the country.

Lancashire played their early round matches at the other Old Trafford on 17th September, where they murdered Yorkshire and saw off Nottinghamshire, before travelling south to play the semi-final against Somerset and the final against Leicestershire at Chelsea's Stamford Bridge ground the following day. Lloyd captained a squad which also included Graeme Fowler, Andrew Kennedy, David Hughes, Paul Allott, Jack Simmons, Michael Holding and Doug Beckett.

"When we played at United, Clive regularly used to hit balls right out of the ground, although the stands aren't as high as they are now," explained Hughes. "It was a synthetic pitch down the centre of the ground, and it was only 25 or 30 yards to go into the stands. A thick top-edge or a mishit usually brought you four or six. You certainly couldn't have a slip in!

"It was almost like playing a game inside the 30-metre circles. The tactics were really to bowl as full as possible. At least then you could defend square and in front of the wicket."

Lancashire proved that anything above 130 was a good score. They twice topped 150, against Yorkshire in the first round and against Leicestershire in the final. Lloyd hit unbeaten scores of 77 and 83 in both matches. Somerset fielded Ian Botham and West Indian Andy Roberts, while Leicestershire were able to call upon David Gower.

"Counties played all their big names," said Hughes. "We didn't know whether it was coming in on a permanent basis, but it turned out to be only a one-off. It was an interesting concept which was ultimately the forerunner to Twenty20 in many ways. It was fairly unique and a bit of fun. It was another trophy, which was great to win."

Not even the part-time overseas employment of West Indies quick Michael Holding, a great of the game, could boost the county's Championship campaign as they slipped one place to 16th. Holding took 40 wickets in seven matches.

The Red Rose also finished joint tenth in the John Player League and were knocked out of the Benson and Hedges Cup prior to the knockout stages.

At least they fared better in the NatWest Trophy, but a thrilling last-ball defeat away to Northamptonshire in the semi-final proved an obvious disappointment.

Holding took five wickets in an innings twice for the Red Rose in the Championship and six wickets twice as well. Aged 27, Holding, nicknamed 'Whispering Death', claimed ten wickets in a match in the 16-run success over Yorkshire at Headingley in late August and early September.

Holding claimed 4-39 from 24 overs in the first innings and 6-76 from 27 in the second. His best haul in a Lancashire shirt came in his last appearance against Glamorgan at Old Trafford. He claimed 6-74 in the first-innings of a drawn game.

Jack Simmons, Graeme Fowler and Clive Lloyd relax during practise at Old Trafford.

Miracle at Southport *1982*

JACK SIMMONS hailed an exceptional County Championship victory over Warwickshire at Southport in late July as the most satisfying of his career. In the midst of a disappointing season, the Red Rose recovered from conceding the highest partnership against them in the county's history to win by an incredible ten wickets. Double centuries from Alvin Kallicharran and Geoff Humpage, who shared a fourth wicket stand of 470, recovered their side from 53-3 to 523-4 declared inside the first day.

Lancashire responded with 414-6 declared before Les McFarlane turned the game on its head with 6-59 as the visitors were skittled for 111, setting Simmons and company 221 to win. Graeme Fowler helped to secure the win with his second hundred of the match in an unbroken first-wicket stand with David Lloyd.

"This was good," recalled Simmons. "They won the toss and elected to bat. Jack Bond was the manager, Clive Lloyd captain and I was vice. It was a hell of a wicket. If it went through the in-field, it was four.

"We were all a bit down when going into the dressing room after that first day, naturally. But Cedric Rhoades, the chairman, was seething. He came across the field saying to Jack 'I'm going to give them a rollocking'. Jack said 'I wouldn't do that chairman. I'd wait until we've batted'. He reluctantly agreed.

"When we went out to bat, we got just over 400. Then when we came to bowl again, the ball just swung and Les ended up getting six wickets. We bowled them out for just over 100, which left us needing 220. Bumble and Graeme Fowler went in again.

"By this time, Jack had to be back at Old Trafford for a meeting. There was a phone in the viewing area at Southport just outside the dressing rooms, and I was sat next to it. Bondy kept ringing up wanting to know the score. He told me to make it clear that he wanted us to win by ten wickets.

"He said 'I want to go and knock on the chairman's door and tell him we've won by ten wickets'. He wanted to make it clear that he was wrong to think about giving us a rollocking on that first day! I think it was (as good as a Championship win as I've been involved in)."

Colin Croft, re-engaged as the club's overseas player having previously spent two seasons at Old Trafford in 1977 and 1978, claimed the club's best ever one-day bowling figures.

The Guyanan quick ripped through Scotland to take 6-10 from ten overs in a

A young Neil Fairbrother, who made his debut in 1982, with Brian Statham, Cyril Washbrook, Paul Allott and Graeme Fowler. Allott and Fowler were current England internationals, Statham and Washbrook were legends for Lancashire and England, whilst Fairbrother would be an England player before the end of the decade.

Benson and Hedges Cup Group B win over Scotland in early May. Lancashire went on to reach the quarter-finals, but the figures still stand as the club's best.

The figures were also the best of Croft's career, although he had taken 6-15 from nine overs at Arnos Vale against England in February of the previous year. Unfortunately for Lancashire, the 29-year-old missed the second half of what turned out to be his final season with the club through injury.

150 LANCASHIRE GREATS
113. Steve O'Shaughnessy

Steve first played for Lancashire in 1980 and was capped in 1985. A right-hand batsman and right-arm medium-pace bowler, he made many valuable contributions with both bat and ball, especially in one-day cricket. In 1983 he scored a sensational first-class century in 35 minutes against Leicestershire at Old Trafford to equal the world record set by Percy Fender in 1920 for the fastest century. He reached his century in 25 scoring stokes off only 54 balls, but the bowling was not of the highest order. He toured West Indies with the Young England side in 1980 and in 1984 he scored 1,167 runs for Lancashire, ave. 34.32, with three centuries. He played 100 first class matches for the county, scoring 3,567 runs, ave 26.61, and took 110 wickets, ave. 35.88. In limited overs cricket he scored over 2,000 runs and took 95 wickets. In 1988 he moved to Worcestershire for two seasons before playing for many years for Cumberland. Since retiring from playing he has become a first-class umpire.

O'Shaughnessy *1983* equals record

Steve O'Shaughnessy pictured with Percy Fender, whose record for the fastest century in first-class cricket he equalled in the last match of the 1983 season.

IN THE season's final County Championship match, all-rounder Steve O'Shaughnessy equalled the world record for the fastest century in 35 minutes against Leicestershire at Old Trafford as the visitors pursued a declaration in a heavily rain-affected contest. O'Shaughnessy shared an opening stand of 201 in 43 minutes with Graeme Fowler as they peppered the short leg-side boundary towards the pavilion off part-time bowlers David Gower and James Whitaker.

In his book *Mods and Blockers*, former Manchester Evening News cricket correspondent Colin Evans recalls how the 22-year-old was "suitably embarrassed" to find his name alongside Percy Fender in the record books. Fender had initially set the record whilst playing for Surrey in 1920.

"O'Shaughnessy would have been far more embarrassed had he beaten Fender's record. And so would the game of cricket. Actually, he did beat it.....," wrote Evans. "Interest grew in the Press Box as ball after ball crossed the rope. Utter nonsense, yes,

but here, after two days of nothing to write about, was the story of the season.

"Wisdens were out, records checked. And when O'Shaughnessy reached his century, my colleague Stan grabbed the internal phone to get the 'hits' (fours and sixes) and the official time from the scorer.

"Stan, a brilliant freelance journalist, knew this could be a big, money-making story. He was excited. So excited that, when scorer Amos Lowe answered the phone, Stan called him Moses.

"When this momentary confusion was cleared up, Amos gave the duration of O'Shaughnessy's innings as 34 minutes. Stan, even more excited, said: "Moses, do you realise that's a world record? Moses – sorry Amos – obviously didn't.

"He was a true cricket lover, the Lancashire scorer, a bluff, heavily built man, an accountant by profession, with whitening hair and cherry red cheeks, which grew crimson when upset or angry. And he was angry at this moment.

"This sort of cricket was sacrilege, and to think it had created history... We could hear him spluttering into the phone... 'world record, no, that's not cricket'. He needed more time to check. Would ring back. We waited anxiously. Then... 'Official time, 36 minutes, not a world record.'

"But we were not prepared to accept that. By my reckoning, O'Shaughnessy's duration was as low as 32 minutes. Eventually, after some argy-bargy, a compromise was reached very reluctantly on Amos's part – 35 minutes, equalling the world record."

The match finished in a draw, one of 17 for Lancashire as they finished (equal) 12th in the Championship for the second year running. The Red Rose won three of their 24 matches. A semi-final finish in the Benson and Hedges Cup was the best showing in a disappointing one-day campaign.

150 LANCASHIRE GREATS
114. John Abrahams

Born in Cape Town, South Africa, he came to England as a boy and played for Milnrow and Radcliffe, where his father Cec was professional. He played for Lancashire between 1973 and 1988 and scored 10,000 first-class runs. He was awarded his county cap in 1982 after completing 1,000 runs in a season and was a consistent performer in the one-day game. In 1983 he captained Lancashire and was re-appointed for the next two seasons. He was a popular leader who led the county to a Benson & Hedges Cup final victory in 1984 and, despite scoring a duck, won the Gold Award for his superb captaincy and fielding. He scored 14 first-class centuries, with a career best 201* v Warwickshire. When he left Lancashire he played for Shropshire and then managed the England A team and then the Under-19 side. His wife Debbie is the Labour MP for Oldham East & Saddleworth.

Birthday boy Abrahams leads Lancs to trophy

1984

LANCASHIRE WON their first Lord's final in nine years as they beat Warwickshire by six wickets with 12.2 overs remaining in pursuit of 140 to claim the Benson and Hedges Cup in late July. John Abrahams won the man-of-the-match award for his excellent captaincy despite scoring no runs on his 32nd birthday. Here, the skipper, now England's under 19s manager, takes us through his memories of another glorious day at the Home of Cricket for the Red Rose.

"It was the first final in nine years that Lancashire had got to, and our spectators were pretty chuffed because one-day finals had been a fairly regular occurrence for the club through the

seventies. The day itself was a bit of a blur because everything happened so quickly. We stayed at the hotel just across the road, so we walked to the ground. People were queuing up with red roses on and starting to enjoy the day.

"The team we had was well suited to a one-day competition because it was young and we were a really good fielding side. We had a bowling attack who could take wickets with the new ball and then squeeze in the middle and at the end with the likes of Jack Simmons, Paul Allott and Steve Jefferies, who was our overseas player at the time. We also had a long batting line-up.

"The tactic in every game if we won the toss was to restrict them to as little as possible. We then felt we could chase anything they set us. Thankfully, it worked well.

"Allott bowled well with three wickets and Jack returned 0-18 off eleven overs, which was brilliant. Alvin Kallicharan on the Warwickshire side scored 70, which was

The pre-season training the Lancashire squad did before the 1984 season paid off with their first major trophy in nine years.

more than half their score. David Hughes and Neil Fairbrother then scored 30-odd not out each to see us home.

"It was a mega shock to me to get the man-of-the-match because it's usually anybody who's contributed with runs or wickets, or even somebody who's come on and bowled a spell to turn the game or scored 20 runs in an over or something similar.

"I had taken the catch to get rid of Kallicharan and not scored any runs. I remember Jefferies bowled a short-ish delivery, which Kallicharan tried to pull with a straight bat. I was fielding at straight mid-wicket, and it came chest height – a very simple catch. We knew at that point that we were in a really good position to restrict them to a low score.

"The presentation was done on the first floor balcony of the pavilion. The PA system goes out towards the crowd, and there's no speaker coming back towards the pavilion. With all the noise going on, with the Lancashire supporters singing, I didn't hear Peter May, the England chairman of selectors at the time, nominate me as the man-of-the-match.

"Steve O'Shaughnessy pushed me forward, but I just thought 'oh it's typical Shauny getting carried away'. Then somebody in the presentation party nodded in my direction.

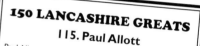

Benson & Hedges Cup final 1984

**Warwickshire 139 (50.4 overs)
(Al Kallicharran 70, PJW Allott 3-15
ST Jefferies 3-28)**

Lancashire 140-4 (42.4 overs)

"As I say, it was a shock to me to get it, though we didn't complain because it was someone on our side and the money went into the players pool, which we shared. As long as it was one of us, it didn't matter who – or the reason why."

Unfortunately, Lancashire endured one of their worst ever Championship campaigns, winning only one of their 24 matches on the way to a 16th placed finish. The only other time the county have failed to win more than once in a season was 1874 when only six matches were played.

Double celebration for Allott

PAUL ALLOTT had plenty of cause for celebration that weekend both on and off the field. The England fast bowler helped to put the skids under Warwickshire with 3-15 from 8.4 overs in the final, less than 24 hours after the birth of his first child, Ben, at

Wythenshawe Hospital.

"It was an interesting one because I played a Test at Headingley against the West Indies the weekend before and got six-for," he recalled. "Then we had a NatWest Trophy game at Bristol a few days later and my wife was pregnant, the baby was due.

"It arrived on the Friday before the final at about five or six o'clock in the evening. Jack Bond stayed behind to drive me down because the rest of the team had gone. You can imagine that having had a first child, I couldn't sleep anyway. My mind was racing and buzzing. I had a few drinks and went to bed about one in the morning.

"The final arrived, and I was still buzzing from everything. It was a great, great day. We all bowled really well, the whole attack." Allott, then aged 27, picked up the wickets of Paul Smith, Geoff Humpage and Bob Willis to wrap up the innings: "I think '84 was about the best I'd ever bowled," he added.

150 LANCASHIRE GREATS
115. Paul Allott

Paul Allott, a powerfully-built, skilful right-arm medium-fast swing bowler, was the mainstay of the Lancashire attack for 14 seasons from 1978. Born in Altrincham, he played minor counties cricket for Cheshire before joining Lancashire. One of the most economical and accurate bowlers in limited overs competitions, he could always be relied upon to produce a perfect off-stump line. He took 549 first-class wickets for Lancashire at 24.30 and 24 times took five or more wickets in an innings. He also took over 250 wickets in one-day competitions, helping Lancashire to win the double in 1990. He made his Test debut at Old Trafford in 1981 against Australia, scoring 52* and also taking four wickets. He played in 13 Test matches and made 13 one-day international appearances for England. He could also bat adequately late in the order and his hard-hitting style helped win many matches. In 1989 he hit a six to win the Sunday League. Known as 'Walt' in the dressing room, he was relied upon by Lancashire for his trademark consistency, bowling a perfect off-stump line day-in, day-out. He is currently working as a commentator for Sky Sports and is on the board of Lancashire.

Wretched season for Lancashire

1985

LANCASHIRE HAD a wretched season in 1985. They finished 14th in the County Championship, 15th in the John Player League, they did not qualify for the knockout rounds of the Benson and Hedges Cup and fell in the second round of the NatWest Trophy. Finishing bottom of the league was, embarrassingly, a realistic prospect heading into the closing stages of the season, but ultimately a win over fellow basement battlers Somerset at Old Trafford, who eventually finished bottom themselves, towards the end of August proved crucial.

The Red Rose actually went six matches unbeaten at the end of the season, although only won one of them. This came from a pulsating rain-affected clash with the Taunton outfit, Lancashire's penultimate home match. The visitors had set the pace with a strong batting performance, led by 88 from opener Peter Roebuck, 120 for Viv Richards and an unbeaten 76 from captain Ian Botham. They contributed to 329-4 declared. But rain early in the match forced captains Botham and John Abrahams to get their heads together. After a couple of innings forfeits, Lancashire responded with their own impressive batting performance to claim 17 points.

The Wisden match report takes up the story: "Lancashire's third win came after the opening day was lost to rain and both teams had forfeited an innings. For Somerset,

Richards hit his sixth century of the season with eleven fours and five sixes, sharing in a stand of 206 in 46 overs with Roebuck, while Botham batted for just 47 balls, striking seven fours and four sixes.

"Lancashire were left with the final day – a minimum of 105 overs – in which to secure victory, which was achieved mainly through a (second-wicket) partnership of 176 between (Kevin) Hayes and (Mark) Chadwick, both uncapped and aged 22. Each scored his maiden Championship century."

Two of Lancashire's three Championship wins had come in the first seven fixtures, but they ended the season with only Neil Fairbrother passing 1,000 runs and no bowler taking 50 wickets. The poor form of experienced batting trio Alan Ormrod, Graeme Fowler and Steve O'Shaughnessy proved particularly costly. At some stage in the season, they were all dropped from the Championship team. The Red Rose only won five one-day matches all summer. One of

those came against Suffolk in the NatWest Trophy.

Fairbrother, capped by the county in 1985, scored two hundreds in Roses Championship matches against Yorkshire, both of which were drawn. The 21-year-old left-hander hit 128 in the first innings of the clash at Old Trafford in late

Graeme Fowler was one of a number of experienced players who found themselves out of the team during this forgettable season.

May and 147 in the first innings of the return at Headingley in early August.

Fairbrother is one of 12 Red Rose players who have achieved the feat of scoring two hundreds against the old enemy in the same season in their first-class history, although we are still awaiting the first player to do it in the same match.

Archie MacLaren, Cyril Washbrook, Geoff Pullar, Jack Bond, Barry Wood, Gehan Mendis, Nick Speak, Michael Atherton, Alec Swann, Mark Chilton and Mal Loye are the other names on the list.

Rhoades resigns *1986*

CEDRIC RHOADES, Lancashire's chairman since 1969, was forced to resign having been caught out about who recommended Clive Lloyd's appointment as captain ahead of a miserable summer for the county as they finished 15th in the County Championship, got knocked out of the Benson and Hedges Cup early on and lost in the NatWest Trophy final to Sussex. After Lloyd retired at the end of a season which saw the sacking of manager Jack Bond and coach Peter Lever, Rhoades misled members about Lloyd's appointment at the AGM in December before coming under increasing pressure in the ensuing months. He resigned in February 1987, with Bob Bennett taking over shortly afterwards.

Rhoades said that Lloyd was recommended by manager Bond, but long-standing member Ken Thomas knew this was nothing to do with Bond. He questioned Rhoades about this at the AGM, which proved to be the beginning of the end for Rhoades. Here, he and Bennett take us through what Thomas described as a "nasty" episode in the club's history.

"At that AGM, no one was very happy about Clive's appointment as captain because, as great a cricketer as he was and as lovely a man as he is, he wasn't the best captain we'd ever had," said Thomas.

"Cedric said Clive was appointed on the specific advice of the then manager Jack Bond. I knew that was not true because I was, and still am, very close to Jack. I got up and said 'Mr chairman, would you mind repeating that. Are you saying that Clive's appointment as captain was on the direct recommendation of Jack Bond?'

"He said 'yes'. It happened very, very late in the meeting under Any Other Business, and I don't think he was expecting this kind of question. I thought 'I'm not having this'."

After the AGM, Rhoades came under intense pressure from the media, and it was a storm he could not ride. Bennett said: "After the AGM, I went off to Australia on holiday and received a call saying that Cedric had resigned. He was being put under pressure because it was all over the media that Jack had said he made

'Lord' Tim attempts to oust committee

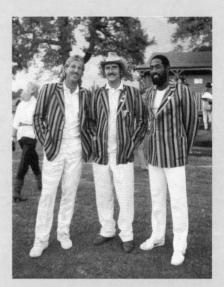

'Lord' Tim Hudson was one of the most colourful characters to stand for the Lancashire Committee. A former 2nd XI player, in 1987 he stood on a mandate which shook the members. Talking about City Cricket, he was an early exponent of what was to become the IPL in India. He was a self-proclaimed hippy eccentric who claimed to have invented the term 'flower-power' whilst working as a DJ in California in the sixties touring with the Beatles. In the 1980s he bought Birtles Old Hall in Prestbury and became Lord of the Manor. It was there he developed Birtles Bowl and brought the cream of English cricket to this ground to play his Hollywood XI, which included Ian Botham, who he managed for a short time in 1986. It had its unique psychedelic pavilion and welcomed the likes of Viv Richards, Gary Sobers and Imran Khan, with rock bands playing in the tea interval. As can be imagined, this picture of the future was too much for Lancashire members and he polled only 273 votes. It was also too much for the residents of Prestbury and in 2004 he sold up and returned the USA. Interestingly, if he attended Twenty20 cricket today it would be something akin to what he was he was proposing 25 years earlier.

no recommendation. In the end, the committee told Cedric he had to resign.

"I received a call at 4am in the morning in Perth from Chris Hassell (secretary) saying 'you will do it, won't you?'. I said 'yes, fine, no problem', but

because of the time of day I didn't really know what I'd agreed to. I ended up cutting short my holiday and coming back ten days later to start the job in late February/early March."

150 LANCASHIRE GREATS
117. Gehan Mendis

Gehan Mendis was born in Columbo, Sri Lanka, and came to Sussex in his teens. He played 201 matches for Sussex between 1974 and 1985, scoring over 11,000 runs. He joined Lancashire in 1986 and became a very dependable opening batsman, scoring over 1,000 runs in a season seven times with a best of 1,551 runs in 1990. Capped in 1986, he and Graeme Fowler formed an opening partnership of contrasting styles which served the county well both in first-class and one-day cricket. A remarkably patient player who was not frightened of the fastest of bowlers, he had quick eyes and nimble feet and was a recognised performer against pace bowlers. He scored 9,815 runs for Lancashire, ave. 38.94, with 18 centuries and centuries in all three one-day competitions. He twice turned down invitations to play for his native Sri Lanka although he lived in England all his life. He can be considered unlucky because of his courage and consistency against fast bowling to not to have been chosen to open the innings for England. He retired from cricket to join the financial world.

Lancs come close to Championship *1987*

IT WAS a tough job to replace Clive Lloyd as Lancashire's overseas player, but somebody had to do it! Step forward Pakistan fast bowler Wasim Akram. Wasim actually debuted for Lancashire at the start of 1988, but he first caught the eye of the county's hierarchy as a tearaway 20-year-old bowling for his country in a triangular one-day international series with England and Australia at Perth in January of this year.

The Benson and Hedges Challenge was being played on Australia's west coast as part of the America's Cup Festival of Sport. And it just so happened that Lancashire's incoming captain David Hughes was Down Under with coach Alan Ormrod. "Alan and myself were in Australia prior to the '87 season watching the Perth Challenge, a one-day triangular competition as part of the Americas Cup yacht race celebrations," explained Hughes.

"I do recall with some fun that Worcester were out there too trying to sign Graham Dilley and Ian Botham. The press had said that it was us in for those two, which gave us a bit of a smokescreen to sign Phil DeFreitas from Leicestershire and Akram.

"We spoke to Was, but Neil Fairbrother and Lawrie Brown, ours and England's physio, were out there too. We used those two to make initial contact with the two of them. When I saw Was bowl I thought 'crikey, this bloke would do a great job for Lancashire'.

"Watching that white ball go through, he was bowling anywhere between 85 and 90mph. He was a superb all-round athlete as well. He was a batter who could get in and get you runs, but he was also a great fielder too. He was the perfect acquisition in many ways."

Hughes's first season in charge oh so nearly brought the club their first outright Championship since 1934. They won the last six matches of the season, but fell four points short of overhauling Nottinghamshire having needed the maximum 24 points from their last match against Essex at Chelmsford to win the league. Unfortunately, they missed out on crucial batting points in their first innings score of 220. Despite going on to win the match, it wasn't enough even though it was a marked improvement on a bottom six finish in each of the previous eleven seasons.

The recruitment of the Pakistan all-rounder Wasim Akram and the second place finish in the Championship hinted at better times to come for the Red Rose.

Another plus point was the form of young top order batsman Michael Atherton, who scored 602 runs in his first eleven Championship matches. Aged 19, Failsworth-born Atherton spent the first half of the season at Cambridge University and the second half of it at Old Trafford, where he established himself at number three in the order. In his maiden Championship innings, he scored 53 in a ten-wicket win over Warwickshire at Southport in late July.

---

150 LANCASHIRE GREATS
118. Ian Austin

Ian Austin was born in Haslingden and was a key member of the Lancashire side in the 1990s. 'Oscar' or 'Bully' as he was nicknamed was a dependable and honest cricketer with a quiet, uncomplicated approach to the game. Broad-chested and with good muscles, he could crack a ball over the boundary with ease. He made his first-class debut in 1987 and remained with the county for his entire career, scoring 3,778 runs at 27.98 and taking 262 wickets at 30.35 with his medium-pace seamers in his 124 matches. Enormously popular with the Lancashire crowd thanks to his uncomplicated batting style and equally old-fashioned waistline, his most successful period came towards the end of his career. He won gold awards at Lord's in two finals and also scored the fastest first-class century of 1991 in a Roses game at Scarborough. He made his one-day international debut against Sri Lanka in 1998. He was made one of Wisden's Cricketers of the Year in 1999. He also played two matches in the 1999 World Cup for England. He played for Cumberland in 2002 and returned to the leagues, playing with distinction. He is currently working for Thwaites brewery as a sales representative.

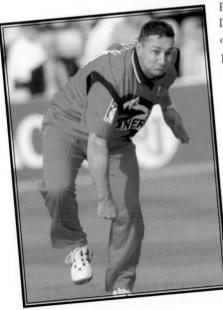

Flat Jack passes 1,000 wickets 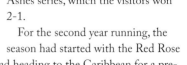 *1988*

JACK SIMMONS became the 13th Lancashire player to take 1,000 first-class wickets when he bowled John Derrick in the first innings of their 72-run County Championship win against Glamorgan at Swansea in June. The Red Rose off-spinning all-rounder, aged 47, followed names such as Brian Statham, Johnny Briggs and Roy Tattersall to that mark, going on to take a total of 1,033 before retiring the following season.

At the age of 47, Jack Simmons became the 13th Lancashire player to take more than 1,000 first-class wickets.

Simmons took 5-53 in the first innings as Glamorgan were bowled out for 199 in response to Lancashire's 155. Gehan Mendis then became the first Red Rose player to carry his bat through an innings for 15 years when he finished 65 not out in a second-innings score of 163, which set the Welshmen only 120 to win.

In a match which also saw Indian slow left-armer Ravi Shastri take eleven wickets,

Simmons finished with nine following four in the second innings as Glamorgan were bowled out for just 47 to seal 21 points. Ian Folley added 6-20 from nine overs to 4-9 from 8.5 for Simmons.

"That was a great game," recalled Simmons. "To get 1,000 wickets was very special. I believe I was the 13th Lancastrian to get to that milestone. To be with all the greats of yesterday was a great feeling. To get it and not just get 1,001 and 1,002, I finished up with quite a few more, was fantastic for me.

"The lads knew that I was getting very, very close, and that I was getting more nervous. Luckily, we went to play at Swansea, which has always been a reputable wicket for spinners. I went there feeling a hell of a lot better and hoping I would get it."

Simmons went on to take 60 wickets in the season as Lancashire finished ninth.

Chris Matthews, a three-time Australian Test fast bowler, endured a frustrating summer as one of the county's two overseas players alongside Wasim Akram, playing only seven matches in all forms of cricket. But at the age of 25, Perth-born Matthews at least wrote himself into the Red Rose record books in a Benson and Hedges Cup Group A tie against Leicestershire at Grace Road in late April.

He still holds the record for the highest score by a Lancashire number eleven batsman in a List A fixture, having hit 43 in a last-wicket stand of 69 with Simmons, who made an unbeaten 31. They helped Lancashire add respectability to their score having been 98-9 in pursuit of 214 in 55 overs. The Red Rose county failed to qualify for the quarter-finals having won only one of four matches.

Two of the three Tests Matthews played were against England at the Brisbane and

Perth in the early stages of the 1986/87 Ashes series, which the visitors won 2-1.

For the second year running, the season had started with the Red Rose squad heading to the Caribbean for a pre-season tour. They even played Jamaica in a three-day first-class match, which they had the better of at Sabina Park in early April.

Neil Fairbrother scored a first-innings century and Mike Watkinson took seven wickets in the match, which finished drawn. In the years to come, Lancashire would tour places such as Zimbabwe, Australia, South Africa and the United Arab Emirates, their preferred destination in the current era.

150 LANCASHIRE GREATS
119. Ian Folley

Ian Folley died tragically at the age of 30 after sustaining a blow on the face while attempting a hook shot. He was taken to the local hospital but died soon afterwards. Born in Burnley, he made his debut for the county in 1982 as a left-arm pace bowler but changed to spin the following year and emerged as a bowler to be reckoned with. His best season was 1987, when he took 70 wickets, ave. 24.40, and was the leading left-arm spinner in the country. He was awarded his county cap and also played for MCC. He took a career best 7-15 against Warwickshire at Southport, going on to take 12 wickets in the match. The following year he took 57 wickets but didn't play in 1989-1990 because of a lack of control in his bowling. He played 135 first-class matches for Lancashire, taking 280 wickets at 31.18, including five or more wickets in an innings ten times. He played for Derbyshire for one season in 1990 before moving to Egremont in Cumberland and combining playing league cricket with his work in the licensing trade. His team-mate John Stanworth said of him: "Everybody in cricket, from teammates to opponents, have memories of his life; most of mine continue to bring a smile to my face."

Hayhurst and Watkinson star in Refuge Assurance Cup triumph

STAR PERFORMANCES from all-rounders Andy Hayhurst and man-of-the-match Mike Watkinson helped David Hughes' side claim the county's first trophy since 1984 by winning the four-team Refuge Assurance Cup with a win over Worcestershire in the final at Edgbaston in mid-September.

The Red Rose qualified for the competition, which saw the use of an orange ball, by finishing third in the Refuge Assurance League.

They won a 40-over semi-final against Gloucestershire at Bristol by chasing down just 118 for the loss of seven wickets. Hughes and Paul Allott had to steer their side home from 99-7.

Worcester were the final opponents having beaten Middlesex in their semi-final at New Road. And although Trevor Jesty top-scored with 59, a brilliantly belligerent 42 from Watkinson helped to post 201-5 having been invited to bat first. The Pears were going reasonably well at 75-2 in response having lost key man Graeme Hick early to Watkinson. But 25-year-old Hayhurst nipped in with 4-46 from eight overs of medium pace as they collapsed to 149 all out.

"I was already a regular in the one-day side. Consequently, establishing yourself as a three-day player, I was doing more bowling," remembered Hayhurst, who joined Somerset ahead of the 1990 campaign.

"What happened was they were doing ok and then Winker got Hick out and we were on top. It was an orange ball, which swung round corners. It was the first time any of us had used that, and it

helped because I swung it anyway. We managed to control it better than they did.

"It was a full house or nearly at Edgbaston with Hick in his prime and two big teams at the time. That was what I remember about it. I had played in one Lord's final, but it was the second or third biggest game I'd played in in terms of crowd.

"I don't think they did it for any other reason than ease of ticketing, but the crowd was segregated. They had Worcester's fans on one side and ours on the other. I was fielding at third man when Winker bowled Hick, and it was the nearest I got to being a footballer because all I saw was the far side of the ground jump up and behind me was quiet. That was fabulous.

"I hadn't had too many big days in my career up until then. I remember getting 4-40 in a NatWest quarter-final at Leicester when I got the likes of Gower out. But I bowled like a drain.

"This one, even though I went for 40-odd, I seem to remember bowling really well, and there were a couple of edges where slip would have been, inside edges – that type of thing. It was going past the bat, which I didn't get it to do that often!"

While Watkinson went on to enjoy a hugely successful career with the county, Hayhurst left Old Trafford at the end of the following season for Somerset due to a lack of first-team opportunities.

He went on to captain the Taunton outfit for three seasons between 1994 and 1996. In all, he scored 13 County Championship hundreds for his second of three counties.

Hayhurst moved to Derbyshire as assistant coach in 1997. He actually played four matches for the Peakites, including one Championship and two Axa Life League fixtures, but got injured early in the season to end his playing days.

Later that summer, Hayhurst was promoted to the role of first-team coach following the departures of Australian Dean Jones and Les Stillman. He appointed Dominic Cork as captain during his reign, but left the County Ground in 1999 following a fall-out with the all-rounder.

Hayhurst returned to Old Trafford in 2002 as the secretary of the Lancashire Cricket Board before graduating through to the role of director, a position he left in the latter stages of 2013.

Andy Hayhurst, left, took four wickets in the Refuge Assurance Cup final. After playing for Somerset and Derbyshire, he returned to Old Trafford to run the Lancashire Cricket Board.

Allott secures Sunday League

1989

PAUL ALLOTT was Lancashire's unlikely hero with the bat as the Refuge Assurance Sunday League title was secured in dramatic fashion against Surrey at Old Trafford in late August. The Red Rose county had been front-runners throughout the competition with eleven wins from their first 13 fixtures, and they needed to win one of their final three – all at Old Trafford – to clinch silverware.

The first of those against Essex was rained off when it looked likely they would lose, then Roses rivals Yorkshire took the points in the second. So it was all to play for when the Oval outfit headed north on August 27. Wasim Akram took 4-21 from eight overs to help bowl Surrey out for 186 inside their 40 overs, but Lancashire were not able to breeze home as they slipped to 170-7 late in their innings. It left Allott and Ian Austin with 17 to get.

"Although we were chasing a modest total, we'd been struggling to get runs in the last three games," recalled Allott. "All of a sudden, we lost a few wickets in the middle and I was batting with Austin.

"There was one over to go with not many to win, and Martin Bicknell was going to bowl it. I'm not exactly sure how many we needed to win. Folklore tells me it was six, but in reality I don't think it was that many. I think it was four or five.

"Anyway, we'd had a mid-pitch conference at the end of the 39th over. I said, 'Right, come on, don't do anything silly. Whatever you do, keep it on the floor and we'll get them in singles'.

"First ball, rush of blood as a number ten batsman, I had a big whoosh and hit it over long-on for six. We didn't have much chance to say anything to each other straightaway because we just ran off celebrating.

"We high-fived each other near the pavilion steps and both nearly fell over. To hit a six in the last over to win the league is a fantastic memory. Batting wasn't my forte, though. I wasn't particularly happy with the batsmen. I came off, went into the dressing room and said 'yes we've won, but don't ever do that to me again!'."

Women were finally admitted into membership of the club after 125 years which meant they could be full members, vote and also enter the club's pavilion.

Refuge Assurance League 1989

	P	W	T	L	N/R	A	Pts	R/R
Lancashire	16	12	0	2	1	1	52	4.722
Worcestershire	16	11	0	4	0	1	46	4.991
Essex	16	11	0	4	1	0	46	4.576
Nottinghamshire	16	9	0	6	0	1	38	4.691
Derbyshire	16	9	0	6	0	1	38	4.257
Hampshire	16	8	1	6	1	0	36	4.339
Northamptonshire	16	8	0	6	1	1	36	4.366
Surrey	16	9	0	7	0	0	36	4.912
Middlesex	16	8	1	7	0	0	34	4.195
Somerset	16	7	1	8	0	0	30	5.030
Kent	16	7	0	9	0	0	28	4.753
Sussex	16	6	1	8	1	0	28	4.751
Yorkshire	16	7	0	9	0	0	28	4.810
Leicestershire	16	5	0	10	0	1	22	4.082
Warwickshire	16	5	0	10	0	1	22	4.730
Glamorgan	16	2	0	12	1	1	12	4.612
Gloucestershire	16	3	0	13	0	0	12	4.342

Chucky equals world record

WARREN HEGG recalls an eventful County Championship draw at Chesterfield in early August when he equalled the world record with eleven catches in the match, which remains a Lancashire record but no longer a world record. The Red Rose wicketkeeper was also witness to a superb 161 in the first innings from captain Neil Fairbrother after being hit by West Indies quick Ian Bishop and also an amusing verbal battle between the left-handed batsman and his former junior team-mate John Morris.

Lancashire, invited to bat first, made 372 before the hosts responded with 354. Hegg and company were then bowled out for 201 in their second innings, which set Derbyshire 220 to win. They finished on 193-8. Phil DeFreitas took nine wickets in the match, including first-innings figures of 6-116 when Hegg took seven catches, also a club record that was equalled by Luke Sutton in 2008. And Hegg, who finished the summer as the country's leading wicketkeeper with 79 dismissals, said: "Chesterfield was fantastic for keeping wicket. It was bouncy and had a bit of pace.

"I remember Ian Bishop bowling at the speed of sound. It was typical West Indies – short, fast, intimidating and violent. He hit Neil Fairbrother flush on the chin. But from then on, Harv smashed him all over the place. He played beautifully.

"It came to our turn to bowl, and we had a really good seam attack. DeFreitas, Akram, Austin, Watkinson, and Dexter Fitton as our off-spinner.

"I was really looking forward to it, and they just kept nicking it to me. I think I had one or two out of the eleven that I had to move slightly to my right for, nothing more. It is nice to think that I was a joint world record holder, but it was real credit to the bowlers for exploiting the conditions.

"Another thing that sticks in my mind from that game was Johnny Morris in the second innings. He and Harv had played together in Cheshire junior cricket, and he kept playing and missing. Harv gave it all the usual 'do you want a bell in it?' and 'it's red and round'.

"Johnny, a school bully like character, was getting more irate. He stopped the game

at one point and stared at Harv. Next ball he nicked Austin to slip. He almost chased Harv off the field. It was the funniest thing."

Pavilion is 1989 beneficiary

LANCASHIRE CELEBRATED their 125th anniversary year by raising £130,000 for Pavilion Restoration. It was the first time in the club's history that a project profited from being handed a benefit year rather than an individual.

A three-man committee, chaired by Bob Wilson, was charged with raising the funds.

"In the main, the money was raised in the same way it would be for a beneficiary," explained Wilson, a Lancashire vice president. "But there was one unusual thing we did, which wouldn't usually happen with beneficiaries.

"We minted a medallion three different ways. We minted a solid gold one that was presented to the Duke of York when he came to visit. There was also a gold plated one and a silver plated one, although they weren't real gold or silver.

"They were given to members who subscribed to donating to the fund. If you paid so much you got the gold one and so much you got the silver. They were basically done to commemorate the 125 years of the club, and virtually every member donated.

"The others on the committee were Paddy Smith, who was also a vice president but has passed away now, and a gentleman called John Downs. We were three business people.

"The electrics in the pavilion were one of the big things done. The wires were all over the place and not connected up properly. The money was used very well, and we were very happy."

A similar thing happened in 2003 when £120,000 was raised for the LCCC Academy.

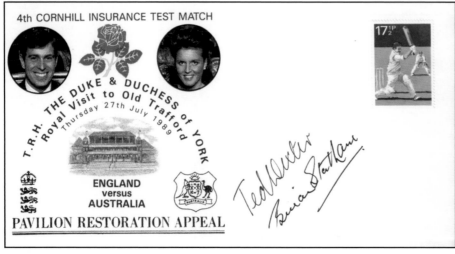

Memorable season for Lancashire

1990

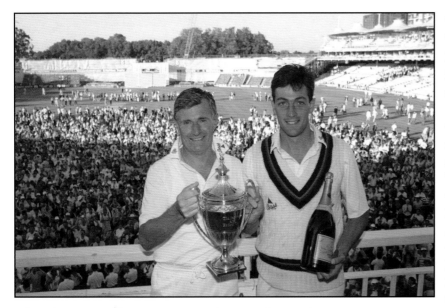

LANCASHIRE RETURNED a 'real good team performance' to beat Worcestershire by 69 runs and win the Benson and Hedges Cup at Lord's in mid-July, according to man of the match Mike Watkinson, who excelled with bat and ball.

The Red Rose, invited to bat first, posted a challenging 241-8 from 55 overs having been in peril at 47-3 and 136-5 thanks to Watkinson's 50 off 78 balls and other useful contributions from Michael Atherton (40), Wasim Akram and Phil DeFreitas (both 28) and Warren Hegg (31 not out). Watkinson and Atherton shared 91 for the fourth wicket before the latter was run out going for a quick single and Watkinson was caught and bowled by Ian Botham as he played to leg.

At that stage, Lancashire needed something special, which Akram, DeFreitas and Hegg provided. Akram even hit two colossal sixes in one Neil Radford over, the biggest over long-on and into the top tier of the pavilion.

"There was great role awareness amongst the side, and everybody settled in for their respective jobs," said Watkinson, who certainly had competition for the personal award. "We had some great fire power at the back end of the innings with Ian Austin, Warren and Was, pace up front with the ball and steady contributions to go with it.

"Should I have been the man of the match or should it have been Akram? That was something that had been debated because he got nearly 30 runs quickly and got Hick out with a great piece of bowling. He went in-swinger, in-swinger, in-swinger, out-swinger and Hick nicked it."

Akram had Tim Curtis caught behind with only his second ball in the 14th over to make the breakthrough before, as Watkinson said, removing Graeme Hick with a beauty. Watkinson (2-37 from eleven overs) bowled Curtis's opening partner Martin Weston and Damian D'Oliveira with balls that nipped back down the slope from the Pavilion End to leave the score at 82-4 and the Pears on the rack. DeFreitas later bowled Botham for an innings-high 38 before Akram (3-30) added his third by bowling Phil Newport.

"I remember looking down the sheet afterwards at names like Botham, Atherton, Fairbrother, Akram, Hick thinking 'you've been picked as man-of-the-match, that's something nice to keep hold of'," added Watkinson.

Benson & Hedges Cup final 1990

Lancashire 241-8 (55 overs)
(M Watkinson 50, MA Atherton 40)

Worcestershire 172 (54 overs)
(Wasim Akram 3-30)

Records galore at the Oval

Lancashire's County Championship draw against Surrey at the Oval in early May was described as "a game for the history books" by Mike Watkinson, who played a small part in the Red Rose's highest innings total in their first-class history.

Neil Fairbrother's 407-ball 366, including a staggering 47 fours and five sixes, contributed to a first-innings score of 863 all out after Surrey had posted 707-9 declared. Surrey's score also remains the most Lancashire have ever conceded in a first-class innings.

Fairbrother's knock, which spanned eight hours and 20 minutes, is the second highest individual score in Lancashire history, while he and Michael Atherton shared a record third-wicket partnership of 364. The total match haul of 1,650 runs – Surrey were 80-1 in their second innings at the end – is also the highest in the county's history.

Red Rose double up

PHIL DEFREITAS starred with five wickets as Lancashire made history by becoming the first county to win the Benson and Hedges Cup and NatWest Trophy in the same season. David Hughes's side hammered Northamptonshire by seven wickets in a one-sided Lord's final in early September, which included the England bowler's 5-26 from 12 overs as the Wantage Road outfit were restricted to 171 all out. Such was Lancashire's early dominance – they had their opponents at 87-7 – some of their supporters were even planning the afternoon's entertainment by looking down the London football fixtures!

DeFreitas took the first five wickets in just over an hour of play. He had Nigel Felton caught at first slip, Alan Fordham lbw, Wayne Larkins and Rob Bailey both caught behind and Allan Lamb lbw. But David Capel's 36 and 48 from Curtly Ambrose prolonged the match: "We got off to the perfect start, and Daffy ripped the heart out of the batting," recalled team-mate Ian Austin.

"He bowled very well on what was a wicket that did a bit. Everyone went on about the 10.30am starts in the NatWest, and yes it was an advantage if you bowled first. But you've still got to bowl well."

There was oh so nearly a sting in the tail as Ambrose, with Lancashire having been reduced to 28-2, dropped Neil Fairbrother at mid-on off Nick Cook's left-arm spin before the left-hander made them pay with 81 off 68 balls, including nine fours and two sixes. When he fell caught at mid-on by Ambrose off the off-spin of Richard Williams, the hard work had been done with the score at 142-3. Mike Watkinson later hit the winning runs with 14.2 overs of the 60 to spare before, not surprisingly, DeFreitas was honoured with the man-of-the-match award.

"When you're playing in a final, nothing's easy. They weren't going to roll over and give it to us even though they'd got a low score. It was tough in the early stages of the innings. But, in reality, the game was over by 12 o'clock," added Austin. "I think you relax a little bit more then and take in more of what's happening around you."

The Manchester Grammar connection

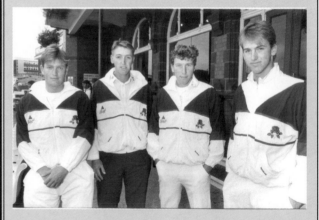

In 1990, Lancashire had no fewer than four contracted players from Manchester Grammar School. Pictured here are Gary Yates, Mark Crawley, Michael Atherton and John Crawley. Atherton was already an England player and would go on to captain his country. Mark Crawley played just this one season for the Red Rose before moving to Nottinghamshire, but younger brother John captained the county and made 37 appearances for England. Yates has had a long career as a player and coach at the club.

Akram on fire *1991*

OVERSEAS STAR Wasim Akram passed 50 Championship wickets for the second year running, including a spectacular run of seven five-wicket hauls or better in eight matches. The Pakistani quick ran into some exceptional form between early June and early August, including an eleven-wicket match haul in a comprehensive six-wicket win over Middlesex at Uxbridge in late July.

It was one of six wins in a disappointing season for the Red Rose, who finished eighth in the table. Lancashire, defending champions, were also beaten finalists in the Benson and Hedges Cup by Worcestershire in July. Akram also took five against

Neil Fairbrother passed 1,000 runs in a season for the eighth time in ten seasons in 1991, and this included centuries in both innings of the game with Somerset.

Hampshire, Leicestershire, Nottinghamshire and Yorkshire as well as six against Kent. Wasim was the county's leading wicket-taker in the Championship with 56 from 14 matches.

"In Championship cricket, in two or three overs Was could stand the game on its head," said team-mate Mike Watkinson, who played with the Lahore-born star right the way through his ten-year Red Rose career between 1988 and 1998.

"A game would be drifting away nowhere and he'd just come on and bowl, perhaps break a partnership and a new batsman would come in. He would make it really, really difficult for them. He bowled quick, but he didn't have to be absolutely rapid quick.

"In one-day cricket, let's say we had Allott and DeFreitas or Chapple and Martin; they could open the bowling and then it would be a case of 'we've seen the new ball off, but who comes on, Wasim Akram'.

"If it was really dry, sometimes he'd be reversing it after a dozen overs. He'd be a real handful. At the end of the innings, he just hit the blockhole. He was pretty good with that. With your overseas players, you don't want to pick up players of inferior quality who will hold back your own. You want them to be someone who can be a role model or a mentor.

"What was good about Wasim was that he'd grown up with us really. He was only 19, 20 or 21 when he first joined up with us. They become one of your own in many ways. You can look at some overseas players nowadays and they've played for five or six counties, whereas players back then only played for one."

Neil Fairbrother continued his excellent form of the previous year by passing 1,000 first-class runs in an English summer for the eighth time in ten attempts, including two centuries in a Championship match against Somerset at Taunton in early July,

The prolific left-hander could not halt Lancashire's slide to defeat, but he joined an impressive list of Red Rose batsmen to have achieved the feat.

Warrington-born Fairbrother hit 109 in the first innings as the visitors posted 326-8 declared, which Somerset responded to with 268-3 declared. Fairbrother added 102 in the second innings as Lancashire posted 235-7 declared, setting their hosts 294 to win. Chris Tavare's men achieved their target inside 61 overs with four wickets to spare.

This season proved to be the last before retirement for captain David Hughes, and he would hand over the reins to Fairbrother ahead of the 1992 campaign. Hughes had been a stalwart of the Lancashire side for more than two decades and under his captaincy the club had again become a major force in one-day cricket.

150 LANCASHIRE GREATS
122. Wasim Akram

Wasim Akram is regarded as one of the greatest fast bowlers in the history of cricket and a magnificent all-rounder. In nine seasons with Lancashire his contribution to the county was immense. In only his second match in 1988 he scored a century against Somerset. He also took 5-15, including a hat-trick, at Southport against Surrey and then hit 98 from 78 balls before being caught on the boundary trying to hit a six to win the game. He played in 91 first-class matches for the club and took 374 wickets at 21.65. He took five wickets or more in an innings 30 times – once every 3 matches! In 1998 he was appointed captain and led Lancashire to a win at Lord's in the NatWest Trophy, one of the proudest moments of his life. Along with Waqar Younis, he formed one of the most formidable and devastating new-ball attacks in Test cricket history. He is considered to be one of the founders and perhaps the finest exponent of reverse-swing bowling. A magnificent striker of the ball, he scored an unbeaten 257 for Pakistan batting at no.8. In 2009, he was one of five new members inducted into the ICC Cricket Hall of Fame.

Four-day cricket gets thumbs up

1992

184 runs at Scarborough in 1989 and Nottinghamshire by ten wickets at Trent Bridge the following summer. Michael Atherton enjoyed a match to remember in the latter, including 81 in the first innings and a career best 6-78 from 21.3 overs as the hosts, following-on in reply to 499 and having been bowled out for 202, were bowled out again for 346. That set the visitors 50 to win, which they achieved in eight overs.

A quarter-final finish in the Benson & Hedges Cup was the standout performance of a forgettable one-day season, which saw Lancashire exit the NatWest Trophy in the second round and finish equal eleventh in the Sunday League.

Wicketkeeper Warren Hegg was one of those who felt that four-day cricket was the right way to go.

IT WAS decided that, at the end of the 1992 season, all future County Championship matches would be played over four days instead of three following a five-season trial period. Counties had been playing six four-day Championship matches per year since 1988, the first and last three games of the season, with the odd exception.

Wicketkeeper Warren Hegg was one player delighted with the decision to change. He said: "In the early stages of my career, I was playing three-day cricket, which was the first two days, then a Sunday League game and finishing off the Championship game on a Monday. So we were still playing four days anyway.

"From that point of view, there was no problem in terms of tiredness. But it was a better format of cricket. You found out over the four days that the better side would win, whereas over three days, if you didn't get four or five wickets in the first session, you were looking for a declaration on day one even at that early stage.

"Four-day cricket was really attacking, positive cricket because you had to bowl a side out rather than maybe wait for a declaration."

Lancashire won nine four-day matches in the five years, including two of those in this season as they finished 12th of 18 counties – the first summer Durham competed in the Championship having been introduced from Minor Counties cricket. Nick Speak scored a superb 232 as Lancashire beat Leicestershire by an innings and 45 runs at Grace Road in mid-May in one of the two four-days win in '92, while slow left-arm Alex Barnett returned figures of 5-78 and 3-74 in either innings.

Other notable four-day wins in the trial period included beating Yorkshire by

Nick Speak made a superb 232 against Leicestershire at Grace Road.

150 LANCASHIRE GREATS
123. Phil DeFreitas

Born in Dominica, 'Daffy' came to London at the age of ten and after a spell on the Lord's groundstaff was offered a contract by Leicestershire in 1985. He played there for four seasons before moving to Lancashire and appeared in 76 matches for the county in five seasons. He made an immediate impact, becoming the leading wicket-taker with 65 wickets at an ave. 24.64, including 7-21 against Middlesex at Lord's. In 1990 he scored 608 runs for the county, including two centuries, and he played a large part in helping Lancashire win the Nat West Cup Final at Lord's when he took 5-26 against Northants and won the Man-of-the-Match award. In one-day games for Lancashire he took 150 wickets and scored useful runs as a middle-order batsman with some explosive displays of hard hitting. He played in 44 Test Matches for England and also 103 one-day Internationals. He was one of Wisden's Cricketers of the Year in 1991 and toured Australia three times. He went on to play for Derbyshire and then returned to Leicestershire, where he became the first player to take 1,000 wickets in first-class cricket in the reduced Championship programme. He coached at Oakham School after retirement.

Crawley ton sinks Aussies

1993

JOHN CRAWLEY scored a superb 109 as Lancashire secured a major scalp by beating the rampant Australians in late July, becoming the first team to do so in a first-class match on that tour. Allan Border's side had just taken an unassailable 3-0 lead in the Ashes with a fourth Test victory at Headingley, but still included seven players from the Test in the side to face the Red Rose, including the Waugh brothers, Mark Taylor and Shane Warne.

At the start of the Ashes summer, Warne had bowled Mike Gatting in the first Test at Old Trafford with 'the ball of the century'. But, coached by Bob Simpson, who would later coach the Red Rose, they were no match for Mike Watkinson's Lancashire in a three-day affair.

Opener Taylor, captaining the tourists, posted 122 in a total of 282-3 declared before Lancashire responded with 250-7 declared during the second day. Another declaration came from the Australians with their second innings at 194-8, which included four wickets for Malaga-born left-arm spinner Alex Barnett.

That set the Red Rose 227 to win in 61 overs, which they achieved for the loss of five wickets. Crawley, aged 21, led the way from the top of the order with eleven fours in 180 balls. Lancashire ended up needing 16 off the last two overs, and Watkinson hit 14 off five balls, including a six, to secure a famous win.

"We had also played them a few years before (in 1989)," recalled wicketkeeper Warren Hegg. "It was also just after a Test match, and our opening attack was Patrick Patterson and Wasim Akram. We played both overseas, and it was the fastest combined spell of bowling I ever kept to.

"They had both played against these guys in Test match cricket, and they were desperate to prove a point. They just wanted to hit them on the head."

The Australians won that match, but revenge was sweet for Hegg and company: "To play against them again in such good form and win was fantastic," he admitted.

"John Crawley was a young player coming into our side, and he'd been bigged up by their coach at the time, who was Simpson. He said 'this boy's the best prospect in English cricket, get him in the team'. It just shows that John was a great player even at that age."

150 LANCASHIRE GREATS
124. Warren Hegg

Warren Hegg was a naturally talented wicketkeeper with an excellent temperament and his energy and enthusiasm helped him to be the perfect team man. He made his first-class debut for Lancashire in 1986 and remained with the county for his entire career. In 1989 he set a Lancashire record when he held 11 catches in a single first-class match. One of Hegg's finest moments came in 1996 when playing against Yorkshire in the semi-final of the Benson & Hedges Cup. Chasing 251 to win, Lancashire were 97-5 when Hegg arrived at the crease. Further wickets tumbled around him, but he scored 81 from 62 balls to help steer his county to victory by one-wicket from the very last ball of the match. He scored over 11,000 first-class runs, ave 27.90, and over 3,000 runs in limited overs cricket. He was selected for two Test matches during the 1998–99 Ashes tour of Australia. He was appointed captain of Lancashire in 2002 and the county finished third and second in the County Championship in 2002 and 2003. A freak accident in 2005 forced his career to end prematurely and he finished with a total of 919 first-class dismissals, just six short of George Duckworth's Lancashire record of 925. He now works at Old Trafford as Business Development Manager.

John Crawley showed what an exciting prospect he was with an accomplished century against the touring Australians, who had just taken a 3-0 lead in the Test series.

Watkinson knocks on England door

1994

Mike Watkinson's all-round contribution to the Lancashire team would see him become yet another Red Rose international.

MIKE WATKINSON spoke of the game of his life after taking eleven wickets, including a career best eight-for, and scoring a second-innings century as Hampshire were hammered by 263 runs at Old Trafford in June. The legendary Red Rose captain revealed a determination to be the best off-spinner in the country, to eclipse Shaun Udal, Robert Croft and Peter Such, which inspired him to play a key role in one of eight four-day wins as the county finished tenth.

A little over a year away from his Test debut against the West Indies on his home ground, this individual performance was a major bright spot for the county in a season that also saw them docked 25 points for preparing an under-used pitch for a clash with Middlesex.

"I suppose what makes that game even more special is that I scored a century (to go along with the eleven wickets)," said Watkinson, one of only five men to achieve the feat in Lancashire's history – and the first since Jack Ikin in 1947.

"It was at a stage of my career just before I got picked for England when I tried to compete against the other off-spinners in the country. I got my highest score of 161 against Essex the year before when Such was bowling for them. But Udal was playing in this game for Hampshire, and it was a spinning pitch.

"I got a dozen runs in the first innings, then I got my 8-30, then I got my hundred, then I got three-for whatever. I thought 'this is game of your life territory'.

"They had Raj Maru and Udal bowling, and I just kept thinking 'Udal, don't let him get you out – score off him'. I had that mentality for a while because there were a few around with people like Crofty as well. I got picked for England in '95, so that performance came at the right time, definitely."

Hampshire were bowled out for 162 in their pursuit of 426 to win. Watkinson added figures of 3-57 from 24.3 overs to 8-30 from 22.3 in the first innings, while he also scored 117 in the second innings.

Lancashire groundsman Peter Marron resigned as the Test and County Cricket Board's assistant inspector of pitches over a row which cost the county 25 points and the chance of finishing third in the Championship.

The Red Rose county hammered Middlesex at Old Trafford in late July by 361 runs, but were docked 25 points for producing a sub-standard pitch. Having been invited to bat first, Lancashire were bowled out for 163 before the visitors replied with 101. In the hosts' second innings, Neil Fairbrother's 204 helped set a target of 546. Middlesex were bowled out for 185.

Ian Austin took five wickets in each innings to complete what proved to be the only ten-wicket match haul of his career, but Lancashire came away with minus five points: "It would now be hypocritical of me to judge other groundsmen," said Marron.

Lancashire bounced back to win their next two matches against Essex at Chelmsford and Yorkshire at Headingley, while the committee firmly defended Marron. The docked points meant Lancashire's players were set to miss out on £14,000 in prize money, but the committee chose to ignore the penalty when their bonus payments were calculated at the end of the season.

Of more national interest, Michael Atherton found himself in hot water less than a week later having been accused of ball tampering during the Lord's Test against South Africa, which England lost by 356 runs. National captain Atherton was pictured applying a substance (it later transpired to be dirt) from his right trouser pocket onto the ball.

He was summoned to explain his actions to match referee Peter Burge at the end of day three, and the opening batsman told him he had only dried his sweaty hands on the floor. However, members of the England management Keith Fletcher and Ray Illingworth were told a different story. Atherton later confessed to applying dirt directly onto the ball from his pocket. He argued that he was only maintaining the condition of the ball rather than changing it.

Critics such as Geoffrey Boycott called for Atherton's sacking, but Illingworth instead fined him £2,000 – £1,000 for using dirt and £1,000 for concealing the story from an International Cricket Council official. When he found out, Burge said Atherton's actions "could not be condoned, particularly when done by a Test captain". Burge had earlier decided not to ban the Lancashire player on the strength of previous evidence. In all, Atherton led England a record 54 times in Test cricket between 1993 and 2001.

150 LANCASHIRE GREATS
125. Peter Martin

For 15 seasons 'Digger' Martin pounded in opening the bowling attack and the familiar dismissal of ct Hegg b Martin appeared with remarkable frequency in the scorebook. Born in Accrington, he was a medium-fast bowler who was able to swing the ball away from the batsman. At 6ft 5in, he had pace and bounce with consistent accuracy, finishing with 606 wickets for the county, ave. 27.51, including a career best 8-32 against Middlesex at Uxbridge in 1997. He helped Lancashire to win three Lord's finals and also the Sunday League twice. He played in eight Tests and 20 ODIs for England from 1995 to 1998. A very decent batsman, he was capable of contributing useful runs from the lower order and scored two first-class centuries for Lancashire, including 133 against Durham at Gateshead Fell in 1992. In retirement he was a bowling coach at Old Trafford and was also involved in the wine trade. His favourite pastime is painting in oils and his originals have attracted much attention.

Calm Yates bowls Red Rose to more Cup success

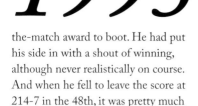

GARY YATES was Lancashire's first name on the teamsheet according to coach David Lloyd. And the Red Rose off-spinner showed just why with three crucial wickets as the county won the Benson and Hedges Cup for the third time by beating Kent at Lord's in July. Aged 27, Yates returned figures of 3-42 from eleven overs as the county defended 275 after posting 274-7 in 55 overs, winning by 35 runs.

"We were star-studded with some fabulous players in that team, but the very first name on the sheet was G Yates," said Lloyd. "You wouldn't put him up alongside the Athertons, Crawleys, Fairbrothers and people like that, but he was still the first name on my sheet. He was just so dependable. He provided us with a much needed change of pace, and he was so unflappable.

"Just look nowadays at David Hussey, who bowls round-arm in limited overs cricket. People see it as something new, but Yatesy was doing that years ago. It's just been recycled."

This final always seems to be remembered as the time when Kent's Sri Lankan batsman Aravinda de Silva scored that fantastic hundred, a 95-ball 112 with eleven fours and three sixes, securing him the man-of-the-match award to boot. He had put his side in with a shout of winning, although never realistically on course. And when he fell to leave the score at 214-7 in the 48th, it was pretty much game over.

"I got prickly in the press conference, as I would do," said Lloyd. "Everybody was talking about this Aravinda innings, which was fabulous. But when he came in, they wanted four and a half an over and when he left, they wanted six and a half. I said 'I think we've done pretty well there'.

"I thought we were the stronger team. Although the bloke got a hundred, I thought we controlled him pretty well."

Gary Yates showed what a valuable asset he was to the team with three wickets in the Benson & Hedges Cup final.

Benson & Hedges Cup final 1995

Lancashire 274-7 (55 overs)
(MA Atherton 93, JP Crawley 83)

Kent 239 (52.1 overs)
(M Watkinson 3-42, G Yates 3-42)

150 LANCASHIRE GREATS
126. Jason Gallian

He was born and raised in Sydney and played youth cricket for Australia before throwing his lot in with England when he signed for Lancashire in 1992, where he played for the second XI to qualify for the county. He was an immediate success, scoring 171 on his Championship debut against Surrey in 1994. He quickly established himself in the Lancashire side, opening the innings with Mike Atherton and proving more than useful with his seam bowling. He scored the slowest ever century, 453 minutes, when his side had their backs to the wall and also a record 312 against Derbyshire at Old Trafford in 1996. He was a technically correct batsman, showing great character and the ability to settle down and amass large scores. He scored centuries in all three one-day competitions. His bowling was good enough for him to once take 6-115 at Southport against Surrey. He played in three Tests and left Lancashire in 1998 to join Nottinghamshire, with a spell as captain, before moving to Essex, where he was involved in winning two trophies in 2008 before he retired.

After Michael Atherton scored 93 and John Crawley 83, the pair sharing 121 for the second wicket to boost the Red Rose, Yates enabled them to take a firm grip on the contest. He bowled Neil Taylor (81-3), trapped Graham Cowdrey lbw sweeping (142-4) and bowled Matthew Fleming (162-5).

Ian Austin later had de Silva caught at deep mid-wicket by Graham Lloyd before Austin caught Tim Wren at long-on off captain Mike Watkinson to complete a famous success.

"Fleming's was the key wicket," recalled Yates. "I always felt Cowdrey was a big wicket, but Fleming and Mark Ealham had been the damgermen for Kent all summer."

Lancashire's current assistant coach continued: "They are very, very fond memories. It was my first final, and I knew I had a great chance of playing. I remember the night leading up to it, being in my room and struggling to sleep. I think I feel asleep well after midnight.

"Then at breakfast, we were given red roses to put on our blazers. We walked across, and there were a few Lancashire supporters wishing us luck.

"My next memory comes when I was given the nod that I'd be bowling the next over at the other end. Mike Watkinson gave me an over's notice.

"I remember saying to myself 'Yatesy, you've worked hard all your life, you've run hard and done all your training for this moment. This is it. Relax, enjoy it and go for it'. It ended up being a good day for me personally and a great win for the team.

"The interesting thing was that there was quite a long delay before they announced the man-of-the-match.

"Apparently, Ian Botham was on the panel with two other ex-players. They felt they should really give the award to a player on the winning team. Botham was keen to give it to me because he felt that my three wickets had turned the game.

"But we had also witnessed one of the best innings played at Lord's by Aravinda. So there's a bit of umming and arrghing, but quite rightly it went to De Silva.

"I went onto the pitch afterwards and spent some time with my girlfriend and now my wife, Christine. Then we went to an Italian, the players and the wives. We had some nice food and a good singalong.

"I remember walking back through Piccadilly in the early hours of the morning seeing on the back pages how we'd won the game. It was a fantastic day."

As aforementioned, Yates has gone on to become a respected and valued member of the club's coaching staff since retiring in 2003, with a particular emphasis on overseeing the running of the second XI.

The England Five

No fewer than five Lancastrians appeared for England in during the 1995 season. From left to right: Jason Gallian, John Crawley, Neil Fairbrother, Peter Martin and Michael Atherton

Kings of one-day cricket at the double again

1996

THIS WAS a great year for Lancashire, who enhanced their reputation as Kings of one-day cricket by winning the knockout double, including the defence of their Benson and Hedges Cup title. But not everything was as rosy, pardon the pun, as you would have expected. Here two Red Rose greats take us back to the B&H and NatWest final wins over Northamptonshire and Essex, with captain at the time Mike Watkinson and then young fast bowler Glen Chapple both having rather different memories.

Benson and Hedges Cup final, Saturday July 13 v Northants, as remembered by Mike Watkinson.

WATKINSON ELECTED to bat first and saw Neil Fairbrother top-score with 63 in a total of 245-9 before Ian Austin returned 4-21 from 9.3 overs as the Wantage Road outfit were bowled out for 214. Lancashire won by 31 runs.

"Peter Martin had been out of the side because he had a badly sprained ankle, so Steve Elworthy had been playing. He'd got wickets in the quarter-final (four against Gloucestershire) and semi-final (one against Yorkshire).

"There was quite a distance between the final and the other matches, however, and Digger was fit again. We had a selection issue.

"This was also the year we had no coach. John Stanworth was helping out by facilitating practice and other things like that, but I was picking the team and doing the captaincy. It was a really challenging year.

"It came to the day before with 12 to pick from, but I still did not know what the right call was. I spoke to a few people who had different views. I even went to bed that night not knowing what the right thing to do was.

"I woke up and thought 'the only way I can play this is that we have junior players

Steve Elworthy, who had done a lot to get Lancashire to the Benson & Hedges Cup final, was left out of the team on the morning of the final. It was a decision which still haunts Mike Watkinson.

inspired by the chance to play in a Lord's final – I can't take the opportunity away from a homegrown Lancastrian'. We went in without an overseas player.

"That's the hardest selection call I've ever made as captain or coach, and I told Steve in the nets beforehand. His family had flown over from South Africa especially, and he just picked up his kit and went back to the hotel. We won the match, but I didn't enjoy it mainly for that reason.

"It was a bombshell for him, but Steve took it like a pro and came back to the ground to celebrate with us. I would expect him to still carry the scars of that day because I know I do. It still does not sit comfortably with me to this day."

150 LANCASHIRE GREATS
127. Mike Watkinson

Born in Westhoughton, 'Winker' was a quality all-rounder, a useful seamer who later turned to off-spin and an aggressive lower middle-order batsman who was a key member of the Lancashire side which enjoyed success in the 1990s. He scored over 10,000 first-class runs, ave 26.84, as well as more than 5,000 in one-day cricket. He took over 700 first-class wickets plus 350 in one-day matches, as well as 156 catches. Appointed captain in 1994, he scored a century and took 10 wickets in a match against Hampshire at Old Trafford. He led Lancashire to double cup final wins at Lord's in 1996 as well as the Benson & Hedges Cup in 1995. International recognition came late - he was almost 34 when first picked in 1995 - but he turned in two solid performances against West Indies and altogether played in four Tests. He was drafted in as England's bowling coach for the tour to Bangladesh in 2003-04 and worked alongside Duncan Fletcher for two winters. After six years as coach at Lancashire, he moved into a new role as Director of Cricket in 2008. He is blessed with a dry sense of humour, accompanied with a determination, purpose and pride in playing and working at Old Trafford.

Benson & Hedges Cup final 1996

Lancashire 245-9 (55 overs)
(NH Fairbrother 63, MA Atherton 48)

Northamptonshire 214 (48.3 overs)
(RG Bailey 46, RR Montgomerie 42, ID Austin 4-21)

NatWest Trophy final, Saturday September 7 v Essex, as remembered by Glen Chapple.

CHAPPLE, AGED 22, picked up the man-of-the-match award for figures of 6-18 from 6.2 overs as Essex, chasing 187, were skittled for just 57 inside 28 overs. Earlier, John Crawley had got Lancashire up to respectability with 66 after they had been 88-4. Lancashire won by 129 runs.

"It was swinging around in the morning, and we grafted. John managed to drag us up to 180ish. There was cloud cover, but we were thinking 'if we don't get 180, we'll get hammered'.

"Peter Martin got three up front, and we were in the game. There was pressure on me when Digger and Ian Austin came off, so I was praying for a good start. I think I went for four in my first couple of balls before Darren Robinson nicked a short one to Fairbrother in the slips.

"That was the boost I needed because I was feeling quite a bit of tension up to that point. After that, they just fell in a heap. Thankfully I got it right.

"I'd played in '95 against Kent and then against Northants in the Bensons. I suppose it was important that I'd been there before on the winning sides, but they'd been high-scoring games. This one was a bit different in terms of pressure.

"By the time I came on to bowl, it was a bit more like four-day cricket because we had to bowl them out rather than defend runs. That was to my strength I guess.

"In terms of personal memories, it's right up there with winning the Championship because it's something you've done on the big stage that everyone remembers. It's not a better achievement than any of the other one-day finals, but I enjoy it more because I took a lot of the credit. I think that's only natural."

At the end of the season Rose Fitzgibbon retired after 40 years involvement at the club. She was the first women cricket secretary and a presentation was made at the Former Players' Association.

> ## NatWest Trophy final 1996
>
> **Lancashire 186 (60 overs)**
> **(JP Crawley 66, RC Irani 3-25,**
> **AP Grayson 3-24)**
>
> **Essex 57 (27.2 overs)**
> **(G Chapple 6-18, PJ Martin 3-17)**

Thriller against Yorkshire

HERO WITH the bat Peter Martin has hailed the county's breathtaking Benson and Hedges Cup semi-final win over Yorkshire at Old Trafford as one of his best ever victories. The Red Rose county beat their White Rose rivals by one wicket as, in pursuit of 251, Martin hit two to deep point off Craig White's last ball of the match.

It was a victory underpinned by a stunning 62-ball 81 from wicketkeeper Warren Hegg as the hosts recovered from 97-5 to get 77 from the last eight overs, including 47 off the last five and eight off the last. What made it just as special for Martin was that it was a team of homegrown Lancastrians aside from overseas player Steve Elworthy.

"That was an underlying theme through the whole team and something we're all massively proud of and will trot out to our heart's content at any given opportunity," recalled the fast bowler. "We had no right to win that match, but Warren played out of his skin. We got over the line, just."

The contest actually went over two days due to rain on the first. Yorkshire finished day one on 198-5 with four overs left of their 50, but ended with 250 the following morning thanks to 95 not out for Australian Michael Bevan and an unbeaten 80 for Richard Blakey.

Lancashire lost Michael Atherton, Mike Watkinson, Elworthy, Nick Speak and Graham Lloyd to leave the score at 97-5 and hamstring their chances before a crucial sixth-wicket stand of 64 between Neil Fairbrother and Hegg reignited their chase. Fairbrother (run out) and Ian Austin fell to leave the score at 174-7 in the 43rd. But, after Gary Yates had lofted left-arm spinner Richard Stemp for a straight six, Hegg peppered the boundary from long-off to cover.

When White bowled Hegg with the last ball of the 48th over, Lancashire were 240-8 needing eleven more to win. And the tension increased dramatically when Anthony McGrath ran Yates (26) out going for two to deep point, leaving the score at 243-9 after 48.5 overs. Glen Chapple hit the first ball of the last over for four before a wide and a single took the target to two off three balls. Martin missed the next two before squeezing the last past Bevan at point to secure the win.

"It's amazing how you go through your whole career taking 950-odd wickets, but the main thing people remember is you hitting two off the last ball!" said Martin.

"One of our strengths as a side was that we could all bat from one to eleven. International Rescue, our nickname for the guys who batted from seven downwards, regularly got us over the line needing 50 off the last seven overs with not many wickets left. It was utterly dramatic. The feeling in the dressing room after that was up there with any other win really."

Lancashire then beat the same opponents by 19 runs in the NatWest Trophy semi-final at Old Trafford in mid-August. Graham Lloyd hit 81 in 293-9 before Martin and Austin took three wickets apiece as Yorkshire replied with 274-8.

"We absolutely murdered them in that one," added Martin. "It looked a lot closer because they walloped loads of runs in the last few overs."

Meanwhile, Jason Gallian scored a superb 312 in a County Championship defeat against Derbyshire in July. It was an innings that lasted 683 minutes, and it remains the highest score in any form of cricket at Old Trafford.

Simmons and Cumbes at helm

1997

ALL-ROUNDER IAN Austin has revealed that he was sceptical of the decision to put players on 12-month contracts during a year of change on and off the field for the Red Rose. Bob Bennett ended his eleven-year spell as chairman as his role in the England team's management increased, while chief executive John Bower also left, citing differences on "issues of philosophy" with some committee members.

The pair were replaced by Jack Simmons and Jim Cumbes before Mike Watkinson resigned to end a successful four-year spell as captain. He was replaced by Wasim Akram ahead of 1998. But, arguably, the most significant news with the club's future in mind was the move from summer contracts.

Austin, 31-years-old and only three years away from retirement, said: "It was the way forward, and it was always going to be. It was just very difficult to change the mentality of doing something completely different to what I'd been doing for the last eleven or 12 years.

"We did two and a half to three weeks of fitness when we came back in early December, then you'd have a week and a half off at Christmas. When you came back, you were probably in worse shape than you were at the start of December!

"In January, it was a case of concentrating on the nets. I'd done all sorts in the previous winters. I worked for a bed company delivering beds and some unloading of animal carcasses from wagons at an abattoir. The full-time contract came late for me. I didn't enjoy the training side at that stage because I couldn't get my head round what we were doing was constructive for cricket.

"I had nothing against Steve Hampson from Wigan Rugby, who was helping us in the gym. I just didn't think it was doing me any good for cricket. I'd been lifting half a cow for five months, so I could do all that! What I needed to do was some cricket.

"It was a learning curve for everybody, and it had to start somewhere. I just don't think enough thought had gone into getting us into cricket specific training. It wasn't massively different financially to what we were on, it was just split over 12 months. I'm sure it's developed massively since the early days."

Lancashire finished outside the top eight in the County Championship for the 20th time in 30 years as they were hampered badly by injuries and international call-ups. The county used 23 players and had four different captains.

The biggest blows were the injury losses of Wasim Akram for all but one match due to a shoulder problem and captain Mike Watkinson, who struggled to make a telling impact, especially with the ball, in the eleven matches he

played. No batsman passed 1,000 Championship runs and only Peter Martin passed 50 wickets.

John Crawley and Michael Atherton, the two England players, played eleven and ten matches respectively, with Crawley's haul of 898 runs being a club high despite his affected availability.

With a more settled team, it would have been no surprise to have seen them challenge for the title. But any hopes of a surprise bid anyway quickly vanished as they had to settle for a first win against Worcestershire at New Road in early June. Lancashire exited both the Benson and Hedges Cup and the NatWest Trophy at an early stage, while they finished third in the Axa Life League. A home defeat against eventual champions Warwickshire at Old Trafford in early August proved to be the killer blow in that campaign.

Coinciding with the introduction of 12-month contracts for Red Rose players was a major revamp of the indoor practice facilities previously built in 1969.

A state of the art Indoor School was built adjacent to the B&Q superstore in the far right-hand corner of the Old Trafford site if you look out from the pavilion, including five bowling lanes designed to suit different conditions such as a spinning pitch and a pitch with more pace and bounce in it. Also included were conference rooms and a club shop.

The initial idea of training indoors came in 1951 when nets were erected in the members' dining room in the pavilion.

150 LANCASHIRE GREATS
128. John Crawley

A product of Manchester Grammar School, he made his debut for Lancashire at the age of 18 before studying for a history degree at Cambridge University, where he played for three seasons. His elegant stroke-making made him a very attractive batsman to watch. He scored 286 for the England 'A' team on their tour of South Africa in 1994. He was also voted Young Cricketer of the Year and topped the Lancashire averages, scoring 281 against Somerset at Southport on a wearing pitch. In 1998 he accumulated 1,850 runs, heading the national averages and scoring 400 runs more than any other player. In 1999 he captained the county and helped win the National League and gain second place in the County Championship. He scored 10,000 runs, ave. 51, for Lancashire and is the only player to average over 50 for the county in a career. He played 37 Tests and 13 one-day internationals, scoring 156* against Sri Lanka. In 2001 he left Lancashire and joined Hampshire, where he continued to score prolifically and finished with over 24,000 career runs. In retirement he taught at Marlborough College and then in 2012 became the Head of Cricket at Magdalen College School in Oxford.

Almost a treble for Wasim's Lancashire

1998

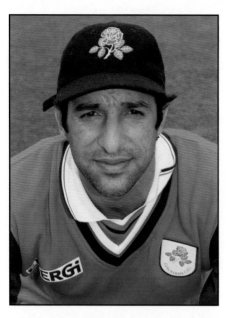

Wasim made an impact as captain every bit the equal to that he had made as a player over the previous decade.

WASIM AKRAM had very little time to make an impact on Lancashire as a captain, but that he certainly did. In fact, so much so that the Pakistani all-rounder has been hailed as one of the county's greatest post war captains. That is the view of long-standing Red Rose member Ken Thomas, who has watched his beloved Lancashire either side of the second world war.

Not only did Was, as he was affectionately known, lead the county to the one-day double, he also led them to second place in the County Championship, a race which went down to the last week of the season. It was their best finish since 1987. The 32-year-old waved goodbye to the Lancashire faithful after ten years at Old Trafford, and had to return to Lahore to fight against allegations of match fixing.

"We've had three great, great captains since the second world war. They are Jack Bond, David Hughes and Wasim Akram," said Thomas. "They were all brilliant captains, and I have to say that Glen Chapple is fast approaching their level as well.

"Wasim was such a brilliant all-rounder, and I mean brilliant. He is the greatest all-rounder I've seen play for Lancashire. Andrew Flintoff is the best English all-rounder I've seen after Botham, but Wasim was something else. He captained by example, and the results under him were wonderful."

Lancashire won 32 of 45 matches in all competitions, including 21 of 28 List A matches. The county won 27 of the 34 matches Wasim captained that summer.

Peter Martin added: "The thing I enjoyed most about Wasim was that he let us be master of our own destiny. We were a very self-propelled group of cricketers, with fine players in there from the top of the line-up to the bottom.

"The last thing you need to do with a group like that is say 'you're doing this, you're doing that'. That team looked after itself, which fitted perfectly with Wasim's style of captaincy. That's fantastic because when you give people the opportunity to look after themselves, they can often really thrive.

"We would all jump through hoops for Was, but he treated us with respect too. He was humble about his performances, which he put in for the team and not himself."

It was oh so nearly the year of all years for the Red Rose, who won their last six County Championship matches only to fall just short of a first outright title since 1934. Lancashire went into their last match of a season in which they only lost five times in all competitions knowing they would have to win and hope other results went their way to secure a terrific treble.

And Wasim's men kept their side of the bargain by beating Hampshire by 161 runs at Old Trafford despite having been bowled out for just 185 inside 69 overs after winning the toss on September 17. Four wickets each for Wasim and Ian Austin helped gain a 13-run first-innings lead before John Crawley and Neil Fairbrother brilliantly put the hosts in the driving seat with 239 and 103 not out respectively.

They shared 261 for the second wicket to underpin a score of 449-4 declared, which meant Hampshire needed 463 in a little over five sessions to win. Gary Yates led the way with 3-86 as Robin Smith's men fell to 301 all out. Unfortunately, their title hopes had ended on day three when Leicestershire beat Surrey by an innings and 211 runs at the Oval. They finished 15 points ahead of second-placed Lancashire.

Another man who had a hugely significant impact on Lancashire's season was prolific batsman John Crawley. He had a point to prove having been dropped from the England Test team midway through the winter tour of the West Indies in the lead-up

to the summer, and he finished the season with 1,681 Championship runs, his most prolific campaign to date.

He scored three successive centuries in that competition, adding an unbeaten 156 on his Test comeback against Sri Lanka at the Oval in late August. Subsequently, the right-hander topped the country's first-class averages with 1,851 runs from 18 matches at an average of 74.04, including eight centuries.

Added to that, the 26-year-old scored 849 runs in List A cricket, including seven fours and two sixes in an Axa League century in a win over Kent at Canterbury in mid-May.

The former Manchester Grammar School pupil was appointed as Wasim's replacement as skipper shortly after the end of the season.

150 LANCASHIRE GREATS
129. Andrew Flintoff

'Freddie' made his Lancashire debut in 1995 and over the following 14 years developed into one of the world's best all-rounders. Born in Preston, he was a tall fast bowler, batsman and slip fielder. Flintoff was consistently rated by the ICC as being among the top international all-rounders in both ODI and Test cricket. Following his debut in 1998, he became an important player for England, serving as both captain and vice-captain of the team. However, he suffered regular injuries throughout his international career, often due to his heavy frame and bowling action. He played in 79 Test matches, scoring 3,845 runs, ave. 31.77, and took 226 wickets, ave. 32.78. His contribution was more than just figures: he inspired England to two Ashes victories in 2005 and 2009. In 1998 he helped Lancashire win two one-day trophies, the AXA League and the Nat West final at Lords. The following year he smashed an unforgettable 143 off 66 balls against Essex at Chelmsford to help retain the one-day title. He played 80 first-class matches, scoring over 4,000 runs, ave. 35.14, and 92 wickets, ave. 29.16. He went on to a media career on TV. He was awarded an MBE in 2005 and also won the BBC Sports Personality of the Year award.

Two trophies in two days

LANCASHIRE WON two trophies in two days in early September, Sunday 6 and Monday 7, to cap off a stunning year for the county. Captained by Wasim Akram for one season only, the Red Rose beat Derbyshire by nine wickets in a rain-affected NatWest Trophy final at Lord's, which went into a second day on the Sunday, before returning to Old Trafford the following day to win the Axa League 40-over title by overturning Hampshire by 16 runs. Lancashire won their fourth 'Sunday League' crown with one game to spare, ending the season 12 points clear of second-placed Warwickshire.

Opening bowler Peter Martin was instrumental in both wins. He took 4-19 from nine overs as Derbyshire were bowled out for 108 at Lord's, having been well placed at 70-0, before adding 3-41 from eight as Hampshire fell short in their pursuit of 203. Martin opened the bowling with Wasim against Derby, a change from the usual new ball attack of Martin and Ian Austin, who came on in a bid to break the dangerous opening partnership brewing between Australian Michael Slater and Kim Barnett. Austin did so with great effect, and his exceptional figures of 3-14 from ten overs earned him the man-of-the-match award. John Crawley's unbeaten 53 anchored the chase.

"I didn't start particularly well in that game," said Martin. "I don't recall getting clattered, but I wasn't buzzing early on. It was only when Wasim brought me back and I got Kim Barnett that I settled.

"I think the change of plan would probably have been because, with Michael Slater opening the batting, who was capable of being very destructive, if we could knock him and Barnett over early with me and Wasim opening, we'd be very happy.

"It clearly wasn't a mistake if we bowled them out for 108, but I guess the plan at the start was slightly flawed."

Funnily enough, on the Monday, Martin and Austin opened the bowling as Lancashire won their eleventh match of 16: "We were playing very well in the Sunday League. We were confident of winning matches," added Martin.

"We knew that if we turned up and played well, we would most likely beat Hampshire. That win was the accumulation of lots of different things through a season which had obviously gone very well for us."

NatWest Trophy final 1998

**Derbyshire 108 (36.4 overs)
(PJ Martin 4-19, ID Austin 3-14)**

**Lancashire 109-1 (30.2 overs)
(JP Crawley 53 not out)**

AXA League 1998

	P	W	T	L	N/R	A	Pts	R/R
Lancashire	17	12	0	2	1	2	54	12.184
Warwickshire	17	9	0	5	1	2	42	4.237
Essex	17	9	1	5	1	1	42	1.275
Leicestershire	17	9	0	6	1	1	40	15.138
Kent	17	8	0	6	3	0	38	3.323
Gloucestershire	17	7	0	6	2	2	36	-1.659
Worcestershire	17	7	1	6	2	1	36	-4.604
Hampshire	17	8	0	8	1	0	34	0.838
Yorkshire	17	8	0	8	1	0	34	-2.477
Glamorgan	17	7	0	8	0	2	32	-0.098
Nottinghamshire	17	7	1	8	0	1	32	-0.675
Middlesex	17	7	0	8	0	2	32	-4.907
Northamptonshire	17	6	1	7	1	2	32	2.805
Somerset	17	6	1	8	1	1	30	-0.102
Derbyshire	17	6	0	8	0	3	30	-5.101
Sussex	17	6	0	9	1	1	28	-3.591
Durham	17	4	1	9	1	2	24	-7.9
Surrey	17	3	0	12	1	1	16	-8.176

Murali replaces Wasim and new legend is born *1999*

The mercurial Muttiah Muralitharan only played in six Championship fixtures in 1999 but still claimed 66 wickets as Lancashire finished as runners-up and claimed the Sunday League title for the second year in a row.

later, the Kandy-born off-spinner took seven wickets in each innings to finish with overall figures of 14-117 from 68.5 overs. They still remain the best figures on that ground in first-class cricket. Ironically, they beat the 13-147 Wasim took in an innings victory against Somerset five years previously.

The only problem was, some questionable batting against the Bears meant Lancashire lost the match by 19 runs. He went on to take 66 wickets in six matches as the Red Rose finished second in the Championship again. There is still a mounted scorecard of that Warwickshire match on the wall in the clubhouse at Southport celebrating Murali's achievements.

MUTTIAH MURALITHARAN made a stunning start to his career as Lancashire's overseas player. The mercurial Sri Lankan off-spinner had been signed as a replacement for Red Rose legend Wasim Akram, whose nine-year association with the county came to an end with an exceptional 641 wickets and 5,689 runs in all cricket to his name. It would take some player to replace Wasim, who had gained a place in the hearts of all associated with the county. But Muralitharan wasn't just any overseas player. He was a superstar too. He had already taken 203 wickets in 42 Test matches for Sri Lanka since debuting in August 1992.

Like Wasim, he was an infectious character. So having been made to wait to get the ball in his hand for Lancashire will have really frustrated him. His first Championship match against Gloucestershire at Bristol in early June was wrecked by rain, meaning there was only enough time for Lancashire's first innings of 351-9, including 158 for Andrew Flintoff. But when he did finally bowl, it was certainly worth the wait.

In a match against Warwickshire at Southport's Trafalgar Road ground a week

Murali, as he was otherwise known, finished his Lancashire career in 2007 with 203 wickets from 28 Championship matches, including 22 hauls of five wickets or more. In all cricket between 1999 and 2007, he took 257 from 67 matches.

150 LANCASHIRE GREATS
130. Mark Chilton

Mark Chilton was born in Sheffield and was educated at Manchester Grammar School and Durham University, where he helped win the Universities tournament in 1997. A right-hand opening batsman who played off the back foot, he could hit the ball hard on the offensive. In 2002 he scored two centuries in the Benson & Hedges Cup and was awarded his county cap. He was appointed Lancashire captain in 2005, leading the county to promotion and to the final of the Twenty20 Cup and the semi-final of the Benson & Hedges Cup. He led the team to within 25 runs of the title in 2007, the closest since 1950. He was in tears afterwards and said "I'm extremely proud of what our guys have achieved though. Our players have risen to an almighty challenge and to come so close is an enormous effort." After a disappointing season with the bat the following year, he came back in 2009 to be named the Club's Player of the Year, and his dedication, commitment and sheer love of Lancashire was rewarded by the club with a benefit in 2011. He scored over 14,000 runs in all forms of the game, including 26 centuries. After retirement, he returned to Manchester Grammar where he took up the position of Director of Cricket.

Sunday League retained

CGU National League Division One 1999

	P	W	T	L	N/R	A	Pts	R/R
Lancashire	16	11	0	2	1	2	50	7.489
Worcestershire	16	10	0	4	1	1	44	8.948
Kent	16	8	0	6	1	1	36	4.300
Gloucestershire	16	8	0	8	0	0	32	3.725
Yorkshire	16	8	0	8	0	0	32	-0.604
Leicestershire	16	6	0	8	1	1	28	-1.518
Warwickshire	16	6	0	8	2	0	28	-6.083
Hampshire	16	5	0	9	2	0	24	-9.441
Essex	16	3	0	12	0	1	14	-6.657

LANCASHIRE RETAINED their National League title, rebranded the CGU League, with an eleventh win in 15 matches against Kent at Old Trafford in mid-September. The Lightning won their penultimate fixture of the campaign by five wickets with two overs to spare in their pursuit of 199.

But wicketkeeper Warren Hegg remembers the match for an unexpected trip to the hospital. The Lightning gloveman was struck in the mouth standing up to Ian Austin in the eighth over of the match, forcing him to hand over the gloves to captain John Crawley. Thankfully, it did not do any damage – to his team's chances that is – as Crawley effected three stumpings off Mike Watkinson, who restricted the Spitfires as he bowled the last seven overs from the Stretford End. Crawley then underpinned the chase with a superb 85 not out, his third score in the eighties in the competition, and Hegg returned to the crease with an unbeaten 19. The pair shared an unbroken 56 for the sixth wicket.

Fifteen minutes after close of play came news of second-placed Worcestershire's defeat against Hampshire at Southampton, sparking celebrations on the pavilion balcony for the second year running.

"I got hit stood up to Ian Austin," said Hegg. "It was a brand new white ball, and it ricocheted into my top set. It split my lip up to right under my nose. I had a gum shield in, so got away with it to a certain degree. But I had padding all under my lip when I came back.

"I had an injection to kill the pain at hospital, and I'm sure I was back in time to see a couple of John's stumpings. He was doing a fine job, and there was no real point me going back out there. He

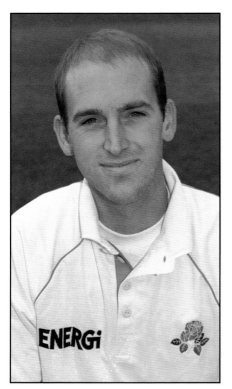

John Crawley had two good reasons to remember his role in the retention of the Sunday League title.

was probably doing better than me to be fair! I went back out to bat later on, and we ended up cruising the game."

This triumph was the last of eight one-day trophies in the nineties, a golden era for the county.

"In that team of the nineties, everybody had a job to do and knew their roles in the side," added Hegg, who would go on to lift the National League Division Two title as captain in 2003. "We always knew how to win from some very tough situations. That's why we were so successful."

The CGU League had started with the county to be known as Lancashire Lightning after the powers that be at the England and Wales Cricket Board opted to introduce nicknames in early March.

It would transpire in later years that nicknames such as Warwickshire Bears, Essex Eagles and Yorkshire Phoenix (now Vikings) would be used in all forms of limited overs cricket. But, for a start, they would only be used in the one competition.

Ken Grime, Lancashire's long-standing marketing services and match manager, explained: "The ECB wanted to 'relaunch' the former Sunday League as the National League with a new sponsor.

"All the counties were asked to come up with a nickname, logo and a mascot, which led initially to Lancashire choosing a somewhat bizarre pink and purple dinosaur called 'Sugar' before we settled on 'Lanky' the giraffe.

"We asked staff, players and ran school competitions to come up with a name, and Lightning got suggested more than most, although 'Lions' was a contender until Surrey pinched it! We liked Lightning because it is quite a dynamic word, and felt we could have a bit of fun with it."

Lancashire came up with the initial Lightning logo before updating it ahead of the 2010 season.

Bridesmaids in Championship for third year running

2000

undermined their chances of County Championship glory, but a second-placed finish for a third year running was a satisfactory outcome. It was the county's best sequence of finishes since 1926 to 1930.

"NOT BAD for a fat lad" was a comment that could have defined Andrew Flintoff's summer. Thankfully a stunning one-day innings for Lancashire ensured he will look back on the Millennium year with plenty of fondness. The Red Rose all-rounder, in the infancy of his international career, had suffered back problems which England's management put down to his being overweight. But he played one of the great knocks in a NatWest quarter-final win over Surrey at the Oval to prove himself arguably the country's finest natural talent.

Dropped from England's Test team after a disappointing couple of Tests against Zimbabwe, which were also county colleague Chris Schofield's only Test appearances, the Preston-born star steered his country to a one-day international win over Zimbabwe on his home ground in July with 42 off 45 balls in pursuit of 115. In a TV interview having been awarded the man of the match, Flintoff responded with the comment above following some cutting newspaper headlines.

Flintoff, who embarked upon a new fitness regime, returned to county colours with devastating effect. In pursuit of 211 in 50 overs against Surrey, and with Mike Atherton out for a three-ball duck to leave the visitors at 0-1, Flintoff strode to the crease at number three, dominated a second-wicket stand of 190 with overseas player Sourav Ganguly and posted a century off 88 balls. He finished with 135 not out off 111 balls, including 19 fours and four sixes. On his Andrew Flintoff Cricket Academy website, the innings makes the list of his top ten memorable career moments.

Unfortunately, Lancashire would go on to lose the semi-final clash with Gloucestershire, who beat them at the same stage of the Benson and Hedges Cup too. Defending champions in the National League, they were also relegated to Division Two having lost half of their 16 matches. A heavy defeat at the Oval in early August also

Not bad for a fat lad! Alec Stewart looks on helplessly as Andrew Flintoff powers to his record-breaking innings against Surrey.

150 LANCASHIRE GREATS
131. Steve Titchard

Loyalty and patience are two of the qualities which spring to mind when the name of Steve Titchard comes up. For nine years he served Lancashire well, although he was never first choice as an opening batsman. Born in Warrington, he was a right-hand batsman and right-arm medium bowler who played for Lancashire from 1990 to 1998. At 6ft 3in he cut an imposing figure and he was also a capable fielder at short leg or slip. He was capped in 1995 after scoring 130 against Essex at Old Trafford and 92 in the Nat West Trophy, winning the man-of-the-match award against Worcestershire. 1996 was his best season, scoring 939 runs, ave. 44.71 with two centuries, including a career best 163 against Essex at Chelmsford. During this innings he put on a Lancashire record of 358 runs for the 4th wicket with Graham Lloyd. Steve served Lancashire loyally and whenever he was brought into the side he responded magnificently and never complained if he was asked to step down. He went on to play two seasons for Derbyshire before returning to Lancashire as batting coach and Performance Manager to the Lancashire Cricket Board.

John Crawley's side won seven, drew eight and lost only one of the 16 Championship matches. Their title bid was hamstrung by a 272-run defeat against Surrey at the Oval in early August – their 12th match of the season. In fact, it was the county's first Championship defeat in 25 matches dating back to the previous June when they were beaten by the same opponents at the same venue.

Later in the month, the Red Rose also failed to beat Leicestershire at Grace Road despite having racked up 574-5 in the first innings. Surrey won the league by ten points having secured a draw at Old Trafford in the final round of matches.

Signing of Anderson and Hogg makes up for disappointing season

2001

A DEPRESSING year in all forms of cricket included two Red Rose youngsters signing professional terms with the county. And one of them would go on to be a star of world cricket! Relegation was only just averted in the Championship, while a Cheltenham & Gloucester Trophy semi-final finish was as good as it got in one-day cricket. But young guns Kyle Hogg and Jimmy Anderson put pen to paper on their first Red Rose senior deals, with the latter going on to play for England the following year and become one of the best swing bowlers on the planet.

Lancashire's Academy director John Stanworth takes up the story of Anderson's path to the county's staff: "Jimmy was recommended to me by Val Brown, the mother of Michael and David Brown, who played at Burnley with Jimmy and had been in our representative sides for several years," he said. "It was winter time of 1997/98, and she rang me unprompted and said 'I don't want to tell you your job, but I think you should have a look at this young lad because the lads are coming back from practice talking about him'.

"So I took her up on the offer. We had some under-17 nets shortly afterwards, and I invited him down. The pace he showed indoors was evident straight away – he had late movement away from the right-hander. His effectiveness in getting top order players out was evident when he first started to play for us at that level."

This was before the days of the club's Academy, and a chance phone call could well have had a huge impact on English cricket.

"Jimmy's success is born out of opportunity," added Stanworth. "In a strange way, it made us question our scouting system. We now have a much more thorough scouting system because how can we have not seen him earlier? What Jimmy has now isn't much different from the Jimmy Anderson that first came onto our radar.

"What he has done is become physically stronger and more robust as an individual. He has also refined a lot of his skills."

Not forgetting Hogg, who has been an excellent performer for the county in domestic cricket, particularly in the Championship.

Thew use of Old Trafford as a music venue was stepped up, with pop superstar Robbie Williams drawing in approximately 150,000 fans over three nights in late July.

Manchester Evening News cricket correspondent Colin Evans described it as "the success of the season" in his report for the Wisden Almanack.

As a result, a number of one-day matches were shifted to outgrounds, with three Benson and Hedges Cup ties being played at Liverpool and the C&G Trophy quarter-final being played at Blackpool.

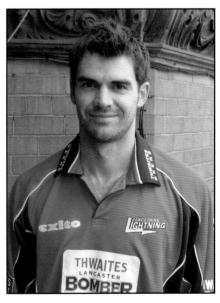

The emergence of Kyle Hogg, above, and Jimmy Anderson, below, made up for a miserable season for the Red Rose.

Although there had been concerts at the ground before, it would be the first of an increasing number of events to be held at Old Trafford as the Lancashire hierarchy tried to gain extra income for the club. Well known names such as Oasis, Arctic Monkeys, Take That and Bon Jovi have all wooed crowds at the ground.

The late Amy Winehouse and Lady Gaga, who have since gained superstar status, supported the Arctic Monkeys and Take That in 2007 and 2009 respectively.

150 LANCASHIRE GREATS
132. Gary Yates

Gary Yates was a dependable off-spinner and often the unsung hero of Lancashire's great one-day side of the 1990s. Born in Ashton-Under-Lyne, he attended Manchester Grammar School and played cricket for them. At the age of 14 he played for Denton St Lawrence before joining Lancashire in 1989. He made a dramatic 106 v Notts at Trent Bridge on his Championship debut in 1990. In 1993 he scored 367 runs in only seven matches with a top score of 134* v North ants at Old Trafford. Capped in 1994, he was instrumental in some of Lancashire's greatest achievements in one-day cricket in the nineties. In 1995 he scored 19 from 14 balls to win the semi-final against Worcestershire and then bowled superbly to take 3-42 in the Lord's final success against Kent. He helped Lancashire to win six titles, including the Lord's double in 1996 when they won the Nat West Trophy and Benson & Hedges Cup. He subsequently became 2nd team captain and coach. He has been assistant coach at Lancashire since 2008.

Exit for Crawley *2002*

LANCASHIRE STEPPED up their drive to produce young stars of the future in November of 2002 with the introduction of their new Academy programme. Twelve players were originally selected, with three more added the following year. Out of that group, Chris Ashling, Karl Brown, Jon Clare, Steven Croft, Andrew Miller, Stephen Mullaney, Stephen Parry, John Simpson, Tom Smith and Vishal Tripathi have all earned county contracts. Brown, Croft, Parry and Smith are currently Lancashire professionals as of 2014.

Academy director John Stanworth was at the head of it, and described this initial intake as arguably the strongest of all when looking back on the ten years of the Academy in 2012. Steve Titchard, the former Lancashire batsman, was involved at the start and remains so to this day as Academy coach.

Blackpool-born all-rounder Croft, who had debuted in the second team aged 16 in 2001, was the first player to earn a professional deal with the Red Rose from the initial intake ahead of his first-class debut against Oxford University in early 2005. "Just before it started, I'd been net bowling with the first team and things like that," explained Croft, who has gone on to captain Lancashire regularly in limited overs cricket.

John Stanworth

"But as a group of youngsters, it was something a bit different really. Usually we'd only have age-group training. But to have Academy sessions in the gym and net sessions was really good for us. In the past you'd have got signed and had a shock as to what professional sport was all about. With the Academy, it gave us an insight before it actually happened.

"I'd just left school, was at Myerscough College and was working part-time in a bar. Stanny and Titch were quite flexible on your personal sessions. Stanny's been a massive part of my development. He's really good at his job. All the players who go through the second team and into the firsts, whether it was in my younger days or now, he's brilliant with."

While gaining some future stars, the year started with Lancashire losing one of their own. England batsman John Crawley left to join Hampshire following a bitter contract row sparked when he was removed from the captaincy after a disappointing 2001.

Lancashire and Crawley parted ways in early March following a legal battle that even involved the barrister-wife of Prime Minister Tony Blair – Cherie. The England batsman, who played in 37 Test matches and 13 one-day internationals between 1994 and 2003, had made clear his desire to leave the Red Rose county having been removed from the captaincy at the end of the previous summer.

Crawley had no intention of seeing out the final three years of a five-year contract having resigned from playing duties due to what he described as "irreconcilable differences". Lancashire had made it clear that despite his removal as captain, they wanted him to stay on as a player. Unfortunately, however, Creepy, as he was affectionately known, had other ideas. With this in mind, the Red Rose county were understandably not prepared to let Crawley, a player who had come through the ranks from his days at Manchester Grammar School, walk away for nothing.

One of their most fluent and eye-catching batsmen of recent times, he had scored 16,043 runs in 331 matches in all forms for his home county at an average of 42.10, including an impressive 35 centuries.

An ECB Contract Appeals panel initially ruled in Lancashire's favour on February 16, insisting Crawley, represented by Blair, should not be released from his contract. But on March 23, an agreement was reached to allow the right-hander to move to Hampshire.

A Lancashire statement read: "Following a period of protracted negotiation, the club has agreed to release John from his contract upon the payment to the club by him and Hampshire of a suitable five-figure compensation payment. The exact terms agreed between the parties are subject to a formal written agreement, which is the subject of a confidentiality obligation. The club wish to place on record their thanks to John for his 12 years of service to the county."

Warren Hegg was appointed Lancashire's new captain for the summer. At the end of it, Lancashire lost two more stalwarts of their batting order as Neil Fairbrother and Graham Lloyd retired.

This was after a campaign which saw Lancashire lose a nerve-shredding Benson & Hedges Cup semi-final against Warwickshire at Old Trafford by one wicket as the visitors chased down 212 off the last ball. The county were knocked out of the Cheltenham & Gloucester Trophy in the fourth round, they finished fifth in Division Two of the National League and fourth in the top tier of the County Championship.

150 LANCASHIRE GREATS
133. Stuart Law

Stuart Law spent seven seasons at Old Trafford, etching his name into Lancashire history by scoring just short of 12,000 runs for the county in all competitions. He came to Lancashire with a tremendous record. He had captained Queensland to seven titles and was Queensland's all-time leading run-scorer. Surprisingly, he only played in one Test but appeared in more than 50 one-day matches as a middle order batsman. He averaged over 55 in all but one of his six seasons with Essex before joining Lancashire in 2002. Awarded his county cap in his first season in 2003, he scored 1,820 runs, ave. 91.00, with seven centuries. He captained the side in 2008 and was popular with players and members, always giving tremendous service to the club. He was a very classical batsmen, scoring 25 centuries in all competitions, including three double-centuries, with a top score of 236* against Warwickshire at Old Trafford in 2005. He was selected as one of the five Wisden Cricketers of the Year in 1998. In 2007, he was awarded the Medal of the Order of Australia. He has represented the Chennai Super Kings in the Indian Cricket League as their captain and was appointed as Sri Lanka's assistant coach in 2011.

New boy Loye stars in vintage year for batsmen *2003*

MAL LOYE, a new signing from Northamptonshire, hailed Lancashire's stunning year with the bat. This was the Northampton-born batsman's first season after a move from Wantage Road, and he scored five out of an incredible 28 hundreds accrued by the team in the County Championship as they finished second. Loye joined Carl Hooper, Stuart Law and Mark Chilton in passing 1,000 runs in the competition, and the quartet broke a 99-year-old record in the latter stages of the season.

In June 1904, Archie MacLaren, Johnny Tyldesley, Albert Henry Hornby and Willis Cuttell all scored hundreds in the same innings during an innings and 136-run victory over Somerset at Old Trafford. Fast forward to August 2003 at the same venue, and Loye, Hooper, Law and Chilton all combined to rack up 734-5 declared in the first innings of a drawn match. Not only that, they went and did it again two matches later against Warwickshire at Edgbaston. Talk about the London Bus syndrome! This time Lancashire won the match by an innings and 145 after replying to 449 with 781 and bowling the Bears out for 187 second time around.

"That year we had the best cricket side on and off the field, in terms of atmosphere too, that I've ever been involved in," said Loye, now the Cricket Master at Wellingborough School near Northampton. "I think it was led by Carl Hooper in terms of his presence.

"That record came in August time. At the end of the season before, when I wasn't on the staff, the lads had spoken about scoring more hundreds as a collective. But to go from five or six to 25 to 30 was incredible.

"There were a lot of things that happened that year which were very satisfying, and being part of that record was right up there. It wasn't just the eight hundreds in those two games, it was getting so many in the whole year. It's amazing what confidence can do."

This year was not just about special batting because Jimmy Anderson took a hat-trick in the early season draw against Essex at Old Trafford, including the scalp of England captain Nasser Hussain. The Twenty20 Cup was also launched, with Lancashire winning only two matches.

It was initially viewed as a hit and giggle by the players. But Twenty20 cricket, a brainchild of the then ECB marketing manager Stuart Robertson, has since become a worldwide phenomenon with competitions such as the Indian Premier League and the Australian Big Bash really capturing the imagination.

Lancashire's first match was a North Division clash with Nottinghamshire at Trent Bridge. The Lightning were bowled out for 120 and lost by seven wickets. They later failed to reach the knockout stages. Since then, Lancashire's performances in Twenty20 cricket have improved markedly. They may never have won the competition, but have won 62 of 109 matches leading into the 2014 campaign.

In an interview published by the Cricketer magazine in the summer of 2013, Red Rose seamer Glen Chapple spoke about how Twenty20 had evolved from 2003 to the present day: "It has

Mal Loye had an outstanding year in his debut season.

changed from something that was almost taken with a pinch of salt as crowd-pleaser, with players not really knowing what the best tactics were," he explained. "It's now a game that all cricketers put hours and hours of practice and thought into. It's certainly a tougher game than it was at the start.

"It's something that players have learnt different methods for, and I went through phases of trying different tactics. I've settled on some that I'm happy with and seem to suit me. Obviously with people playing the scoop and hitting the ball over the wicketkeeper's head, it's a bit of a problem for bowling at the death. Death bowling is not really seen as my strength anymore, and thankfully I don't do too much of it. You accept that players can do different things from the past, and there's no real stigma attached to going for runs. You just have to rock up next ball and try and remain calm under pressure. You've certainly got to have a thick skin."

150 LANCASHIRE GREATS
134. Carl Hooper

Carl Hooper joined Lancashire at short notice in 2003 and his impact was immediate as Lancashire supporters were treated to some marvelous and memorable innings from the former West Indies skipper. In 14 first-class matches he scored six centuries and three fifties, scoring 1,219 runs, ave. 67.72. He was also prolific in the one-day game, passing 50 on eight occasions as Lancashire gained promotion in the National League. Hooper became only the second player to have scored a century against all 18 county teams. He was a right-handed batsman and off-spin bowler who came to prominence in the late 1980s and he represented the West Indies over a 21-year international career. His highest innings score of 233 was made against India in 2001 and he has made 5,762 runs in his Test cricket career. In ODIs, Hooper's aggressive style of batting saw him average 35.34 in 227 matches. He holds the accolade of being the first cricketer in the world to have scored 5,000 runs, taken 100 wickets, held 100 catches and received 100 caps in both ODIs and Tests. He has lived in Adelaide since the late 1990s and was coach for the Woodville District Cricket Club in Adelaide in 2012.

Lanky the Giraffe spares Red Rose blushes

2004

A SOBERING Twenty20 semi-final defeat to Surrey at Edgbaston in early August summed up a forgettable summer for Lancashire, which culminated in County Championship relegation despite having won two of their first four matches. Warren Hegg's side were installed as pre-season title favourites having bolstered their squad with the signing of former England bowler Dominic Cork from Derbyshire.

In fact, former Manchester Evening News cricket correspondent Colin Evans wrote in Wisden that one of the Northamptonshire players had said during the first game of the season at Wantage Road: "Millionaire

Even the best efforts of Dominic Cork were not enough to beat Surrey in the T20 semi-final.

club. Bought a team to win the Championship. If they don't, they will have to take a long hard look at themselves". The Red Rose were relegated on September 17 having been top after beating Worcestershire by 219 runs at Old Trafford in mid-May.

But, in the glare of the television cameras, it was their Finals Day failure that really caught the headlines. With Andrew Flintoff, Dinesh Mongia, Carl Hooper, Glen Chapple, Cork and Jimmy Anderson in the side, Lancashire were hot favourites to beat the defending champions, especially having bowled them out for 133. But the Lightning struggled with the bat throughout their reply, slipping from 22-0 to 63-4.

Chapple and Hooper shared 31 for the fifth wicket to get their side back on track, but both fell in quick succession. Cork

hit 25 off 13 balls to put Lancashire back on track, but he skied Adam Hollioake to Rikki Clarke at cover in the penultimate over with ten needed.

That equation was brought down to seven from the final over, or even six to tie and progress to the final by virtue of losing fewer wickets. It got down to three needed off the last ball to win and two to tie with Chris Schofield, partnered by skipper Hegg at the time, on strike. Schofield was run out having picked up a single and Surrey went on to lose against Leicestershire in the final. At least Lanky the Giraffe won the Mascot Derby!

150 LANCASHIRE GREATS
135. Dominic Cork

Dominic Cork was a right-hand lower order batsman who bowled right-arm fast-medium, and was renowned for his swing and seam control. He made his debut for Derbyshire in 1990 and played 13 seasons for them before joining Lancashire in 2004. He made 69 appearances for England from 1992 to 2002. He took a hat-trick against West Indies at Old Trafford in 1995. In his five seasons with Lancashire, he played 64 first-class matches, scoring 1,822 runs at an average of 24.95, with three centuries, eight half centuries and a highest score 154. In the field he took 49 catches. The Old Trafford pitches suited his pace and bounce and he took 173 wickets at a bowling average of 28.29, with four five-wickets hauls and best innings figures of 7-120. In List A cricket he played 57 matches, scoring 749 runs at an average of 22.69. With the ball he took 58 wickets at an average of 28.98, with best figures of 4-14. Leaving Lancashire after the 2008 season, he joined Hampshire, who he played for from 2009 to 2011. In an interview in Lancashire Spin he once admitted, "I should have joined Lancashire years ago." In retirement he works for Sky Sports.

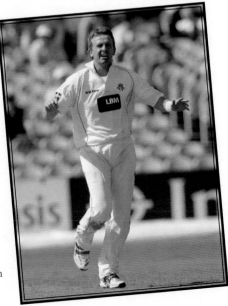

Having spent heavily on players, the Red Rose suffered the ignominy of relegation, but at least the mascot, Lanky the Giraffe brought some silverware back to the club.

Secret spinner takes ten wickets on debut

2005

A MAN Lancashire players nicknamed 'Pirate' would star for them as an immediate return to the County Championship's top tier was secured with a convincing eight-wicket win inside three days over Essex at Chelmsford with a match to spare.

The Red Rose headed south in early September with a secret weapon up their sleeve. Indian international left-arm spinner Kartik Murali had been playing in the Lancashire League for Ramsbottom, but he was called upon to take advantage of a turning track prepared for home leggie Danish Kaneria.

Cricket manager Mike Watkinson kept the signing under wraps until the last minute, having got an idea that Essex would prepare a turner, and it was a ploy that worked a treat. With Gary Keedy injured, Kartik joined in-form Australian Andrew Symonds as the club's second overseas player following the absence of Marcus North and Brad Hodge from earlier in the season. And he became the first player to take ten wickets on his first-class debut for the county since 1914. It was a match that saw the premature retirement of wicketkeeping legend Warren Hegg, who broke a finger on day one, leaving youngster Gareth Cross to take the gloves after a dash down the motorway.

Kartik, whose nickname was revealed by Mal Loye due to long hair, a pierced ear and bangles around neck and wrist, took five wickets in each innings to finish with 10-168 as the Red Rose went top of the table and out of sight of third place.

"Within two or three balls of him coming on, I knew we were in business," admitted captain Mark Chilton. "I just remember thinking 'this guy's got it on a string'. He was definitely one of the best spinners I played with.

"To come into a new team and settle straightaway like he did was fantastic. His signing was a real stroke of luck."

The season had started with former leg-spinner Chris Schofield winning his claim for unfair dismissal against the club after being released midway through 2004. His argument was that he had been given no prior notice of the club's decision. Lancashire were also beaten in the Twenty20 Cup final by Somerset.

Chilton's side had topped the North Division with six wins from eight matches, including the double over Yorkshire. Loye and Stuart Law scored the county's first Twenty20 centuries in home wins over Durham and Yorkshire, while Symonds inspired a quarter-final victory over Derbyshire at Old Trafford with 57 not out, a wicket, a catch and a run out.

The Red Rose then gained revenge for the previous year's semi-final defeat to Surrey by beating the same opponents on their own patch at the Oval to advance to the evening's final against Graeme Smith's Somerset.

Symonds again scored an unbeaten half-century as Lancashire posted more than 200 for the fourth time in the season. Six bowlers, including England duo Jimmy Anderson and Andrew

Flintoff, then took a wicket apiece as Surrey posted 195-7 in their pursuit of 218.

Early evening rain delayed the start of the final and reduced it to a 16 overs per side contest. And Lancashire, who opted to bat first, were never really at the races as they could only post 114-8 having been 41-5.

The Pirate – Kartik Murali made an immediate impact for the Red Rose.

Graeme Smith underpinned a routine chase with 64 not out as the Taunton side won by seven wickets with eleven balls to spare.

Unfortunately, it was not the end of the limited overs disappointment for the county as they lost in the semi-final of the Cheltenham and Gloucester Trophy to Warwickshire following a batting collapse at Edgbaston three weeks later.

The Bears having been reduced to 155-7, Michael Powell and Tony Frost shared an unbroken 81 for the eighth wicket to set Lancashire 237 win from their 50 overs. It was a task that looked incredibly stiff once Lancashire were reduced to 31-3 in response.

Only Loye and Law made any headway with 40 and 47 respectively as the Lightning were bowled out for just 137 in 38 overs. Earlier in the competition, opener Andrew Crook's unbeaten 162 against Buckinghamshire at Wormsley set the record for the county's highest individual one-day score. The record still stands.

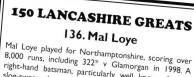

150 LANCASHIRE GREATS
136. Mal Loye

Mal Loye played for Northamptonshire, scoring over 8,000 runs, including 322* v Glamorgan in 1998. A right-hand batsman, particularly well known for his slog-sweep shot against fast bowlers, he represented England U19 and England A and made his one-day international debut against Australia in 2007 aged 34. He transferred to Lancashire in 2003, scored a century on debut and scored another in his next match. He was an ever-present during Lancashire's march to the County Championship Division Two title in 2005 and was the county's leading run-scorer with 1,198, including a knock of 200 against Durham. He almost became the first Lancashire batsman ever to score consecutive double centuries, but was dismissed for 194 in his next match against Essex. Loye also made a century in the Twenty20 Cup for the first time when he hammered exactly 100 against Durham, including five sixes and 10 fours. A mainstay in the Lancashire top order, Loye was rewarded with a benefit season for 2008. He was plagued with back problems during his career and was released in 2009 when he returned to Northants for two seasons before playing for Buckinghamshire.

Championship challenge ends in controversy

2006

ASIDE FROM leaving Lancashire for Surrey at the end of 2012, Gary Keedy made arguably the biggest decision of his career in a season of disappointment for the county in two competitions. The experienced left-arm spinner, born in Yorkshire, was on course to play against Sussex in the Cheltenham and Gloucester Trophy final in August, which would have been the first Lord's showpiece appearance of his career.

But Keedy picked up a late knee injury and ruled himself out of the game, with Indian overseas player Kartik Murali having returned to the club earlier in the week with the primary objective of maintaining their Championship challenge.

"I'd played in all the group stages in 2006, but I picked up an injury and wasn't 100 percent fit," explained Keedy. "Had Kartik not been with us, I'd have probably played. To leave myself out of the final is maybe something I regret.

"We had Kartik come in for the second half of the season as an overseas. Just the kind of person I am, I knew I wasn't fully fit even though I could have got through. I just thought 'we've got an overseas bloke here who does the same job; it would be crazy for me to not make way'.

"I think Mike Watkinson (cricket manager) had said at the time that we'd be going in with the team that got us there. I was in that team. It was the right thing to do at the time, but when I look back on it you wonder how many opportunities you'll get."

Lancashire lost a low-scoring final to Sussex after bowling their opponents out for 172, and they were also edged out of a tight race for the County Championship title by the men from Hove the following month even though they narrowly led the race in June.

A season which included a two-day Championship hammering of Sussex at Liverpool, and three of their last six matches – all drawn – badly affected by rain, ended in controversy during the final match against Hampshire. Sussex beat Worcestershire at Hove to render Lancashire's match at the Rose Bowl irrelevant, and the visiting camp declined Shane Warne's invitation to set up a competitive finish on the final afternoon. Needless to say, the Australian was not too chuffed.

Lancashire fielded Jimmy Anderson at the Rose Bowl for his only Championship appearance of an injury-ravaged season. The England bowler had returned from a winter tour of India early in the year with a stress fracture of the back, ruling him out of the vast majority of the home summer. Incidentally, Red Rose team-mate Sajid Mahmood benefited by impressing for England in home Tests against Sri Lanka and Pakistan.

Anderson played some league cricket for Burnley before playing in a Pro40 League match against Glamorgan at Old Trafford on September 17. Having been named in the squad for England's winter Ashes series, the ECB were desperate to get the fast bowler some first-class match action prior to the tour. And they believed that with Lancashire in a title-decider, it would be unfair to force them to pick him with a restriction on how many overs he could bowl.

So, with that in mind, they organised a one-game loan spell with Glamorgan, who had nothing to play for in their final fixture of the season. As it happened, Lancashire opted to pick Anderson anyway. He bowled ten wicketless overs at a cost of 38 runs in the first innings and did not bowl again because of the decision to bat on during the final day. Anderson went on to play three of the five Tests in Australia as England lost the series 5-0.

There was also mixed news off the field for the Red Rose. It was announced in April that Cardiff's Sophia Gardens had been preferred as an Ashes venue in 2009 to Old Trafford, despite the success of the previous summer's Test. But, determined not to be defeated, the club ended nearly three years of speculation about potential moves to East Manchester or Wigan by announcing that they would be remaining at Old Trafford and redeveloping their famous home at a cost in the region of £30m.

Injury to Jimmy Anderson gave Saj Mahmood his chance to shine at international level.

---

150 LANCASHIRE GREATS

137. Gary Keedy

Despite being born in Yorkshire and playing once for that county, Keedy established himself as the leading spinner in the Lancashire team for 17 years. A slow left-arm spinner, he was admired for his simple no-nonsense bowling action. He was Lancashire's player of the year in 2004 after taking 72 wickets. And was also the club's leading bowler in 2009 with 42 wickets after missing the first half of the season. In the last seven matches of that season he took 31 wickets and said that the spell was as well as he had ever bowled. He became an important force in Lancashire's one-day squad and helped them get to the 2006 C & G Trophy Final and also four Twenty20 finals days. He took 654 first class wickets for Lancashire and 840 in all forms of the game. In the 2011 Championship-winning season he was the leading wicket–taker with 62 wickets, but it will be his direct hit from cover point to run out the last Somerset batsman to end the innings that will be remembered. He was unlucky to have been on the verge of England selection during his career without winning a cap. He moved to Surrey in 2013.

Final day run chase falls short

2007

VVS LAXMAN GENERALLY did his talking with the bat. One of the game's greats, when the exquisite Indian retired in 2012 he had 19,730 first-class runs to his name, including 8,781 in 134 Test matches. But, as Lancashire chased an unlikely 489 against Surrey at the Oval in their last County Championship match of the season to clinch the victory they needed for the title, Laxman made an exception.

Their target was 462 in a minimum of 96 overs during the final day of the campaign having been outplayed for the three previous days. They had gone into the clash top of the table, leading Sussex by six points, so basically needing to match the Hove side's result in their final game against Worcestershire at home.

150 LANCASHIRE GREATS
138. Muttiah Muralitharan

Muttiah Muralitharan was a Sri Lankan cricketer who was rated as the greatest Test match bowler ever by Wisden Cricketers' Almanack in 2002. He retired from Test cricket in 2010, registering his 800th and final wicket on 22nd July 2010 from his final ball in his last Test match. He is also the leading bowler in one-day internationals with 534 wickets. He made his debut for Lancashire in 1999 and had four spells with the club, finishing with 203 wickets at an ave. of 15.96. He reached 100 wickets in only his 14th match and took five or more wickets in an innings 22 times. In his first season, his 66 wickets in the six first-class matches won him the Player of the Year award. His enthusiasm and commitment to playing for Lancashire was evident. With his extravagant wrist-action, every muscle in his arm assisted the viciousness of the spinning ball, but his career was beset by controversy over his bowling action. Due to an unusual hyper-extension of his congenitally bent arm during delivery, it was called into question on a number of occasions by umpires and sections of the cricket community. Through all this, the bowler remained patient and mentally strong with a dignified silence until he was finally cleared by the ICC.

Generally in the Lancashire camp before a day's play, captain and coach speak to their team, which Mark Chilton and Mike Watkinson did on the outfield. But then the team talk was opened up to the floor. Step forward Laxman. Chilton takes up the story: "VVS was a very quiet man, somebody of very few words – but someone we all had a massive amount of respect for. Because he hadn't really spoken before, his words meant so much more," he said.

"He has achieved so much in the game, but you could see winning the Championship with Lancashire meant a lot to him. He had previous experience of chasing down big targets with India, and he just made us believe that the total was definitely gettable."

They showed it definitely was possible with a spirited performance in the London sunshine, which included 100 for Laxman, only falling an agonising 25 runs short. Having lost to Sussex at Liverpool in early August, they looked out of the title race, and had been written off before winning three of their next five to leave them eyeing a first title since 1934.

"Where we did so well was to score the amount of runs we did in the day," added Chilton. "I was very proud of the guys after a monumental effort, but it was gutting to get so close without getting over the line." Lancashire finished third behind Sussex and Durham.

Just two days after the aforementioned Sussex match at Liverpool, Lancashire travelled to Edgbaston for Twenty20 Finals Day and a semi-final appearance with Gloucestershire. Unfortunately, it proved to be a nightmare experience for the Lightning.

With England's Andrew Flintoff available, skipper Chilton had decided to leave himself out of the team. But, within an hour of the game starting, Mal Loye suffered a back spasm in the nets and could not play. Chilton had to step back into the side.

Things went from bad to worse for the Red Rose, whose total of 148-6 was well below par. Only Brad Hodge and Steven Croft passed 30, and the Gladiators had little trouble knocking off the runs. Former New Zealand opening batsman Craig Spearman smashed 86 off 55 balls, including eight fours and five sixes, as they won at a canter by eight wickets with 19 balls to spare.

Indian master VVS Laxman made a huge contribution to the Red Rose cause in 2007, but it was ultimately in vain as the club fell 25 runs short of their first outright Championship title since 1934.

Chilton makes way for Law

LANCASHIRE WERE searching for a new captain at the end of 2007 following Mark Chilton's decision to resign from the role he had held for three seasons in order to concentrate on improving his form with the bat. But in truth, the club's hierarchy did not have to look too far as waiting in the wings was veteran Australian star Stuart Law, who had served the Red Rose with great distinction since arriving at Old Trafford from Essex ahead of 2002.

Chilton only won one trophy during his tenure – the 2005 County Championship Division Two title – but came close to a number of other successes. However, he only scored 616 Championship runs at an average of 28 in 2007, and hit only 92 runs in nine completed innings in limited overs cricket.

"I just feel that my own game has not produced what it should have done over the past year or two," he said having relinquished the job in mid-October. "People have not been seeing the best of me out on the pitch. I have come through the Lancashire set up myself, but I just wanted to take a step back and analyse where I was at with my own personal game.

"I have been pretty happy with the way things have gone as a whole with the captaincy, but personally I have been below par. I am just looking forward to getting back to doing what I was signed to do, which is score runs for Lancashire.

Disappointment is etched all over the face of skipper Mark Chilton after his team just failed to make the 489 runs needed to land Lancashire's first Championship title in 73 years. With his own form suffering under the pressures of captaincy, he decided to return to the ranks for the 2008 season and Australian overseas star Stuart Law took over.

"There is the expectation with a club such as Lancashire, and you have to deal with that as well. A lot of time I enjoyed that challenge, but there were also times when it weighed heavily on my shoulders.

"Last season I certainly felt that a little bit, especially when my form was not quite where I wanted it to be. Ultimately it was very difficult, but I had to do everything logically and come to the right decision."

Law was appointed to his second major captaincy job in cricket just under a month later. He still remains Australia's most successful domestic captain having led Queensland to five four-day Pura Cup titles and two one-day trophies between 1994 and 2002.

Upon his appointment, Law, who had gained UK citizenship ahead of 2005, said: "I've been around Lancashire nearly six years now, and it's a great honour just to be asked. I was offered the job before, but it maybe wasn't the right time.

"I'd just come back from nearly 12 years with Queensland, and I felt I just needed a break. Now I'm ready to grab it with both hands and hopefully win something. It feels like we've been on the verge of something special for the last two or three years.

"The captain is the one who makes the decisions, but there should be eleven captains out there making choices and trying to get the game done and dusted."

Upon retirement from the game, Chilton (2011) and Law (2009) both went into coaching. Chilton joined the staff at Manchester Grammar School, while Law coached the national teams of Sri Lanka and Bangladesh before heading back to Queensland as their head coach in 2013. He won his first trophy – the one-day Ryobi Cup – less than three months after being appointed.

New skipper Stuart Law in typically aggressive mode.

All change at 2008 Old Trafford

JACK SIMMONS stepped down as the club's chairman with a tear in his eye after eleven years in office. The former Red Rose off-spinner announced his intentions at the club's AGM in April, with Michael Cairns appointed as his successor.

Cairns, Levenshulme-born and renowned for his work in the hotel and tourism industry, had only just been awarded an OBE in the Queen's New Year's Honours List, and Simmons felt the time was right to hand over the reins. The plans for Old Trafford's redevelopment were also unveiled, including a reorientated square from east to west to north to south, a revamped pavilion, new player and media facilities directly opposite and a new conference and banqueting suite called The Point.

New Lancashire chairman Michael Cairns unveiled some ambitious plans for the club's future.

"We have to go forward," said an emotional Simmons, who would continue as a member of the cricket committee and as the chairman of the ECB's cricket committee.

"I never used to get any sleep when we were borrowing a couple of million, but Michael is more used to the sort of figures we are dealing with now."

There were a host of personnel changes at Old Trafford, including the departure of long-standing groundsman Peter Marron, who was to go freelance after 30 years on the groundstaff – 25 of them as head of the operation. Matt Merchant was to be his replacement.

"To my mind, he has been the best groundsman in the country for years," said chief executive Jim Cumbes. "And I know he doesn't win the top awards, but they tend to go to those with the flattest pitches, not necessarily the best cricket pitches!

"You just need to read the comments made by the England team and touring sides over recent years, and they are always full of praise for the pitches at Old Trafford."

On making the decision, Marron said: "Not many people can come to work each morning and honestly say they love their job, but I can. However, when you've been doing it for as long as I have, you get to a point when you need a new challenge and want to use your knowledge in a different capacity. Lancashire CCC and Old Trafford is a massive part of who I am. I've had the best and the worst of times whilst working here, and over the years some work colleagues have become my closest friends. But there is a big wide world out there, and you just know when it's time to pass over the reins and try something new."

Australian batsman Stuart Law spent just a year in the captaincy hot-seat before being relieved of his duties following a distinctly middle of the road season saw the team flirt with relegation in the Championship and disappoint in the three limited overs competitions, even if they were on the wrong end of a brutal century from Middlesex's Dawid Malan in the Twenty20 quarter-final. The club's decision to release Dominic Cork did not sit well with Law, who was replaced by Glen Chapple in December. Mike Watkinson would also change his title from cricket manager to cricket director, with a new first-team coach to be appointed ahead of 2009.

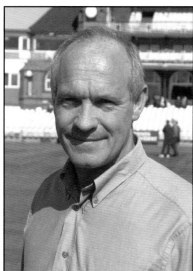

Groundsman Peter Marron, who had made an invaluable contribution to the club over three decades, retired in 2008.

150 LANCASHIRE GREATS
139. Jimmy Anderson

Jimmy Anderson was born in Burnley and played cricket for his home-town club. A right-arm fast bowler, he made his first-class debut for Lancashire in 2002, playing 13 matches that season and taking 50 wickets at an average of 22.28, including three five-wicket hauls. He was awarded the Denis Compton Award for Lancashire's most promising young county player. In 2003, he became the youngest player to take a hat-trick for Lancashire just a week before his Test match debut against Zimbabwe and in 2004 there was also his first ten-wicket haul against Worcestershire. He has represented England in more than 80 Test matches and over 160 one-day internationals. He is England's all-time highest wicket-taker in all three formats and only the fourth English bowler to take 300 Test wickets. In 2009 he took career best first-class figures with 11-109 against Sussex. He has become one of the world's leading fast bowlers on the back of being an integral part in two Ashes-winning campaigns, the first of which led to him being named as one of Wisden's Cricketers of the Year in 2009. Lancashire awarded him a benefit in 2012 and he was also given the Freedom of Burnley.

Bowl-out agony *2009*

LANCASHIRE WOULD find a couple of strange ways to exit the Twenty20 Cup in the space of three years. In 2011, it would be at the semi-final stage to Leicestershire via English cricket's first ever Super Over Eliminator, the decider following tied matches. And in 2009, Peter Moores' first year as head coach, it would be at the quarter-final stage to Somerset after a bowl out at Old Trafford on the back of three rainy days at the end of July.

Lancashire were the country's most successful team through the group stages, with nobody else matching their haul of eight wins from ten matches. But in the eerie atmosphere of the Indoor School, with no spectators watching and only being

The new men in charge: coach Peter Moores and skipper Glen Chapple face the media

150 LANCASHIRE GREATS
140. Saj Mahmood

Saj Mahmood was born in Bolton, the cousin of boxer Amir Khan. Saj played club cricket in the Bolton League with Astley Bridge well enough to be signed by Lancashire in 2002. A fast bowler with a potent combination of a full length, late swing and high pace, he showed great promise. Within a year he was selected to train with England's National Academy and went on to play eight Tests for England, 26 one-day internationals and four Twenty20 matches. He toured Australia in 2006/7 but had few opportunities. 2009 was his most successful season for Lancashire with 38 wickets and he also took 33 Championship wickets in 2010. His potential with the bat was evident when he scored 94 against Sussex at Old Trafford early in his career. Aside from his undoubted skill as a cricketer, Mahmood was the life and soul of the Lancashire dressing-room. Rarely without a huge grin on his face, practical jokes were his thing. He played 92 first-class matches for Lancashire, taking 260 wickets at 31.62. He also played 95 limited over games, taking 137 wickets at 25.40. He was released at the end of the 2012 season and moved to Essex.

informed of events in the stands outside via PA Announcer Matt Proctor, the Lightning were comfortably beaten 5-1. Only rookie pace bowler Steven Cheetham, who was not due to play in the tie, hit the stumps for the hosts. Alfonso Thomas was on target twice for Somerset, with Peter Trego, Charl Willoughby and Ben Phillips also hitting the unguarded stumps once apiece.

Aside from the arrival of Moores, it was also Glen Chapple's first summer as captain. Moores joined in early February on the back of a re-jigging of the coaching department that saw Mike Watkinson move from a more hands on cricket manager role to that of cricket director, which would see him head up the club's cricket department.

Lancashire also topped their Friends Provident 50-over Trophy group with six wins from eight matches. They went on to win a home quarter-final against Essex thanks to a spectacular 113 from South African Francois du Plessis, but they lost a semi-final against Hampshire, failing to chase down 272 at Old Trafford in early July.

Lancashire, whose brilliant fielding was highlighted by du Plessis's excellence and two memorable boundary catches in Twenty20 by Steven Croft and Stephen Parry, raised expectations of a Championship challenge by winning

two of their first three matches. But seven straight draws during the second half of the season meant they were closer to relegation than they would have liked again. There was good news for popular ex-captain Mark Chilton, whose 777 Championship runs were a factor in his Player of the Year Award.

Lancashire's players look on nervously during the bowl-out in the quarter-final of the T20 competition against Somerset. Only Steven Cheetham (right) managed to hit the stumps in a 5-1 defeat.

Flintoff retires *2010*

IT WAS the sight Lancashire fans had waited for decades to see! A team celebrating a County Championship title win on the Old Trafford outfield. Unfortunately however, Nottinghamshire were the ones popping the champagne corks after a dramatic finale to the season. On the day that Andrew Flintoff announced his retirement from all forms of professional cricket (September 16), Notts secured the bonus points they needed in a draw to clinch their second title in six seasons. It was also a day that signalled the end of an era for Old Trafford, with this match being the last played with the square running from east to west before its reorientation during the winter months.

In many ways, it was an injury ravaged summer for the Red Rose, who finished fourth for the second successive year. Added to Flintoff's retirement due to knee problems, Gary Keedy missed nine Championship matches with a broken collarbone suffered during pre-season before taking 31 wickets in the last seven matches,

while new signing Stephen Moore badly dislocated his shoulder in a fielding accident at Chelmsford during a Twenty20 quarter-final defeat against Essex in July.

Lancashire still managed progress in coach Peter Moores's second season, with five fifties for Sajid Mahmood a factor in five wins. There was a simple explanation for the fast bowler's improvement with the willow: "I've started to watch the ball!" he said.

The challenges posed to counties signing overseas player were highlighted in this season. By and large, gone were the days of being able to sign a

Clive Lloyd, Wasim Akram or Farokh Engineer for a whole summer. Lancashire contracted no fewer than seven overseas players in all competitions. Ashwell Prince, Shivnarine Chanderpaul, Simon Katich, Kumar Sangakkara, Nathan McCullum and Shoaib Malik were all signed, but Sangakkara and Malik were not able to fulfill their deals because of international commitments.

Off the field, there was the bizarre sight of Lanky the Giraffe sitting through a planning meeting in the council chambers at Trafford Town Hall in March as the club tried to convince Trafford's Planning Committee to give their redevelopment plans the green light.

150 LANCASHIRE GREATS
141. Ashwell Prince

Ashwell Prince remains an integral part of the Lancashire team. The left-hand batsman from South Africa had his fourth spell at Old Trafford in 2013, but this time as a local player rather than an overseas. A middle order batsman, he has a high batting stance and is strong through the offside. He is noted for his gritty style of batting and also for being an athletic fielder in the covers. Feisty, brave, tough, combative are all apt descriptions for the Port Elizabeth-born star. The owner of 119 international caps in all forms of cricket - 66 of them in Test matches - at the age of 29 he became the first non-white man to captain the South African cricket team when he stood in for the injured Graeme Smith in two Tests. He has scored 11 Test match centuries. He was the only Lancashire player to top 1,000 County Championship runs in 2012 and repeated this in 2013, being awarded the Championship Player of the Year accolade. Peter Moores said: "Ashwell's a very competitive player. He is a product of not potential but performance. He's tough, hard, finds a way to adapt and deliver something on a given day however he's feeling or how the conditions are. That's a really powerful thing to have in your side."

After a distinguished career with Lancashire and England, injuries forced Andrew Flintoff's retirement at the end of the 2010 season.

Champions at last *2011*

IT WAS as good as done and dusted! The Championship title was Warwickshire's to lose as the season's final day dawned. On course for a tenth Division One victory against Somerset at Taunton on the morning of Thursday September 15, Lancashire simply had to dot the i's and cross the t's at their end and pray for a draw down at the Rose Bowl in Southampton, where Hampshire were in trouble against the table-topping Bears.

Somerset started the day with a five-run lead in their second innings with only five wickets left, while Warwickshire had their hosts 43-3 having followed on. Events elsewhere looked like rendering famous Lanky wins over Yorkshire twice and Hampshire at Liverpool meaningless, and even captain Glen Chapple, who performed heroically despite a hamstring injury, knew it – even if he didn't admit it.

Long-serving chief executive Jim Cumbes was among those who aborted plans to travel to the West Country on the Wednesday night. A meeting planned to discuss the publication of the club's celebratory book was even cancelled. Thankfully, things did not go to script as Hampshire centurions Michael Carberry and Neil McKenzie shared a fourth-wicket stand of 182 to secure an unlikely draw.

But now things were in the balance back at Taunton. Peter Trego hit his own hundred, sharing in partnerships of 75 and 95 for the eighth and ninth wickets to leave the visitors chasing a tricky 211 in 34 overs during the final session to win the title. As the day unfolded, Cumbes was frantically looking at flights to Bristol or Exeter, while that book meeting was hastily reconvened at tea.

Openers Paul Horton and Stephen Moore got Lancashire ticking along nicely.

Steven Croft and Karl Brown celebrate after their partnership against Somerset saw Lancashire to their first Championship title in 77 years.

And, as they approached the latter stages of a 131-run opening stand, the excitement built. Chants of 'oh Lanky, Lanky' and 'Champions' rang out from sections of the visiting support, whose numbers have been

150 LANCASHIRE GREATS
142. Glen Chapple

Glen Chapple capped off a memorable 2011 by being crowned as Lancashire's Player of the Year for the third time in his career. The Lancashire skipper led Lancashire to the Championship title for the first time in 76 years with 55 wickets, bravely battling through the pain barrier for the team cause on numerous occasions. He made his debut for Lancashire in 1992 and shot to fame four years later when he claimed 6-18 to skittle Essex for just 57 to help win the NatWest Trophy at Lord's. His best bowling of 7-53 came against Durham at Blackpool in 2007, contributing to best match figures of 10-86. He formed a devastating new ball alliance with Peter Martin for many seasons. Chapple is part of an elite group of cricketers to pass 7,000 runs and taken 800 wickets for Lancashire. A one-time He can be considered very unlucky not have played Test cricket. Talismanic is the perfect way to describe the Skipton-born player, who has returned many a valuable contribution with both bat and ball. He was awarded the captaincy in 2009 and has formed a close bond with coach Peter Moores, who has often hailed Chapple's dedication to fitness and his desire to succeed. 2014 will be his sixth season as Lancashire's captain.

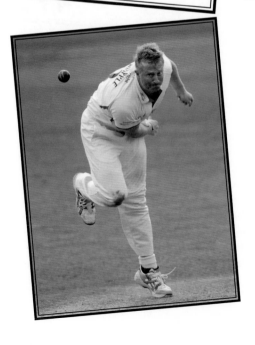

Final LV= County Championship table

	P	W	L	D	BaP	BoP	Pts
Lancashire**	16	10	4	2	37	44	246
Warwickshire*	16	9	4	3	46	45	235
Durham	16	8	4	4	47	45	232
Somerset	16	6	7	3	45	39	189
Sussex	16	6	6	4	34	40	182
Nottinghamshire	16	5	6	5	35	43	173
Worcestershire	16	4	11	1	31	44	142
Yorkshire+	16	3	6	7	34	37	138
Hampshire++	16	3	6	7	30	36	127

* Warwickshire deducted eight points for poor pitch and one point for slow over rate
** Lancashire deducted one point for slow over rate
+ Yorkshire deducted two points for slow over rate
++ Hampshire deducted eight points for poor pitch

since quoted as anywhere between 200 and 2,000 – it was more like the former.

As the chase unfolded, players and coaches bowed to superstition and refused to move from their original dressing room seats. For example, Gary Keedy, who had earlier effected the crucial run out of last man Gemaal Hussain, had no view of the action and relied on cheers or jeers for news. Luke Procter was locked in the toilets. When Steven Croft hit those winning runs with 29 balls left, celebrations finally began. For Cumbes, he ended up sharing a bottle of champers with Lanky the Giraffe in the Old Trafford offices. It was the day we had waited 77 years for!

Moores best in the world

ENGLAND'S LOSS was definitely Lancashire's gain as they were led to their ninth outright County Championship title by the best coach in world cricket, according to Red Rose all-rounder Kyle Hogg. Macclesfield-born Peter Moores watched the county as a youngster, even heading down to Old Trafford to play in an under

13s tournament on the Nursery Ground and train in the nets under the guidance of Jack Bond. He would have dreamt of being involved in a Championship win with his county. But he certainly could not have dreamt about the way he arrived at Old Trafford, having been sacked as coach of England following a breakdown in his relationship with controversial national captain Kevin Pietersen in early 2009.

Moores, a wicketkeeper in his playing days with Sussex and Worcestershire, had plenty of success as a coach prior to returning to the North West. He led Sussex to the Championship in 2003 before being appointed as the head of the ECB's National Academy and graduating to become his country's head coach in 2007. He gave Stuart Broad and Matt Prior their international chance, while re-invigorating the careers of Jimmy Anderson and Ryan Sidebottom amongst others.

Upon arriving at Old Trafford on February 11 2009, he was an instant hit in the Lancashire dressing room, as Hogg explains. The all-rounder told the book *Champions...about bloomin' time!*: "I remember training in the Indoor Centre, and he was watching us from the balcony having just taken over. I'd never met him before, but I felt like I'd known him for ages as soon as he introduced himself.

"When he finished with England, he could have come and just had three years on auto pilot, but he took this job on with the same enthusiasm as he must have done with England. In fact, it was almost as if it was his first ever job. I've never met anybody who's on the same level with regards to his enthusiasm. His knowledge is also different class.

"Some say he's the best coach in county cricket, but I'd say world cricket. There's not a lot of other international coaches who would have done that."

Winning the Championship was not the only thing Lancashire were celebrating in September. They were also given the final go ahead for the entire redevelopment of Old Trafford after a bitter dispute with rival developers Derwent Holdings as well as being awarded an Ashes Test match in 2013.

Relegation blow softened by rise of Kerrigan

2012

THERE WERE not too many highlights and plus points from 2012 as Lancashire became the third county since the turn of the century to win the County Championship one year and then get relegated the next. At least Yorkshire were amongst the group from 2002! Ten Championship wins the season before were followed by just one as the Red Rose were hampered by a combination of poor cricket and bad weather, culminating in a drop in divisions alongside Worcestershire.

South African overseas Ashwell Prince was the only batsman to pass 1,000 Championship runs, while no bowler reached 50 wickets after an encouraging start to the domestic campaign with a comprehensive victory in the first-class champion county match against the MCC at Abu Dhabi in March.

The development of Simon Kerrigan was one of the few plus points in a wet season that was to end in relegation.

One of the pluses was the form of young left-arm spinner Simon Kerrigan, who had taken over the role of number one spinner from Gary Keedy, who left for Surrey at the end of the season in search of regular first-team cricket as his career comes to a close. Left-arm spinner Kerrigan had shot into the limelight with hauls of 5-7 against Warwickshire the previous May and then a record-breaking 9-51 later in the season to clinch a crucial and last gasp win against Hampshire to help secure the famous title success. And Kerrigan made significant strides in his development by taking 44 wickets during this summer, more than any other Lancashire bowler. He also took six wickets for the Lions against Australia A at Old Trafford.

Another highlight was a stunning Clydesdale Bank 40 innings by Tom Smith in an abandoned match against Worcestershire at New Road in August. The Lightning had already secured a semi-final tie against Warwickshire at Old Trafford, which they eventually lost, but Smith ensured a damp day was brightened up with a 44-ball hundred on the way to 106 off 46. He hammered eight fours and ten sixes in equalling the fifth fastest List A innings of all time and equalling the third fastest in domestic cricket. He underpinned a 37-over total of 324-4, putting Stephen Moore's 113 in the shade. It came after a five-week injury lay-off for Smith, who helped celebrate 50 years of one-day cricket in some style.

"It's not often I stand at the other end and see the ball sail over my head like that," admitted Moore. "The last person I batted with who did that was Chris Gayle, and Tom played a very Chris Gayle like innings there. It was striking of world-class calibre."

Smith even revealed: "At one stage I was trying to hit six sixes in an over, but just to get a hundred was great. I got to 50 off 24 balls and decided to keep going. It came off for me."

The season had started with the club's members voting in favour of plans to abolish the committee system in favour of a new ten-man board at a Special General Meeting in April. It was a move chairman Michael Cairns described as "essential" for the future of the club.

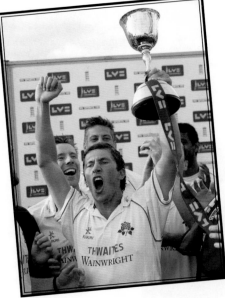

150 LANCASHIRE GREATS
143. Simon Kerrigan

Simon Kerrigan, a slow left-arm orthodox spinner who was born in Preston, started his cricket career at Fulwood & Broughton before moving on to Ormskirk. In 2009. An injury to Gary Keedy in 2010 meant he made his first-class debut in Lancashire's first match of the season and he claimed his maiden five-wicket haul to help Lancashire to victory over Warwickshire. He played 13 first-class matches in his first full season, taking 30 wickets, ave.32.23, including three five-wicket hauls. In 2011 he took 5-7 in Warwickshire's second innings to take his team to a 147-run victory. Despite limited opportunities in the County Championship, he played 10 matches in the CB40 and six twenty20 games. In the penultimate County Championship match of the season he took career best bowling figures of 9-51 to take Lancashire to a 222-run win over Hampshire. This was the best bowling figures for Lancashire since Roy Tattersall's 9-40 in 1953. He was also included in the 16-man England Lions squad to tour Bangladesh in January 2012. He made his Test debut against Australia in the fifth Ashes Test of 2013.

Essex shot out for 20

2013

LANCASHIRE ENJOYED one of the most spectacular days in their history in mid-June when Essex were bowled out for just 20 in the second innings at Chelmsford on the way to LV= County Championship promotion. The year started with the Red Rose announcing a ground breaking ten-year sponsorship deal with Dubai-based airline Fly Emirates for the naming rights of Old Trafford and the shirt sponsorship for Twenty20 worth up to £10m. And it ended with the success on the field as Glen Chapple's side won Division Two at a canter ahead of promoted Northamptonshire, including a spectacular three-day victory in the south when the skipper and Kyle Hogg shared nine second-innings wickets.

Lancashire took a lead of 125 into the afternoon session of day three, but the Essex second innings lasted just 14.4 overs and 68 minutes. Not only had Lancashire never

Old Trafford

because the new man is under pressure, but you don't often see the whole team succumbing in that sense."

Hogg, who finished the season as the club's leading Championship wicket-taker with 60, said: "We've been involved in a piece of history, and that's what you play the game for. This kind of day makes up for all the bad days. That was unreal. It will

Left-arm spinner Simon Kerrigan finished the season with 57 Championship wickets, the most by any spinner in county cricket. He also made his Test debut for England in the final Ashes Test of the summer at the Oval in August, although things did not quite go to plan for him. He returned first-innings figures of 0-53 from eight overs. His disappointing display meant he missed out on a winter tour place with England, but everybody at the club is confident he will bounce back and star at the top level for years to come.

After the retirement of Jim Cumbes ahead of the 2013 summer, the club appointed Daniel Gidney as their new chief executive. Gidney arrived at Emirates Old Trafford having worked in the same post at Coventry's Ricoh Arena

Glen Chapple in action as the county defeated nearest challengers Northants inside two days. The skipper and his opening partner Kyle Hogg had many great days during the season, not least when they skittled Essex out for just 20.

150 LANCASHIRE GREATS
144. Kyle Hogg

Born in Birmingham, Kyle Hogg's family moved to Oldham when he was a child. He is the son of former Lancashire player Willie and the grandson of former West Indies legend Sonny Ramadhin. A right-arm fast-medium bowler and a hard-hitting left-hand batsman, he has proved himself to be one of the best number tens in county cricket, often getting Lancashire out of a hole with entertaining cameos. He made his debut in 2001 but found himself in and out of the side and struggling with injuries. He enjoyed success in 2006, playing his part as the Red Rose reached the 40-over competition final, but 2007 didn't quite go as planned due to a lack of opportunities. He was awarded his county cap during the 2010 summer, forming a dangerous new ball alliance with skipper Glen Chapple. The 2011 season was Hogg's most successful. He took 50 wickets in the County Championship for the first time and also scored 300 first-class runs at an average of 21.47, contributing greatly to the club winning the County Championship. He was crowned as Player of the Year for the County in 2013 after his 60 wickets helped Lancashire to the Second Division title.

bowled a side out for fewer in their history, it was also county cricket's lowest total since 1983, when Surrey scored 14 against Essex on the same ground. Before Chapple returned 5-9 from 7.2 overs and Hogg 4-11 from seven, Lancashire had increased the pressure on Essex by adding 190 runs for the last three wickets in their first innings.

"There's no point trying to explain what happened," said Chapple. "Everything that could have gone for us did. It's definitely one of the best days of cricket I've had in my career because things just don't happen like that. We know that wickets can go quickly

probably sink in in a few weeks."

Lancashire, who added international duo Kyle Jarvis and Jos Buttler to their squad ahead of 2014, clinched promotion with two matches to go and the Division Two title in their penultimate fixture of the season at Gloucestershire. Unfortunately, the season ended with defeat against Kent at Canterbury as they failed to remain unbeaten through a campaign for the first time since 1974. Kent's successful chase of 418 was the highest fourth-innings against Lancashire in their history.

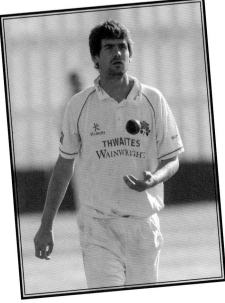

Lancashire's biggest battle

By Chris Ostick

Cricket correspondent, *Manchester Evening News*

WHEN JIM Cumbes walked into his office, Geoff Durbin could tell by the look on his face something was wrong. Just minutes earlier, the then Lancashire chief executive Cumbes had taken a bombshell phone call. It was from the chairman of the ECB David Morgan, who revealed Old Trafford would not be getting an Ashes Test in 2009 and that instead Cardiff would be hosting the biggest series in cricket.

That was the moment which changed the direction of the club. It was the catalyst which started an amazing seven years that saw Lancashire go through plenty of soul-searching, planning battles and financial nightmares. But now, after a £45m redevelopment, the club today proudly shows off its new-look Emirates Old Trafford. And for the club's commercial director Durbin, that pivotal day in 2006 is still fresh in his mind.

"I remember the day very well," said Durbin. "I can still see Jim Cumbes coming into my office with a look on his face saying he had some bad news and told me we hadn't got the Ashes. I felt shocked, numb, disbelief, anger. It was one of those defining moments.

"But I honestly believe it was that moment that fostered everything that has now happened. We didn't know it at the time but it was the catalyst. We had sunk to a very low place and we had to put it right. Little did we know how many battles and obstacles we would have. But that was the day we had to do something about it. It was the marker in the sand.

"We didn't react the wrong way, moaning and whingeing, we got up off our backsides and did something about it. Now we have produced this fantastic venue. It was probably the wrong reason why it happened, but I am glad it did because that's why we are here where we are now.

"Old Trafford was tired, it was an old lady that on her day could produce a fantastic show. We had some amazing moments in that old stadium and that is what masked the reality of what we had to do. Our customers put up with the fact the toilets weren't that good and

Commercial director Geoff Durbin.

the facilities weren't up to scratch because they still had a great day. Maybe we were a bit guilty of using that as a reason for not to do things. Was there some complacency in the old days? There probably was. But we have dealt with it now, have learnt from it and, in a special way, it has bonded a lot of people who came through that journey."

After three years of posting multi-million pound losses, the return of the Ashes in 2013 put Lancashire into profitability, with the club banking over a seven-figure profit from just the game itself. Plus the coffers have been boosted by increased sponsorship becoming a Test venue brings with it. After a 10-year deal worth up to £10m having been completed with Emirates early in 2013, the club also signed a three-year deal with financial services company AJ Bell for the naming rights of the new players and media centre.

But Durbin insists the club want to ensure they make enough money from non-cricketing activities to guarantee their financial future if they ever lose Ashes cricket again. "An Ashes Test will make us a significant amount of money," he said. "We will have our first big profit this year after several years of losses. But we are not complacent. We want to ensure our non-match day income will be the core bread and butter that makes sure Lancashire has a viable and sustainable future. The day you start relying on an Ashes Test to survive is the day venues tend to get into trouble."

Getting to this point was hardly a breeze for Lancashire, with the redevelopment opposed at almost every level by local businessman Albert Gubay. Although they won that fight, it cost them close to £4m and around 18 months. But now, says Durbin, it is time for the club – and the whole region – to enjoy the rewards of all the hard work and perseverance that has gone into transforming the stadium.

"There were times when I thought it might not happen, but I couldn't believe it wouldn't happen," he said. "We got the champagne out at one

150 LANCASHIRE GREATS

145. Jim Cumbes

Jim Cumbes had a remarkable 50-year sporting career in both cricket and football. Born in East Didsbury, he played for four counties, including Lancashire, and also had a substantial career as a professional footballer, playing in goal for Aston Villa, Tranmere Rovers and West Brom. He was commercial manager at Warwickshire before moving to Lancashire, where he became the longest-serving chief executive from 1998 to 2012. He oversaw the rebuilding of Old Trafford from a run-down stadium to a world-class international venue. He also led the fight for the redevelopment of the ground through many difficult court battles when the whole future of Old Trafford was under threat. He said, "In terms of achievement and satisfaction, I think sowing the seeds of the redevelopment in 2003, and then seeing it through with everyone else associated at the club, has given me the most satisfaction. At no stage was the process easy, and at times the difficulties almost overwhelmed us. But everyone stuck at it. We had no alternative, no Plan B."

point thinking it was all over, only to hear we had another challenge and another court battle. You felt this massive concern, but there was always this inner belief that it had to happen, even though we didn't know how. The Ashes was something we had been preparing for seven years. It has been a hard slog and a battle on many occasions.

"Showing the world what we had done was more important to us than saying this is the culmination of all our dreams, because we have an awful lot more dreams. This is about showcasing to the world what we are all about. We believe the stadium is one of the finest in the world now and it was for other people to tell us that, and The Ashes was the opportunity for them to do so. Whether it be fans facilities, media facilities, player facilities, corporate hospitality facilities – Emirates Old Trafford is among the finest now of any of the grounds in world cricket.

"In 2005 cricket knocked everything off the back pages and you talk about Ashes Fever, but it was. And that came back in 2013, but it was even more exciting because of the redevelopment of the stadium and what we have been through to get here. And it also reminded us what we might have lost. We, our members and everyone who loves their cricket in the north west know how close we were to not having all this and that's what makes it really special.

"The first ball of a Test is very special anyway, but this was a hugely symbolic moment. A lot of people who have been through this journey found it a very emotional moment. We can't take our eye off the ball for too long, but I think we should enjoy that very special moment. It was fitting that Jimmy Anderson bowled the first ball of the Test, and it was also fitting that we retained the Ashes here. It was just reward for everything the club has gone through."

Finance Director and Secretary Lee Morgan, who will play a key role in the club's future.

Lancashire County Cricket Club
OLD TRAFFORD

1857   1957

Dinner to Commemorate One Hundred Years of Cricket at Old Trafford

Manchester Town Hall
6th June 1957

President:
The Rt.Hon.The Earl of Derby M.C.

MENU

Lancashire County and
Manchester Cricket
Club ❖ Old Trafford

OPENING DAY LUNCHEON
GIVEN BY DR. H. H. I. HITCHON, J.P.

CLEAR ROYAL SOUP.
CREAM OF TOMATO SOUP.
———
SCOTCH SALMON AND CUCUMBER.
MAYONNAISE SAUCE.
———
BRAISED CHICKEN.   YORK HAM.
QUARTER OF LAMB.
VEGETABLES.
———
APPLE TART AND CREAM.
PARISIAN CREAM TRIFLES.

CHEESE.   BISCUITS.   BUTTER.
———
COFFEE.

MONDAY, 16th APRIL, 1934.   [over

LANCASHIRE COUNTY CRICKET CLUB

*John Player League Champions
and Gillette Cup Winners*
1970

CELEBRATION DINNER

♕ ♕

Old Trafford February 24th, 1971

LANCASHIRE COUNTY AND
MANCHESTER CRICKET CLUB
OLD TRAFFORD
———
Opening Day Luncheon
GIVEN BY SIR THOMAS ROBINSON
K.B.E.,J.P.

Menu

Creme à la Portuguaise
—
Saumon au Concombre
—
Bouchées Volaille
—
Selle à Agneau
Verts—Pomme Novelle
—
lace-a-l' Ananas
npote de Fruits
—
Coffee

19th April, 1939

[over

The Grounds before Old Trafford

By Rev. Malcolm G Lorimer

OLD TRAFFORD is the 'home' of Lancashire cricket and many supporters could not imagine the county ground being situated anywhere else. But it wasn't always so! Old Trafford is Manchester's fourth ground and the club is only based at Old Trafford because of the Art Treasures Exhibition in 1857.

Cricket in the county has a romantic beginning. Manchester Cricket Club was originally called 'The Aurora' from the fact that players used to meet at dawn in the Adelphi, which was a green oasis

Old Trafford as it looked in the 1850s.

opposite The Crescent in Salford (where the River Irwell bends). Some great matches took place, among them against Liverpool in 1823 and in a scorebook which has been preserved from the time we have the scores. Manchester all out for 24 and 25 and Liverpool, despite scoring only 70, managing to win by an innings!

Two other great clubs played at the same time: Broughton Cricket Club, where WG Grace played as well as the touring Australians and which for a time went on to rival Old Trafford for crowds and prominence. The other great club was the Western club, situated in Eccles (the De La Salle College sports fields are on the site now). Western was a breakaway from the Manchester

club. It became a strong and exclusive club with a splendid pavilion. John Wisden and one Julius Caesar played as professionals in the three-run win against Surrey in 1857.

In 1832 Manchester CC established themselves at Moss Lane in Hulme in the vicinity of Chalk Farm, where a variety of sports took place and which was called, 'The Battersea of Manchester'. They continued to play against Liverpool and in 1844 first played Yorkshire in Sheffield and won.

The greatest match on the Moss Lane ground was undoubtedly the All-England X1 against the 18 of Manchester in 1846. Fuller Pilch, Joseph Guy, Alfred Mynn and William Clarke graced the ground and caused great interest, with huge sums being wagered on the match. A regimental band played during the play, which caused some distraction, and Manchester lost the game. In the return match the following year the Manchester club acquitted themselves much better, and with the England Xl in sight of defeat, they caused consternation by refusing to play on because they wanted to see Jenny Lind, 'The Swedish Nightingale', perform in Manchester that evening. Almost £40,000 in bets depended on the result and they were declared null and void.

After 14 years the ground was required for building as the Manchester suburbs expanded (St Mary's church is now on the site) and

150 LANCASHIRE GREATS
146. Sam Swire

Samuel Swire was an excellent organiser who became the first Hon. Secretary of the Manchester Club in 1862. He was an amateur all-rounder for the club and attended the famous meeting in January 1864 to consider forming a county club. He played in the first match at Warrington in 1864 against Birkenhead Park when a team officially used the name Lancashire (it wasn't deemed first-class) and he played in Lancashire's first county match against Middlesex in 1865. Though never a prominent cricketer, he played occasionally for Lancashire in the early days of the county. He was joint secretary of the club with AB Rowley in the formative years of the club and then sole secretary for 33 years from 1873 until his death in 1906. Before his death, he was presented with a silver tray with a picture of the Old Trafford Pavilion engraved on it for his long service, which is now in the museum, and a dinner was held in his honour at the Queen's Hotel, where the club was formed.

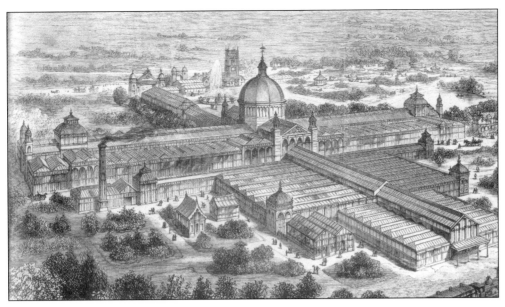

*The Art Treasures Exhibition at White City in 1857, for which
the club was forced to move to the Old Trafford site.*

ground would be required for the National Art Treasures Exhibition, which was coming to the Botanical Gardens the following year, so the ground was surrendered for £1,000 with £300 compensation for the pavilion. Two fields were leased a short distance away for £37 6s 6d a year from the De Trafford estate and no-one could have imagined that it would become one of the finest and most famous cricket grounds in the world. A small local cricket club played on the ground and the land was used as a racecourse, the Stretford Steeplechase being run on New Year's Day. The land was bordered by the railway on one side and Manchester Gun Club on the other (which is now the site of B&Q).

so the club moved again, this time to the Botanical Gardens about a mile away (where the White City stadium stood). On 18th July, 1847 it was announced: "The ground of the Manchester club being required for building, the club has leased from the De Trafford's a large field of 17 acres situated at the back of the Botanical Gardens, Stretford Rd." A pavilion was erected and it was regarded as one of the most picturesque cricket grounds in England. Important fixtures were played against Sheffield and for the first time in 1849 'Lancashire' was used in the scorebook in a match against Yorkshire. Matches were played against England XIs and in a salutary piece the Manchester Guardian reflected in 1849, "We must seek for a solution of the fact that Manchester, with its very great superiority in many respects, is still, in the name of cricket, inferior to many provincial towns."

In 1853 it had 230 members and began to grow in playing strength and influence. In 1856 it was realised that the cricket

The ground opened in 1857 with a match between Manchester and Liverpool and it is surprising to think that many people thought that it was situated too far out in the country from the centre of Manchester! Early maps show space for three cricket grounds, a polo ground and also two football pitches. The great decision which we need to thank our predecessors for is that in 1898 they took the bold decision to buy the ground, including the gun club, for £24,732. It was a big step at the time, but one which in later years was to secure the prosperity and future of the club.

Lancashire have come a long way since those players from the Aurora Cricket Club got up before dawn to play their cricket on the Adelphi before they went to work. Perhaps we owe it to them and all those involved in the history of this great club for their foresight and imagination in re-building a ground which has become the envy of many.

Award for Merchant

MATT MERCHANT, the Head Groundsman at Lancashire County Cricket Club, was named 2013 Groundsman of the Year in the four-day category at an awards ceremony held by the ECB in December 2013. Matt has been Head Groundsman for five years having joined the groundstaff in 1990 and played a major role in the preparation of wickets following the reorientation of the square in 2010.

Cricket Director Mike Watkinson said: "The award is worthy recognition for Matt and his team, especially given the challenges of recent years. The square was turned through 90 degrees in 2010. This was a major project which was managed in house and created 11 new pitches along with the refurbishment of the existing five. The success of the project is demonstrated in the quality of recent international pitches and this award recognises the outstanding four-day surfaces this year. I am delighted for Matt and we look forward to an exciting season of domestic and international cricket at Emirates Old Trafford in 2014."

Matt added: "I am pleased to have picked up this award, which is a great credit to our team of ground staff who work extremely hard throughout the year."

Red Rose can continue to bloom

By Graham Hardcastle

THE FUTURE of Lancashire cricket is bright, says Gary Yates, a man who has played a significant role in the county's history, both as a trophy-winning player and a trophy-winning coach. Yates, a former off-spinner and the Red Rose's current assistant coach, has tasted success with both the first team and the second team, most recently as the latter's coach.

First of all, evidence both on and off the field suggests that Lancashire's short-term future is healthy. Off the field, the club have navigated recent financial issues to emerge with an Emirates Old Trafford cricket ground to be proud of. On the field, the first team are back in Division One of the County Championship and, as alluded to above, the second team have had plenty of recent success with silverware. For example, in the 2013 summer, they shared the three-day Championship title with Middlesex and won the one-day Trophy for the second year running.

A number of young players enhanced their reputations through their performances, most notably Luis Reece, Arron Lilley, Alex Davies and Liam Livingstone, and ahead of the 150th anniversary season, 15 players signed contract extensions. Fourteen of those came through the Lancashire system, while Cypriot Andrea Agathangelou has taken to life in the North West like a duck to water.

More experienced players such as Paul Horton, Tom Smith, Kyle Hogg, Simon Kerrigan and Luke Procter also thrived under the pressure of having to drive the side back up to Division One. Stephen Parry also excelled as the second XI captain. And then there is captain Glen Chapple, who heads into 2014 aged 40 and leads the side for a sixth year. He continues to set the standards for the rest to follow.

"I think the fact that we've signed so many players up on long-term contracts, the vast majority of those being homegrown, shows a lot of confidence from the coaching staff. That's not just myself, that's Peter Moores as well," said Yates. "Some of our younger players who haven't yet broken through to the first team, in my opinion, would be

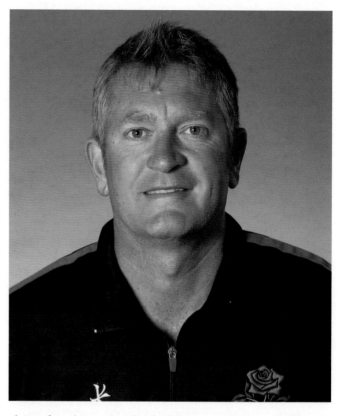

playing first-class cricket already if they were at other counties.

"We have belief in these players to come through. We think there's enough talent there to show that these players will break through to become very, very exciting first-class cricketers, for sure. The majority of those players are all a work in progress. But in recent times, as well as improving their skills, they have also played in winning teams and are learning how to win. That's also very important. It's part of your make-up in becoming a great player.

"The group of players who went on to win the Championship a couple of years ago, the bulk of them were consistently finishing in the top two or three of the Second XI Championship, which was a good guide for us as coaches to see where they were at. The current group in the seconds have had a lot of success recently, particularly in one-day finals. The signs are good."

The majority of Lancashire members will look to the Championship as the title they want to win again – the Holy Grail. It has the most history and prestige. But Yates, who was instrumental in the club's Kings of One-Day Cricket 'mark II' era through the 1990s, sees it slightly differently.

150 LANCASHIRE GREATS
147. Michael Cairns

In 2008 Mike Cairns became chairman of Lancashire CCC after Jack Simmons stepped down. With a background in the international hotel sector, he was the ideal person to oversee the £45 million development of the ground, the complex building programme and the re-shaping of the club. Born and bred in Levenshulme, he always harboured ambitions to make it as a cricketer and at 15 captained both the Manchester and Lancashire schoolboys teams as a wicketkeeper/batsman, playing alongside Jack Simmons. By 19, however, he knew his talents lay elsewhere and decided to study at Hollins College in Manchester. It was inevitable that a man who loves Lancashire and cricket so much would return and in 2001 he became chairman of the Business Committee. Awarded an OBE for services to English Heritage in 2007, he oversaw the complete re-development of the ground, including re-orientating the cricket square, re-vamping the pavilion, new player and media facilities and a new 1,000-seater banqueting suite, The Point. With a successful return of an Ashes Test to Old Trafford in 2013, he has built a powerful legacy on which to build for the future.

"Under Peter Moores in the first team, there has been a certain consistency in terms of amount of games won during his reign, which has put us in the top four teams in four-day cricket and probably the top three or four in limited overs cricket," he continued. "I think the signs for success in the short-term are very healthy. Obviously, there's no guarantee, but you have to say you would expect us to be challenging.

"I think the aim for this group of players is to be the top limited overs team in the country because that's what you need to be to be the best team overall. That's because of the dynamism you need to have and because two of the three domestic competitions are one-dayers. People will always see the Championship as the main one, but to be regarded as the best team you have to be winning one-day competitions.

"As a coach, you are always trying to improve individuals and the team, and you can't get away from the fact that two of three competitions are played as one-dayers. Teams in this day and age, whether it be cricket or football, are judged on the amount of games you win and the trophies you win. If you win two trophies, you are going to be the best team."

Obviously, it gets harder to predict what the long-term future holds for the club – what will happen in another 50 years, 100 years, 150 years? But, bearing in mind a host of areas where the club has moved forward, we can take an educated guess. The players were netting in the members' dining room during the winter in 1951, for example. In 1997, the club built a state of the art Indoor School. There are plans to increase its size further. In 2002, the Lancashire Academy was formed. In 2013, Simon Kerrigan became its first Test cricketer. How many will there be in 2050? And Clive Lloyd has always said that we should build a roof to go over Old Trafford to combat the weather. In 2075, you never know, it might well have happened!

"Where will the club be in 50 years? That's one of the toughest questions I've ever been asked! Looking into the future with a crystal ball is very difficult," continued Yates. "I think you almost get trends in sport. Where something becomes fresh and new, people tend to catch up with it and then something else comes along. But what is new is maybe a skill that's been recycled."

It is quite ironic that Yates should say this given that in the 1995 piece you will have read, then Lancashire coach David Lloyd

said of the former off-spinner: "The very first name on the sheet was G.Yates. He was just so dependable. He provided us with a much needed change of pace, and he was so unflappable. Just look nowadays at David Hussey, who bowls round-arm in limited overs cricket. People see it as something new, but Yatesy was doing that years ago. It's just been recycled."

"I'm sure there will be an element of full circle in some departments of the game. The wheel's always spinning," said Yates. "Although I don't really know, you would expect the game to become even more dynamic. You would also expect equipment to become better, bats thicker and lighter for example. There's enough areas to see where Lancashire could move forward. Things like a larger indoor school, better equipment, more coaches working with younger age-groups, a second ground that becomes a home for junior cricket. They are all things that I think will help the development of players in the long term."

Yates first got into cricket as a youngster in the 1970s and came through the Lancashire system, which has been modernised through the years with the introduction of the Academy in 2002 and the Colts team ahead of the 2010 summer. (The Colts team gives emerging players in and around the Lancashire system the opportunity to play match cricket in the Northern League, whilst enabling LCCC to develop this talent pool.)

"My father was a coach, and I went with him as an 11-year-old to sessions he ran with adult teams. I was tapping into that as a bowler. I would be bowling at adults when I was aged 13 and 14," explained the former Manchester Grammar School pupil. "I went through a system at Lancashire which I don't see changing much, although there have been welcome additions to it with things like the Academy programme and also the Colts team. Strong performances from youngsters in that team will get you opportunities at a higher level. The Lancashire way is to give as much opportunity to young homegrown players as we can.

"From a personal point of view, it's been a wonderful journey. To be involved in Lancashire for so many years, I am very proud to be associated with a great and wonderfully caring county. I have no regrets. I have played with and against some of the best players in the world, and I have moved on to an exciting period of my career in terms of coaching and bringing on young players. I have nothing but praise for Lancashire."

Unsung hero

One of Lancashire's unsung heroes of recent years has been the treasurer, David Hodgkiss. Never one to take the centre stage, his quiet diplomacy, especially with the banks and the business world, has helped smooth Lancashire's ground development. As Lancashire's treasurer for ten years he has presided over Lancashire's largest profit and also the largest loss. His calm assurance at Annual General Meetings has re-assured members that the club has been in safe hands. As Managing Director of William Hare Construction, he could talk to the banks with some confidence and he has managed the club's finances, along with Lee Morgan, over one of most difficult periods in Lancashire's history. David has also been pivotal along with Michael Cairns in helping re-shape the governance of the club and the resulting board. His good stewardship of the club means that Lancashire enter its 150th year in a very confident and robust manner able to face the future with great confidence.

150 years

By Keith Hayhurst

LANCASHIRE COUNTY Cricket Club's rich and eventful heritage over 150 years has included a vast number of cricketing characters who have played their part in creating its long history. They form the extended web that continuously links the story of Lancashire cricket celebrated in this book.

From the inception of the Players' Association, I visited senior former players who were unable to attend our functions at Old Trafford. Many of them had extraordinary tales to tell, some relating hardships, others humorous incidents, but all fascinating stories. One such character was Steve Preston, a medium-fast bowler who opened the bowling with the great Ted McDonald in 1928 against Leicestershire. Preston took the first two wickets, McDonald the next six. Heading the bowling averages for the seconds the previous year, Steve Preston joined the Championship-winning side which included Ernest and Richard Tyldesley, Charlie Hallows, Frank Watson, Len Hopwood and Harry Makepeace. I visited Steve regularly in his nursing home in Hambleton near Blackpool. Approaching 90 years of age, his memory was sharp and he articulated dozens of amusing stories about those cricketers he played with and against. Wages were low and competition for places rigorous.

On a rainy day in the 1920s, his coach Arthur Paul would gather the second XI together in the old pros' room and relate enthralling and captivating stories about cricketers he played with in the 1890s. He had partnered Archie MacLaren in his famous record innings of 424 at Somerset in 1895. Arthur scored 177 himself in the partnership and was greatly admired by Preston. He related stories about Paul who, besides being a great cricketer, played rugby for Swinton and kept goal for Blackburn Rovers. To crown it all he trained as an architect but loved the camaraderie of sporting people. He was born in 1864, which brings the connection stretching back to the formation of the Club.

As a collector I have kept many letters from Steve Preston and read them to members of our Players' Association, which caused continuous laughter throughout the luncheon events. I quote an example: 'Dear fellow members, tampering with the cricket ball has made the news recently – what a fuss about nowt. In my day we used to raise the seam with our thumb. I well remember a bowler who sucked the ball in his mouth with his false teeth in. Then, taking them out would suck the ball again. When asked why he did this he replied – Steve, it makes the ball swing both ways at the same time. There was a lot of skulduggery in my day regarding ball tampering.' In my final visits he would tell me he was fit enough to chase the nurses but forgot what to do when he caught them.

In the early days of Lancashire cricket, Richard Barlow was the first major professional amongst a team of gifted amateurs. Barlow was a gifted all-rounder, opening the bowling and batting for Lancashire and England. He took 7 for 40 to win the first Ashes series, his name appearing on the original Urn. The Lancashire club presented him with a stained-glass window in his benefit year, 1886, which was Barlow's choice of gift. It displayed his revered Captain AN Hornby at the wicket with himself and Lancashire and England keeper Richard Pilling. All played in the first Test Match at Old Trafford. It took me seven years hard searching to find this window and I brought it to the club over 30 years ago. It is exhibited in the members' suite in the pavilion.

Two sample stories from many in our impressive history help to join the threads that complete the historical web. Our heritage is all around us to be enjoyed and appreciated. This book pulls together most of those threads to witness this tapestry which displays a rich, captivating picture.

Old Trafford through the years

LANCASHIRE CCC OFFICIALS 1864-2013

President

1873	Mark Phillips
1874-80	A.B. Rowley
1881-86	Sir Humphrey deTrafford, Bart
1887-93	Sir Humphrey Francis de Trafford
1894-1916	A.N. Hornby
1917-18	Lord Ellesmere
1919-20	Sir Frank Hollins, Bart
1921-22	Lord Derby
1923-24	O.P. Lancashire
1925-26	Sir Edwin Stockton
1927-28	Lord Ashton
1929	Rev. V.F.P.A. Royle
1930-31	Lord Derby
1932-33	Lord Colwyn
1934-35	Dr H.H.I. Hitchon
1936-37	Myles N. Kenyon
1938	Lord Stanley
1939-40	Sir Thomas Robinson
1941-42	Sir Christopher Needham
1943-44	Sir R. Noton Barclay
1945-46	R.H. Spooner
1947-48	W. Findlay
1949-50	Sir Edward Rhodes
1951-52	Colonel L. Green
1953-54	T. Stone
1955-56	Dr J. Bowling Holmes
1957-58	The Rt. Hon. The Earl of Derby MC
1959-60	R.A. Boddington
1961-62	Stanley Holt
1963-64	Rev. Canon F. Paton-Williams
1965-66	J.S. Cragg
1967	G.O. Shelmerdine
1968	J.S. Cragg
1969-70	W.H.L. Lister
1971-72	Sir Neville Cardus
1973-74	P. Higson
1975-76	F.D. Beattie
1977-78	T.A. Higson
1979-80	W.D. Crumblehulme
1981-82	J.L. Hopwood
1983-84	E. Kay
1985-86	C.D. Peaker
1987-88	B.J. Howard
1989-90	C.Washbrook CBE
1991-92	A.J. Leggat
1993-94	K. Cranston
1995-96	Sir B. Lovell OBE, FRS
1997-98	J.B. Statham, CBE
1999-2000	Sir Patrick Russell
2001-02	J.F. Blackledge
2003-06	Sir Dennis Landau
2007-09	Lord Steinberg
2010-	J. Livingstone OBE

Chairman

1869-77	A.B. Rowley
1878-98	A.N. Hornby
1899-1912	E. Roper
1913-27	O.P. Lancashire
1928-31	Sir Edwin Stockton
1932-49	T.A. Higson
1950-54	Dr J. Bowling Holmes
1955-64	T.A. Burrows
1965-68	T.P. Higson Jnr
1969-86	C.S. Rhoades
1987-97	R. Bennett
1998-2009	J. Simmons MBE
2009-	MA Cairns OBE

Treasurer

1874-76	John Holt
1876-79	A.H.Wolff
1879-81	J.A. Bannerman
1881-1900	James MacLaren
1900-09	James Horner
1910-17	Talbot Fair
1918-24	Sir Edwin Stockton
1925-32	T.A. Higson
1932-37	A.F. Stockton
1938-45	John Boddan
1946-48	J.C. Fallows
1949-58	R.A. Boddington
1959-72	C.R. Davies
1973-87	A.J. Leggat
1988-97	C.D. Peaker
1998-2002	Sir Dennis Landau
2005-	D.M.W. Hodgkiss

Secretary

1873-1906	S.H. Swire (Hon)
1906-21	T.J. Matthews
1921-32	H. Rylance
1932-48	R. Howard
1949-64	C.G. Howard
1965-74	J.B. Wood
1975-77	A.K. James
1978-91	C.D. Hassell
2013-	L. Morgan

Secretary/ Chief Executive

1991-97	J.M. Bower
1998-2012	J. Cumbes

Chief Executive

2013-	D.G. Gidney

---

150 LANCASHIRE GREATS
148. Cedric Rhoades

Cedric Rhoades never scored a run or took a wicket for Lancashire, but for 20 years he was a dynamic chairman of the club. He came on the committee in dramatic fashion, putting forward a motion of no confidence in the then committee in 1964, which was passed by 656 votes to 48. He brought in a new regime at the club and was a dominant and forceful character, always ready to stand his ground. But behind a stern exterior there was a warmth, an understanding and an appreciation of others. He was a friend to many of the players and staff and his support for them was always firm. His term of office saw Lancashire's resurgence under Jack Bond, with the team winning numerous one-day competitions and improving in the County Championship. It was ironic that someone who had led a revolution was himself the victim of a coup by members. He was forced to resign in February 1987 amidst poor results from the team and doubts about his judgment over the appointment of a captain. He died two years later aged 69 after being taken ill on holiday in Egypt.

LANCASHIRE FIRST-CLASS CRICKETERS 1864-2013

1	R. Blackstock	1865	64	W. Rawlinson	1870-1871	120	A.W. Brooks	1877
2	E.J.Bousfield	1865-1878	65	R.W.B. Sanderson	1870	121	R. Pilling	1877-1889
3	F.J. Crooke	1865	66	J.R. Hillkirk	1871-1877	122	S.S. Schultz	1877-1882
4	R.Iddison	1865-1870	67	W.G. Mills	1871-1877	123	A.G. Steel	1877-1893
5	J.F.Leese	1865-1881	68	E.Wadsworth	1871-1879	124	H.Wall	1877
6	J.Makinson	1865-1873	69	T.Whatmough	1871	125	J.Dixon	1878
7	W. Perry	1865	70	S. Corlett	1871-1875	126	E. Holroyd	1878
8	F.R. Reynolds	1865-1874	71	J.Taylor	1871-1873	127	O.P. Lancashire	1878-1888
9	A.B.Rowley	1865-1871	72	J. Unsworth	1871	128	J. Crossland	1878-1885
10	S.H. Swire	1865-1868	73	R.G. Barlow	1871-1891	129	J. Briggs	1879-1900
11	E.Whittaker	1865-1868	74	G. Hartley	1871-1872	130	G. Nash	1879-1885
12	C. Coward	1865-1876	75	E. Jackson	1871-1885	131	W.E. Openshaw	1879-1882
13	L.H.Moorsom	1865	76	J.T.Ashworth	1871-1873	132	C.H.Haigh	1879-1887
14	E.B. Rowley	1865-1880	77	R.W.D. Hill	1871	133	S. Palmer	1879-1880
15	R. Slater	1865	78	A.Watson	1871-1893	134	R. Horrocks	1880-1882
16	J.Smith	1865-1869	79	R. Dewhurst	1872-1875	135	E. Leese	1880-1884
17	E. Storer	1865-1878	80	W. McIntyre	1872-1880	136	H. Miller	1880-1881
18	H.N. Tennent	1865-1870	81	R.Roberts	1872-1874	137	W. Robinson	1880-1888
19	G. Holgate	1866-1867	82	H.B. Parr	1872-1876	138	R.Wood	1880-1884
20	J. Leach	1866-1877	83	Rev V.P.F.A. Royle	1873-1891	139	G. Bird	1880
21	A.Appleby	1866-1887	84	E. Moorhouse	1873-1875	140	F. Isherwood	1881
22	H.W. Barber	1866-1867	85	J. Braddock	1873			
23	G.A.Campbell	1866	86	A. Ollivant	1873-1874			
24	T.O. Potter	1866	87	W.R. Craig	1874			
25	W. Burrows	1867-1873	88	J. Harrop	1874			
26	F. Coward	1867-1868	89	W.S. Jervis	1874			
27	W. Hickton	1867-1871	90	H. Mellor	1874-1875			
28	J. Ricketts	1867-1877	91	R.Walker	1874-1875			
29	T. Smith	1867	92	G.Walsh	1874-1877			
30	G.Hibberd	1867	93	F.Taylor	1874-1888			
31	A.N. Hornby	1867-1899	94	C.W. Landon	1874-1875			
32	E.C. Leventon	1867	95	W.S. Patterson	1874-1882			
33	E.B.Rawlinson	1867	96	W.A. Scott	1874			
34	W.H.Iddison	1867-1868	97	E.H. Porter	1874-1882			
35	W.M.Tennent	1867	98	J.B.Barber	1874-1876			
36	J. Jackson	1867	99	H.Thornber	1874			
37	J.L. Kaye	1867	100	J.Melling	1874-1876			
38	A. Smith	1867-1871	101	E.Tranter	1875-1876			
39	C.Wardle	1867-1872	102	E.L. Chadwick	1875-1881			
40	M.Walton	1867	103	J.H. Kevan	1875			
41	H.J. Ramsbottom	1868	104	E. Kewley	1875			
42	W. Richmond	1868	105	F. Stephenson	1875-1877			
43	G.C.H.Dunlop	1868	106	W.S. Butterworth	1876-1882			
44	F.S. Head	1868-1869	107	W. Rickman	1876			
45	R.Leach	1868-1876	108	E. Roper	1876-1886			
46	D. Rowland	1868	109	J. Schofield	1876			
47	H.A.H. Hulton	1868	110	R. Howe	1876-1877			
48	F.J.Rutter	1868	111	C.L. Jones	1876-1888			
49	T.Wall	1868	112	D.Q. Steel	1876-1887			
50	G.H. Grimshaw	1868	113	F. Melhuish	1877			
51	J. Smalley	1869	114	W.Wall	1877			
52	Rev F.W.Wright	1869-1875	115	R. Boyes	1877			
53	W.M.Hardcastle	1869-1874	116	C.L. Hornby	1877			
54	F.Hardcastle	1869	117	B. Harwood	1877			
55	F. Carlisle	1869	118	J.E. Kershaw	1877-1885			
56	G.A.Winder	1869	119	W. Blake	1877			
57	C.A.G.Hulton	1869-1882						
58	W.J. Marchbank	1869-1870						
59	A. Seymour	1869						
60	F.H. Birley	1870-1872						
61	D.W. MacKinnon	1870-1871						
62	T.H. Rushton	1870						
63	W.H. Potter	1870						

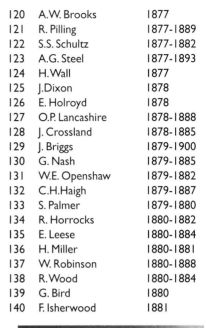

Fred Isherwood was asked to play against Kent, at Old Trafford, starting on the 9th June 1881. He scored a duck. That was the limit to his first-class career – but he kept the letter from the Lancashire Secretary inviting him to play for the rest of his life as a valued possession.

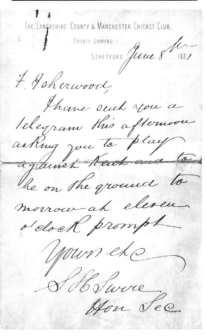

141	H. Leach	1881
142	F.W. Hargreaves	1881
143	H.C.R. John	1881
144	T.F. Bradbury	1881
145	R.O. Milne	1882
146	C. Yates	1882
147	G.M. Harper	1883
148	S.M. Crosfield	1883-1899
149	W.M. Massey	1883
150	J.H. Payne	1883
151	H.B. Steel	1883-1896
152	H. Hibbard	1884
153	E.E. Steel	1884-1903
154	S. Haggas	1884-1885
155	L.D. Hildyard	1884-1885
156	F.D. Gaddum	1884
157	E. Ratcliffe	1884
158	F. Ward	1884-1896
159	D. Whittaker	1884-1888
160	C.E. de Trafford	1884
161	J.G. Heap	1884
162	H. McIntyre	1884
163	C.M. Sawyer	1884
164	T. Whitehead	1884

165	L. Sanderson	1884
166	A. Price	1885
167	G.H. Biddolph	1885
168	W.E. Leach	1885
169	G.W. Littlewood	1885
170	G.E. Jowett	1885-1889
171	R.C. Leach	1885
172	H. Eccles	1885-1886
173	G. Yates	1885-1894
174	W.H. Bower	1885-1886
175	E.C. Hornby	1885-1887
176	G. Kemp	1885-1892
177	W. Copeland	1885
178	A.T. Kemble	1885-1894
179	J. Mayall	1885
180	E. Nutter	1885
181	A.P. Smith	1886-1894
182	A. Teggin	1886
183	A. Champion	1886
184	P. Dobell	1886-1887
185	J. Eccles	1886-1889
186	B. Hudson	1886-1888
187	C. Shore	1886
188	G.R. Baker	1887-1899
189	A. Durandu	1887
190	G.A. Bigg	1887
191	A.B.E. Gibson	1887
192	F.H. Sugg	1887-1899
193	J. Leigh	1887
194	Rev J.R. Napier	1888
195	A. Knowles	1888
196	J.P. Whiteside	1888-1890
197	H.G. Barchard	1888
198	R.W. Kentfield	1888
199	A.W. Mold	1889-1901
200	A.G. Paul	1889-1900
201	J. Mills	1889
202	A. Ward	1889-1904
203	F. Crabtree	1890
204	A. Tinsley	1890-1895
205	C. Holden	1890
206	J. Hewitson	1890
207	A.C. MacLaren	1890-1914
208	R.G.E. Mortimer	1891
209	J.A. MacLaren	1891-1894
210	W. Pilling	1891
211	C.H. Benton	1892-1901
212	J. Ellis	1892-1898
213	T.R. Hubback	1892
214	W. Oakley	1983-1894
215	C. Smith	1893-1902
216	W.H. Houldsworth	1893-1894
217	E.B. Rowley,jr	1893-1898
218	R. Smith	1893
219	G.E. Wharmby	1894
220	W. Brown	1894
221	F.H. Goodwin	1894
222	R. Thomas	1894-1902
223	T. Ainscough	1894-1906
224	H.S. Bennett	1894
225	S.M. Tindall	1894-1898
226	G.R. Bardswell	1894-1902
227	T. Lancaster	1894-1899
228	H.J. Tinsley	1894-1896
229	A.W. Hallam	1895-1900
230	J.T. Tyldesley	1895-1923

231	C.C. Pilkington	1895
232	W.R. Cuttell	1896-1906
233	J. l'Anson	1896-1908
234	J.F. Arnold	1896
235	C.R. Hartley	1897-1909
236	L. Radcliffe	1897-1905
237	J. Hallows	1898-1907
238	W.B. Stoddart	1898-1899
239	R.J. Taylor	1898
240	A. Eccles	1898-1907
241	J. Payne	1898
242	J.L. Ainsworth	1899
243	A.H. Hornby	1899-1914
244	W. Silcock	1899-1902
245	C.W. Ingleby	1899
246	J. Sharp	1899-1925
247	S. Webb	1899-1903
248	R.H. Spooner	1899-1921
249	S.F. Barnes	1899-1903
250	H.G. Garnett	1899-1914
251	W. Huddleston	1899-1914
252	J. Holland	1900-1902
253	W.J. Hibbert	1900-1901
254	H. Pennington	1900
255	J. Stanning	1900-1903
256	H. Cudworth	1900
257	J.J. Broughton	1901-1902
258	G. Potter	1902
259	F.H. Hollins	1902-1904
260	H. Crabtree	1902-1908
261	W. Findlay	1902-1906
262	W. Brearley	1902-1911
263	G. MacLaren	1902
264	G.H. Littlewood	1902-1904
265	A. Kermode	1902-1908
266	B. Blomley	1903-1922
267	W. Haggas	1903
268	F.W. Baucher	1903
269	W. Worsley	1903-1913
270	J.S. Heap	1903-1921
271	F.G. MacLaren	1903
272	G. Radcliffe	1903-1906
273	A.R. Sladen	1903-1904
274	F. Harry	1903-1908
275	L.S. Rowlands	1903-1910
276	T.G.O. Cole	1904
277	L.O.S. Poidevin	1904-1908
278	W. Phillips	1904-1908
279	H.L. Farrar	1904
280	F.N. Miller	1904
281	W. Parker	1904
282	W. Cook	1905-1907
283	E.L. Wright	1905-1910
284	C. Clarke	1905
285	T.A. Higson	1905-1923
286	H. Dean	1906-1921
287	H.D. Stanning	1906-1908
288	F.H. Mugliston	1906-1908
289	A.F. Spooner	1906-1909
290	W.R. Gregson	1906
291	J.W.H. Makepeace	1906-1930
292	R.G. Boden	1907
293	L.W. Cook	1907-1923
294	M.C. Bird	1907
295	A. Hartley	1907-1914
296	W.K. Tyldesley	1908-1914

150 LANCASHIRE GREATS
149. Tommy Higson Snr.

For 49 years Tommy Higson served on the Lancashire committee during the county's most successful period. He was treasurer between 1924-1932 and then chairman between 1932-49. A solicitor in Manchester who because of his place of birth played for Derbyshire, he made five appearances for Lancashire between 1905 and 1923. He was a distinguished administrator with great energy, keen insight and a wide knowledge of the game, which helped him become a well-respected chairman of the club. He had a firm grip on the club's affairs, but he also possessed a warm humanity when it came to helping cricketers or clubs in distress. He presided over Lancashire during the difficult time during the Second World War and the re-building of the club afterwards. He was on the MCC selection committee during the Bodyline series and the soundness of his judgement was reflected in his remark, "If a game of cricket leaves us worse friends than when we started, then it isn't worth a damn!" Though he had the knack of getting his own way in many things, he failed in one: he could not convince other counties that single-innings matches were a worthwhile proposition 30 years before one-day cricket began. He died in Grange-over-Sands in 1949 aged 75.

297	R. Whitehead	1908-1914
298	K.G. MacLeod	1908-1913
299	J.S. Cragg	1908
300	G.E. Tyldesley	1909-1936
301	J.L. Jones	1910
302	J.D. Tyldesley	1910-1922
303	R.V. Bardsley	1910-1920
304	P.M. Fairclough	1911-1923
305	B. Barrell	1911-1923
306	C.P. Leese	1911
307	F.B. Scholfield	1911
308	F.R.R. Brooke	1912-1913
309	A.E. Lawton	1912-1914
310	B.A. Boddington	1913-1924
311	H.E. Edge	1913
312	J. Nelson	1913
313	E. Bowden	1914
314	J.C.H.L. Hollins	1914-1919
315	J. Bullough	1914-1919
316	F.W. Musson	1914-1921
317	C.H. Parkin	1914-1926
318	H. Tyldesley	1914-1922
319	C. Hallows	1914-1932
320	H. Spencer	1914
321	M.N. Kenyon	1919-1925
322	D.V. Norbury	1919-1922
323	G.S. Rawstorne	1919
324	C.S. Marriott	1919-1921
325	R.K. Tyldesley	1919-1931
326	A.W. Farnsworth	1919
327	A.W. Pewtress	1919-1925
328	E.O. Bleackley	1919
329	G.O. Shelmerdine	1919-1925
330	J.R. Barnes	1919-1930
331	W. Brown	1919-1922
332	J. Coulthurst	1919
333	F. Taylor	1920-1922
334	W. Ellis	1920-1923
335	H. Douthwaite	1920-1921
336	F.B. Watson	1920-1937
337	J.W. Whewell	1921-1927
338	R.A. Lloyd	1921-1922
339	R. Howard	1922-1933
340	H.B. Parkinson	1922-1923
341	L. Green	1922-1935
342	A. Rhodes	1922-1924
343	A.E. Hall	1923-1924
344	G.H. Rogerson	1923
345	P.T. Eckersley	1923-1935
346	W.E. Hickmott	1923-1924
347	J.L. Hopwood	1923-1939
348	G. Duckworth	1923-1938
349	E.L.C. Leach	1923-1924
350	S. Ellis	1923-1924
351	J. Iddon	1924-1945
352	H.D. Davies	1924-1925
353	E.A. McDonald	1924-1931
354	W. Farrimond	1924-1945
355	M.L. Taylor	1924-1931
356	D.M. Ritchie	1924
357	F. Hartley	1924-1925
358	R. MacNairy	1925
359	F.M. Sibbles	1925-1937
360	T.M. Halliday	1925-1929
361	F. Webster	1925-1927
362	A. Woolley	1926

363	E. Paynter	1926-1945
364	F.S. Booth	1927-1937
365	J. Holroyd	1927-1933
366	L. Horridge	1927-1929
367	P. Higson	1928-1931
368	G. Hodgson	1928-1933
369	S. Preston	1928-1930
370	F. Rushton	1928-1929
371	L. Warburton	1929-1938
372	H. Elliott	1930
373	J.R. Latchford	1930-1932
374	C. Hawkwood	1931-1935
375	H.R.W. Butterworth	1931-1936
376	W.J. Horrocks	1931-1933
377	R.H. Parkin	1931-1939
378	A. Bennett	1932-1933
379	L.W. Parkinson	1932-1936
380	F.D. Beattie	1932
381	E.A. Barlow	1932
382	W.E. Phillipson	1933-1948
383	C. Washbrook	1933-1959

384	A.D. Baxter	1933-1934
385	W.H.L. Lister	1933-1939
386	R. Pollard	1933-1950
387	N. Oldfield	1935-1939
388	E.W. Greenhalgh	1935-1938
389	A.E. Nutter	1935-1945
390	C.A. Edge	1936-1938
391	F. Harrison	1936
392	G.N. Hudson	1936
393	D.M. Matthews	1936-1938
394	T.A. Higson, jr	1936-1946
395	T. Jaques	1937
396	W. Place	1937-1955
397	L.L. Wilkinson	1937-1947
398	C.A. Rhodes	!937-1938
399	A.J. Birtwell	1937-1939
400	R.G. Garlick	1938-1947
401	J.B. Bowes	1938-1948
402	J. Briggs	1939
403	S.T. Banham	1939
404	J.T. Ikin	1939-1957
405	W.B. Roberts	1939-1949
406	S.F. Hird	1939
407	J.M. Brocklebank	1939

408	W. Barron	1945
409	R.B. Rae	1945
410	T.L. Brierley	1946-1948
411	J.A. Fallows	1946
412	B.P. King	1946-1947
413	A. Wharton	1946-1960
414	G.A. Edrich	1946-1958
415	F. Cooper	1946
416	E.J. Price	1946-1947
417	N.D. Howard	1946-1953
418	L. Bulcock	1946
419	E.H. Edrich	1946-1948
420	M.J. Hilton	1946-1961
421	K. Cranston	1947-1948
422	B.J. Howard	1947-1951
423	A. Barlow	1947-1951
424	W.T. Jolley	1947
425	J.M. Kelly	1947-1949
426	P. Greenwood	1948-1952
427	R. Tattersall	1948-1960
428	A. Wilson	1948-1962
429	W. Lawton	1948
430	R. Alderson	1948-1949
431	J.H.G. Deighton	1948-1950
432	R. Berry	1948-1954
433	K.J. Grieves	1949-1964
434	J.G. Lomax	1949-1953
435	D.H. Stone	1949-1950
436	J.B. Statham	1950-1968
437	A. Booth	1950-1951
438	T.E. Dickinson	1950-1951
439	F.D. Parr	1951-1954
440	D.J. Smith	1951-1952
441	E.F.W. Highton	1951
442	T. Greenhough	1951-1966
443	C.S. Smith	1951-1957
444	S. Smith	1952-1956
445	J. Hilton	!952-1953
446	P.T. Marner	!952-1964
447	R.W. Barber	1954-1962
448	F. Moore	!954-1958
449	J. Dyson	1954-1964
450	K. Bowling	1954
451	G. Pullar	1954-1968
452	R. Collins	1954-1962
453	H. Farrar	1955
454	J. Jordan	1955-1957
455	K.B. Standring	1955-1959
456	F. Goodwin	1955-1956
457	J.D. Bond	1955-1972
458	J. Wood	1956
459	P. Barcroft	1956
460	C. Burton	1956
461	B.J. Booth	1956-1963
462	E.A. Kelly	1957
463	W. Heys	1957
464	J.F.E. Roberts	1957
465	Alan Bolton	1957-1961
466	C. Hilton	1957-1963
467	P. Whiteley	1957-1958
468	R. Bowman	1957-1959
469	K. Higgs	1958-1969
470	N.H. Cooke	1958-1959
471	G. Clayton	1959-1964
472	D.M. Green	1959-1967
473	P. Lever	1960-1976

474	K. Goodwin	1960-1974	540	N.H. Fairbrother	1982-2002	606	S.G. Law	2002-2008
475	K. Howard	1960-1966	541	M. Watkinson	1982-1999	607	A.J. Swann	2002-2004
476	D.R. Worsley	1960-1967	542	R.G. Watson	1982-1985	608	J.M. Anderson	2002-
477	G. Houlton	1961-1963	543	S.T. Jefferies	1983-1985	609	M.R. Currie	2002-2003
478	E.J. Craig	1961-1962	544	S.M. Nazir Zaidi	1983-1984	610	S.I. Mahmood	2002-2012
479	K. Tebay	1961-1963	545	J. Stanworth	1983-1992	611	T.M. Rees	2002
480	J.F. Blackledge	1962	546	M.R. Chadwick	1983-1987	612	M.B. Loye	2003-2008
481	R. Bennett	1962-1966	547	J.A. Ormrod	1984-1985	613	I.J. Sutcliffe	2003-2008
482	J.M. Cownley	1962	548	D.W. Varey	1984-1987	614	C.L. Hooper	2003-2004
483	R. Entwistle	1962-1966	549	D.J. Makinson	1984-1988	615	S.P. Crook	2003-2005
484	A.M. Beddow	1962-1966	550	B.P. Patterson	1984-1990	616	P.J. Horton	2003-
485	H. Pilling	1962-1980	551	S.W. Henriksen	1985-1986	617	O.J. Newby	2003-
486	I.M. Chappell	1963	552	I.C. Davidson	1985-1987	618	D.G. Cork	2004-2008
487	J. Sullivan	1963-1976	553	A.J. Murphy	1985-1988	619	D. Mongia	2004
488	J. Cumbes	1963-67/71	554	A.N. Hayhurst	1985-1989	620	A.R. Crook	2004-2005
489	S. Ramadhin	1964-1965	555	G.D. Mendis	1986-1993	621	B.J. Hodge	2005-2008
490	G.K. Knox	1964-1967	556	W.K. Hegg	1986-2005	622	S.J. Croft	2005-
491	K. Shuttleworth	1964-1975	557	N.J. Speak	1986/7-96	623	G.D. Cross	2005-2013
492	D. Lloyd	1965-1983	558	K.W. McLeod	1987	624	S.J. Marshall	2005-2008
493	K.L. Snellgrove	1965-1974	559	I.D. Austin	1987-2000	625	T.C. Smith	2005-
494	G. Hodgson	1965	560	M.A. Atherton	1987-2001	626	A. Symonds	2005
495	B.E. Krikken	1966-1967	561	J.D. Fitton	1987-1992	627	M.J. North	2005
496	A. Thomas	1966	562	T.E. Jesty	1987/88-91	628	M. Kartik	2005-2006
497	B. Wood	1966-1979	563	C.D. Matthews	1988	629	L.D. Sutton	2006-2008
498	G. Atkinson	1967-1969	564	Wasim Akram	1988-1998	630	K.R. Brown	2006-
499	J.S. Savage	1967-1969	565	G.D. Lloyd	1988-2002	631	S.J. Mullaney	2006-2008
500	D.P. Hughes	1967-1990	566	P.A.J. DeFreitas	1988/9-93	632	N.J. Astle	2006
501	D.S. van der Knapp	1967	567	P.J. Martin	1989-2004	633	S.P. Cheetham	2007
502	F.M. Engineer	1968-1976	568	J.P. Crawley	1990-2001	634	S.D. Parry	2007-
503	C.H. Lloyd	1968-1986	569	R.C. Irani	1990-1993	635	S.T. Jayasuriya	2007
504	D. Bailey	1968-1969	570	S.P. Titchard	1990-1998	636	V.V.S. Laxman	2007
505	J. Simmons	1968-1989	571	G. Yates	1990-2002	637	F. duPlessis	2008
506	P.A. Gooch	1970	572	J.E.R. Gallian	1990-1997	638	Mohammad Yousuf	2008
507	F.C. Hayes	1970-1984	573	S.N.V. Waterton	1990	639	L. Vincent	2008
508	M.W. Staziker	1970	574	S. Bramhall	1990	640	A.G. Prince	2009-
509	A. Kennedy	1970-1982	575	M.A. Crawley	1990	641	T. Lungley	2009
510	R.H. Tattersall	1971	576	T.M. Orrell	1991	642	S.C. Kerrigan	2010-
511	P.G. Lee	1972-1982	577	M.A. Sharp	1991	643	S.C. Moore	2010-2013
512	R.M. Ratcliffe	1972-1980	578	M.J.P. Ward	1991	644	D.B.L. Powell	2010
513	B.W. Reidy	1973-1982	579	A.A. Barnett	1992-1994	645	L.A. Procter	2010-
514	J. Lyon	1973-1979	580	D.K. Morrison	1992	646	S.M. Katich	2010-2013
515	A.J. Good	1973-1976	581	S.D. Fletcher	1992-1993	647	S. Chanderpaul	2010
516	J. Abrahams	1973-1988	582	G. Chapple	1992-	648	A.P. Agathangelou	2011-
517	J.W. Edmonds	1975	583	N.A. Derbyshire	1994	649	M.F. Maharoof	2011
518	G.E. Trim	1976-1980	584	J.M. Fielding	1994	650	Junaid Khan	2011
519	R. Arrowsmith	1976-1979	585	M.E. Harvey	1994-1999	651	A. Shahzad	2012
520	W. Hogg	1976-1980	586	G. Keedy	1995-2012	652	T.E. Bailey	2012-
521	C.E.H. Croft	1977-1982	587	D.J. Shadford	1995-1998	653	A.L. Davies	2012-
522	C.J. Scott	1977-1982	588	A. Flintoff	1995-2010	654	W.A. White	2013-
523	P.J.W. Allott	1978-1991	589	R.J. Green	1995-2000	655	L.M. Reece	2013-
524	R.J. Sutcliffe	1978	590	S. Elworthy	1995/6-96	656	A.M. Lilley	2013-
525	G. Fowler	1979-1992	591	N.T. Wood	1996-2000	657	K.M. Jarvis	2013-
526	G.F. Lawson	1979	592	P.C. McKeown	1996-2000			
527	P.A. Robinson	1979	593	J.J. Haynes	1996-2004			
528	M.F. Malone	1979-1980	594	P.M. Ridgway	1997-1999			
529	I. Cockbain	1979-1983	595	M.J. Chilton	1997-2011			
530	K.A. Hayes	1980-1986	596	C.P. Schofield	1998-2004			
531	S.J. O'Shaughnessy	1980-1987	597	M.P. Smethurst	1999-2002			
532	N.V. Radford	1980-1984	598	M. Muralitharan	1999-2007			
533	M.A. Holding	1981	599	J.C. Scuderi	2000-2001			
534	G.J. Speak	1981-1982	600	S.C. Ganguly	2000			
535	T.J. Taylor	1981-1982	601	R.C. Driver	2001-2002			
536	L.L. McFarlane	1982-1984	602	T.W. Roberts	2001-2002			
537	I. Folley	1982-1990	603	K.W. Hogg	2001-			
538	M.A. Wallwork	1982	604	J. Wood	2001-2004			
539	C. Maynard	1982-1986	605	D. Byas	2002			

LANCASHIRE'S YEAR BY YEAR CHAMPIONSHIP RECORD

Year	Capt	Pos	P	W	L	D	T	A
1865	-	-	2	1	1	0	0	0
1866	EB Rowley	-	4	0	3	1	0	0
1867	EB Rowley	-	6	0	4	2	0	0
1868	EB Rowley	-	6	1	5	0	0	0
1869	EB Rowley	-	5	2	3	0	0	0
1870	EB Rowley	-	4	3	1	0	0	0
1871	EB Rowley	-	6	3	3	0	0	0
1872	EB Rowley	-	4	4	0	0	0	0
1873	EB Rowley	-	7	4	3	0	0	0
1874	EB Rowley	-	6	1	3	2	0	0
1875	EB Rowley	-	6	4	1	1	0	0
1876	EB Rowley	-	10	5	5	0	0	0
1877	EB Rowley	-	10	6	4	0	0	0
1878	EB Rowley	-	10	5	3	2	0	0
1879	EB Rowley	=1st	10	5	1	4	0	0
1880	AN Hornby	4th	12	6	3	3	0	0
1881	AN Hornby	1st	13	10	0	3	0	0
1882	AN Hornby	=1st	14	10	1	3	0	0
1883	AN Hornby	5th	12	6	5	1	0	0
1884	AN Hornby	3rd	10	5	4	1	0	0
1885	AN Hornby	4th	11	6	3	2	0	0
1886	AN Hornby	4th	14	5	5	4	0	0
1887	AN Hornby	2nd	14	10	3	1	0	0
1888	AN Hornby	5th	14	4	5	5	0	0
1889	AN Hornby	=1st	14	10	3	1	0	0
1890	AN Hornby	2nd	14	7	3	4	0	0
1891	AN Hornby	2nd	16	8	4	3	0	1
1892	AN Hornby SM Crosfield	4th	16	7	5	4	0	0
1893	AN Hornby SM Crosfield	2nd	16	9	5	2	0	0
1894	AC MacLaren	4th	16	7	7	1	1	0
1895	AC MacLaren	2nd	22	14	4	3	0	1
1896	AC MacLaren	2nd	22	11	4	7	0	0
1897	AN Hornby	1st	26	16	3	7	0	0
1898	AN Hornby	6th	26	9	6	11	0	0
1899	AC MacLaren GR Bardswell	4th	26	12	6	7	0	1
1900	AC MacLaren	2nd	28	15	2	11	0	0
1901	AC MacLaren	3rd	28	11	5	12	0	0
1902	AC MacLaren	5th	24	7	5	11	0	1
1903	AC MacLaren	4th	26	10	5	11	0	0
1904	AC MacLaren	1st	26	16	0	10	0	0
1905	AC MacLaren	2nd	26	12	3	10	0	1
1906	AC MacLaren	4th	26	15	6	5	0	0
1907	AC MacLaren	6th	26	11	7	8	0	0
1908	AH Hornby	7th	26	10	9	6	0	1
1909	AH Hornby	2nd	24	14	4	6	0	0
1910	AH Hornby	4th	30	14	5	11	0	0
1911	AH Hornby	4th	30	15	7	8	0	0
1912	AH Hornby	4th	22	8	2	10	0	2
1913	AH Hornby	8th	26	7	11	8	0	0
1914	AH Hornby	11th	26	6	9	11	0	0

Year	Capt	Pos	P	W	L	D	T	A
1919	MN Kenyon	5th	24	8	4	12	0	0
1920	MN Kenyon	2nd	28	19	5	4	0	0
1921	MN Kenyon	5th	28	15	4	9	0	0
1922	MN Kenyon	5th	30	15	7	8	0	0
1923	J Sharp	3rd	30	15	2	13	0	0
1924	J Sharp	4th	30	11	2	17	0	0
1925	J Sharp	3rd	32	19	4	9	0	0
1926	L Green	1st	32	17	2	13	0	0
1927	L Green	1st	32	10	1	20	0	1
1928	L Green	1st	30	15	0	15	0	0
1929	PT Eckersley	2nd	28	12	3	13	0	0
1930	PT Eckersley	1st	28	10	0	18	0	0
1931	PT Eckersley	6th	28	7	4	15	0	2
1932	PT Eckersley	6th	28	8	6	13	0	1
1933	PT Eckersley	5th	28	9	1	18	0	0
1934	PT Eckersley	1st	30	13	3	14	0	0
1935	PT Eckersley	4th	28	12	6	10	0	0
1936	WHL Lister	11th	30	7	6	17	0	0
1937	WHL Lister	9th	32	9	5	18	0	0
1938	WHL Lister	4th	32	14	6	12	0	0
1939	WHL Lister	6th	32	10	6	14	0	2
1946	JA Fallows	3rd	26	15	4	7	0	0
1947	K Cranston	3rd	26	13	1	11	1	0
1948	K Cranston	5th	26	8	2	16	0	0
1949	ND Howard	11th	26	6	7	13	0	0
1950	ND Howard	=1st	28	16	2	10	0	0
1951	ND Howard	3rd	28	8	2	18	0	0
1952	ND Howard	3rd	28	12	3	12	1	0
1953	ND Howard	3rd	28	10	4	14	0	0
1954	C Washbrook	10th	28	6	3	16	0	3
1955	C Washbrook	9th	28	10	9	9	0	0
1956	C Washbrook	2nd	28	12	2	14	0	0
1957	C Washbrook	6th	28	10	8	10	0	0
1958	C Washbrook	7th	28	9	7	10	0	2
1959	C Washbrook	5th	28	12	7	9	0	0
1960	RW Barber	2nd	32	13	8	11	0	0
1961	RW Barber	13th	32	9	7	16	0	0
1962	JF Blackledge	16th	32	2	16	14	0	0
1963	KJ Grieves	15th	28	4	10	14	0	0
1964	KJ Grieves	14th	28	4	10	14	0	0
1965	JB Statham	13th	28	5	13	10	0	0
1966	JB Statham	12th	28	6	11	11	0	0
1967	JB Statham	11th	28	4	3	19	0	2
1968	JD Bond	6th	28	8	6	14	0	0
1969	JD Bond	15th	24	2	1	21	0	0
1970	JD Bond	3rd	24	6	2	16	0	0
1971	JD Bond	3rd	24	9	4	11	0	0
1972	JD Bond	15th	20	2	3	14	0	1
1973	D Lloyd	12th	20	4	6	10	0	0
1974	D Lloyd	8th	20	5	0	15	0	0
1975	D Lloyd	4th	20	9	3	8	0	0
1976	D Lloyd	16th	20	3	7	10	0	0
1977	D Lloyd	16th	22	2	4	15	0	1
1978	FC Hayes	12th	22	4	8	9	0	1
1979	FC Hayes	13th	22	4	4	14	0	0

Year	Capt	Pos	P	W	L	D	T	A
1980	FC Hayes	15th	22	4	3	13	0	2
1981	CH Lloyd	16th	22	4	7	11	0	0
1982	CH Lloyd	12th	22	4	3	15	0	0
1983	CH Lloyd	12th	24	3	4	17	0	0
1984	J Abrahams	16th	24	1	9	14	0	0
1985	J Abrahams	14th	24	3	7	14	0	0
1986	CH Lloyd	15th	24	4	5	14	0	1
1987	DP Hughes	2nd	24	10	4	10	0	0
1988	DP Hughes	9th	22	6	7	9	0	0
1989	DP Hughes	4th	22	8	5	9	0	0
1990	DP Hughes	6th	22	6	3	13	0	0
1991	DP Hughes	8th	22	6	9	7	0	0
1992	NH Fairbrother	12th	22	4	6	12	0	0
1993	NH Fairbrother	14th	17	4	8	5	0	0
1994	M Watkinson	10th	17	8	6	3	0	0
1995	M Watkinson	4th	17	10	4	3	0	0
1996	M Watkinson	15th	17	2	6	9	0	0
1997	M Watkinson	12th	17	5	6	6	0	0
1998	Wasim Akram	2nd	17	11	1	5	0	0
1999	JP Crawley	2nd	17	8	4	4	0	1
2000	JP Crawley	2nd	16	7	1	8	0	0
2001	JP Crawley	6th	16	4	5	5	0	2
2002	WK Hegg	4th	16	6	4	6	0	0
2003	WK Hegg	2nd	16	6	2	8	0	0
2004	WK Hegg	8th-rel	16	2	4	10	0	0
2005	MJ Chilton	1st-div 2	16	7	3	6	0	0
2006	MJ Chilton	2nd	16	6	1	9	0	0
2007	MJ Chilton	3rd	16	5	2	9	0	0
2008	SG Law	5th	16	5	2	9	0	0
2009	G Chapple	4th	16	4	2	10	0	0
2010	G Chapple	4th	16	5	3	8	0	0
2011	G Chapple	1st	16	10	4	2	0	0
2012	G Chapple	8th-rel	16	1	5	10	0	0
2013	G Chapple	1st-div 2	16	8	1	7	0	0

Two of Lancashire's great captains: Albert Neilsen 'Monkey' Hornby and Glen Chapple.

LANCASHIRE CCC FIRST-CLASS PLAYING RECORD

	P	W	L	D	T
Derbyshire	214	96	32	86	0
Durham	26	14	5	7	0
Essex	150	51	29	69	1
Glamorgan	121	38	20	63	0
Gloucestershire	180	80	27	73	0
Hampshire	144	64	19	60	1
Kent	223	89	56	78	0
Leicestershire	161	79	20	62	0
Middlesex	188	54	54	80	0
Northamptonshire	126	50	18	58	0
Nottinghamshire	230	68	55	107	0
Somerset	153	80	25	48	0
Surrey	212	58	64	89	1
Sussex	202	81	45	76	0
Warwickshire	194	69	33	92	0
Worcestershire	159	64	30	65	0
Yorkshire	265	55	79	131	0
Australia	43	5	17	21	0
Australian Imperial Forces	1	0	1	0	0
Cambridge MCC University	1	0	0	1	0
Cambridge University	47	14	7	26	0
Combined Services	2	2	0	0	0
Durham UCCE	7	2	0	5	0
England XI	4	0	2	2	0
India	13	2	3	8	0
Jamaica	4	0	1	3	0
London County	1	0	0	1	0
MCC	32	12	16	4	0
Minor Counties	2	0	0	2	0
New Zealand	12	3	2	7	0
New Zealand A	1	0	0	1	0
Oxford MCC University	1	0	0	1	0
Oxford UCCE	1	1	0	0	0
Oxford University	83	46	7	30	0
Pakistan	7	0	2	5	0
Philadelphians	2	1	1	0	0
Rest of England	6	0	4	2	0
Scotland	5	2	0	3	0
Sir Julien Cahn's XI	1	0	0	1	0
South Africa	17	5	3	9	0
Sri Lanka	2	0	0	2	0
Sri Lanka A	1	0	1	0	0
Wales	1	1	0	0	0
West Indies	15	1	4	10	0
West Indies A	1	0	0	1	0
Zimbabwe	2	0	1	1	0
Total	**3263**	**1187**	**683**	**1390**	**3**

Totals exclude matches abandoned without a ball being bowled

MOST APPEARANCES FOR LANCASHIRE

573	GE Tyldesley	391	J Briggs
518	J Sharp	378	D Lloyd
507	JT Tyldesley	374	RK Tyldesley
500	C Washbrook	370	C Hallows
487	JWH Makepeace	344	JD Bond
483	J Iddon	337	NH Fairbrother
456	FB Watson	337	WK Hegg
452	KJ Grieves	330	A Ward
436	DP Hughes	323	H Pilling
430	JB Statham	322	GA Edrich
429	J Simmons	312	G Pullar
424	G Duckworth	308	FM Sibbles
397	JL Hopwood	307	AC MacLaren
392	A Wharton	306	K Higgs

150 LANCASHIRE GREATS

150. Sir Neville Cardus

Neville Cardus was neither Lancashire cricketer nor administrator, but by the very power of his pen he made a unique contribution to Lancashire cricket, to cricket in general, to the sphere of classical music, and to the world of letters. He was only partly tongue-in-cheek when he intimated that the Presidency of LCCC, which came to him in 1971-72, was the crowning achievement of a long and illustrious life, the public honours of which had also included a CBE in 1964 and a knighthood in 1967. Cardus was humbly born in Rusholme, Manchester. His native genius, a thirst for learning and self-education somewhat improbably carried him onto the staff of the Manchester Guardian in March 1917. Cardus developed as a brilliantly original writer on the game of cricket, a role in which he chronicled the great Lancashire teams and players of the 1920s and the 1930s. But he was never parochial and he celebrated the game as a whole, hymning all cricketers of character in a prose that was elevated but also shrewd, muscular and humorous, carrying its learning lightly. The Neville Cardus Archive, devoted to perpetuating his works and his memory, is based at the LCCC Library, Old Trafford.

BATSMEN WHO HAVE SCORED OVER 10,000 RUNS FOR LANCASHIRE

	Runs	Ave
GE Tyldesley	34,222	45.20
JT Tyldesley	31,949	41.38
C Washbrook	27,863	42.15
JWH Makepeace	25,207	36.37
FB Watson	22,833	37.06
J Sharp	22,015	31.18
J Iddon	21,975	37.05
KJ Grieves	20,802	33.39
C Hallows	20,142	39.72
NH Fairbrother	19,603	42.43
A Wharton	17,921	33.55
D Lloyd	17,877	33.41
G Pullar	16,853	35.18
E Paynter	16,555	41.59
AC MacLaren	15,772	33.34
JL Hopwood	15,519	30.01
A Ward	15,392	30.96
H Pilling	14,841	32.26
GA Edrich	14,730	34.74
W Place	14,605	36.69
JT Ikin	14,327	37.70
G Fowler	13,453	36.55
B Wood	12,969	35.24
CH Lloyd	12,764	44.94
JD Bond	11,867	26.60
GD Lloyd	11,038	38.06
WK Hegg	11,027	28.27
FC Hayes	10,899	37.45
J Briggs	10,707	19.01
M Watkinson	10,683	26.84
AN Hornby	10,649	24.25
JP Crawley	10,533	51.17
PT Marner	10,312	29.21
DP Hughes	10,126	22.01

HIGHEST INNINGS TOTALS BY LANCASHIRE

863	v Surrey (Oval)	1990
801	v Somerset (Taunton)	1895
781	v Warwickshire (Edgbaston)	2003
734-5d	v Middlesex (Old Trafford)	2003
686	v Essex (Chelmsford)	1996
676-7d	v Hampshire (Old Trafford)	1911
655-6d	v Essex (Old Trafford)	2005
640-8d	v Sussex (Hove)	1937
627	v Nottinghamshire (Trent Bridge)	1905
601-8d	v Sussex (Hove)	1905
600-6d	v Northamptonshire (Old Trafford)	2001

LOWEST INNINGS TOTALS BY LANCASHIRE

25	v Derbyshire (Old Trafford)	1871
27	v Surrey (Old Trafford)	1958
28	v Australia (Liverpool)	1896
30	v Yorkshire (Holbeck)	1868
33	v Northamptonshire (Northampton)	1977
34	v Yorkshire (Holbeck)	1868
35	v Surrey (Old Trafford)	1888
35	v Derbyshire (Derby)	1894

RECORD PARTNERSHIPS FOR LANCASHIRE

1st	368	AC MacLaren & RH Spooner	v Gloucestershire (Liverpool)	1903
2nd	371	FB Watson & GE Tyldesley	v Surrey (Old Trafford)	1928
3rd	364	MA Atherton & NH Fairbrother	v Surrey (Oval)	1990
4th	358	SP Titchard & GD Lloyd	v Essex (Chelmsford)	1996
5th	360	SG Law & CL Hooper	v Warwickshire (Edgbaston)	2003
6th	278	J Iddon & HRW Butterworth	v Sussex (Old Trafford)	1932
7th	248	GD Lloyd & ID Austin	v Yorkshire (Headingley)	1997
8th	158	J Lyon & RM Ratcliffe	v Warwickshire (Old Trafford)	1979
9th	142	LOS Poidevin & A Kermode	v Sussex (Eastbourne)	1907
10th	173	J Briggs & R Pilling	v Surrey (Liverpool)	1885

Archie MacLaren's 424

Match played at Taunton between Lancashire & Somersetshire

Lancashire — First Innings

	Name of the Batsman	How out	Total	Remarks
1	A.C. MacLaren	c Fowler b Gamlin	424	
2	Ward (A.)	c R. Palairet b Tyler	64	
3	Paul	c Gamlin b L. Palairet	177	
4	Hallam	c Fowler b do	6	
5	C.H. Benton	c & b Fowler	43	
6	Sugg (F.H.)	c Wickham b Woods	41	
7	Tinsley (A.)	c Gamlin b do	0	
8	Baker	st Wickham b L. Palairet	23	
9	Briggs	Not Out	9	
10	Smith (C.)	c Trask b L. Palairet	0	
11	Mold	c R. Palairet b Gamlin	0	
	Byes		9	
	Leg Byes		4	
	Wide Balls		1	
	No Balls			
	Total of first Innings		**801**	

Runs at the fall of each Wicket: 1 for 141 2 for 501 3 for 530 4 for 637 5 for 732 6 for 738 7 for 792 8 for 792 9 for 98 10 for 801

Analysis of the Bowling — First Innings

	Bowlers	Overs	Maidens	Runs	Wickets	Wides	No Balls
1	Tyler	59	5	212	1	–	–
2	Woods	46	5	163	2	–	–
3	L. Palairet	44	10	133	4	1	–
4	Gamlin	26	8	100	2	–	–
5	Fowler	23	5	97	1	–	–
6	R. Palairet	11	3	41	0	–	–
7	Trask	2	0	9	0	–	–
8	Porch	5	0	16	0	–	–
9	Bartlett	6	0	16	0	–	–
10							

This Match was concluded at   o'clock on

LANCASHIRE v. SOMERSET,

AT TAUNTON, JULY, 1895.

Mr. MacLaren ran up the biggest individual score (424)
ever secured in first-class Cricket.

No season can prove barren
To Sportsmen like MacLaren,
If they at times are beaten, they count defeat no crime
With energies undying,
They bravely keep on trying.
They have no time for sighing, they calmly bide their time.
We boast of history makers,
Of previous record breakers,
Our northern hero puts them all completely in the shade ;
If your inclined to doubt it,
Ask Somerset about it,
They won't forget, at least just yet, the historic score he made.
If Lancashire in chorus,
Puts this grand feat before us,
And tells how her illustrious son has glorified the game,
We'll swell the chorus louder,
Make Lancashire feel prouder,
And when they praise their famous bat we'll gladly do the same
We'll laud his great endurance,
His patience and assurance,
Place him amongst Brittania's gems, more precious far than gold,
Like Maurice Read, undaunted,
May he repeat when wanted,
The brilliancy of Albert Ward, the pluck of Arthur Mold.
A.C.

Colonnade Hotel and Restaurant,

NEW STREET, BIRMINGHAM.

Caterer to the Warwickshire County Ground.   Luncheons provided daily.   Proprietor—W. H. COX.

HIGHEST INDIVIDUAL SCORES FOR LANCASHIRE

424	AC MacLaren	v Somerset (Taunton)	1895
366	NH Fairbrother	v Surrey (Oval)	1990
322	E Paynter	v Sussex (Hove)	1937
312	JER Gallian	v Derbyshire (Old Trafford)	1996
300*	FB Watson	v Surrey (Old Trafford)	1928
295*	JT Tyldesley	v Kent (Old Trafford)	1906
291	E Paynter	v Hampshire (Southampton)	1938
281*	JP Crawley	v Somerset (Southport)	1994
280	JP Crawley	v Northamptonshire (Old Trafford)	2001
272	JT Tyldesley	v Derbyshire (Chesterfield)	1919
268*	MA Atherton	v Glamorgan (Blackpool)	1999
266*	W Place	v Oxford University (Oxford)	1947
266	E Paynter	v Essex (Old Trafford)	1937
256*	GE Tyldesley	v Warwickshire (Old Trafford)	1930
253	JT Tyldesley	v Kent (Canterbury)	1914
251*	C Washbrook	v Surrey (Old Trafford)	1947
250	JT Tyldesley	v Nottinghamshire (Trent Bridge)	1905
250	JP Crawley	v Nottinghamshire (Trent Bridge)	1994

5,000 RUNS AND 300 WICKETS FOR LANCASHIRE

		Runs	Ave	Wkts	Ave
RG Barlow	1871-1891	7,765	20.43	735	13.60
J Briggs	1879-1900	10,707	19.01	1,696	15.60
WR Cuttell	1896-1906	5,389	20.41	760	19.59
J Sharp	1899-1925	22,015	31.18	434	27.23
JS Heap	1903-1921	5,146	18.98	412	23.08
RK Tyldesley	1919-1931	6,126	15.78	1,449	16.65
FB Watson	1920-1937	22,833	37.06	402	31.86
JL Hopwood	1923-1939	15,519	30.01	672	22.18
J Iddon	1924-1945	21,975	37.05	533	26.66
DP Hughes	1967-1991	10,126	22.01	637	29.78
J Simmons	1968-1989	8,773	22.61	985	26.89
M Watkinson	1982-1999	10,683	26.84	720	33.64
G Chapple	1992-2013	8,056	24.41	899	26.35

BOWLERS WHO HAVE TAKEN OVER 500 WICKETS FOR LANCASHIRE

	Wkts	Ave
JB Statham	1,816	15.12
J Briggs	1,696	15.60
AW Mold	1,543	15.15
RK Tyldesley	1,449	16.65
A Watson	1,308	13.39
H Dean	1,267	18.01
R Tattersall	1,168	17.39
EA McDonald	1,053	20.96
K Higgs	1,033	22.90
R Pollard	1,015	22.15
J Simmons	985	26.89
FM Sibbles	932	22.03
MJ Hilton	926	18.81
CH Parkin	901	16.12
G Chapple	899	26.35
LW Cook	821	21.36
WR Cuttell	760	19.59
RG Barlow	736	13.60
M Watkinson	720	33.64
P Lever	716	24.64
T Greenhough	707	21.98
W Brearley	690	18.70
W Huddleston	684	17.55
JL Hopwood	672	22.18
G Keedy	654	31.19
DP Hughes	637	29.78
PJ Martin	584	27.23
PJW Allott	549	24.46
WE Phillipson	545	24.78
J Iddon	533	26.66

WICKETKEEPING IN FIRST-CLASS MATCHES FOR LANCASHIRE

		M	Ct	St	Total
G Duckworth	1923-1938	424	635	290	925
WK Hegg	1987-2005	337	825	94	919
R Pilling	1877-1889	177	333	153	486
FM Engineer	1968-1976	175	429	35	464
C Smith	1893-1902	167	312	119	431
G Clayton	1959-1964	183	390	32	422
A Wilson	1948-1962	171	287	59	346
W Farrimond	1924-1945	134	232	65	297
W Worsley	1903-1913	136	239	45	284
K Goodwin	1960-1974	122	227	26	253
LD Sutton	2006-2010	73	227	15	242
GD Cross	2005-2013	58	152	23	175
C Maynard	1982-1986	91	145	23	168
J Lyon	1973-1979	84	153	11	164
A Barlow	1947-1951	74	104	47	151
B Blomley	1903-1922	69	109	33	142
AT Kemble	1885-1894	76	97	45	142
J Jordan	1955-1957	62	104	24	128
W Findlay	1902-1906	58	101	12	113
CJ Scott	1977-1982	46	94	10	104
L Radcliffe	1897-1905	50	69	34	103
HG Garnett	1899-1914	144	87	14	101

Catches and stumpings totals relate only to those matches in which the player kept wicket.
WK Hegg also took one catch as a fielder, not included in the above figures.

AUTOGRAPHS